ORNAMENT OF REASON

Ornament of Reason

THE GREAT COMMENTARY TO NĀGĀRJUNA'S
Root of the Middle Way

by Mabja Jangchub Tsöndrü

Translated by the Dharmachakra
Translation Committee

SNOW LION
Boulder

Snow Lion
An imprint of Shambhala Publications, Inc.
2129 13th Street
Boulder, Colorado 80302
www.shambhala.com

Snow Lion is distributed worldwide by Penguin Random House, Inc., and its subsidiaries.

Library of Congress Cataloging-in-Publication Data
Rma-bya Byang-chub Brtson-'grus, d. 1185.
  [Dbu ma rtsa ba shes rab kyi 'grel pa 'thad pa'i rgyan. English]
Ornament of reason : the great commentary to Nāgārjuna's Root of the middle way / by Mabja Jangchub Tsöndrü ; translated by the Dharmachakra Translation Committee.
    p. cm.
  Includes translations from Tibetan.
  Includes bibliographical references and index.
  ISBN 978-1-55939-368-3 (alk. paper)

  1. Nāgārjuna, 2nd cent. Madhyamakakārikā. 2. Mādhyamika (Buddhism)—Early works to 1800. I. Nāgārjuna, 2nd cent. Madhyamakakārikā. English. II. Dharmachakra Translation Committee. III. Title.
    BQ7479.8.N344M333713 2011
    294.3'85—dc22
2010037413

Designed and typeset by Gopa & Ted2, Inc.
Visual outline on pp. 533–75 created for the Tsadra Foundation by Rafael Ortet.

Contents

THE DALAI LAMA

Foreword

I AM OFTEN reminded of the great kindness of the scholars and translators of the past who translated a vast array of Buddhist literature into Tibetan. Through their persistent efforts, working in small teams, they made books available to Tibetans that allowed a deep understanding of the Buddha's teachings to take root in Tibet. It was this understanding that later found expression in the many books composed by Tibetan authors. Therefore, it gives me great pleasure to know that there are groups of experienced translators today, similar to those of the past, such as the Dharmachakra Translation Committee, who are working steadily to translate Buddhist books from Tibetan into English and other Western languages. Undoubtedly these will make an invaluable contribution to a deep and lasting understanding of the Buddhist tradition.

The revered Indian master Nāgārjuna was extremely kind, like a second Buddha. He was a scholar of high distinction, who was renowned for his spiritual realization. The Buddha made a prophecy in the *Lankavatara Sutra* about his coming and what he would do to preserve and propagate Buddhism. He restored the declining Mahayana tradition and his six works on the Madhyamika view laid the basis for the Madhyamika School. Even to this day we regard Arya Nāgārjuna as the final authority concerning the Madhyamika point of view.

Nāgārjuna's *Root of the Middle Way* presents a clear, firm philosophical thesis with respect to things' lacking true existence. It argues that just as sentient beings are devoid of innate existence, so are all Buddhas, the cycle of existence, and the tranquility of nirvana. Such assertions are a great source of inspiration, for they suggest that each of us has the opportunity to scale the greatest spiritual heights, provided we tread the right path.

I am pleased to know that great care has been taken in preparing this translation along with the early Tibetan commentator Mabja Jangchub Tsöndrü's explanation of the *Root of the Middle Way*. I have no doubt that readers interested in the development of the Madhyamika view will derive great benefit from this work. I congratulate all who have participated in this translation and offer my prayers that the good you have done will make a far-reaching contribution to peace and enlightenment in the world.

11 September 2008

Translators' Introduction

IN THE *Root of the Middle Way,* Nāgārjuna presents a magical method of reasoning, inviting everyone who encounters these lucid and fearless contemplations to follow him on a journey to the heart of transcendent insight. Inspired by the Buddha's teachings on profound emptiness in the Prajñāpāramitā Sūtras, Nāgārjuna sets out to probe what appears to be the most fundamental facts of the world, challenging us to question even our most deeply ingrained ideas and what seem to be self-evident facts.

In a series of unassuming and penetrating investigations, he asks basic questions. What does it mean for something to occur, for something to take place? What is meant by "going" or by "coming"? What is an "action" and who or what might perform such an act? Does the eye see? Does fire burn fuel? What is an example of being right? What does it mean to be wrong? What is confinement? What is freedom? Nāgārjuna extends an invitation to open-minded and unprejudiced inquiry, and from his reader he asks for nothing more and nothing less than sincere and honest answers. Yet where are our answers? Once we begin to follow Nāgārjuna's clear and direct steps, the gateway to the inconceivable emerges. Perhaps unexpectedly.

In the nearly two thousand years since these verses first appeared,[1] the *Root of the Middle Way* (or *Mūlamadhyamaka-kārikās* as they are known in their original Sanskrit) has continued to provoke and inspire, and its place among our world's great literary treasures cannot be questioned. First in Asia, and more recently throughout the world, these verses have continued to serve as a vexing nexus of philosophical inquiry, just as they have emerged as a timeless source of liberating insights.

The present work contains Nāgārjuna's verses on the Middle Way (Skt.

---

1. Nāgārjuna's dates are unresolved. Recently scholars tend to suggest that the *Root of the Middle Way* was composed in the second century CE.

Madhyamaka, Tib. dBu ma), accompanied by Mabja Jangchub Tsöndrü's famed commentary, the *Ornament of Reason*.[2] Active in the twelfth century, Mabja was among the first Tibetans to rely on the works of the Indian master Candrakīrti,[3] and his account of the Middle Way exercised a deep and lasting influence on the development of Madhyamaka philosophy in all four schools of Buddhism in Tibet.[4] Sharp, concise, and yet comprehensive, the *Ornament of Reason* has been cherished by generations of scholar-practitioners. The late Khunu Lama Tenzin Gyaltsen Rinpoche,[5] a renowned authority on the subject, often referred to this commentary as "the best there is."[6] We are delighted to present here an English translation of Nāgārjuna's classic treatise in the company of Mabja's dynamic explanations.

Technical Notes and Acknowledgments
Our translation of the *Root of the Middle Way* is based on the Tibetan version contained in the Derge (sDe dge) edition of the Tibetan Tripiṭaka, and for the *Ornament of Reason* we have relied on the woodblock prints prepared under the auspices of the sixteenth Gyalwang Karmapa.[7] In working with Nāgārjuna's verses, we have benefited greatly from the scholarly works of others, and we wish in particular to thank professors Shoryu Katsura and Mark Siderits for making a draft of their lucid translation and commentary on the *Root of the Middle Way* available to us.[8] It has likewise been a great advantage to have access to the comprehensive work of Jay

---

2. rMa bya byang chub brtson 'grus 1975. On Mabja (?–1185 CE) and his Madhyamaka interpretation, see Williams 1985, Ruegg 2000, Vose 2009, Doctor 2009, and Doctor n.d.
3. Sixth century CE.
4. See Doctor n.d.
5. 1894–1977. Khunu Rinpoche was a teacher of many of the foremost Tibetan masters of recent times, including His Holiness the Fourteenth Dalai Lama. His teachings on the bodhisattva path are translated in Khunu Rinpoche 1999.
6. Chökyi Nyima Rinpoche, who himself studied with Tenzin Gyaltsen Rinpoche, mentioned this to us.
7. Available in electronic format through the Tibetan Buddhist Resource Center (www. tbrc.org). This edition, prepared at the Dharma Chakra Center at Rumtek, Sikkim, in 1975, is based on an earlier print produced in sDe dge in the nineteenth century under the editorship of Jamyang Khyentse Wangpo ('Jam dbyangs mkhyen brtse dbang po). We have not had access to this earlier edition.
8. Katsura and Siderits forthcoming.

Garfield and Ngawang Samten.[9] Particularly challenging points were discussed with the kind and expert help of Khenpo Sherab Sangpo, Khenpo Jampa Donden, professor Tom Tillemans, professor John Dunne, and Dr. Mattia Salvini. We are most grateful to them all. The entire production of the manuscript for this book was sponsored by a grant from the Tsadra Foundation. We sincerely thank the Foundation for their generous and inspiring support.

Personally, I wish to express my gratitude to Tulku Chökyi Nyima Rinpoche, himself known as an emanation of Nāgārjuna, for his clear and profound Madhyamaka teaching, and to Khenpo Chöga, Lobpön Yeshe Trinley, Khenpo Sherab Öser, Tulku Sang-ngag Tendzin, and Khenpo Sherab Sangpo (here mentioned in the order that I was able to learn from them at Ka-Nying Shedrub Ling Monastery) with whom I have had the fortune of studying a few Indian Madhyamaka treatises, including the *Root of the Middle Way*.

Tulku Chökyi Nyima Rinpoche conceived the present translation of Nāgārjuna's verses and Mabja's commentary, and the Dharmachakra Translation Committee produced it under Rinpoche's guidance and supervision. I prepared the translation, and Cortland Dahl subsequently edited and compared it against the Tibetan. Rafael Ortet created the reproductions of Mabja's multilayered "topical outline" (sa bcad) that appear in the appendix. Michael Wakoff copyedited the book and prepared the index. The responsibility for any errors and shortcomings of this book is my own.

For those wishing to read the *Ornament of Reason* back to back with the original, we have made a cross-referenced version of the Tibetan text, prepared by Karma Öser, available for download on the Web site of the Dharmachakra Translation Committee, www.dharmachakra.net.[10]

We are all deeply thankful to His Holiness the Fourteenth Dalai Lama for blessing this book with a foreword.

May whatever goodness there may be in producing this book become a perfect circumstance for happiness and awakening throughout the world. In particular, may it serve to ensure the auspicious and continuous presence

9. Tsong khapa 2006.
10. The original Tibetan text assumes that the reader is already familiar with Nāgārjuna's stanzas, and in general it therefore does not cite them separately in the course of the explanation. In the English version, we have however chosen to insert Nāgārjuna's verses at the relevant places.

of our lord of refuge, Chökyi Nyima Rinpoche, and of all other masters who flawlessly uphold the sacred Dharma—scripture and realization.

On behalf of the team,
Thomas H. Doctor, on the full moon day
of the 2nd of December 2009

*Insight—The Stanzas
of the Root of the Middle Way*

by Nāgārjuna

Homage

That which originates dependently
Does not cease and does not arise,
Does not come and does not go,
Is not annihilated and is not permanent,

Is not different and not the same.
To the true teacher who reveals this peace,
The complete pacification of constructs,
To the perfect Buddha I bow down.

CHAPTER I

Analysis of Conditions

Not from itself, not from another,
Not from both, and not uncaused—
Nowhere does anything
Ever arise. [I.1]

There are four conditions:
Causal, objective, immediately preceding,
And, likewise, the ruling.
There is no fifth condition. [I.2]

The nature of things is not
In conditions and so forth.
If there is no thing itself,
How could there be anything other? [I.3]

Actions do not have conditions,
Yet there are no actions without conditions.
Without an action there are no conditions,
Yet no conditions are involved in an action. [I.4]

They are known as conditions
Because things arise in dependence on them.
Yet as long as nothing arises,
Why would they not be nonconditions? [I.5]

Neither for the nonexistent, nor for the existent,
Could there possibly be conditions.

For the nonexistent, what would be conditioned?
For the existent, what role could conditions play? [I.6]

If no existent, nonexistent, or both existent and nonexistent
Phenomenon comes into being,
How can we speak of "effectuating conditions"?
When this is the case, they do not make sense. [I.7]

It is explained that, with existent phenomena,
There are no observations whatsoever.
How could a phenomenon for which there is no observation
Ever relate to an observation? [I.8]

If phenomena have not arisen,
Cessation makes no sense.
Hence, an immediately preceding condition is untenable.
If it has ceased, how could it be a condition? [I.9]

Since there is no existence
Of things that have no nature,
Saying, "this occurs because of that"
Would not make any sense. [I.10]

In separate conditions and their gathering,
The effect is entirely absent.
How could something that does not exist in the conditions
Ever arise from them? [I.11]

If, without being present there,
It were still to arise from conditions,
Why would it not also arise
From that which is not a condition? [I.12]

The effect may be of its conditions' nature,
But these conditions have no nature of their own.
How could the effect of that which is not an entity itself
Be of the nature of that which conditions it? [I.13]

Hence, it is not of the nature of its conditions,
Nor of the nature of that which are not its conditions.
As there is no effect, how could there be
Conditions as well as nonconditions? [I.14]

CHAPTER TWO

Analysis of Going and Coming

Where there has been going, there is none;
Where it has yet to occur, there is no going either.
Aside from what has been traversed and what has not,
No place where walking occurs can be identified. [II.1]

Where there is movement, there is going,
And movement is found where walking takes place,
Not where going has been, nor where it has yet to occur.
Hence, going is found where walking takes place. [II.2]

Going where walking takes place,
How could that make sense,
When, without going, there cannot reasonably be
Any place where walking takes place? [II.3]

For whomever there is going where walking takes place,
It then follows
That there is no going where walking takes place
Because "going is found where walking takes place." [II.4]

If going took place where walking takes place,
It would follow that there are two acts of going:
One due to which there is a place with walking
And another that is the going that happens there. [II.5]

When it follows that there are two acts of going,
It follows that there are two agents of going,

Because without something that goes,
It makes no sense for there to be going. [II.6]

If there is nothing that goes,
Going makes no sense.
In the absence of any going,
How could there be one who goes? [II.7]

One who goes does not go,
Nor does one who does not go.
Other than goers and nongoers,
What third party could be going? [II.8]

When, in the absence of going,
A goer does not make sense,
The statement "going is engaged in by the one who goes"—
How could that possibly make sense? [II.9]

For those who hold that going is engaged in by one who goes
It would then follow that there is
One who goes in the absence of going,
For it is asserted that going is performed by one who goes. [II.10]

If going is engaged in by the one who goes,
It follows that there are two acts of going:
One that characterizes the one who goes,
And another going in that capacity. [II.11]

Going does not begin where it has been,
Nor does it begin where it has yet to occur.
Going does not begin where walking takes place,
So where does going begin? [II.12]

Before going has been initiated,
There is no place where walking occurs or has taken place
Upon which going could begin.
And how could there be going where there is none yet? [II.13]

Since we never witness a beginning of going
How can we conceive of the traversed,
Of what is being traversed,
And what has yet to be traversed? [II.14]

The one who goes does not stand still,
Nor does one who does not go.
Aside from those that do and do not go,
What third party could stand still? [II.15]

In the absence of going,
There cannot reasonably be anyone who goes.
How, then, could it reasonably be said
That it is the one who goes who stands still? [II.16]

Stopping does not occur where walking takes place,
Where going has been, or where it has yet to occur.
With going, beginning, and stopping,
The case is the same as with going. [II.17]

The act of going and the one who goes
Cannot rightly be said to be the same.
The act of going and the one who goes
Cannot rightly be said to be different. [II.18]

If that which is the going
Were also the one who goes,
It would follow that agent and act
Would be one and the same. [II.19]

Yet if the going and goer
Are thought to be different,
There could be going without something that goes
And someone who goes in the absence of going. [II.20]

When two things cannot be
Established as identical,

Yet not as different things either,
How can they be established at all? [II.21]

The one who goes does not engage in the going
That characterizes him as someone who goes,
Because there is no one who goes before going.
Someone goes somewhere. [II.22]

The one who goes does not engage in going other than
The going that characterizes him as someone who goes,
The reason being that for a single agent of going,
It does not make sense for there to be two acts. [II.23]

Someone who goes does not engage
In any of the three kinds of going.
Someone who does not go does not engage
In any of the three kinds of going. [II.24]

Someone who does and does not go does not engage
In any of the three kinds of going either.
There is, therefore, no going,
No one who goes, and nothing traversed. [II.25]

CHAPTER THREE

Analysis of the Sense Sources

Sight, hearing, smell,
Taste, touch, and cognition—
The experiential domain of these six faculties
Are the objects that are seen and so forth. [III.1]

Sight does indeed not see
Its own identity.
How can something that does not see itself
See anything else either? [III.2]

A solid establishment of sight cannot
Be provided through the example of fire.
With what was, has yet to be, and is being traversed
We have replied to that along with sight. [III.3]

When nothing at all is seen,
Neither is there one that sees.
"Sight is what performs seeing,"
How could this be right? [III.4]

Sight does not see,
Yet nonsight does not see either.
Know that sight itself
Also explains the one that sees. [III.5]

Whether seeing is involved or not,
There is nothing that sees.

Without the one that sees,
How could there be something seen and seeing? [III.6]

As there is nothing to see and no sight,
The four, such as consciousness, do not exist.
How could appropriation and other
Such factors come into existence? [III.7]

Hearing, smell,
Taste, touch, and cognition;
The hearer, the heard, and so forth—
Know that all are explained through sight. [III.8]

CHAPTER FOUR

Analysis of the Aggregates

Apart from the cause of form,
Form is not observed.
Likewise, aside from so-called form,
No cause of form can be observed either. [IV.1]

If there were form apart from its causes,
It would follow that form has no cause.
Yet there are no objects at all
That do not have causes. [IV.2]

If, aside from form,
There were a cause of form,
There would be a cause with no effect,
Yet there are no causes without effects. [IV.3]

When form exists,
A cause of form does not make sense,
Yet when form does not exist,
A cause of form doest not make sense either. [IV.4]

A form without a cause is impossible,
Utterly impossible.
Therefore, do not give rise
To any thoughts about form at all. [IV.5]

It is not right to say
That effects resemble their causes.

It is not right to say
That effects do not resemble their causes. [IV.6]

With feeling, identification, formation,
Mind, and all things
The steps are, in all regards,
The same as in the case of form. [IV.7]

When a critique is made using emptiness,
Whatever may be replied
Will not be a reply,
But the same as what is still to be proven. [IV.8]

When an explanation is given using emptiness
Whatever flaws one may find
Will not be found to be flaws,
But the same as what is still to be proven. [IV.9]

CHAPTER FIVE

Analysis of the Elements

Before the characteristics of space,
There is no space whatsoever.
If it existed before its characteristics,
It would follow that it has no characteristics. [V.1]

Something without characteristics
Does not exist anywhere at all.
Since there is no thing without characteristics,
To what do the characteristics apply? [V.2]

Characteristics do not apply to what has them,
Nor do they apply to what does not.
Neither do characteristics apply to something
Other than what does or does not have them. [V.3]

If characteristics have no application,
It makes no sense that there should be bearers of them.
If the bearers of characteristics are unreasonable,
Their characteristics cannot exist either. [V.4]

Therefore, the bearers of characteristics do not exist,
And characteristics themselves have no existence either.
Yet aside from bearers and characteristics
There are no entities. [V.5]

If there is no entity,
Of what would there be no entity?

What entity, nonentity, or otherwise
Would be the knower of entity and nonentity? [V.6]

Space, therefore, is not an entity, not a nonentity,
Not a bearer of characteristics, not a characteristic.
As for the other five elements,
The case is the same as with space. [V.7]

The feebleminded who see
Things in terms of existence and nonexistence
Fail to see what is to be seen—
The peace of complete pacification. [V.8]

CHAPTER SIX

Analysis of Desire and the Desirous One

If, before the presence of desire,
The desirous one exists without desire,
Based on that, there would be desire.
When the desirous one exists, so does desire. [VI.1]

Yet if the desirous one does not exist,
How could there possibly be desire?
Given the presence or absence of desire,
This follows also in the case of the desirous one. [VI.2]

Desire and the desirous one
Cannot reasonably arise together.
In this case, desire and the desirous one
Would not depend on one another. [VI.3]

Identical things are not coexistent,
As nothing is coexistent with itself.
Yet if they are different,
How could they be coexistent? [VI.4]

If a single thing were coexistent,
This would occur in isolation as well.
If the different were coexistent,
This would occur in isolation as well. [VI.5]

If they are different and coexistent,
How could desire and the desirous one

Be established as two different things
That would then be present together? [VI.6]

If desire and the desirous one
Are established as different,
Then why would you think of them
As being coexistent? [VI.7]

If they are asserted to be coexistent
Because their difference lacks establishment,
Would you also assert their difference
To prove their coexistence? [VI.8]

When things are not established as different,
Neither are they established as coexistent.
When there is a thing that is different,
It may be claimed that it is coexistent. [VI.9]

Therefore, desire and the desirous one
Are not established as coexistent or otherwise.
As is the case with desire and the desirous one,
No phenomena are established as coexistent or otherwise. [VI.10]

CHAPTER SEVEN

Analysis of the Characteristics of the Conditioned

If arising were conditioned,
It would possess these three characteristics.
If arising were unconditioned,
How could it be a characteristic of the conditioned? [VII.1]

Arising and the other two are each
Incapable of characterizing the conditioned.
But how could they simultaneously
Come together anywhere? [VII.2]

If arising, abiding, and cessation themselves
Bear further characteristics of the conditioned,
There will be an infinite regress.
Yet if they do not, they are not conditioned. [VII.3]

Due to the arising of arising,
There arises only fundamental arising,
Yet fundamental arising is responsible
For the arising of arising as well. [VII.4]

If your "arising of arising"
Produces fundamental arising,
How could it do so when not produced
By this "fundamental arising?" [VII.5]

If the product of this "fundamental arising"
Itself produces fundamental arising,

Then how could fundamental arising produce it,
When it has not been produced by that? [VII.6]

If that which has not yet arisen
Were capable of production,
Your assertion of production by the currently arising
Would have been acceptable. [VII.7]

Just as a light illumines
Both itself and other things,
Birth produces both itself
As well as other things. [VII.8]

Light itself and the place where it is—
Neither of these have any darkness.
What does light illuminate?
Illumination occurs by dispelling darkness. [VII.9]

When light that is currently arising
Does not encounter darkness,
How could the currently arising light
Illuminate the darkness? [VII.10]

If light were to dispel darkness,
Even without encountering it,
Then the one right here would dispel
All the darkness in the world. [VII.11]

If light could illumine
Both itself and other things,
Darkness would undoubtedly conceal
Both itself and other things as well. [VII.12]

When it has not arisen itself,
How could arising produce its own nature?
If it does so having already arisen,
Having arisen, what is it that is produced? [VII.13]

The arisen, unarisen, and arising
Are not produced in any way.
This was explained before
By what was, will be, and is being traversed. [VII.14]

When there is arising,
Current arising occurs,
Yet, when there is none, how can you claim
That this current arising is based on arising? [VII.15]

That which originates dependently
Is peace by its very essence.
Arising and the currently arising as well
Are, therefore, peace itself. [VII.16]

If an unarisen entity were to exist somewhere,
Then that could arise.
But, when it does not exist,
What sort of thing could then arise? [VII.17]

If arising gives rise
To the currently arising,
Then what, in turn,
Gives rise to arising? [VII.18]

If arising is due to a separate arising
There will be an infinite regress.
If it arises without arising,
Then so does everything else. [VII. 19]

The existent and nonexistent cannot reasonably arise.
Something that is both
Cannot do so either.
Indeed, this has already been explained. [VII.20]

A thing that is currently ceasing
Cannot reasonably arise.

A thing that is not currently ceasing
Cannot reasonably be a thing. [VII.21]

A thing that has abided does not abide,
A thing that has yet to abide does not abide,
And no currently abiding thing abides either.
What thing abides that does not arise? [VII.22]

A thing that is currently ceasing
Cannot reasonably abide.
A thing that is not currently ceasing
Cannot reasonably be a thing. [VII.23]

All things, at all times,
Are subject to aging and death.
What thing then remains
Free from aging and death? [VII.24]

Abiding cannot reasonably abide
Due to itself, or due to another.
The case was the same with arising,
Which arises neither by itself nor through another. [VII.25]

A thing that has ceased does not cease,
A thing that has yet to cease does not cease,
And no currently ceasing thing ceases either.
What thing ceases that did not arise? [VII.26]

A thing that abides
Cannot reasonably cease,
Yet a thing that does not abide
Cannot reasonably cease either. [VII.27]

The same state does not
Bring an end to itself,
Nor is it that a different state
Makes the initial one cease. [VII.28]

When no phenomenon's arising
Makes any sense,
No phenomenon's cessation,
Makes any sense either. [VII.29]

A thing that exists
Cannot have a cessation,
Because the same thing cannot
Be both thing and no thing. [VII.30]

A thing that does not exist
Cannot have a cessation,
Just as it is impossible
To cut off a second head. [VII.31]

Cessation is neither brought about
By itself nor by anything else,
Just as arising is not produced
By itself or something else. [VII.32]

As arising, abiding, and cessation are not established,
There is nothing that is conditioned.
Since the conditioned lacks any establishment,
How could the unconditioned be established? [VII.33]

Like a dream, like an illusion,
Like a city of scent-eaters—
This is how arising, abiding,
And cessation are taught to be. [VII.34]

CHAPTER EIGHT

Analysis of Action and Agent

That which is an agent does not
Perform something that is an action.
A nonagent does not
Perform a nonaction. [VIII.1]

That which is an agent would have no activity.
There would also be action without an agent.
That which is an action is not performed,
So the agent would be lacking its action. [VIII.2]

If a nonagent were to perform
That which is not an action,
The action would have no cause
And the agent would have no cause either. [VIII.3]

If there is no cause,
Cause and effect become untenable.
Without these, action, agent, and activity
Will all be nonsensical as well. [VIII.4]

If action and so forth are unreasonable,
There can be no Dharma and non-Dharma,
And without Dharma and non-Dharma,
Their effects do not exist either. [VIII.5]

Without such effects, paths to liberation
And to the higher realms do not make sense.

All activities would indeed
End up entirely meaningless. [VIII.6]

That which both is and is not an agent
Does not perform something that both is and is not.
Since being and not being are incompatible in one thing,
How could this ever be the case? [VIII.7]

One that is an agent does not perform
Something that is not an action,
Nor does one that is not perform something that is
Because the same flaws would ensue. [VIII.8]

The agent involved does not
Perform any nonaction,
Or something that both is and is not an action.
The arguments have already been given. [VIII.9]

That which is not an agent
Does not perform any action,
Or something that both is and is not an action.
The arguments have already been given. [VIII.10]

One that both is and is not an agent
Does not perform an action or a nonaction.
Here as well it should be understood
That the arguments have already been given. [VIII.11]

Agent comes about in dependence on action,
And action, in turn, in dependence on agent.
Apart from that we do not see
Any cause of their establishment. [VIII.12]

Appropriation should be understood in the same way,
As here action and agent have been excluded.
Agent and action will provide
Understanding of the remaining issues. [VIII.13]

CHAPTER NINE

Analysis of Prior Existence

Some assert that sight, hearing, and the rest,
As well as sensation and so forth,
Are in the possession of, and belong to,
Something that precedes them. [IX.1]

If there was no thing,
How could there be sight and so forth?
Hence, prior to these factors,
There is an abiding entity. [IX.2]

Before sight, hearing, and the rest,
And before sensation and so on,
What are your grounds for speaking
Of that abiding entity's existence? [IX.3]

If this remains in the absence
Of sight and these other factors,
Then they will undoubtedly be present
Even in the absence of that. [IX.4]

Something manifests somebody,
And somebody manifests something.
How could somebody exist in the absence of anything?
How could something exist in the absence of anybody? [IX.5]

This is not present before
The totality of sight and so forth.

Yet each factor among sight and the rest
Individually makes it manifest. [IX.6]

Unless it precedes the totality
Of sight and the rest,
How could it possibly precede
Each of them individually? [IX.7]

If that which sees were that which hears,
And what hears were that which senses,
This would exist before every one of them,
Yet that does not make sense. [IX.8]

If the seer, the hearer, and the one that senses
Were all different from each other,
The hearer could be present at the time of the seer
And there would be multiple selves. [IX.9]

Sight, hearing, and the rest,
As well as sensation and so forth—
Among the causes from which these emerge,
There is no existence of that. [IX.10]

Sight, hearing, and the rest,
As well as sensation and so forth—
If there is no one to whom these belong,
Then they do not exist either. [IX.11]

That which does not exist
Before, together with, or after sight and the rest
Will no longer be thought about
As existent or nonexistent. [IX.12]

CHAPTER TEN

Analysis of Fire and Fuel

If fuel were the same as fire,
Then agent and object would be the same.
If fire were different from fuel,
Then it would burn even without it. [X.1]

Fire would burn forever,
It would not arise from what causes it to burn,
Trying to light it would be pointless,
And it would not relate to any object. [X.2]

Because it would not depend on anything else,
It would not arise from what causes it to burn.
Because it would burn eternally,
Lighting it would be pointless. [X.3]

It may be thought that the fuel
Is that which is burning,
But if that is all that it is,
What is it that burns the fuel? [X.4]

If they are distinct, they do not touch;
If they do not touch, nothing is burned;
If nothing is burned, nothing dies out;
If nothing dies out, it will remain with its mark. [X.5]

Just as a woman touches a man
And a man touches a woman,

Fire can be different from fuel,
And yet still touch it. [X.6]

If fire and fuel,
Would exclude each other,
Fire would be different from fuel,
And so fire could touch fuel. [X.7]

If fire depends on fuel
And fuel depends on fire,
Of fire and fuel, the two dependents,
Which is established first? [X.8]

If fire depended on fuel,
An established fire would be reestablished,
And fuel would end up
Existing without fire. [X.9]

If an entity is established in dependence,
And is itself depended on
By that upon which it depends,
What is established in dependence on what? [X.10]

How could an entity that is established in dependence
Depend on something when it is not established?
If it is said that it depends while established,
Its dependence does not make any sense. [X.11]

There is no fire that depends on fuel,
There is no fire that does not depend on fuel.
There is no fuel that depends on fire,
There is no fuel that does not depend on fire. [X.12]

Fire does not come from anything else,
Nor is there any fire in the fuel.
The rest about fuel has been explained
By what was, will be, and is being traversed. [X.13]

Fuel is not the same as fire,
Nor is there fire apart from fuel.
Fire does not possess fuel.
Fuel is not in fire, nor is fire in fuel. [X.14]

Through the treatment of fire and fuel,
The self and its appropriation,
Along with vases, woolen garments, and so forth,
Have all been explained without exception. [X.15]

Those who teach that self and entities
Are the same or different
I do not consider knowledgeable
About the meaning of the teachings. [X.16]

CHAPTER ELEVEN

Analysis of Beginnings and Ends

When asked whether any beginning can be seen,
The Able One answered in the negative.
Cyclic existence has no beginning or end;
There is no before and there is no after. [XI.1]

When something has neither beginning nor end,
How could it possibly have a middle?
Therefore, cyclic existence cannot
Be either sequential or simultaneous. [XI.2]

If birth came first
And aging and death followed later,
There would be birth without aging and death,
As well as birth without anyone having died. [XI.3]

If birth occurred later,
And aging and death before,
How could this causeless aging and death
Happen to someone who was never born? [XI.4]

Birth, aging, and death
Cannot occur simultaneously,
For the one being born would then be dying,
And both would be lacking their cause. [XI.5]

As it is impossible for them to occur
In sequence or simultaneously,

Why would anyone think
In terms of birth, aging, and death? [XI.6]

Not only does cyclic existence
Have no beginning,
But also cause and effect,
Characteristics and their bearers, [XI.7]

Feelings and those that feel—
Whatever there may be.
The same applies to all things;
None have a beginning. [XI.8]

CHAPTER TWELVE

Analysis of Suffering

Some say that suffering is produced by itself,
By something other, by both,
Or that it arises without a cause.
Such production is not possible. [XII.1]

If suffering were produced by itself,
It could not arise in dependence,
Because, based on these aggregates,
Those aggregates arise. [XII.2]

If those were something other than these,
And these were something other than those,
Suffering would be produced by something other,
And they would produce something other. [XII.3]

If the person itself
Produces suffering,
Then what, apart from suffering,
Is this person who produces suffering? [XII.4]

If suffering comes from a different person,
Then how, when produced by another person,
Could it be given to somebody
Who is something other than suffering? [XII.5]

If suffering occurs because of another person,
Then who is this producer,

This other who gives suffering to another,
Yet who is not that very suffering? [XII.6]

As it cannot be established to be produced by a self,
How could suffering be the product of another?
The suffering produced by the other
Is the product of that other itself. [XII.7]

Suffering is not self-produced;
It is not its own product.
If the other is not the product of itself,
How could suffering be produced by another? [XII.8]

If suffering were produced by each of these,
Then suffering would be the product of both.
Neither produced by self nor other,
How could suffering be uncaused? [XII.9]

Not only does suffering
Not exist in any of these four ways,
External entities as well
Do not exist in any of the four ways. [XII.10]

CHAPTER THIRTEEN

Analysis of the Conditioned

The Transcendent Conqueror has taught
That all deceptive phenomena are false.
All conditioned phenomena are deceptive,
And, therefore, they are false. [XIII.1]

If a phenomenon that is deceptive is also false,
Then what is it that deceives?
With this, the Transcendent Conqueror
Has fully revealed emptiness. [XIII.2]

Things are devoid of essence
Because they are perceived to change.
There are no entities without essence
Because entities possess emptiness. [XIII.3]

If there is no essence,
To what does change pertain?
If there were essences,
How could there be change? [XIII.4]

Change is not in that itself,
Nor is it in something else,
Because the young do not age,
And because the aged do not age. [XIII.5]

If that itself changes,
Then milk itself is yogurt.

What, other than milk,
Would turn into yogurt? [XIII.6]

If there were a bit of something that is not empty,
There could be a bit of something that is empty.
As there is not a bit that is not empty,
How could there be anything that is empty? [XIII.7]

The Victorious Ones have taught emptiness
As a deliverance from all views.
For those whose view is emptiness, they teach,
Nothing can be accomplished. [XIII.8]

CHAPTER FOURTEEN

Analysis of Contact

The seen, sight, and the seer
Do not, either in pairs
Or as a group,
Ever come into contact. [XIV.1]

The same goes for desire, the desirous one,
And the object of desire, the other afflictions,
The remaining sense sources,
And for all such triads. [XIV.2]

Contact occurs between different things,
So because the seen and so forth
Do not exist as different things,
They do not come into contact. [XIV.3]

It is not only the seen and the rest
That do not differ from each other;
Wherever there is coexistence
There cannot reasonably be difference. [XIV.4]

That which is different differs in dependence on something else.
It does not differ without that different thing from which it differs.
Where something depends on something else,
The two cannot reasonably be different. [XIV.5]

If the different differed from something different,
It would be different even without anything different.

But nothing differs without something different,
And, hence, this is not the case. [XIV.6]

Difference does not exist in the different,
Nor does it exist in what is not different.
As difference as such does not exist,
Nothing is different and nothing is the same. [XIV.7]

Nothing comes into contact with itself,
Nor do different things come into contact.
Contacting, contacted, and contactor
Do not exist either. [XIV.8]

CHAPTER FIFTEEN

Analysis of Nature

Nature cannot reasonably occur
Due to causes and conditions.
A nature that arises due to causes and conditions
Would be a nature that is produced. [XV.1]

"A nature that is produced,"
How could that be right?
The natural is not fabricated,
And does not depend on anything else. [XV.2]

If nature does not exist,
How could there be other-nature?
It is the nature of other-nature
That is identified as "other-nature." [XV.3]

Apart from nature and other-nature,
What entity could there possibly be?
If there were nature and other-nature,
Entities would be established. [XV.4]

If entity is not established,
Then neither is nonentity.
It is the transformation of entity
That people call nonentity. [XV.5]

Those who believe in nature or other-nature,
In entity or nonentity,

Fail to see reality
Within the teachings of the Buddha. [XV.6]

The Transcendent Conqueror,
With knowledge of both entities and nonentities,
Refuted, in his Instructions to Kātāyana,
Both existence and nonexistence. [XV.7]

If something is existent by nature,
It would never become nonexistent.
A nature that undergoes change
Would never make any sense. [XV.8]

If no nature exists,
To what does change pertain?
Even if nature exists,
To what could change pertain? [XV.9]

"Existence" is apprehension of permanence,
"Nonexistence" a view of annihilation.
The wise, therefore, ought not to adhere
To either existence or nonexistence. [XV.10]

That which exists by nature
Is not nonexistent—this is permanence.
"It existed before, but now it does not"—
That implies annihilation. [XV.11]

CHAPTER SIXTEEN

Analysis of Bondage and Liberation

If it is claimed that formations cycle,
They cannot do so if permanent,
Nor can they if impermanent.
In the case of sentient beings, the steps are the same. [XVI.1]

It might be said that the person cycles,
But when we search the aggregates, elements, and sense sources,
Using the five steps and there is nothing,
What is it, then, that cycles? [XVI.2]

If there is cycling from appropriation to appropriation,
Then there cannot be any becoming.
Without becoming there can be no appropriation,
So what kind of cycling is this? [XVI.3]

Formations that transcend suffering
Do not make sense in any way.
Sentient beings that transcend suffering
Do not make sense in any way either. [XVI.4]

Formations that are subject to arising and ceasing
Are not bound and will not be freed.
As before, sentient beings as well
Are not bound and will not be freed. [XVI.5]

If bondage is due to appropriation,
Since nothing is bound in the presence of appropriation,

And there is no bondage in the absence of appropriation,
When, then, is it that bondage occurs? [XVI.6]

If the bond existed prior to the bound,
There could be bondage, yet it does not.
The rest has already been explained
By what was, will be, and is being traversed. [XVI.7]

That which is bound is not freed,
Yet the unbound is not freed either.
If the bound were being liberated,
Bondage and liberation would be simultaneous. [XVI.8]

"Without appropriation, I shall transcend suffering;
The transcendence of suffering, that shall be mine!"
Those who grasp in this way
Are engaged in severe appropriation. [XVI.9]

Where the transcendence of suffering is not produced
And cyclic existence is not dispelled,
How to conceive of cyclic existence,
And how of the transcendence of suffering? [XVI.10]

CHAPTER SEVENTEEN

Analysis of Action and Its Results

Restraining oneself properly,
Helping others, and a loving mind—
These are Dharma, seeds that bear fruit
Both here and hereafter. [XVII.1]

The Supreme Sage has taught
That action is volition and the willed.
The subdivisions of these actions
Are set forth in great detail. [XVII.2]

That which is taught as "actions of volition"
Is asserted to be mental,
While the so-called "intended actions"
Are physical and verbal. [XVII.3]

Speech and movement;
Imperceptible nonabstinence
And imperceptible abstinence—
These are similarly asserted. [XVII.4]

The merit that arises from enjoyment
And the demerit, in a similar manner,
Along with volition—
These seven principles are held to be action. [XVII.5]

If an action would remain until ripening,
Then it would be permanent.

If it ceases, then having ceased,
How could it produce an effect? [XVII.6]

The continuum of the sprout and so forth
Manifests from the seed,
Due to which the fruit comes about;
Without the seed, it would not arise. [XVII.7]

The continuum arises from the seed,
And from the continuum comes the fruit.
Therefore, the seed precedes the fruit.
Hence, there is no annihilation or permanence. [XVII.8]

That which is the continuum of mind
Manifests from the mind,
And from that emerges the effect.
Without this mind, it would not occur. [XVII.9]

The continuum arises from the mind,
And from the continuum comes the effect.
Therefore, the action precedes the effect
And there is no annihilation or permanence. [XVII.10]

The ten avenues of wholesome action
Are the means for performing Dharma.
Here and hereafter, the fruits of Dharma
Are the five sense pleasures. [XVII.11]

When it comes to this account,
There are numerous and significant flaws.
Hence, this account
Is untenable here. [XVII.12]

The account given by the Buddhas,
The self-realized buddhas, and the listeners
Is the one that is tenable here.
That, then, shall be set forth. [XVII.13]

Nondissipation resembles a promissory note.
The action then is the debt.
It is fourfold with reference to the realms
And its nature is neutral. [XVII.14]

It is not eliminated by elimination,
Yet it is eliminated through cultivation.
Therefore, it is due to nondissipation
That the effects of action are produced. [XVII.15]

If it were eliminated by elimination
Or destroyed by a transference of action,
Various flaws would ensue,
Such as the destruction of action. [XVII.16]

All those associated with realm-specific actions,
Whether congruent or incongruent,
Manifest as only one
When linking takes place. [XVII.17]

During the present life it arises
Separately with each instance
Of the two types of action,
Remaining even after the ripening. [XVII.18]

It ceases at transference
To the fruition or at death.
It should be understood that it is divided
In terms of the defiling and undefiling. [XVII.19]

Emptiness and absence of annihilation,
Cyclic existence and absence of permanence—
The phenomenon of nondissipation
Is the teaching of the Buddha. [XVII.20]

Why does action not arise?
Because it has no nature.

Because it does not arise,
Action does not dissipate. [XVII.21]

If action had a nature,
It would, undoubtedly, be permanent.
Action would not be created
Because the permanent cannot be active. [XVII.22]

If action were uncreated, there would be fear
Of encountering that which had not been done.
A lack of pure conduct
Would follow as a flaw as well. [XVII.23]

Undoubtedly, this would
Contradict all conventions.
The distinction between virtuous persons and sinners
Would no longer make sense. [XVII.24]

The ripening that has already ripened
Would go on ripening again and again.
For if it possessed a nature,
Action would remain present. [XVII.25]

Action is constituted by the afflictions,
But the afflictions are not real.
If afflictions are not real,
How could action be so? [XVII.26]

Action and affliction are taught
To be conditions for the body.
If action and affliction are empty,
Then what can be said of the body? [XVII.27]

The consumer is that being
Who is obscured by ignorance and has craving.
This being is not different from the agent,
Yet neither are these two identical. [XVII.28]

Because action does not arise
Based on conditions
Or based on nonconditions,
There is no agent either. [XVII.29]

If there is no action and no agent,
How could there be a result produced by action?
If there is no result,
How could there be a consumer? [XVII.30]

The Teacher, in a perfect miracle,
Creates emanations,
And these emanations again
Create further emanations. [XVII.31]

Likewise, the act performed by the agent
Resembles an emanation,
Just as when one emanation
Gives rise to another. [XVII.32]

Affliction, action, the body,
The agent, and the result
Are all like a city of scent-eaters,
Like an illusion, and like a dream. [XVII.33]

CHAPTER EIGHTEEN

Analysis of Self and Phenomena

If the self were the aggregates,
It would arise and cease.
If it were different from the aggregates,
It would have none of their characteristics. [XVIII.1]

When the self does not exist,
How could that which belongs to it?
Due to the pacification of self and that which belongs to it,
The belief in an "I" and a "mine" will cease. [XVIII.2]

The one who does not grasp at "I" or "mine"
Does not exist either.
The one who sees what lacks the grasping of "I" and "mine,"
That one does not see. [XVIII.3]

When the sense of "I" and "mine" that is based
On the inner and outer is exhausted,
Appropriation comes to an end.
As that is exhausted, so is birth. [XVIII.4]

Liberation follows from the exhaustion of action and affliction.
Action and affliction are due to thought,
And thoughts proliferate due to mental construction.
They are brought to an end by emptiness. [XVIII.5]

"Self" is stated
And also "no self" is taught.

The Buddhas even teach that there is neither
Self nor absence of self. [XVIII.6]

The expressible is annulled
Because the domain of the mind is annulled.
The intrinsic nature, unarisen and unceasing,
Equals the transcendence of suffering. [XVIII.7]

Everything is real and unreal,
Real and indeed not real,
Not unreal and not real—
That is the thorough teaching of the Buddha. [XVIII.8]

Not known by anything else, peace,
Not constructed through constructs,
Absence of concepts, and absence of a different meaning—
These are the characteristics of reality. [XVIII.9]

That which arises in dependence on something else
Is not identical with it,
Nor is it something other.
Hence, it is neither annihilated nor permanent. [XVIII.10]

The Buddhas, protectors of the world,
Grant the elixir of teaching
Without sameness or difference of meaning,
Without annihilation and without permanence. [XVIII.11]

Where a perfect Buddha has not appeared
And the listeners have disappeared,
The wakefulness of self-realized buddhas
Will, in the absence of a teacher, arise in full. [XVIII.12]

CHAPTER NINETEEN

Analysis of Time

If the present and the future
Depend on the past,
The present and the future
Exist in the past. [XIX.1]

If the present and the future
Do not exist in the past,
How can the present and future
Be dependent on it? [XIX.2]

If the two do not depend on the past,
Then they are not established.
The present and future
Therefore, do not exist. [XIX.3]

By these very same steps, the other two,
The supreme, the middling, and the inferior,
    and so forth;
As well as singularity and so on
Can also be understood. [XIX.4]

A time that does not endure is not apprehended.
Since a time apprehended as enduring
Does not exist, how can one speak
Of a time that is not apprehended? [XIX.5]

If time is based on entities,
And there are none, how could there be time?
When there are no entities at all,
How could there be any time? [XIX.6]

Analysis of the Assembly

If effects are produced by an assembly
Of causes and conditions
And are present in those assemblies,
How could they be produced by those assemblies? [XX.1]

If effects are produced by the very assembly
Of causes and conditions,
And are not present in those assemblies,
How could they be produced by those assemblies? [XX.2]

If effects are present in the assemblies
Of their causes and conditions,
They should be perceptible in those assemblies,
And yet they are not perceptible in those assemblies. [XX.3]

If effects are not present in the assemblies
Of their causes and conditions,
Then the causes and conditions
Equal what are not causes and conditions. [XX.4]

If the cause ceases to be,
Having been supplied to its effect,
It follows that the cause has two identities,
One supplied and another that ceases. [XX.5]

If a cause ceases to be,
Without having been supplied to its effect,

The effects that arise when it has ceased
Do not have any cause. [XX.6]

If effects arise together
With their assemblies,
The producer and produced
Will then be simultaneous. [XX.7]

If effects arise
Before their assemblies,
The absence of causes and conditions
Implies that effects are uncaused. [XX.8]

If a cause ceases,
Yet is transferred to its effect,
It follows that a cause already arisen
Would arise once more. [XX.9]

How could that which has ceased and disappeared
Be the producer of an arisen effect?
An enduring cause that is connected to its effect,
How could that produce it? [XX.10]

If cause and effect are not connected,
What effect would then be produced?
Whether seen or unseen by the cause,
No effect is produced. [XX.11]

A past effect is never in contact
With a cause that has passed,
Nor with one that has not arisen,
Or one that has already arisen. [XX.12]

An effect that has arisen
Is never in contact
With a cause that has not arisen,
That has passed, or that has arisen. [XX.13]

An effect that has not arisen
Is never in contact
With a cause that has arisen,
Has not arisen, or that has passed. [XX.14]

If there is no contact,
How could a cause produce its effect?
Even if there is contact,
How could a cause produce its effect? [XX.15]

If empty of an effect,
How can a cause produce its effect?
If not empty of an effect,
How can a cause produce its effect? [XX.16]

An effect that is not empty does not arise.
An effect that is not empty does not cease.
It follows that what is not empty
Has not ceased and has not arisen. [XX.17]

How can the empty arise?
How can the empty cease?
It follows that the empty
Has not ceased and not arisen. [XX.18]

Cause and effect being identical
Will never make sense.
Cause and effect being different
Will never make sense. [XX.19]

If cause and effect were identical,
Produced and producer would be the same.
If cause and effect were different,
Cause and noncause would be equal. [XX.20]

If an effect is existent by nature,
Then what could its cause produce?

If an effect is nonexistent by nature,
Then what could its cause produce? [XX.21]

If it does not produce any effect,
The cause does not make sense.
If the cause does not make sense,
Of what, then, is the effect? [XX.22]

If the assembly of causes and conditions
Does not itself
Produce its own identity,
How could it produce an effect? [XX.23]

Therefore, nothing is produced by an assembly,
And yet there is no effect made by anything else.
When no effect exists,
How can there be an assembly of conditions? [XX.24]

CHAPTER TWENTY-ONE

Analysis of Arising and Disintegration

Disintegration occurs neither apart from
Nor together with arising.
Arising occurs neither apart from
Nor together with disintegration. [XXI.1]

Disintegration without arising,
How could this occur?
There would be dying without birth.
Without arising, there is no disintegration. [XXI.2]

Disintegration together with arising
How could this occur?
Death does not take place
At the very same time as birth. [XXI.3]

Arising without disintegration,
How could this occur?
It is not that things
Ever lack impermanence. [XXI.4]

Arising together with disintegration,
How could this occur?
Birth does not occur
At the very same time as death. [XXI.5]

When two things are neither
Established as coexistent,

Nor as not coexistent,
How can they be established? [XXI.6]

There is no arising of the ceased,
Nor is there arising of the not ceased.
There is no disintegration of the ceased,
Nor is there disintegration of the not ceased. [XXI.7]

Where there is no thing,
There is no arising and no disintegration.
Without arising and disintegration,
There is no thing. [XXI.8]

With respect to the empty,
Arising and disintegration make no sense.
With respect to the not empty,
Arising and disintegration make no sense either. [XXI.9]

Arising and disintegration
Do not make sense if the same.
Arising and disintegration
Do not make sense if different. [XXI.10]

If you think,
"I see arising and disintegration,"
Then know that what you see
Is due to ignorance. [XXI.11]

Things do not arise from things.
Things do not arise from nonthings.
Nonthings do not arise from nonthings.
Nonthings do not arise from things. [XXI.12]

Things do not arise from themselves
Nor from something other than themselves.
When nothing arises from either self or other,
How could there be arising? [XXI.13]

If the existence of things is claimed,
Views of permanence and annihilation follow
Because these things must then
Be permanent or annihilated. [XXI.14]

Although the existence of things is claimed,
Permanence and annihilation do not follow
Because existence is the continuum of effects and causes
That arise and disintegrate. [XXI.15]

If a continuum of arising and ceasing
Causes and effects constitutes existence,
That which is destroyed does not arise again
And so causes are annihilated. [XXI.16]

If things have an essential nature,
They cannot reasonably become nonexistent.
When suffering is transcended there is annihilation,
For the continuum of existence is then entirely pacified. [XXI.17]

If the last ceases,
The first existence does not make sense.
When the last does not cease,
The first existence does not make sense. [XXI.18]

If the last is in the process of ceasing
While the first arises,
There is one that is ceasing
And another that arises. [XXI.19]

Hence, it does not make sense either
For ceasing and arising to occur together.
Could the aggregates with which one dies
Be the ones with which one is born as well? [XXI.20]

Therefore, nowhere in the three times,
Could there reasonably be any continuum of existence.
How could something outside of the three times
Be the continuum of existence? [XXI.21]

CHAPTER TWENTY-TWO

Analysis of the Thus-Gone

He is not the aggregates, nor is he different from them.
He is not in them, nor are they in him.
Neither does the Thus-Gone possess the aggregates.
Who, then, is the Thus-Gone? [XXII.1]

If the Buddha exists dependent on the aggregates,
And thus not by his own nature,
How could that which does not exist in terms of its own nature
Exist through the nature of another? [XXII.2]

That which depends on the nature of another
Cannot reasonably have an identity of its own.
How could something lacking an identity
Turn out to be the Thus-Gone? [XXII.3]

If he does not exist by his own nature,
How could there be the nature of something else?
Apart from what is of the nature of self and other,
What sort of Thus-Gone could there be? [XXII.4]

If, independent of the aggregates,
There were a Thus-Gone,
Then he could now rely on the aggregates
And, based on them, become that. [XXII.5]

Yet, independent of the aggregates,
There is no Thus-Gone at all.

When there is no one who exists independently,
How could there be any appropriation? [XXII.6]

Without any appropriation,
There cannot be something appropriated.
Not involved in appropriation—
Such a Thus-Gone does not exist at all. [XXII.7]

When examined in the five ways,
He exists neither as identical nor different.
How, then, could a Thus-Gone who does not exist like that
Be spoken of by virtue of appropriation? [XXII.8]

That which is appropriated
Does not exist by its own nature.
That which does not exist by itself,
Can definitely not exist due to other things. [XXII.9]

Thus, the appropriated and the appropriator
Are empty in all regards.
Given their emptiness, how to speak
Of an empty Thus-Gone? [XXII.10]

Do not say "empty,"
And do not say "not empty" either.
Do not say "both" and do not say "neither."
These are to be stated for the sake of designation. [XXII.11]

Permanence, impermanence, and the other two—
How could they pertain to this peace?
Limited, limitless, and the other two—
How could they pertain to this peace? [XXII.12]

One seized by the dense fixation
That the Thus-Gone exists
Will think that, upon his transcendence,
The Thus-Gone no longer exists. [XXII.13]

As for a Buddha empty of nature,
To declare that, upon transcendence,
He exists or does not exist
Would not make any sense. [XII.14]

Those who create constructs about the Buddha,
Who is beyond construction and without exhaustion,
Are thereby damaged by their constructs;
They fail to see the Thus-Gone. [XXII.15]

That which is the nature of the Thus-Gone
Is also the nature of this world.
There is no nature of the Thus-Gone.
There is no nature of the world. [XXII.16]

Analysis of Error

It is taught that desire, anger, and stupor
Originate in dependence on thought.
Their arising depends
On the attractive, unattractive, and mistaken. [XXIII.1]

That which originates in dependence
On the attractive, unattractive, and mistaken
Cannot be due to its own nature.
Hence, the afflictions are not real. [XXIII.2]

The existence or nonexistence of the self
Is not established in any way.
How can the existence or nonexistence
Of the afflictions be established without it? [XXIII.3]

The one to which the afflictions belong
Is not in any way established.
When they do not pertain to anything at all,
The afflictions cannot exist in any way either. [XXIII.4]

As in the case of the view regarding one's body,
The afflictions are absent in the afflicted in five ways.
As in the case of the view of one's body,
The afflicted is absent in the afflictions in five ways. [XXIII.5]

If the attractive, unattractive, and mistaken
Are not due to their own nature,

Then what are those afflictions that depend
On the attractive, unattractive, and mistaken? [XXIII.6]

Form, sound, taste, tactility, smell,
And phenomena—these six
Are believed to be the bases
For desire, anger, and stupor. [XXIII.7]

Form, sound, taste, tactility, smell,
And phenomena are all without exception
Like a city of scent-eaters,
Like an optical illusion, like a dream. [XXIII.8]

They resemble an illusory person
And are similar to reflections.
How could there be any real element
Of the attractive or unattractive in them? [XXIII.9]

The unattractive upon which
The designation "attractive" depends
Does not exist independently of the attractive.
Hence, the attractive does not make sense. [XXIII.10]

The attractive upon which
The designation "unattractive" depends
Does not exist independently of the unattractive.
Hence, the unattractive does not make sense. [XXIII.11]

When there is nothing attractive,
How could there possibly be desire?
When there is nothing unattractive,
How could there possibly be anger? [XXIII.12]

If thinking the impermanent
To be permanent is an error,
Then why, since the empty is not impermanent,
Would that thought be in error? [XXIII.13]

If thinking that which is not permanent
To be permanent is an error,
Then why would thinking the empty
To be impermanent not also be in error? [XXIII.14]

The means for apprehending, the apprehension,
That which apprehends, and what is apprehended
Are all completely pacified.
Hence, there is no apprehending. [XXIII.15]

Given that there is neither mistaken
Nor unmistaken apprehension,
Who could be in error?
Who could be correct? [XXIII.16]

The mistaken cannot
Become mistaken,
Nor can the unmistaken
Become mistaken. [XXIII.17]

That which is becoming mistaken
Cannot become mistaken either.
Where is error possible?
Investigate that. [XXIII.18]

Since they have not arisen,
How could there be errors?
Given that no error has occurred,
How could there be one that is mistaken? [XXIII.19]

Things do not arise from themselves,
Nor do they arise from anything else.
As things do not arise from self and not from other either,
How could there be one that is mistaken? [XXIII.20]

If there is a self, something clean,
Something permanent, and something delightful,

The apprehending of self, clean, permanent, and delightful
Are not mistakes. [XXIII.21]

If there is no self, nothing clean,
Nothing permanent, and nothing delightful,
There cannot be any absence of self, anything unclean,
impermanent, and painful. [XXIII.22]

As error in this way ceases,
Ignorance comes to an end.
As ignorance ceases,
Formations and so forth end. [XXIII.23]

If someone's afflictions
Are existent by nature,
How can they be eliminated?
Who can eliminate the existent? [XXIII.24]

If someone's afflictions
Are nonexistent by nature,
How can they be eliminated?
Who can eliminate the nonexistent? [XXIII.25]

CHAPTER TWENTY-FOUR

Analysis of the Noble Truths

If all of this were empty,
Nothing would arise or be destroyed.
For you it follows that
There are no four noble truths. [XXIV.1]

Since there are no four noble truths,
Complete understanding and elimination,
As well as familiarization and actualization,
Do not make any sense. [XXIV.2]

Without these,
The four fruitions do not exist either.
Without fruition, there is no one abiding in that,
Nor anyone who has gained entry. [XXIV.3]

If the eight persons do not exist,
Then there is no Sangha.
Because there are no noble truths,
There is no sacred Dharma. [XXIV.4]

If there is no Dharma and no Sangha,
How could there be any Buddha?
This teaching of emptiness
Invalidates the three jewels. [XXIV.5]

Likewise, the existence of results,
Non-Dharma and Dharma,

And all the conventions of the world
Would likewise be invalidated thereby. [XXIV.6]

To explain, you have not understood
The purpose of emptiness,
Emptiness itself, or its meaning.
Therefore this is damaging to you. [XXIV.7]

The Dharma taught by the Buddhas
Is genuinely based on the two truths:
The relative truth of the world
And the truth of the ultimate meaning. [XXIV.8]

Those who do not understand
The distinction between these two truths,
Fail to comprehend the profound reality
Of the Buddha's teaching. [XXIV.9]

Without relying on convention,
The ultimate cannot be shown.
Without realizing the ultimate,
Suffering cannot be transcended. [XXIV.10]

When viewing emptiness incorrectly,
Those with little insight will be ruined,
As when a snake is caught in the wrong way,
Or a knowledge mantra is used incorrectly. [XXIV.11]

Hence, knowing that the depth of this Dharma
Would be hard for the feebleminded to understand,
The realized mind of the Able One
Turned entirely away from teaching the Dharma. [XXIV.12]

The flaws that ensue in consequence
Are not reasonable with respect to emptiness.
Hence, your discarding emptiness
Is not reasonable to me. [XXIV.13]

Everything is possible
For those for whom emptiness is possible.
Nothing is possible
For those for whom emptiness is impossible. [XXIV.14]

All your own faults
You project onto me,
As if, while riding your horse,
You had forgotten all about it. [XXIV.15]

If you view things
As existent by nature,
Then for you there are
No causes and conditions. [XXIV.16]

Effect and cause;
Agent, means, and action;
Arising, cessation, and result—
These are invalidated as well. [XXIV.17]

That which originates in dependence
Is taught to be emptiness.
This itself is dependent imputation
And so the path of the Middle Way. [XXIV.18]

Apart from what originates dependently,
There are no phenomena at all.
Therefore, apart from emptiness,
There are no phenomena at all. [XXIV.19]

If all of this were not empty,
Nothing would arise or be destroyed.
For you it follows that
There are no four noble truths. [XXIV.20]

As it would not originate dependently,
How could there be suffering?

The teaching that the impermanent is suffering
Cannot be relevant where nature exists. [XXIV.21]

Given natural existence,
What could originate?
Hence, for those who deny emptiness,
There cannot be any origin. [XXIV.22]

If suffering exists by nature,
There can be no cessation.
As it would remain completely,
Cessation would be invalidated. [XXIV.23]

If there were a nature of the path,
It could not reasonably be cultivated.
If the path is to be cultivated,
Then this nature of yours does not exist. [XXIV.24]

If there is neither suffering
Nor its origin and cessation,
What cessation of suffering
Do you assert is achieved by the path? [XXIV.25]

If complete understanding
Were absent by nature,
How could complete understanding occur?
Does nature not remain? [XXIV.26]

The same with your elimination,
Actualization, familiarization,
Cultivation, and four fruitions—
They are as impossible as complete understanding. [XXIV.27]

Since they retain their own nature,
How could fruitions that are
By nature unachieved
Ever be achieved? [XXIV.28]

Without fruition, there is no one abiding in it,
Nor anyone who has gained entry.
If the eight persons do not exist,
Then there is no Sangha. [XXIV.29]

Because there are no noble truths,
There is no Dharma either.
If there are no Dharma and Sangha,
How could there be any Buddha? [XXIV.30]

For you it follows that the Buddha
Does not depend on enlightenment.
For you it follows that enlightenment
Does not depend on the Buddha. [XXIV.31]

For you, the one who by nature is no Buddha
May pursue the conduct of enlightenment
In order to attain enlightenment,
Yet all such efforts will be in vain. [XXIV.32]

Nobody would ever perform
Dharma or non-Dharma.
What can be done to the not empty?
There can be no action in relation to nature. [XXIV.33]

In the absence of Dharma and non-Dharma,
For you, there are still effects.
Effects caused by Dharma and non-Dharma
For you, do not exist. [XXIV.34]

If, for you, there are effects
That arise from Dharma and non-Dharma,
Why, then, would these effects
Of Dharma and non-Dharma not be empty? [XXIV.35]

The one who denies
The emptiness of dependent origination

Will, likewise, be denying
All conventions of the world. [XXIV.36]

A denial of emptiness
Will preclude all action.
There will be actions without initiation,
As well as agents without anything done. [XXIV.37]

If beings had any nature,
They would not be born or die.
Indeed, they would remain immutable
And would not know a variety of states. [XXIV.38]

Were it not for emptiness,
The unattained could not be attained,
There would be no liberation from suffering,
And no elimination of action and affliction. [XXIV.39]

The one who sees
Dependent origination
Sees suffering, its origin,
Cessation, and the path. [XXIV.40]

CHAPTER TWENTY-FIVE

Analysis of the Transcendence of Suffering

If all of this were empty,
Nothing would arise or be destroyed.
Which elimination and cessation is it
That you assert leads to the transcendence of suffering? [XXV.1]

If all of this were not empty,
Nothing would arise or be destroyed.
Which elimination and cessation is it
That you assert leads to the transcendence of suffering? [XXV.2]

No elimination and no attainment,
No annihilation and no permanence,
No cessation and no arising—
This is termed the transcendence of suffering. [XXV.3]

Now, the transcendence of suffering is not an entity,
For it would then be characterized by aging and death.
There is no entity that is free
From aging and death. [XXV.4]

If the transcendence of suffering were an entity,
The transcendence of suffering would be conditioned.
An entity that is not conditioned
Does not exist anywhere at all. [XXV.5]

If the transcendence of suffering were an entity,
Why would it not be dependent?

An entity that is not dependent
Does not exist at all. [XXV.6]

If the transcendence of suffering is not an entity,
How could it be a nonentity?
When the transcendence of suffering is not an entity,
Neither is it a nonentity. [XXV.7]

If the transcendence of suffering is not an entity,
Why would it not be dependent?
Indeed, there is no nonentity at all
That is not dependent. [XXV.8]

Entities that come and go
Are dependent and caused.
Their being independent and not caused
Is taught to be the transcendence of suffering. [XXV.9]

The Teacher has declared
The abandonment of arising and disintegration.
Thus, it makes sense that the transcendence of suffering
Is not an entity or a nonentity. [XXV.10]

If the transcendence of suffering
Were both entity and nonentity,
Entity and nonentity would be liberation,
Yet this does not make sense. [XXV.11]

If the transcendence of suffering
Were both entity and nonentity,
The transcendence of suffering would not be independent,
Because these two are dependent. [XXV.12]

How could the transcendence of suffering
Be both entity and nonentity?
The transcendence of suffering is unconditioned,
Entity and nonentity are conditioned. [XXV.13]

How could the transcendence of suffering
Possess both entity and nonentity?
These two cannot coexist,
Just like light and darkness. [XXV.14]

The teaching that the transcendence of suffering
Is neither entity nor nonentity
Would be established
If entity and nonentity were established. [XXV.15]

If the transcendence of suffering
Were neither entity nor nonentity,
Who would perceive that
"It is neither entity nor nonentity"? [XXV.16]

When the Transcendent Conqueror has gone beyond,
He is not perceived as "existent,"
Nor as "nonexistent,"
As "both," or as "neither." [XXV.17]

Even as the Transcendent Conqueror remains,
He is not perceived as "existent,"
Nor as "nonexistent,"
As "both" or as "neither." [XXV.18]

Cyclic existence is not the slightest bit
Different from the transcendence of suffering
Transcendence of suffering is not the slightest bit
Different from cyclic existence. [XXV.19]

That which is the condition of transcendence
Is the condition of cyclic existence as well.
Between these two there is not
The slightest bit of difference. [XXV.20]

Views of what follows the passing, of the finite and so on,
Along with those on permanence and so forth,

Are based on the transcendence of suffering,
The limit of the future, and the limit of the past. [XXV.21]

When all things are empty,
What is finite and what is infinite?
What is both finite and infinite?
What is neither finite nor infinite? [XXV.22]

What is identical and what is different?
What is permanent, what is impermanent?
What is both permanent and impermanent?
What is neither permanent nor impermanent? [XXV.23]

Complete pacification of all observations,
The complete pacification of constructs, peace—
Nowhere did the Buddha
Teach any Dharma to anyone at all. [XXV.24]

CHAPTER TWENTY-SIX

Analysis of Dependent Origination

Due to the obscuration of ignorance, there occurs, directed at rebirth
The conditioning of the action
Of the three types of formation.
Thus, there is migration between the realms. [XXVI.1]

Consciousness, conditioned by formation,
Enters the realms.
Once consciousness has entered,
Name and form will manifest. [XXVI.2]

When name and form have manifested,
The six sense sources will develop.
Dependent on the six sense sources,
Contact comes into being. [XXVI.3]

It arises exclusively in dependence
On eye, form, and consciousness.
Thus, dependent on eye and form,
Consciousness will occur. [XXVI.4]

Contact is the meeting
Of eye, form, and consciousness.
Out of this meeting
Arises sensation. [XXVI.5]

Conditioned by sensation, there is craving,
Craving with respect to sensation.

When there is craving, there will be grasping,
Grasping in the fourfold way. [XXVI.6]

Grasping will initiate
The becoming of the grasper.
Absence of grasping will result
In liberation free from becoming. [XXVI.7]

Becoming is the five aggregates.
From becoming follows birth.
Aging and death, grief,
Lamentation, pain, [XXVI.8]

Mental unrest, disturbance—
All of this occurs due to birth.
Thus arises this mass
Of nothing but suffering. [XXVI.9]

Formation is the root of cyclic existence,
Therefore, the wise do not form.
The agents of that are the unwise;
Not the wise, for they see reality. [XXVI.10]

When ignorance has ceased,
Formation does not arise either.
The cessation of ignorance is accomplished
By meditating on reality through insight. [XXVI.11]

As each of them ceases,
None of them will occur.
Thus, this mass of nothing but suffering
Will actually come to an end. [XXVI.12]

CHAPTER TWENTY-SEVEN

Analysis of Views

Past existence and nonexistence,
A permanent world, and so forth—
These views depend
On the extreme of the past. [XXVII.1]

The views of existence and nonexistence
At a different time in the future,
Of the end of the world, and so forth
Depend on the extreme of the future. [XXVII.2]

Saying "It existed in the past"
Indeed, does not make sense.
Whatever occurred in past lives
Is not the same as this. [XXVII.3]

If you think, "That itself is the self,"
The appropriated would be different.
Apart from appropriated,
What is this self of yours? [XXVII.4]

When it is held that there is no self
Apart from the appropriated,
If the appropriated is itself the self,
Your self does not exist. [XXVII.5]

The appropriated is not the self,
For it arises and disintegrates.

How could the appropriated
Ever be the appropriator? [XXVII.6]

It does not make sense for there to be
A self that is different from the appropriated.
If different, it could reasonably be perceived
In the absence of appropriation, yet it cannot. [XXVII.7]

Thus, it is not other than appropriation,
Nor are these two the same.
The self does not exist without appropriation,
Yet neither can it be ascertained as nonexistent. [XXVII.8]

Saying "It did not exist in the past,"
Does not make sense either.
Whatever was there in past lives
Is not different from this. [XXVII.9]

If it were something other,
It could arise even in its absence.
Likewise, that would remain
And there could be birth without death there. [XXVII.10]

There would be annihilation, action would be wasted,
The action done by one
Would be experienced by another—
These and other flaws would ensue. [XXVII.11]

Something previously nonexistent does not arise
Because flaws would follow:
The self would be a product
And its arising would lack a cause. [XXVII.12]

Thus, that the self existed, did not exist,
That it both existed and did not,
Or neither existed nor did not exist—
These views on the past are untenable. [XXVII.13]

The views that "it will exist
At a different time in the future,"
Or that, "it will not exist in the future,"
Are equal to those about the past. [XXVII.14]

If the god were the human,
It would be permanent.
The god would be unborn,
For the permanent has no birth. [XXVII.15]

If the god were different from the human,
It would be impermanent.
If god and human were different,
There could not reasonably be one stream of being. [XXVII.16]

If one part were divine
And another part human,
It would be permanent and impermanent.
That is not reasonable either. [XXVII.17]

If permanent and impermanent
Were both established,
It would be possible to establish
The neither permanent nor impermanent. [XXVII.18]

If something came somewhere from somewhere
And then would go somewhere else,
Then cyclic existence would have no beginning,
Yet that is not the case. [XXVII.19]

When nothing is permanent,
What could be impermanent?
Permanence, impermanence,
And both have been dismissed. [XXVII.20]

If the world had an end,
How could there be another world?

If the world had no end,
How could there be another world? [XXVII.21]

This continuity of the aggregates
Is just like an oil lamp's light.
Hence, neither finitude
Nor infinitude makes sense. [XXVII.22]

If the previous were to cease,
And if, based on these aggregates,
Those aggregates would not arise,
The world would have an end. [XXVII.23]

If the previous were not to cease,
And if, based on these aggregates,
Those aggregates would not arise,
The world would be endless. [XXVII.24]

If one part were finite
And another part infinite,
The world would and would not have an end.
This does not make sense either. [XXVII.25]

How could one part
Of the appropriator be destroyed
And another part not be destroyed?
This does not make sense. [XXVII.26]

How could one part
Of the appropriated be destroyed
And another part not be destroyed?
That does not make sense either. [XXVII.27]

If the finite and infinite
Were both established,
It would be possible to establish
The neither finite nor infinite. [XXVII.28]

Alternately, because all things are empty,
How could views of permanence and so on,
Occur in any form, anywhere,
And to anyone at all? [XXVII.29]

By the love of his heart, he accepts us
And, so that all views may be relinquished,
Reveals the sacred Dharma.
To the teacher, Gautama, I prostrate. [XXVII.30]

Colophon to the Tibetan Translation

This completes the root stanzas of the Middle Way, entitled "Insight," which belong to the Abhidharma of the Great Vehicle and which truly reveal ultimate reality. This elucidation of the way of transcendent insight was composed by the great being and noble Master Nāgārjuna, possessor of inalienable knowledge and compassion. Illuminating the way of the supreme vehicle of the Thus-Gone One, he accomplished the ground of great joy and departed for the Realm of Bliss. In the world called Clear Light, he will become a Thus-Gone One, known by the name "Light of the Source of Wakefulness."

As instructed by the great king, Pal-lha Tsenpo, Lord of Perfect Majesty, this translation was prepared, revised, and established by the great Indian preceptor and representative of the Middle Way, Jñānagarbha, and the lotsāwa and editor, the monk Chokru Lui Gyaltsen. The twenty-seven chapters and 449 *śloka*s are contained in one and a half *bampo*.

Subsequently, the translation was revised based on the *Clear Words* commentary during the reign of Āryadeva, Lord of Men, in the Temple of Hidden Jewels, a monastic college situated in the center of the city of Anupamanagara in Kashmir. This revision was undertaken by the Kashmiri preceptor Hasumati and the Tibetan lotsāwa, the translator Patsab Nyima Drakpa. The Indian preceptor Kanaka and the same lotsāwa later prepared a final revision in the Temple of Rasa Trülnang.

Saṃgatālaṃkāra Madhyamakamūlaprajñāyāḥ vṛtti[11] nāma viharati sma

dBu ma rtsa ba shes rab kyi 'grel pa 'thad pa'i rgyan ces
bya ba bzhugs so

A Commentary on *Insight—Root of the Middle Way*

entitled the

Ornament of Reason

11. In an apparent error, the original here reads *prajñāsya pratti*.

Homage to the noble youthful Mañjuśrī!

Having seen the perfectly genuine, the definitive meaning of the
    Victor's teaching,
You light the lamp of genuine reasoning for wandering beings
With a compassion that is free of focal point—
Homage to you, lord Nāgārjuna, son of the Victorious Ones

Completely crushing the mountain of the two imputed extremes,
His profound and extensive vajra words, the root of insight,
Illumine the Middle Way, beyond permanence and annihilation, exis-
    tence and peace,
Revealing its ground, path, and fruition just as they are.

Relying on scripture, reasoning, and the guru's instructions,
I shall respond to the request of those intelligent and committed,
And so, with an approach that neither exaggerates nor denigrates,
Here explain for the benefit of others.

PRELIMINARY DISCUSSION

Generally speaking, those who teach the sūtras and treatises should precede their explanation with a consideration of three main topics: (1) an identification of the Dharma that is being taught and listened to, (2) how to teach and listen to this Dharma, and (3) the result of teaching and listening in this manner.

THE DHARMA

The first of these topics includes three further topics: (1) the various uses of the word "dharma," (2) an explanation of this term, and (3) an identification of the dharma that is relevant in the present context.

Uses of the Term "Dharma"

Regarding the first topic, it is taught:

> Dharma can mean object of cognition, path,
> Transcendence of suffering, object of the mind,
> Merit, life, excellent discourse, what will happen,
> That which is certain, and spiritual tradition.[12]

As indicated here, each occurrence of the word "dharma" found in the sūtras and the treatises should be understood with reference to this set of ten meanings.

---

12. From Vasubandhu, *Reasoned Exposition.*

EXPLANATION OF THE TERM "DHARMA"

Second, the term "dharma" derives from the Sanskrit word *dharaṇa*, which means to hold. This can be understood to mean the holding of specific characteristics and also holding in the sense of protecting from a fall. In the first case, the word "dharma" is used to denote that all defiling and undefiling objects of cognition hold their own characteristics. An example of this usage would be the sentence "all dharmas are devoid of self."

In the second case, holding has the specific meaning of protecting one from falling into the lower realms, and, more generally, of keeping one from falling into the cyclic existence of the five classes of wandering beings. An example of the first usage is found in the following verses:

> The one who practices Dharma rests at ease,
> Both in this world and beyond.

As indicated here, the word "dharma" may refer to the practice of the ten forms of virtue. Such virtuous activity may be instigated by the faith of conviction in karmic action and its effects, or based on the authentic views of worldly beings (which may also be found among certain non-Buddhists). This usage can also refer to mundane forms of concentration, such as the cultivation of the meditative absorptions associated with the formless realms.

The second sense of holding can be illustrated by statements such as, "I go for refuge in the Dharma, supreme among all that is free from attachment." Here, the reference is to the unique Dharma in which Buddhists take refuge. This refers to the Dharma of realization (the two truths of complete purification) and the Dharma of scripture that applies to this realization. As is taught:

> The sacred Dharma of the Teacher is twofold:
> It is of the nature of scripture and realization.[13]

THE DHARMA BEING TAUGHT IN THE PRESENT CONTEXT

Third, in this particular context we are concerned with the Dharma of the excellent discourses, the Dharma of scripture. On this topic, it is taught:

13. Vasubandhu, *Treasury of Abhidharma*, VIII.39a–b.

The entire Dharma is contained in the words of the Buddha and
the treatises,
The excellent statements and the commentaries on their
intent.[14]

As stated here, there are two divisions: (1) the words of the Buddha, the
excellent statements made by the truly and completely enlightened one,
and (2) the treatises that definitively explain their meaning. The first category, the words of the Buddha, can be understood with reference to (1)
its defining characteristics, (2) the meaning of the defined term, and (3) a
classification of that which bears these characteristics.

The Words of the Buddha

The Defining Characteristics of the Words of the Buddha
First, regarding the defining characteristics of the words of the Buddha,
it is taught:

That which holds meaning, closely connected with the Dharma,
And which is a speech that eliminates the afflictions of the three
realms,
While revealing the benefits of peace—
That is the speech of the Sage, and anything else is not.[15]

As indicated here, the words of the Buddha are stainless words and syl-
lables. Their subject matter is the three precious trainings. In terms of
function, they completely eliminate the afflictions of the three realms. As
their result, they reveal, or bring about, the attainment of the three forms
of the transcendence of suffering. Thus, the defining characteristics of the
words of the Buddha lie in their being endowed with these four aspects
of confident speech. This formulation simply goes to show how the
teachings found in the sūtras and treatises are distinguished from those
of non-Buddhist scriptures. Hence, from the point of view of excluding
that which does not fall into this category, the words of the Buddha can
also be defined as Dharma that arises directly from the Buddha as its ruling condition.

14. From the *Sūtra Requested by the Son of the Gods, Susthitamati.*
15. Maitreya, *Supreme Continuity,* V.18.

The Defined Term
Second, the Buddha's "words" are referred to as such because they are verbal expressions.

Classifications of the Words of the Buddha
Third, of the various ways to classify the words of the Buddha, one popular threefold division distinguishes them with reference to their ruling conditions. Here, the three divisions are those that were actually spoken, those of blessings, and those of acceptance.

The words of the Buddha can also be divided in terms of when they were spoken. In order to tame individuals inclined to the Lesser Vehicle, such as the excellent retinue of five, the Buddha turned the Dharma wheel of the initial teachings of the four truths. He turned this wheel of Dharma using a twelvefold sequence at the Deer Park of the Forest of the Falling Sages in Varanasi. The content of these teachings covers both conduct and view. Conduct, here, involves not harming sentient beings. In terms of the view, he simply taught the sixteen aspects of the four noble truths or, in other words, that the aggregates are merely impermanent phenomena, empty of any personal self in the form of an agent or consumer.

To tame individuals with a potential for the Great Vehicle, the Buddha turned the intermediate wheel of Dharma on the absence of characteristics, thus teaching the extensive, middling, and concise Sūtras [on Transcendent Insight]. The setting for these teachings was Vulture Peak Mountain. In terms of content, the vast conduct presented in these teachings consists of working for the welfare of others with great compassion, while the profound view is taught to be emptiness free from all the constructs associated with persons and phenomena.

For those individuals with a potential to be inclined toward a diversity of vehicles, the Buddha turned the final wheel of Dharma on the definitive meaning at locations such as Laṅkapūri. In terms of content, these teachings explain the conduct as consisting in working for the welfare of others on vast scale, and with respect to the view, they address a qualm that is based on a perceived contradiction between the initial and intermediate teachings. The initial teachings explain that, while there is no person, the mere phenomena of the five aggregates, or those associated with the four truths, do exist. The intermediate teachings, meanwhile, claim that these phenomena are nonexistent as well. Addressing this problem, the followers of the Yogic Practice School consider the intent of the third set of teachings to be the mind only [position]. When stating that these phenomena are nonexistent, they explain, the second set of teachings intends to show the nonexistence of the imaginary object-subject duality. This does not, however, mean that the dependent, nondual cognition that is the support for the afflictions and their purification is also nonexistent. Therefore, they say, these two do not contradict one another.

The learned followers of noble Nāgārjuna, however, employ scripture and reasoning to explain the intent of the sūtras without error. They resolve the message of the first and second sets of teachings in the following way: In the initial set of teachings, the aggregates, elements, and sense sources (or the mere phenomena associated with the four truths, the dependently originated phenomena that are devoid of a person and subsumed by affliction and purification) are said to exist. This statement is made in consideration of the relative, deluded perspective. On the other hand, in the second set of teachings these are all said to be nonexistent. This statement accords with the ultimate, rational perspective that is free from delusion. Hence, they say, there is no contradiction. Together, these are the three stages of the words of the Buddha.

With respect to their content, one may make a twofold distinction between the sūtras of expedient meaning, which explain the vast relative truth, and the sūtras of definitive meaning, which teach the ultimate truth of profound emptiness. With reference to the expressions that convey this content, one may distinguish Sūtra from the other categories that make up the twelve aspects of melodious speech. In terms of their respective focus, the teachings can be divided into the Three Precious Collections with regard to which of the three precious trainings they emphasize. Alternatively, Sūtra can be seen to concisely teach the nature of all three precious trainings, while the Vinaya sets forth the training of discipline in detail, and the Abhidharma gives an elaborate presentation of the training of insight.

In terms of inferiority and superiority, the words of the Buddha can also be divided into the Lesser Vehicle and Great Vehicle. The Great Vehicle can be further divided into the Causal Vehicle of Characteristics and the Resultant Vehicle of Secret Mantra.

The Treatises
To ascertain the general nature of the treatises, we shall consider (1) their defining characteristics, (2) the meaning of the defined term, and (3) a classification of the bearers of the characteristics.

Defining Characteristics of the Treatises

Regarding the first topic, a treatise is written by a fully qualified individual based on the teachings of the truly and completely enlightened one. The following passage explains further:

> That which assumes the perspective of the Victor's teachings alone,
> Was written by one with an undistracted mind,
> And accords with the path through which liberation is achieved
> Should be venerated with the crown of one's head, just like the
> Sage's teachings.[16]

The Defined Term

Second, the term "treatise" derives from the Sanskrit word *śāsana*,[17] meaning conquering, dispelling, or healing. Hence, a *śāstra,* or treatise, is something that thoroughly conquers the enemy of the afflictions, dispels concepts, or, through these two, heals the mind of the student. Alternatively, [the term "treatise" is also associated with the Sanskrit] word *trāṇa*,[18] meaning protection. Hence, a treatise can also be taken to refer to something that protects one from both the lower realms and existence. Thus, it is taught:

> It is *śāstra* since it dispels concepts,
> And because it heals grasping

And:

> Conquering all the enemies, the afflictions, without exception,
> While protecting from the lower realms and existence,
> The treatises possess the qualities of being able to protect
>   and heal,
> Two qualities that are absent in the traditions of others.[19]

These qualities are also found in the words of the Buddha. This does not

16. Maitreya, *Supreme Continuity*, V.19.
17. In what appears to be an error, the Tibetan text here reads *śāstrayā*.
18. In what appears to be an error, the Tibetan text here reads *styāna*.
19. Vasubandhu, *Reasoned Exposition*.

pose a problem, however, because this explanation of the term is meant to show the decisive superiority of Buddhist treatises over non-Buddhist ones, rather than their defining characteristics.

Classification of the Treatises
Third, of the various ways to classify the treatises, one popular approach is to distinguish the treatises with respect to the words of the Buddha they explain, in which case there are two divisions. The first group of treatises presents general comments on the common meaning of the words of the Buddha, while the second explains the intent of particular teachings. The first category contains treatises that clarify the words and meanings that relate to the words of the Buddha in general, such as those on linguistics and reliable means of cognition.

The second category can be further classified with reference to the three wheels of Dharma. First we have the treatises that clarify the view and conduct associated with the wheel of Dharma of the four truths. This includes the *Vinaya-sūtra* and the *Treasury of Abhidharma*. Second are the treatises that clarify the meaning of the sūtras on the absence of characteristics, within which there are two categories. One is constituted by the master Nāgārjuna's *Six Collections of Reasoning* and the treatises that adhere to them. These are works that use reasoning to explain what is taught explicitly by the Sūtras [of Transcendent Insight], namely, the natural emptiness of all phenomena that is observed by insight, or the view. The second category contains the noble Maitreya's *Ornament of Manifest Realization* and the treatises that adhere to it. Distinguishing between eight manifest realizations, these works clarify the implicit teaching of the sūtras. They are thus concerned with the subject and the stages of manifest realization that comprise the path and fruition.

The treatises associated with the third wheel of Dharma explain the intent of the final teachings of definitive meaning. Among these treatises, some rely upon the view of the Mind Only School to explain numerous principles associated with the view and conduct. In this category we find the noble Maitreya's *Distinguishing the Middle from Extremes, Ornament of the Sūtras*, and *Distinguishing Phenomena from Their Intrinsic Nature*. This also includes the treatises that adhere to these three, such as the master Asaṅga's fivefold *Grounds of Yogic Practice* and his two compendia, as well as the master Vasubandhu's eightfold *prakaraṇa*. There are also treatises that explain the intent of the final set of teachings to be the Middle

Way. These include the noble Maitreya's *Supreme Continuity* and the master Candrakīrti's *Entering the Middle Way*.

In terms of function, treatises can be divided into three categories: those that discern the profound, those that summarize the vast, and those that systematize the scattered. With respect to their particular focus, there are the aforementioned three categories of treatises that clarify the meaning of the three collections. In terms of content, treatises can be categorized as those that explain the sūtras of expedient meaning and those that explain the sūtras of definitive meaning. A distinction may also be made between those that clarify the nature of the Lesser Vehicle and those that pertain to the Great Vehicle. With regard to quality, treatises can also be divided into nine categories, as explained in the following passage:

> Meaningless, mistaken, and meaningful;
> Deceitful, unkind, and relinquishing suffering;
> In pursuit of learning, argument, and practice—
> Treatises are held to be threefold and free from six.[20]

The Significance of the Present Treatise

In this way, the Dharma of scripture consists of the words of the Buddha and treatises. Here it is the latter that will be explained. The meaning of this particular treatise will be ascertained under three headings: (1) the uniqueness of the author, (2) his literary corpus, and (3) the nature of his treatise [on the Middle Way].

The Author

This treatise was composed by the master Nāgārjuna. According to some scholars, there are five features that distinguish Nāgārjuna: (1) He took birth as the Licchavī youth, Sarvalokapriyadarśana, (2) as the monk Matidhara, and (3) as the master Nāgārjuna; (4) he attained the first ground of the Truly Joyous; and (5) he was prophesied in various sūtras and tantras taught by the Bliss-Gone One. The first three of these are held to be circumstantial distinctions, whereas the last two distinguish his nature. Other scholars mention three distinctions: the qualities Nāgārjuna attained, the enlightened activities he performed, and the praises he received.

---

20. Vasubandhu, *Reasoned Exposition*.

Nāgārjunaʾs Qualities

The qualities achieved by this master relate to his extraordinary abandonment and realization. A member of the Brahmin caste, Nāgārjuna left home without taking even a needle; he was completely unattached to the pleasures of household life. Having become a fully ordained monk and completing the preliminary process of training, he underwent fifty-three trials without becoming tainted by even the slightest evil deed. He then beheld the intrinsic nature, which is empty of both the self of the person and of phenomena, and thereby eliminated the relevant afflictive and cognitive obscurations that are to be overcome. This was his extraordinary abandonment.

In terms of realization, Nāgārjuna had a universal insight into the five fields of learning, yet his particular achievement was an illuminated realization of the inner science, the full range of the Bliss-Gone One's teachings. More specifically, he internalized the Dharma of scripture by flawlessly realizing the definitive meaning of the Great Vehicle's sūtras and tantras. He likewise directly perceived and realized the omnipresence of the basic field of phenomena on the first ground and achieved its twelve hundred qualities, which includes being able to simultaneously behold the face of one hundred Buddhas. With this, he internalized the Dharma of realization. This was Nāgārjuna's extraordinary realization.

Nāgārjunaʾs Activities

As for Nāgārjuna's extraordinary activities, let us recall the following verses:

> At this time, for such an individual generosity is predominant
> As the initial cause of complete Buddhahood.[21]

As outlined here, Nāgārjuna trained specifically in transcendent generosity, which is the main activity of the first ground. He also established supports for the three jewels, the perfect cause of accomplishing the welfare of both oneself and others. Concerning the first of these, Nāgārjuna was generous with material things. He used his abilities as an alchemist, for example, to gain mastery over outer, material necessities, which he then distributed without attachment. With respect to internal things, he even

---

21. Candrakīrti, *Entering the Middle Way*, I.9a–b.

gave away his own head to someone who wanted it. In healing the sick and protecting others from nāgas and other malevolent forces, he also generously gave the gift of fearlessness and protection. Finally, Nāgārjuna generously gave the undefiled gift of Dharma. He retrieved the scriptures on transcendent insight, such as the *One Hundred Thousand Verse Sūtra*, from the realm of nāgas, while from the land of Oḍḍiyāna he revealed numerous tantras of secret mantra that he had received from the hands of the ḍākinīs. All of these teachings he then propagated extensively, in addition to composing treatises that flawlessly clarify their meaning.

As shown above, Nāgārjuna also established supports for the three jewels. He constructed ten million temples, for example, in accord with the instructions of the preceptor Rāhulabhadra, thus erecting supports of the Buddha's body, speech, and mind. In this way, he established supports for the jewel of the Buddha. As just mentioned, Nāgārjuna also revealed many classes of sūtra and tantra and wrote treatises to clarify their meaning. Moreover, he also achieved the first ground and the path of seeing. In this way, he established supports for the jewel of the Dharma in terms of both scripture and realization. As a monk who had completed the preparatory steps, and as a bodhisattva abiding on the first ground, Nāgārjuna was himself a member of the Sangha. In this capacity, he served to establish others in these positions, thus establishing supports for the jewel of Sangha.

Praises of Nāgārjuna

We shall consider the extraordinary praise that Nāgārjuna received in terms of (1) the name for which he was naturally qualified, (2) his renown throughout the world, and (3) his being praised by the Buddha in many sūtras and tantras. Concerning the first, the syllable *ga* in the name *Nāgārjuna* contains a long syllable *a* as the result of the joining of *nāga* and *arjuna*. Thus, *Nāga-arjuna* literally means "nāga-existence-accomplisher." Although "existence" is not explicit, it is nevertheless implicitly contained in the name. His name begins with the word "nāga" because he has five qualities in common with the nāgas: (1) He does not adhere to extreme inferior views; (2) he lives in the ocean of wakefulness pertaining to the first ground; (3) he is the master of the jewels of profound dependent origination free from arising and cessation, which is the subject matter expressed in the treasury of the Bliss-Gone One's excellent discourses; (4) with the fire of reason arising from the view of selflessness, he completely incinerates the firewood of mistaken philosophies that are poisonous to perception, those constructed by non-Buddhists and Buddhists alike; and (5) he dispels the darkness in the mind of ordinary mundane individuals who are not spoiled by philosophy.

["Arjuna," which literally means] "existence-accomplisher," is also part of Nāgārjuna's name. This is due to the two qualities that he shares with Arjuna: First, his speech of nondual wakefulness is straight and piercing, as if it were the arrow of King Arjuna. Second, for the sake of his disciples throughout the world, including the gods, he uses [this weapon of nondual wakefulness] to vanquish any enemy within the three realms of existence, and so he establishes the reign of the great King of Dharma.

Concerning the second point, we may note that Nāgārjuna became renowned throughout the world as a second Buddha.

Third are the many prophecies about Nāgārjuna. The *Sūtra of the Great Cloud*, for example, states:

> Ānanda, four hundred years after I have completely transcended suffering this Licchavī youth, Sarvalokapriyadarśana, will become a monk by the name of Nāga. He will teach my doctrine thoroughly and completely, before finally departing to a realm known as Perfectly Clear Light. There he will become fully and completely enlightened as a thus-gone one, a foe destroyer, a truly and completely enlightened one known as Light of the Source of Wakefulness.

In the *Journey to Laṅkā*, Mahāmati asks:

> Once the Bliss-Gone One has transcended suffering,
> Who will uphold the teachings?

And in reply:

> Once the Bliss-Gone One has transcended suffering,
> The one who will uphold the teachings
> Will appear after some time has passed.
> Know this, Mahāmati.
> In the southern land of Bheta,
> There will be a glorious monk of great renown

Known by the name Nāga.
Concerning my teachings in this world,
He will destroy positions of existence and nonexistence,
Thoroughly teaching the unsurpassable Great Vehicle.
Having reached the ground of the Truly Joyous,
He will depart for the Realm of Bliss.

The *Root Tantra of Mañjusrī* states:

Once I have transcended suffering
Four hundred years will pass,
Then one who works to benefit my teachings,
A monk known as Nāgārjuna, will appear.
Accomplishing the insight of "the peacock,"
[He will compose] numerous treatises on the meaning
    of the element.
Aware of thatness, the nature devoid of entity,
He will live for six hundred years.
Once he has left this body behind,
He will leave for the Realm of Bliss.
Immediately thereafter, he is sure
To accomplish Buddhahood itself.

While in the *Sūtra of the Great Drum*, it is taught:

Ānanda, eighty years after I have gone completely beyond suffering, this Licchavī youth, Sarvalokapriyadarśana, will become a monk named Matidhara, a holder of this *Sūtra of the Great Drum*.

And:

Then, four hundred years after I have gone beyond suffering, he will become a monk known as He Who Sustains and will spread my teachings.

Nāgārjuna's Literary Corpus

Second, we shall consider the character of Nāgārjuna's literary corpus. In a general sense, the treatises composed by this master can be grouped into (1) those that explain the Causal Vehicle of Characteristics, (2) those that explain the Resultant Vehicle of Secret Mantra, and (3) those that show these two vehicles to be identical in meaning. The first category contains the following works: The Sixfold Collection of Middle Way Reasoning, which is composed of treatises that primarily explain the view; the extensive *Accumulations of Enlightenment,* the moderate-length *Compendium on the Sūtras,* and the concise *Letter from a Friend,* which are treatises that primarily explain conduct; and the *Jewel Garland,* which places equal emphasis on view and conduct in the form of advice to a king.

The Sixfold Collection of Reasoning

The first group contains a definitively numbered body of six treatises. This collection resolves flawlessly what is observed through the view, or insight, namely, the natural emptiness of all phenomena, or the two truths. Of these six, there are two primary treatises that teach all aspects of this content, and which thus resemble a complete body. The remaining four were written to dispel mistaken ideas with regard to isolated aspects of this content. These subsidiary treatises, therefore, resemble limbs.

The first of these two groups is definitively composed of two treatises: the *Fundamental Insight*[22] and the *Sixty Stanzas on Reasoning.* Some explain the *Fundamental Insight* to be a teaching on dependent origination free from arising, cessation, and the rest of the eight constructed extremes and the *Sixty Stanzas* to be a teaching on the absence of the four constructed extremes of arising, cessation, existence, and non-existence. Nevertheless, what appears to be supported by the texts themselves is that the former teaches natural emptiness by means of eliminative negation, while the latter also teaches natural emptiness, yet by way of determinative affirmation in terms of mere convention.

The four subsidiary treatises are likewise definitively numbered at four. The *Rebuttal of Objections* is an appendix that addresses a perceived contradiction in the refutation of origination from other that is found the

---

22. Tib. *rtsa ba'i shes rab.* An alternative title to the *Root of the Middle Way.*

Root of the Middle Way's analysis of conditions. On this topic, the *Root of the Middle Way* teaches:

> The nature of things is not
> In conditions and so forth.
> If there is no thing itself,
> How could there be anything other?[23]

Here, it is argued that external and internal effects cannot be present in their individual causes and conditions, in a conglomeration of such causes and conditions, or in anything else before they themselves arise. If they were, they would appear to us, and yet we do not observe them. Such an arising would also be meaningless. For this reason, if one thing is absent in something else, the latter cannot be the basis for the arising of the former, just as oil cannot be produced from sand. Therefore, since things do not arise from something other than themselves, they are emptiness and devoid of nature.

Others may object to this, saying: "Well, if things could not arise from something other than themselves, as you proponents of the Middle Way suggest, this very line of reasoning would also affect your thesis that negates the nature of things. Since this would also prove that your own argument does not arise, it would itself end up being emptiness devoid of nature. As such, it would be incapable of refuting the positions of others. If, on other hand, your words do have their own nature, your previous thesis concerning the absence of nature would be undermined. Moreover, you would also have to state the specific reason that shows why words alone possess a nature." Hence, we find the objection:

> If all of these things
> Did not have a nature,
> Your words would also lack nature,
> And thus be incapable of refuting nature.
>
> If, on the other hand, things do have nature,
> Your previous thesis will be undermined.

---

23. Nāgārjuna, *Root of the Middle Way*, I.3.

If there is, indeed, a difference,
Then present an argument for this distinction.[24]

In response, it is taught: "Since my words do not have any nature, there is no contradiction in teaching the emptiness of all phenomena. For the same reason, there is no need to account for a difference either. Because they lack nature, my words cannot, in reality, refute the position of others. Hence, since both the object and the agent of negation are not established in reality, I do not claim that a negation of the positions of others takes place either. Nevertheless, although no nature exists, this does not mean that another's position cannot be refuted in terms of mere convention, just as an illusory person may defeat another illusory person, and the water in a dream may seem to extinguish fire." Addressing this issue, the *Rebuttal of Objections* states:

As there is nothing whatsoever to negate,
I myself negate nothing at all.
Therefore, when accusing me of negation,
It is you who are guilty of denigration.[25]

And:

An emanation may refute an emanation;
An illusory being may refute an illusion.
Just like these forms of refutation
Do I assert this negation to be.[26]

Seventy Stanzas on Emptiness addresses an objection to the *Fundamental Insight's* analysis of the conditioned. In this analysis, the natural establishment of the characteristics of the conditioned, that is, arising, abidance, and cessation, is refuted. Some, however, object that this refutation conflicts with the following statement from the *Sūtra of the Great Cloud*:

---

24. Nāgārjuna, *Rebuttal of Objections*, 1–2.
25. Ibid., 63.
26. Ibid., 23.

Monks, these three are the characteristics of the conditioned. Conditionality, disintegration, and the transformation of what abides are all evident.

In reply, it is said: "This statement takes into account the deluded perspective of conventional cognition. From this perspective, arising, abiding, and cessation *seem* to take place, though these do not possess any nature. Rather, they are dreamlike and illusory. Therefore, since this passage is not stating that these are established by nature, it does not contradict our refutation of natural existence." Thus the *Seventy Stanzas on Emptiness* states:

> Abiding, arising and cessation; existence and nonexistence;
> The inferior, mediocre, and exceptional—
> The Buddha spoke of these from the perspective of mundane convention,
> Not from that of ultimate reality.[27]

Detailed Examination is likewise a reply to an objection. Some may object that if things have no nature of their own, it would contradict the establishment of such natures by reliable means of cognition. In reply, it is said: "To establish that things possess their own natures using reliable means of cognition, we must be able to examine these reliable means of cognition themselves and find no contradiction, yet we are not able to. Instead, what we find is that the reliable means of cognition, the object of evaluation, and the rest of the sixteen topics that logicians conceive of are themselves unreasonable." Hence, we find the statement:

> So that those intent on dispute,
> Priding themselves in their expertise in logic,
> May give up this pride,
> I shall explain this detailed examination.[28]

The treatise then proceeds to examine in detail, and consequently refute, reliable means of cognition, objects of evaluation, and the other principles that are appealed to in order to prove that things have their own nature.

---

27. Nāgārjuna, *Seventy Stanzas on Emptiness*, 1.
28. Nāgārjuna, *Detailed Examination*, 1.

Establishing Conventions replies to the objection that, in the absence of nature, the categories of the conventional would be as unreasonable as donkey horns and the like. In response it is taught: "While devoid of nature, it is feasible for fabrications to arise interdependently. For this reason, the categories of convention are indeed totally reasonable."

Some scholars of times past considered the *Jewel Garland* part of this sixfold collection. Others claim that there is no definitive sixfold enumeration and that instead we should simply speak of the "collection" or "compilation" of reasoning. Still more assert that five treatises constitute the Collection of Reasoning that demonstrates the absence of nature. The presentation given here should serve to dispense with all of these claims. Furthermore, this approach is addressed in the *Commentary on the Sixty Stanzas of Reasoning.*[29] Explaining why an initial homage is included in the *Sixty Stanzas of Reasoning* but not in treatises such as the *Rebuttal of Objections*, this text states that the former is a primary treatise, as is the *Fundamental Insight*, whereas the remaining [four texts] are appendices. Thus, the *Commentary on the Sixty Stanzas of Reasoning* clearly demonstrates the relationships between the treatises explained here.

Works on Secret Mantra

The second group includes the *Five Stages* and other works that explain the Vehicle of Secret Mantra.

Demonstration of Single Meaning

Third we have the *Commentary on the Enlightened Mind*, a work that shows the Causal and Resultant Vehicles to be identical in meaning. This can be understood from the fact that this commentary explains a portion of the *Guhyasamāja Root Tantra* in which Vairocana proclaims the greatness of the ultimate mind of enlightenment in terms of the Vehicle of Characteristics.

The Root of the Middle Way

Third, we shall discuss the nature of the treatise. This section identifies: (1) the meaning of the treatise's title, (2) the categories to which it belongs, and (3) the body of the treatise itself.

---

29. This is a reference to Candrakīrti's commentary.

The Title
The treatise bears the title:

Insight—The Stanzas of the Root of the Middle Way.

The first topic includes the following divisions: (1) an explanation of the words in the title, (2) the reasons for giving the treatise this title, and (3) the purpose that it serves. Concerning the first of these, the term "middle way" is derived from the Sanskrit word *madhyama*, signifying that which is beyond all extremes. "Root" is a translation of the word *mūla*. This indicates that the full significance of the Middle Way, the topic under discussion, is contained in this treatise. "Insight" is a translation of the term *prajñā*. This indicates that by studying and reflecting on this treatise one will develop a flawless insight into the two truths, free from the extremes of one-sided existence and nonexistence. "Stanzas" derives from the word *kārikā*, showing that the treatise is written in verse. The dash in the title renders the word *nāma*, which shows that the preceding word is a name.

Concerning the second topic, the title is given in consideration of the treatise's subject matter, the expressions it employs, and its function.

Third, we have the purpose of the title, which is fourfold: (1) Generally speaking, the significance of a text can be seen to be essentially contained in its title, and so the title can make one aware of the way one should relate to the text. (2) More specifically, a title concerns a text's subject matter, expressions, and function. That is to say, for those of the sharpest faculties, simply hearing the title will engender knowledge of the text's content, the expressions it employs, as well as its function. (3) Stating the title at the outset serves to minimize hardship for the reader. (4) Finally, rendering the title in Sanskrit serves to create a karmic affinity with this language and establish the pure origins of the Buddha's teachings. It also serves to demonstrate the lotsāwas' and paṇḍitas' expertise in accurate translation. Furthermore, one will come to understand what it was that these lotsāwas and paṇḍitas did, thus inspiring one to repay their kindness. Of these four purposes, the first two concern what was written by the author and the latter two what was written by the lotsāwas and paṇḍitas.

Categorization
This second section addresses the various categories to which the treatise belongs. As explained earlier, in terms of scripture, of the words of

the Buddha and treatises, the *Root of the Middle Way* is categorized as a treatise. Furthermore, among treatises this work clarifies the explicit statements of the sūtras that belong to the intermediate teachings, those on the absence of characteristics. It thus explains the focal point of the view. In terms of import, of the Great and Lesser Vehicles, it pertains to the former. Within the Great Vehicle, moreover, it relates to the Causal Vehicle of Characteristics and Transcendent Insight. In terms of genre, of the Three Collections, it is part of the Abhidharma Collection, which primarily explains the training in superior insight.

Aware of this, the lotsāwas and paṇḍitas who translated this work began their translation by paying homage, in accordance with royal edict, to pacify obstacles. Since the *Root of the Middle Way* reveals the essential reality that is the final, core meaning of all the collections, homage is paid in a general manner to the three jewels. More specifically, because the *Root of the Middle Way* conveys the insight that all phenomena are ultimately free from all conceptually constructed extremes, homage is paid to the deity of insight, noble Mañjuśrī. Further, because he is superior to others, homage is also paid to the author himself.

The Body of the Treatise
This third section addresses the body of the treatise. As has been taught: "The body, divided in chapters, has two aspects: word and meaning." As shown here, the body of this treatise consists of both subject matter and the expressions used to convey this subject matter. The subject matter of this work is dependent origination free from the eight conceptually constructed extremes or, in other words, the two truths. The expressions used to communicate this subject matter are embodied in 449 stanzas that are divided into twenty-seven chapters.

This completes the identification of the Dharma that is to be taught and listened to.

TEACHING AND STUDYING THE DHARMA

The second section addresses how the Dharma should be taught and listened to. This includes two topics: (1) how the teacher should explain the Dharma and (2) how the student should listen.

The Teacher

The first of these concerns (1) the type of individual who is a suitable support to offer Dharma teachings, (2) the various methods through which the teachings may be imparted, and (3) how to use these methods when giving a teaching.

Regarding the first topic, it is said that for a teaching to be meaningful:

> One must rely on a spiritual friend who is completely peaceful,
>   at peace, and gentle;
> Who has superior qualities, diligence, and wealth of scriptural
>   transmission;
> Who has a thorough realization of reality and is eloquent;
> Whose nature is loving and who has given up weariness.[30]

While it is taught that a spiritual friend must possess ten unique qualities, as mentioned above, there are three indispensable qualities one must have as a minimum. First, a spiritual friend must be learned, both in terms of the nature of the subject matter as well as the expressions used to communicate. Concerning the former, a teacher must have a general knowledge of all the subjects addressed in the five fields and [Three] Collections. In particular, a teacher must be knowledgeable concerning the specific teaching he or she is giving. One must also be a skilled communicator. He or she must speak with a pleasant voice and make the meaning clear and accessible. The explanation must also be relevant, reasonable, and of appropriate length. Second, in terms of conduct, a spiritual friend must avoid doing anything evil, and thus be capable of eliciting faith in the listener. Self-reliant, he or she must in this way be fit to be taken as a guru. Third, teachers should be unconcerned with material wealth and possess a loving heart. Without concern for fame, wealth, and honor, they must not lose heart when faced with the blatant ingratitude of those around them.

Second, there are three methods that can be used to teach: First, the subject matter is set forth by identifying the background of the teaching, its intended purpose, and its contents. Second, the means used to express

---

30. Maitreya, *Ornament of the Sūtras of the Great Vehicle*, XVIII.10.

this subject matter are explained by setting forth the topic through a gradual presentation of the basic issues, by clarifying the words with reference to their distinctive features, and by showing what is directly or indirectly implied by the words and sentence structures in their particular context. Third, one resolves the nature of the subject matter by means of objections and replies. Thus, one first sets forth objections, claiming that the meaning and the explanation of the text is flawed. Subsequently, one replies to these objections by showing how there is no such flaw and presenting arguments to this end.

These methods are to be used during the teaching in three ways: In terms of purpose, they can be used to ascertain defining characteristics or explain the process of gaining experience in practice. With respect to those in need of guidance, one may offer concise, moderate, or detailed explanations, depending on whether the student is of sharp, mediocre, or dull faculties. In terms of one's own teaching process, explanations should be presented within the framework of a preparation, main part, and conclusion.

THE STUDENT

Second we have the student. This discussion addresses (1) the type of individual who is a [suitable] support for listening to the Dharma and (2) how such a student should listen. Concerning the first, a great deal is taught in both the sūtras and treatises. However, for the process of listening to the Dharma to be meaningful, the student must possess a minimum of three indispensable qualities: intelligence that facilitates realization, faith that engenders the wish to practice, and diligence in the form of untiring commitment. On this topic, it is taught:

> To summarize their practice,
> In brief, it is faith and insight.
> With faith one follows the Dharma
> And with insight one recognizes reality.[31]

Likewise:

---

31. Nāgārjuna, *Jewel Garland*, I.4c–5b.

When sincere, bright, and committed,
A listener is taught to be "a vessel."[32]

Second, when receiving a teaching, the listener should think of himself or herself as a patient stricken with the disease of the afflictions. The teacher should be regarded as the doctor who is treating the disease, and the Dharma as the medical treatment. Finally, one's practice of the path should be viewed as the process of recovery. Furthermore, having given rise to the mind of enlightenment of the Great Vehicle as a preliminary step, in the main part of the session the student should listen carefully with an undistracted mind, regarding the Dharma and the teacher with respect. To conclude the session, he or she should dedicate the virtue that has been gathered to great enlightenment, yet without maintaining a reference point. In summary, the master Asaṅga explains:

> There are five factors that cause the instructions to be internalized: listening with the attitude of universal understanding, listening attentively, concentrating on what is heard, summoning the mind back when distracted, and listening with an attitude of veneration for the Dharma and teacher.[33]

THE RESULTS OF TEACHING AND LISTENING

Third, regarding the results of these activities, generally speaking, the result of listening and teaching the Dharma is that the insight of realizing the subject matter will arise in the listener's mind-stream. In particular, when the Dharma is taught and listened to in the manner outlined above, this subject matter will be realized flawlessly and with ease.

This completes the survey of how one should teach and listen to the Dharma.

---

32. Āryadeva, *Four Hundred Stanzas*, XII.1a–b.
33. From Asaṅga, *Grounds of the Bodhisattvas*.

THE MEANING OF THE SCRIPTURE

Next is the explanation of the meaning of the scripture that was summarized above. This section contains three divisions: (1) the meaning of the opening lines, (2) the meaning of the main body of the treatise, and (3) the meaning of the postscript.

THE MEANING OF THE OPENING LINES

The treatise opens with two stanzas of homage:

> *That which originates dependently*
> *Does not cease and does not arise,*
> *Does not come and does not go,*
> *Is not annihilated and is not permanent,*
>
> *Is not different and not the same.*
> *To the true teacher who reveals this peace,*
> *The complete pacification of constructs,*
> *To the perfect Buddha I bow down.*

These verses can be explained in two ways: either in terms of their explicit or implicit meaning. Here, we will take the first approach and explain their explicit meaning. Since this statement pays homage to the precious teacher, we will (1) consider the purpose of paying homage to the teacher at the outset of the treatise, (2) provide a summary of the text, and (3) elaborate on the meaning of its words.

The Purpose of the Homage

The rational purpose of paying homage is threefold. One general aspect concerns homage to something extraordinary; another relates to beginning the composition of a treatise; and a third relates to the homage being entered into the text. As for the first, when one feels inspired and pays homage to the Teacher, one takes hold of the cause of enlightenment because this brings an end to negativity and obscurations and allows one to gain merit. Regarding the second purpose, by paying homage the author will obtain merit and pacify conflicting factors. Through this, any outer or inner obstacles that may hinder the composition's completion will be thoroughly pacified and the author will abide by the conduct of holy beings.

The third purpose relates to the welfare of others, and here again there are three aspects: First, judging by the way he or she engages in the conduct of a holy being, the author can be seen to be a holy person himself or herself. Understanding this, others will take an interest in the treatise that is composed. Secondly, the fact that the author begins by paying homage to his or her chosen deity makes it apparent that the treatise itself has a sublime purpose. Again, understanding this will cause others to take an interest in his or her text. Finally, when those who teach or study the treatise first engage the homage, they will be able to bring the process [of teaching or study] to completion. The homage also provides a valuable example to others, such that they will first pay homage to the Jewels before writing a treatise or commencing any other work or project. Furthermore, those who see, chant, or otherwise concern themselves with the homage will thereby acquire merit. Thus, the homage is a way of caring for disciples.

These points are identical with the Master's[34] own teaching on the purpose of the focal points. In his *ṭīka* on the great dependent origination, he writes:

> When the author of a treatise pays homage
> To the Teacher, it is not in vain.
> It arouses respect for the treatise and the Teacher;
> It is not for any other purpose.

---

34. Here and elsewhere, "the Master" refers to Nāgārjuna if not further specified.

SUMMARY

The summary concerns *who* pays homage *to what*, and *in which way*. The one who pays homage is the author of the present work. For Buddhists, the objects of homage are generally the Three Jewels. The Three Jewels are worthy of both homage and of being taken as a source of refuge. Here, homage is paid to the foremost of all that are suited to be taken as a source of refuge—the perfect Buddha. The homage is made through praise and prostration; it is an offering of veneration without any hope for material acquisitions, reverence, and the like.

THE WORDS OF THE HOMAGE

Taking the word "prostration" as a basis for making distinctions, we can again consider the words of the homage in terms of (1) *who* prostrates, (2) *to what*, and (3) *how*. The one who is prostrating we can understand from the line that reads "I," that is, the master Nāgārjuna, "bow down." The second issue we shall explore with reference to the Buddha's essence, superiority, and the reasons for this superiority. Concerning the first, as explained above, here homage is being paid to the "perfect Buddha," foremost among the Jewels that are suitable to be taken as sources of refuge. The word "buddha" denotes an awakening from the sleep of ignorance, as well as an opening of the eye of wisdom with respect to the objects of cognition. Hence, it refers to the possession of the qualities of abandonment and realization. The word "perfect" indicates that the Buddha dwells on the eleventh ground of Universal Illumination and is superior to the listeners, self-realized buddhas, and all others who have not yet perfected the qualities of abandonment and realization.

In terms of the second topic, the Buddha's distinct superiority is referred to with the words "the true teacher ... the perfect Buddha." The Buddha is referred to as a "teacher" because he reveals to others what he himself has realized. Moreover, he is also the "true teacher," insofar as his teachings possess seven superior features that distinguish them from those of mundane, non-Buddhist, and other Buddhist teachers. These seven are as follows: (1) they are motivated by compassion; (2) they are melodious and gentle in essence; (3) the meaning they express is the truth; (4) they propel one to the fruition; (5) they are in tune with those in need of guidance; (6) they are timely; and (7) they are able to decisively answer everyone's questions. Therefore, some also explain this to mean that the Buddha is a "Lion among Teachers," "Moon among Teachers," "Leader of Teachers," and "King of Teachers."

Concerning the third topic, it is the teaching of dependent origination that makes the Buddha the true teacher. To ascertain the meaning of this statement, we shall consider (1) the nature of this teaching, that is, dependent origination, (2) how this teaching makes him the true teacher, and (3) the purpose of this teaching.

The first of these contains three further divisions: (1) the basis for distinctions, (2) the distinctive qualities of dependent origination, and (3) a consideration of the difference between the basis and its qualities.

Basis for Distinctions

As for the first, the basis for distinctions is what we refer to as "dependent origination." This can be ascertained by considering (1) the literal meaning of the term "dependent origination" and (2) what this term refers to.

Pratītyasamutpāda

The term "dependent origination" is a translation of the Sanskrit word *pratītyasamutpāda*. Let us consider each of the five elements contained in this word. *Prati* has the sense of contact, dependence, and reliance, while *i* or *iṇ* denotes going, departure, or destruction. Generally, the connective *ya* syllable carries the meaning of an indeclinable or the absolutive, "having." In this particular case *iti*, which has the sense of the verbal root, or the so-called *dhātu*, is governed by the prepositional affix *prati*, yielding *pratītya*, Hence, what is implied is an encounter with causes and conditions, or a dependence and reliance on causes and conditions.

Sam can be seen to provide the affix for *samyak*, and so mean "authentically." Others, however, hold that this syllable supplies the affix for *sambandha*, thus expressing the idea of relation. This latter explanation is the better of the two.

There is no difference in meaning with respect to *ud*. *Pāda* generally means "stage" or "foot," yet because of the prefix *samud*, it comes to mean "origination." Hence, *samutpāda* becomes "origination in relation." Together, *pratītyasamutpāda* then means "origination that has encountered, and is related to, causes and conditions" or "origination that is related to, and dependent on, causes and conditions." In this way, the term can be seen to exclude that which never occurs, that which occurs without causes and conditions, and that which occurs with an indefinite causal relationship.

What Does "Dependent Origination" Refer To?

Second, regarding the referent of the term "dependent origination," we shall identify (1) its defining characteristic and (2) the bearers of that characteristic. "Dependent origination" is a term that is explicable to the same extent that it is applied. Therefore, the defining characteristic of dependent origination is, as discussed above, "that which originates in dependence on causes and conditions." Some understand this in terms of causes and conditions giving rise to particularly characterized entities. Thus, they teach that those entities that are grouped into the five aggregates are the bearers of the characteristic of dependent origination. Here, however, origination in dependence on causes and conditions is held to be a mere appearance. Therefore, the bases that possess this characteristic include all cognizable phenomena. A sūtra teaches:

> Aside from the dependently originated, a bodhisattva does not see any phenomena whatsoever.

And:

> The wise realize that phenomena are dependently originated,
> And so do not adhere to extreme views in any way.
> The cognized are phenomena with causes and conditions;
> There is no cognition of any phenomenon without causes and conditions.[35]

While this treatise states:

> Apart from what originates dependently,
> There are no phenomena at all.[36]

Similarly, it is taught:

---

35. From the *Sūtra Requested by Anavatapta, King of the Nāgas.*
36. *Root of the Middle Way*, XXIV.19a–b.

Nowhere does there ever exist
Anything at all that is not dependent.

The Qualities of Dependent Origination
Second, the distinctive qualities of dependent origination are not positive
properties. Instead, there are eight distinctive negative qualities, such as
the absence of cessation. We shall examine these by (1) identifying the
essence of each of these eight, (2) contemplating the way in which these
qualities are definitively numbered, and (3) deflecting any critique that
their sequence is unreasonable.

The Essence of the Eight Distinctive Qualities
All negative qualities depend on an identification of that which is negated.
Thus, in the present context, the negated quality of cessation is not established as an agent or object. Rather, here cessation means "to cease," that
is, the action that is the momentary cessation of a substance. Likewise,
arising means "to arise," that is, the coming into being of something that
previously was not. Annihilation means "to be annihilated," that is, the
annihilation of an entity's continuity.
   Permanence is as stated in the verses:

   That which has a nature that never ceases
   Is what the wise refer to as permanent.[37]

Hence, something permanent remains immutable; it is a substance that
neither disintegrates momentarily nor does so in terms of having a continuity [that comes to an end]. Coming means "to come," the approach of
something from a distant location, while going is the departure of something nearby to a location farther away. Difference does not imply different conceptual distinctions or the mere negation of sameness. Instead, it
means difference in terms of essence or the difference between [distinct]
entities. Sameness does not refer to the sameness of conceptual distinctions, but again, to sameness in terms of essence or entities that are the
same and not different.
   Are the eight conceptually constructed extremes, which are negated
in relation to the basis of negation (that is dependent origination), ulti-

---

37. Dharmakīrti, *Commentary on Reliable Means of Cognition*, II.204c–d.

mately nonexistent, or are they nonexistent even conventionally? Some explain permanence and annihilation to be nonexistent even conventionally, whereas the rest are ultimately nonexistent. Nevertheless, arising, cessation, and so forth are dreamlike and illusory. They are merely apparent from the perspective of the deluded mind. Particular characteristics, such as those that the Middle Way Autonomists believe in, do not even exist conventionally. The *appearance* of arising, cessation, and so forth, meanwhile, should be understood to be ultimately nonexistent.

It could then be argued: "It may indeed be the case that no negandum, in the form of true arising, cessation, and so forth, is established, but is there, or is there not, a presence of the qualities of their mere negation? If there is, it follows that these negative conceptual constructs are ultimately established. Yet if not, dependent origination will be established to have qualities such as true arising and cessation."

Let us examine and reply to this concern: First, it is taught:

> Here the intent is to negate existence,
> Not to prove nonexistence.[38]

And:

> Since there is nothing to negate,
> It is clear that in reality nothing is negated.[39]

Thus, not only are there ultimately no conceptual constructs to be negated, even the qualities of their negation are not established. Since, moreover, the qualities that negate true arising, cessation, and so forth are present relatively, we are free from both of the aforementioned inconsistencies. The ultimate freedom from all negative and positive constructs is termed "the natural absence of arising" and "the uncategorized ultimate." The mere negation of true arising, cessation, and so forth that is relevant in the context of the relative is conventionally termed "absence of arising *qua* negation" and "the categorized ultimate." Concerning the latter, it is taught:

---

38. From the *Investigation of the World (Lokaparikṣa)*, a lost text attributed to Nāgārjuna by Bhāvaviveka.
39. Jñānagarbha, *Discerning the Two Truths*, 9c–d.

Since the negation of arising and so on
Accords with reality, it too is accepted.[40]

The Enumeration of Distinctive Qualities
Second, the eight negative distinctive qualities presented here are merely
representative; they are not an exhaustive enumeration. Thus, the *Commentary*[41] explains, "These alone are the primary bases of dispute." Some
take this to mean that because the features of these eight objects of negation are readily apparent, the fixation toward them is intense. That, then,
is why these eight negated qualities are the bases of dispute. Others claim
that the first two are misconceptions held by our own tradition and the
second two by other traditions, while the final four are commonly held
worldly notions. This, they say, is why these eight negative distinctive
qualities are specifically mentioned.

Is the Sequence of the Qualities Unreasonable?
Third, it may be thought that since cessation follows arising, it would
make more sense to mention arising first. However, although arising does
indeed precede cessation, the arising of an effect must be preceded by the
cessation of its cause. Hence, the point here is that there is no definite
sequence with respect to arising and cessation and, therefore, this presentation is not problematic. As is explained:

> If birth came first
> And aging and death followed later,
> There would be birth without aging and death,
> As well as birth without anyone having died.[42]

Distinguishing between the Basis and Its Qualities
Third, the natural absence of arising, or the uncategorized ultimate, which
was mentioned earlier, and the subject, dependent origination, cannot
be said to be the same or different in essence. The absence of arising as a
negation, or the categorized ultimate, is in essence the same [as dependent
origination], yet a different conceptual distinction.

---

40. Ibid., 9a–b.
41. Candrakīrti, *Clear Words.*
42. *Root of the Middle Way,* XI.3.

How This Teaching Makes the Buddha the True Teacher
Second, dependent origination free from the eight conceptually constructed extremes is the structure that permeates all objects of cognition. Therefore, this teaching is an expression of the truth. Just as a lion's roar overwhelms deer, the Buddha's teaching dispels the notions of permanence, annihilation, and other inferior views, and so vanquishes those in need of guidance who harbor misguided ideas. Likewise, as this teaching serves as a remedy for the stupor that lies at the root of all shortcomings, he provides for those in need of guidance who lack realization. Finally, this dependent origination is taught exclusively by the Thus-Gone One, who realizes it in all its aspects with individual self-awareness. As is taught:

> The Knower of the World, without having heard this from others,
> Teaches by means of these very two truths.

And:

> Who could teach me, one with peerless great wisdom?
> Because without any teacher he teaches Dharmas in the best way,
> The Thus-Gone is the teacher of gods and humans.

The Purpose of the Teaching
Third, dependent origination is taught for the sake of "peace, the complete pacification of constructs." Hence, the direct purpose of this teaching is to elicit a precise realization in those in need of guidance through the insight that arises from study. Having applied the insight born of reflection to ascertain the meaning of what one has studied, one can then familiarize oneself with that meaning over an extended period. The following passage highlights the effects of this process:

> Therefore, whether real or unreal,
> Whatever is an object of intense meditation
> Will, once the meditation has been perfected,
> Be cognized clearly and nonconceptually.[43]

---

43. Dharmakīrti, *Commentary on Reliable Means of Cognition*, III.285.

Hence, while resting in equipoise, insight without appearance allows one to directly perceive, by way of not seeing anything at all, the intrinsic nature of dependent origination—an existential negation that is ultimate freedom from the eight constructed extremes. Likewise, by means of the pure, subsequently attained wakefulness that involves appearance, one perceives the subject, illusion-like dependent origination, directly and precisely. This is a predicative negation, which is again free from the eight conceptually constructed extremes. Through this, the apprehension of true marks with respect to consciousness and its objects, expressions and their meanings, and so forth is completely pacified and the causal wakefulness of the ten grounds is attained. This is the temporary purpose of teaching dependent origination.

From the perspective of such a mind, dependent origination is, by nature, present as the complete pacification of mentally constructed reality. Therefore, dependent origination is itself referred to as "the complete pacification of mental constructs."

By continuing this process of familiarization through the tenth ground, causal ignorance, along with the habitual tendencies, will eventually be eliminated. This results in the attainment of the ground of Buddhahood, where even the consciousness that is deluded with respect to the appearing object withdraws. Hence, even the activity of the supportive mind and its mental states vanishes. The withdrawal of all activity associated with consciousness and its objects completely pacifies birth, aging, sickness, death, and all other such resultant factors. Thus, the Buddha body of qualities is attained. This is the ultimate purpose of the teaching on dependent origination.

From the perspective of such a mind, dependent origination itself remains the natural pacification of even the marks of appearance. Thus, dependent origination is itself also referred to as "peace." This has, for example, been taught as follows:

These are deluded appearances,
Like those experienced in a dream.
When awoken from the dark sleep of ignorance,
None of the features of cyclic existence are observed.
Hence, when the mind does not arise
In regard to anything at all, that is Buddhahood.

THE MEANING OF THE SCRIPTURE 119

Thus, the fact that the Buddha has actively taught dependent origination implies a compassionate motivation, a compassionate intent. These two factors, intent and action, explain the perfect benefit for others. The abandonments and realizations described above explain the perfect benefit for oneself.

How Homage Is Paid

The third topic concerns how homage is paid. The expression "I bow down" implies an act of physical, verbal, and mental veneration. Another way of explaining the homage is to say that the energy, or force, of the words encapsulates the treatise's four related elements. This can be appreciated by considering (1) the purpose of stating the four related elements at the beginning of the treatise, (2) a summary of the four, and (3) the words and their meaning.

The Purpose of the Four Elements

As for the first, some say that the four elements play a rhetorical role, in that they enhance the aesthetic value of a treatise. Others claim that stating the four aspects is a means for countering the mistaken idea that, like an examination of crow teeth, the given treatise serves no purpose and should not have been composed. These explanations are not reasonable because both fail to explain why these related elements are definitively numbered at four. Likewise, discerning individuals are not interested in superficially attractive appearances. On the other hand, when it is said that "this treatise is endowed with the four related elements," discerning and faithful followers of the Dharma will respond. Those who readily trust will think that the treatise is, therefore, definitely endowed with the four aspects, while those who do not will think that this is likely to be the case. The latter will thus engage the treatise based on the arising of meaningful doubt. As is said:

> The related and the appropriate methods,
> The words that express what is meaningful for humanity,
> Are taken possession of by those who thoroughly discern;
> They are not the possession of anyone else.[44]

44. Dharmakīrti, *Commentary on Reliable Means of Cognition*, I.216.

Likewise:

> So that hearing a sūtra's magnificent meaning
> Can lead to its being comprehended and upheld
> Through the listeners' veneration
> The purpose should be explained in the beginning.[45]

In order to show that this account is above reproach, we may consider the following objections. First, it may be argued that these statements concerning the related elements are unable to produce any certainty about their meaning because the words and their meaning are unrelated, as is the case with the words of a liar. Second, it may likewise be objected that words are not necessary to produce doubt since it is through the receding of a reliable means of cognition of an examined meaning that one comes to doubt. To this, we reply that although the words are not able to engender the certainty of reliable means of cognition, this does not mean that certainty as such cannot arise. Moreover, while words are not necessary for the production of doubt, the author's speech is required for the arising of this particular doubt, which takes the form of thinking "the four aspects of the related purpose are quite likely to be present." Hence, there are no such flaws at all.

Summary of the Four Related Elements

This summary includes (1) an identification of the four related elements as contained in the meaning of the opening statement, (2) a consideration of the manner in which this statement presents these four, and (3) a contemplation of the reasons why the elements are definitively numbered at four.

First, a treatise's four related elements are its (1) subject matter, (2) purpose, (3) inner purpose, and (4) relationship. In general, these four refer respectively to (1) that which the text is primarily meant to resolve, (2) the realization of that through reading and listening to the text, (3) the essential purpose that eventually ensues from this realization, and (4) how realization relies and depends on the treatise. In terms of this particular treatise, these four are (1) dependent origination free from the eight constructed extremes, (2) realization of that by means of this scripture alone, (3) the temporary attainment of the ten grounds and the final attainment

---

45. Vasubandhu, *Reasoned Exposition.*

of Buddhahood that come about through cultivating this realization, and (4) how the purpose, realization, depends on this treatise.

The Presentation of the Four Related Elements
Second, the subject matter is covered in the lines that end with the words "and not the same." The phrase "who reveals" indicates the purpose, meaning the realization that results from the teaching, while the words "this peace, the complete pacification of constructs" present the essential purpose. The relationship is as taught in the following verses:

> There may indeed not be any words
> That directly show the relationship.
> Nevertheless, by discerning . . .

Hence, the relationship between this treatise and its purpose is implicit in its words. Moreover, all four of these elements are implicitly stated in the praise to the Teacher.

Some say that the phrase "the complete pacification of constructs" is meant to explain the specific subject matter, whereas the phrase "who reveals this peace" shows how this subject matter is presented. The phrase "to the perfect Buddha," they assert, is a presentation of the essential purpose.

Definitive Enumeration
Third, since this treatise possesses countless positive qualities, why is this fourfold purpose and relationship alone presented as the definitive enumeration? The reason is that only these four are suited to serve the purpose of the stated homage. As already explained, the purpose of this statement is to provide the means whereby discerning individuals can access this treatise, and there are, moreover, four thoughts that are sure to prevent discerning individuals from accessing it. Any fifth such thought is impossible. Hence, to avert these obstructive ideas anything less than the four aspects would be insufficient, and anything more would be superfluous.

It is possible for one of the following four thoughts to manifest: First, reasonable individuals may think that there is no special purpose to access this treatise, just as though the topic of the treatise were an investigation of crow teeth. Second, they may think that although there may indeed be such a purpose, it may not be a desirable one, as would be the case with a teaching on how to get married. Third, it may be thought that although there is a special purpose that is also desirable, it might not be achievable by relying on the treatise in question, as in the example of the jewel ornament instructions.[46] Finally, although this purpose may be achievable, one may think that perhaps there is an easier way to accomplish it without any connection to this particular treatise.

Respectively, these four thoughts are averted by stating the purpose's essence, the essential purpose, the subject matter, and the relationship. Thereby, it will be understood that the treatise does have a special purpose, that this purpose is desirable, that it can be achieved by means of this particular treatise, and that this achievement is strongly related to it. Thus, since a discerning individual will engage this treatise through these factors alone, there is no fifth obstructive thought that is sure to hinder access to a given treatise.

The meaning of the words of the homage was already explained above.

THE MEANING OF
THE MAIN PART OF THE TREATISE

We shall now turn to the significance of the composition that concerns us here. To explain the meaning of this profound teaching, we must (1) ascertain the meaning of the chapters and (2) explain the progression of the text.

ASCERTAINING THE MEANING
OF THE CHAPTERS

The first of these involves (1) contextualizing the chapters and (2) ascertaining their subject matter, the nature of the two truths. The first includes (1) explanations of the general context of the chapters and (2) their specific contexts.

---

46. Instructions on the manufacturing of an ornament that displays the precious jewel contained within the head of the king of the nāgas would be relevant if they would also explain how we might obtain that jewel. In the classical example of "the jewel ornament instructions," the latter information is absent, however. Hence, the instructions turn out to be wholly irrelevant.

The General Context of the Chapters

First, one may wonder what particular meaning is conveyed by the twenty-seven chapters in this text. What is taught here is the two truths, or alternatively, dependent origination empty of all mental constructions of ultimate truth, along with the results of realization. Hence, the chapters explain what was presented in the homage, as well as the subject matter of all the precious sūtras.

There are three issues here: (1) the distinctive qualities of dependent origination, (2) the basis for these qualities—dependent origination itself, and (3) the result of realizing [the nature of] dependent origination, that which possesses these distinctive qualities. The first topic is subdivided into (1) the primary distinctive qualities of dependent origination, (2) its subsidiary distinct qualities, and (3) immunity to the charge of absurdity.

The Distinctive Qualities of Dependent Origination

As for the first, the primary distinctive qualities of dependent origination are the absence of cessation and the rest of the eight factors mentioned above. These eight serve to remedy the primary misconceptions commonly held in the treatises and worldly life. Hence, when arising, going, and coming are explicitly negated, cessation and the remaining five will be implicitly negated as well. This is what takes place in the *analysis of conditions* and *analysis of going and coming*.

The subsidiary distinctive qualities are treated in five sections. The first group of six chapters shows dependent origination to be devoid of the nature of the aggregates, elements, and sense sources, and thus empty of the self of phenomena. The *analysis of the sense sources, analysis of the aggregates,* and *analysis of the elements* refute the natural establishment of the essence of these factors, while the *analysis of desire and the desirous one, analysis of the characteristics of the conditioned,* and *analysis of action and agent* refute the arguments advanced to prove this natural establishment. To elaborate, the *analysis of desire and the desirous one* refutes the natural establishment of the afflicted subject; the *analysis of the characteristics of the conditioned* refutes the arising, remaining, and destruction that characterize the aggregates, elements, and sense sources as conditioned; and the *analysis of action and agent* refutes action and its agent being the cause of these factors.

The second group consists of four chapters. These show that dependent origination is empty of a self in the form of a person that appropriates the aggregates. *Analysis of prior existence* refutes the natural establishment of the essence of an individual, whereas the *analysis of fire and fuel*, *analysis of beginnings and ends*, and *analysis of suffering* refute the arguments advanced to prove the natural existence of such a personal self. The *analysis of fire and fuel* refutes the example of fire and fuel, the *analysis of beginnings and ends* refutes the notion that the cyclic existence of birth, aging, and death is the activity of the person, and the *analysis of suffering* refutes the idea that naturally existent suffering is supported by the person.

Without differentiating the person and phenomena, the third group of six chapters explains how dependent origination is empty of the nature of mere things. The *analysis of the conditioned* refutes any natural establishment of the essence of things as such, without differentiating between the person and phenomena. The *analysis of contact, analysis of nature, analysis of bondage and liberation*, and *analysis of action and its results* disprove the arguments advanced to prove this natural establishment. In other words, the natural establishment of contact, of the causes and conditions of appropriation, and so forth of cyclic existence, and of action and its results (as that which proves the latter) are all refuted. Finally, the *analysis of self and phenomena* presents, as a mere convention, the Middle Way's own account of the real nature of things.

The fourth group of three chapters shows dependent origination to be empty of the nature of time. The *analysis of time* refutes the natural existence of the essence of the three times, whereas *the analysis of the assembly* and the *analysis of arising and disintegration* refute the arguments advanced to prove this form of existence. More specifically, the *analysis of the assembly* refutes the notion that time is a cooperating condition in the production of external and internal effects, while the *analysis of arising and disintegration* disproves the idea that time is the cause of these two events.

The fifth group of two chapters demonstrates how dependent origination is empty of the nature of the continuum of existence. The *analysis of the Thus-Gone* disproves that the Thus-Gone is naturally established as the result of the continuum of existence, whereas the *analysis of error* disproves that affliction is naturally established as its cause.

This presentation of the distinctive qualities of dependent origination as natural emptiness may be taken to involve absurd consequences. Hence, there are two chapters that dispense with such charges. First, it may be argued: "If all phenomena are emptiness, it would render all the topics that are presented in the scriptures nonexistent. This would include the four noble truths, the four types of subjective wakefulness, the resultant Three Jewels, the causes and effects of actions, and so forth. Moreover, it would also turn all mundane conventions into nothing."

In response, the *analysis of the noble truths* states: "We do indeed accept the consequence that all of these have no nature. However, dependent origination is still feasible as a conventional principle in light of this position on the absence of nature. Hence, all of these are perfectly feasible as conventional principles." Thus, this reply is given in terms of the relative.

Second, it may be objected: "If all phenomena were emptiness, it would not be possible to eliminate the causal afflictions by means of the path that remedies them, nor would it be possible to thereby bring an end to the continuum of the resultant aggregates and achieve the transcendence of suffering with or without remainder."

In response, the *analysis of the transcendence of suffering* states: "For us, the transcendence of suffering refers to the absence of the nature of suffering and its causes within the real condition of things. We do indeed accept the consequence that there is no transcendence of suffering to be attained by using remedies to eliminate previously existing causal afflictions and resultant aggregates." Hence, this reply is given in terms of the ultimate.

These twenty-five chapters show how the distinctive qualities of dependent origination are, in fact, natural emptiness. These chapters are followed by the *analysis of dependent origination*, which presents the basis for these distinctions, namely, the dependent origination of affliction and purification. Finally, the *analysis of views* explains how one will relinquish all views and ultimately achieve the nonabiding transcendence of suffering as the result of realizing this distinctive dependent origination.

The particular contexts of the chapters are discussed elsewhere.[47]

The Two Truths

This second section deals with the subject matter of these chapters, the nature of the two truths. Ascertaining this nature involves (1) setting forth the characteristics of each of the two truths, (2) identifying the bearers of these characteristics, and (3) presenting the means for validly cognizing the presence of the characteristics upon their bearers.

---

47. In his treatment of the twenty-seven chapters below, Mabja always begins with a discussion of the relevant chapter's particular context.

Concerning the first, it is taught:

> The object of genuine seeing is the ultimate.
> False perception is taught to be relative truth.[48]

As stated here, the relative truth is characterized by being true as the object of conventional, deluded consciousness. Regarding the ultimate truth, any mental examination of its nature will fail to find any established characteristics and so on. We may, however, employ superimpositions as mere conventions to explain the defining characteristic of the ultimate truth to be that which is true in being the object of a mind free from delusion. In other words, it is that which is true from the perspective of either the nonconceptual wakefulness of the noble ones' equipoise or the final consciousness that has employed reasoning to examine the nature of reality using the three modes as proof.

The Bearers of the Relative Truth's Defining Characteristic

Concerning the second issue, it is taught:

> The ultimate is not an object of the mind;
> Mind is held to be relative.[49]

As mentioned here, all objects of a mind that involves appearance, the entire range of cognizable phenomena, are bearers of the defining characteristics of the relative truth. There are two kinds of relative truth: the mundane relative truth and the relative truth of noble beings. The first includes all delusions created by afflictive ignorance, whatever is established as an object of the deluded mind of an ordinary immature individual. The second consists of all the delusions created by nonafflictive ignorance. This refers to all that is established as a deluded object to the appearance-based minds of the noble beings of the three classes during their subsequent attainments.

The mundane relative truth can itself be divided into two categories: the authentic and mistaken. The authentic relative truth consists of that which is true in the sense of being accepted by the world as an object of a

---

48. Candrakīrti, *Entering the Middle Way*, VI.23c–d.
49. Śāntideva, *Entering the Activity of the Bodhisattvas*, IX.2c–d.

mind that is not deluded about the object it apprehends. Mistaken relative truth, on the other hand, consists of that which is true in the sense of being accepted as the object of a mind that *is* deluded about its apprehended object.

The distinction between a mundane consciousness that is deluded and one that is not is as follows. Mundane nondelusion includes both self-awareness, the inward-directed consciousness that experiences its own essence, as well as the outward-directed consciousness that is aware of other. With the latter, consciousness must be mediated by unimpaired faculties, which is to say that any factors that cause the six sense faculties to misapprehend their respective objects must be absent. Such factors may be associated with the internal faculties and immediately [preceding conditions], with the external objects, or otherwise. An example of that which is classified as an undeluded consciousness would be the perception of a single moon in the sky. Whenever the mind is influenced by factors that cause the sense consciousnesses to engage their objects in a distorted manner, as when two moons are perceived, that consciousness is considered mistaken. On this point, it is taught:

> False perception, moreover, is of two kinds:
> Some have keen faculties while those of others are impaired.
> The consciousness of one with impaired faculties is considered
>   mistaken
> Relative to the consciousness of one whose faculties are sound.[50]

Therefore, the authentic relative truth includes two types of entity. The first category consists of inner mental entities, the primary minds and subsidiary mental states that are the objects of inward-directed self-awareness. The second includes external objective entities, the forms and other objects that are cognized by the outward-directed six sense consciousnesses when unimpaired.

The mistaken relative is also of two types. Nonconceptual deluded observations are objects of the six sense consciousnesses when the latter are in a deluded state. An example of this is the appearance of a double moon. The second type includes conceptually apprehended features of

---

50. Candrakīrti, *Entering the Middle Way*, VI.24.

object universals, such as those associated with the self or the primary principle. Hence, it is taught:

> That which the world realizes by apprehending it
> Through the six sense faculties when unimpaired
> Is true from the perspective of the world itself.
> The rest is classified, according to the world itself, as mistaken.[51]

Moreover, according to this twofold division of the mistaken relative, it is taught:

> That which the extremists conceive of,
> Heavily disturbed in their sleep of ignorance,
> And that which is thought of as illusion, visual distortion, and so
>   forth,
> Do not even exist from the perspective of the world.[52]

Therefore, the mind that involves appearance may be divided in terms of the presence and absence of delusion, while its objects may be classified as either true or false. Yet, since these divisions are known among worldly, childish, ordinary individuals, they belong to the relative truth of such individuals.

There is also the so-called relative truth of the noble ones. This includes whatever may appear during the subsequent [attainment] of the three types of noble beings, their appearance-based minds' perception of the way the relative truly is. In the subsequent attainment, the noble ones see everything to be false, like a dream or illusion, and experience it all as one taste, appearing, yet devoid of nature. Since there is no distinction between true and false, or authentic and mistaken, this is also referred to as the "mere relative." Furthermore, the followers of the Middle Way hold that, in terms of the real nature of things, all objects of a mind that involves appearance are false and all minds are deluded. For this reason, this is also spoken of as the "relative for followers of the Middle Way." As is taught:

51. Ibid., VI.25.
52. Ibid., VI.26.

In being bewilderment, an obscuration of the natural, it is relative.
That which is made to appear real thereby
The Able One has termed "relative truth."
Thus, fabricated entities belong to the relative.[53]

This completes the explanation of the bearers of the characteristic of the relative and their respective divisions.

The Bearers of the Ultimate Truth's Defining Characteristic
Second, as for the bearers of the defining characteristic of the ultimate truth, it is taught:

When these apparent entities
Are analyzed by reasoning, nothing is found.
That lack of finding is itself the ultimate,
The intrinsic nature that is primordially present.[54]

As stated here, all that appears is unestablished, both from the perspective of the nonconceptual wakefulness of a noble one's equipoise, as well as from the viewpoint of a consciousness that has employed reason to analyze and investigate. The appearances themselves are neither existent nor nonexistent, neither true nor false. They entirely lack any essential establishment, such as being an object of cognition, expression, or evaluation. They are, hence, beyond all conceptual constructs. The conventional term "ultimate truth" is applied in consideration of this alone. Therefore, the explanation of the ultimate is similar to saying that the real condition of the visual distortions experienced by a person suffering from a phlegm disorder is simply the way such distortions are from the perspective of somebody with healthy eyesight, someone to whose mind the distortions would not in any way be established as objects. As is taught:

A person may imagine hair tufts and other such things due to
    a visual disorder,
Though, in essence, they are errors.

---

53. Ibid., VI.28.
54. Almost identical verses appear in Dīpaṅkaraśrījñāna, *Accessing the Two Truths*, 21.

As their nature would be seen by one with healthy sight,
Here, that is how reality should be known.[55]

How the Two Truths Are Known

Third is the reliable means of cognizing the characteristics of the two truths. One may argue: "It may be the case that mere objects of cognition are the bearers of the aforementioned characteristics of the relative truth. Likewise, it may be the case that the characteristics of the ultimate truth that were discussed earlier pertain to bearers that are free from mental construction and beyond being cognizable phenomena. But what reliable means of cognition, or what type of mind, would then be able to ascertain that this is the case?"

In response, we shall (1) identify the mind, or reliable means of cognition, that ascertains the characteristics of the two truths and (2) show how this mind ascertains them. The first of these involves (1) refuting the positions of others and (2) setting forth our own position.

Refuting the Positions of Others

First, the Middle Way Autonomists say that the defining characteristics of the two truths are ascertained by a reliable means of cognition brought about through the power of facts agreed upon by both parties in a debate. In other words, they claim that the ascertaining reliable means of cognition apprehends in a way that is not deluded. This account, however, is untenable. Generally speaking, reliable means of cognition by the power of fact can be refuted by showing its untenability in terms of the meaning of the term "reliable means of cognition," the defining characteristics of reliable means of cognition, and the process of ascertainment. In particular, the principle of reliable means of cognition by the power of fact is disproved because direct perception, inference, scripture, and analogy become untenable when conceived of in terms of that paradigm. These refutations are discussed at length in *The Essential Reality of the Middle Way*.[56]

---

55. Candrakīrti, *Entering the Middle Way*, VI.29.
56. Mabja's own *The Appearance of Reality*. Tibetan root text and auto-commentary in rMa bya byang chub brtson 'grus 2006a and 2006b. A translation of the root verses and the topical outline of the commentary can be found in Doctor n.d.

Others take a different position, basing their view on the following statement:

> If I were to have a thesis,
> Then that would be my flaw.
> Yet since I have no thesis,
> I am flawless in all regards.[57]

This is interpreted to mean that, since followers of the Middle Way do not accept any views, there is, for them, no reliable means of cognition whereby views can be proven either. Instead, the follower of the Middle Way refutes all extreme beliefs as held by others by showing the consequences of the internal contradictions in their claims.

This account is also untenable. From the rational perspective based on having examined the ultimate, no claim can be established. It is, therefore, also true that no probative reliable means of cognition can exist from such a perspective either. However, from the merely relative perspective of a mind that has not engaged in such analysis, the Middle Way means dependent origination; there are followers of the Middle Way; and such people advance Middle Way arguments. It could, therefore, not reasonably be the case that a follower of the Middle Way does not have any view.

If even reliable means of cognitions that are acknowledged by the world or agreed upon by others cannot be accepted, our own position cannot be set forth. We cannot, then, maintain that although things lack any nature, they appear merely relatively as illusion-like dependent origination. Nor will there be any way to induce the understanding that the positions of others, the extreme beliefs in conventional nonexistence or actual existence, are false. Hence, the wish to refute the positions of others would not arise. Likewise, there would be no way to ascertain whether or not the property of the position, entailment, and exclusion have been claimed. Hence, the object of attack through consequential argumentation would remain unestablished. Finally, since there would be no way to see the contradictions between the various elements of an opponent's statement, the consequential argument would itself remain unestablished. Thus, using consequences to refute another's position would be unreasonable. All of this is discussed in the aforementioned work.

57. Nāgārjuna, *Rebuttal of Objections*, 29.

Our Own Position

Second, in presenting our own position it must first be acknowledged that a reliable means of cognition by the power of facts is not tenable even conventionally. Next, if even reliable means of cognition that are acknowledged by the opponent, or by the world, cannot be accepted, all principles that are negated and affirmed in terms of the mere relative will lack establishment as well. Therefore, it is held that in terms of mere convention, both parties of the debate realize the negated or affirmed points through four reliable means of cognition (perception, inference, scripture, and analogy) that are acknowledged by the world.

As a reliable means of cognition, *perception* is the experiential realization of that which has not been realized before. Through this, one sees the mere dependent origination that is unexamined, manifest, and subsumed under the external and the internal. Thus, it primarily serves to rule out the extreme view of conventional nonexistence.

In the case of *inference*, a proof that displays the three features brings about a realization of that which is not evident. [58] One type of inference provides conventional affirmations. Based on the three kinds of proof, one may realize that, for example, there are minds other than one's own, that conditioned things are impermanent, or that there are phenomena devoid of self. Hence, it excludes the extreme belief that such things do not exist even conventionally.

Another kind of inference performs negations in terms of reality. Through arguments, such as the absence of one and many, one may real-

---

58. According to Buddhist logicians such as Dharmakīrti (seventh century), a genuine proof must display three features known as 1) the *property of the position*, 2) the *forward entailment*, or just the *entailment*, and 3) the *reverse entailment*, which is also called the *exclusion*. These three features are determined in terms of the relation between the argument's three basic elements: the *subject*, the *evidence*, and the *property of the probandum*. In Tibet the textbook example of an argument that displays the three features is often this one: "There is fire on the hill because there is smoke." In this example, the *subject* of the argument is the hill, while the fact that there is smoke is the *evidence*. Finally, the inferred presence of fire is the *property of the probandum*. First of all, the argument displays the *property of the position* because the evidence relates to the subject: Smoke is indeed seen on the hill. Second, it also displays the *forward entailment* because the evidence entails the property of the probandum: Wherever there is smoke, there is also fire. Finally, it likewise displays the *reverse entailment* because the negation of the property of the probandum entails the negation of the evidence: Wherever fire is absent, there is no smoke. Hence, we can conclude that the argument is genuine. For a presentation of the structure of inference according to Dharmakīrti, see Dunne 2004, 25–35.

ize, for example, that there is no real establishment for any of the conceptually constructed marks. This form of inference eliminates the extreme
superimposition that phenomena exist in reality. For the most part, the
inferences explained in the scriptures of the Middle Way are seen to be
primarily refutations that concern reality.

As explained above, the three features of a proof involved in such inferences cannot reasonably be due to the power of facts that are established
for both parties. There is no such proof that can establish autonomously
the truth of the position that one seeks to prove. Therefore, the proofs,
here, are consequential, and the three features are accepted, either explicitly or implicitly, by the other party [alone]. Likewise, the type of mind
that ensues from such proofs is inferential insofar as it is acknowledged
as such by the opposing party. (As for implicit acceptance, this is the case
when the other side has not explicitly accepted [the elements one employs
in the argument], yet would still have to be committed [to them].) When
unexamined, these arguments may appear to be established by reliable
means of cognition, yet upon investigation, [it is seen that] that [only] in
dependence on the claims of the other side [can] the mind grasping the
evidence [be said to produce] a reliable means of cognition that apprehends in way that is free from delusion.

There are four types of consequential argument. In an *inference acknowledged by others*, the property of the position and the entailment are established for the opponent. Based on that, the thesis is then proven definitively
from the perspective of the opposing side, thereby causing them to reject
their own position. In a *consequential argument that expresses contradiction*, an opponent's position is dispensed with by letting the opponent
come to the conclusion that the way the property of the position, the
entailment, and the exclusion are established to him or her makes him
or her implicitly committed to the opposite of his or her own position.
Equivalence of identical reasons is used against someone who applies the
same reason to reach two different conclusions. This consequence serves
to show that since the reason he or she applies is the same in both cases,
the conclusions one draws cannot be differentiated and must, hence, be
identical as well. Finally, *lack of establishment due to [the proof] being equal
to the proven* is applied to show that the realist's proof lacks establishment
because it takes for granted that which has yet to be proven. Moreover, it
also reveals that the flaws perceived by the realist in the Middle Way position are just as devoid of establishment as the realist's own probandum.

Hence, it shows that an element applied in the debate lacks establishment in the object of the debate.

In the context of the relative, definitive proofs and refutations are used from the perspective of the Middle Way follower. However, such proofs and refutations are established merely through the reliable means of cognition acknowledged by the other side. Unequivocal and definitive ascertainments by the power of facts, including consequential reversals, do not occur even relatively. It must, therefore, be understood that these consequences are not autonomous arguments and that they do not entail affirmative proof.

Scriptural reliable means of cognition refers to the realization of extremely hidden objects by means of trustworthy statements. This includes both the words of the Buddha and treatises by noble masters. In both cases, the statements are found to be pure when subjected to the threefold analysis of perception, inference, and scripture. That is, when examined by means of these three, which respectively reveal the three fields of objects of evaluation, such statements are seen to be both flawless and established. The scriptures of expedient meaning, which teach the vast relative, eliminate the extreme of conventional nonexistence. The scriptures of definitive meaning, on the other hand, teach the ultimate profound emptiness, thereby dispensing with the extreme superimposition that phenomena exist in reality.

Analogical reliable means of cognition considers the resemblance between an example that can be observed and something else that cannot, using the former to get at the latter. Since illusions and other such examples appear, while at the same time they are devoid of nature, they exclude the belief that phenomena exist in reality. Since they also exemplify that which has no nature yet still appears conventionally, they also exclude the extreme of denigration, which holds that things do not even exist in terms of convention.

The Presence of the Defining Characteristics of the Two Truths
Second, how do these minds ascertain the presence of the defining characteristics in the aforementioned bearers of the characteristics of the two truths? Once all outer and inner entities have been dismantled by the rational cognitions described above, no truly existent entities, nonentities, or other such mental constructions will be found at all. Thus, it is impossible for there to be a bearer of the characteristic of the ultimate that resists

examination. In the absence of their support, there can be no characteristics either, so it is established that the ultimate truth is free from all mental constructions in the form of defining characteristics, definienda, and bearers of characteristics. Moreover, true existence is refuted when examined from the perspective of reasoning, yet from an unexamined perspective appearance may be established by, for example, mundane perception. All objects of a mind that involves appearance are, therefore, false and illusory. From the perspective of a mind that is established to be delusional, the bearer, that is, the mere object of cognition, therefore definitely bears the defining characteristic, being true as the deluded object of conventional cognition.

This concludes the general survey of the treatise.

EXPLAINING THE PROGRESSION OF THE TEXT

CHAPTER ONE

Analysis of Conditions

WE SHALL NOW turn to the individual chapters of the text. Each of these chapters should be understood in terms of (1) their context, (2) the explanation of their content, and (3) a summary of their general significance.[59]

THE CONTEXT OF CHAPTER 1

Chapter 1 presents an analysis of conditions. This chapter can be contextualized in terms of its connection to the profound sūtras and its relationship to the other chapters in the treatise. Concerning the first issue, the Transcendent Conqueror himself prophesied the master Nāgārjuna as one who would clarify the Great Vehicle's principle of transcendent insight. Accordingly, each of the chapters in his text employs reasoning to resolve the essential meaning of the extensive, medium-length, and concise Mother Scriptures. In this way, their concern is with the natural emptiness of all phenomena, which is observed by insight. In particular, this first chapter is concerned with the meaning of the statement that no phenomena arise by nature. It proves that this is the case through a rational refutation of the beliefs in real arising in any one of the four extreme ways. In doing so, it proves that teachings on the absence of arising are of definitive meaning, showing how this is a teaching that reveals the ultimate intrinsic nature as supported by reason. It also proves that the teachings on arising

---

59. Mabja refers to this framework of context, explanation, and summary at the beginning of each of the chapters in the *Root of the Middle Way*. Despite this continuous reference, however, his treatment of certain chapters does not contain a separate summary at the end.

and other such principles are of expedient meaning and concerned with what is false and relative.

Second is this section's relationship to the other chapters in the treatise. Something that knows no arising, such as the horn of a donkey, cannot reasonably be said to cease, or to possess any other distinctive properties. Therefore, once the mental construct of arising has been refuted from the perspective of reasoning, cessation and every other construction will be implicitly refuted as well. It is with this in mind that the refutation of arising is taught first.

The present chapter engenders two types of insight, one that is beyond appearance and one that is not. The former is the realization of the ultimate intrinsic nature that is similar to space. This realization is produced by invalidating all mental constructs from the perspective of reason. The latter is the realization of the relative and illusory subjects. This is elicited by showing that, while all phenomena that appear to arise, cease, and so forth do not make sense when examined, their relative appearance is established. This is applicable to the other chapters as well.

THE CONTENT OF CHAPTER 1

Second, explaining the meaning of the content of chapter one will involve (1) a general refutation of the four extreme modes of arising and (2) a specific refutation of arising from other. The first of these will be discussed by (1) presenting the thesis, (2) proving it with reasoning, and (3) showing how the refutation is immune to criticism.

The Thesis
Concerning the first issue, the treatise states:

> *Not from itself, not from another,*
> *Not from both, and not uncaused—*
> *Nowhere does anything*
> *Ever arise. [I.1]*

Others consider the second half of the stanza to be a probandum and the first half to be its proof. In this way, they see the reference to the absence of arising in the manner of the four extremes as providing an agentive sense.[60] This, however, is not appropriate. No one imputes any fifth form of arising, aside from the four extremes. Hence, when it is established that nothing arises in any of these four extreme ways, it will automatically be established that arising as such does not occur at all. Therefore, it does not make sense to posit the absence of arising in these four extreme ways as evidence to prove that there is no arising as such. Furthermore, since the stanza does not contain any words that indicate an agentive sense, this cannot be the meaning of the statement.

Therefore, what is being said here is that "Nowhere is it ever the case that anything arises from itself" and so forth. In other words, this establishment of an object is a stated claim. For this reason, the stanza should be read as it is rendered in certain scriptures:

> Anything that could be held to exist
> At any place and at any time
> Would not be due to itself, to another,
> To both, nor would it be uncaused.

This may be ascertained by (1) explaining the words of the four theses, (2) contemplating how the theses that negate arising are definitively numbered at four, and (3) dispensing with the criticism that this contradicts the Middle Way's lack of a thesis.

The Words of the Four Theses
In the first stanza, "anything" refers to supported outer and inner entities and is synonymous with "whatever thing." "Nowhere" is [the negation] of a supportive location or philosophical system, while "ever" denotes any possible time.

Definitive Enumeration
Second, the Enumerators, the realists within our own tradition, the proponents of a primary principle that involves an almighty, and the Far-Throwers and Ritualists, each profess one of the four extreme positions on arising. Since no one actually professes a fifth misconception with respect

---

60. With this sense, the absence of arising in the four ways becomes a reason that is set forth to prove that nothing arises.

to arising, there are only four refutations of the misconceptions that are actually maintained. Thus, there are four theses that negate them. Alternatively, we may say that these four theses are employed because refuting the extreme imputation of arising involves exactly four elements. Arising as such may be either dependent on a cause or not. If there is such dependence, the cause as such[61] must be either identical in substance with its effect or different. Because these two options are directly contradictory, there is no third option. The effect may then be thought to arise from a cause that is of the exact same substance as itself, from one that is of an entirely different substance, or, finally, from a cause that is both. Any other imputation would be impossible.

How the Middle Way Has No Thesis

Third, some may propose: "When it is said that the Middle Way has no thesis, it means that there is no thesis that takes the form of a determinative affirmation. This does not, however, necessitate the absence of a thesis that is a mere eliminative negation." Others claim: "Even a thesis that is an eliminative negation would be set forth merely with the wish to dispel the misconceptions of the opposition, and in consideration of their perspective alone. Representatives of the Middle Way have no thesis of their own, not even an eliminative negation."

Neither of these explanations is reasonable. They are not the intent of the Master either, who states:

> Since there is nothing at all to negate,
> I do not negate anything.[62]

Hence, since ultimately there is nothing to be negated and nothing that negates, it does not make sense for there to be a thesis in the form of an eliminative negation either. However, concerning the relative he teaches:

> From ignorance up to the culmination of aging,
> The dependent workings

---

61. "The cause as such" (Tib. *rgyu tsam*), or perhaps more literally, "the mere cause," is the cause not qualified or specified in any particular way. The same goes for "arising as such" in the preceding sentence; the reference is to the unspecified, bare phenomenon of arising.
62. Nāgārjuna, *Rebuttal of Objections*, 63.

Of these twelve links I hold
To be like dreams and illusions.[63]

Thus, it is necessary to accept illusion-like dependent origination, which even involves a thesis in the form of determinative affirmation. Moreover, when representatives of the Middle Way wish to reverse the misconceptions of their opponents and so speak in a way that considers their perspective, the statements that they make express theses that are eliminative negations in terms of the relative.

Therefore, the intent of the Master, and the real reply [to the question of whether or not the Middle Way has a thesis], is as follows: For a follower of the Middle Way, there are ultimately no positive or negative theses at all. In terms of the ultimate, therefore, we do not create any affirmative or negative theses whatsoever either. As for the mere relative, however, in the present context we present a thesis that is a mere eliminative negation, whereas in general we also set forth theses that are determinative affirmations. On this point, it is taught:

We do not explain
Without accepting conventions.[64]

Hence, we do not accept that the representatives of the Middle Way have neither positive nor negative theses in terms of the relative.

Furthermore, relative theses may concern relative issues (as when it is said, for example, that relatively phenomena are like an illusion, apparent yet devoid of nature), as well as ultimate issues (such as the statements, "Ultimately phenomena do not arise" or "They are beyond mental constructions and transcend all claims"). In the first case, a genuine thesis is sincerely asserted. In the second, however, the thesis is a superimposition. One is concerned with the mistaken beliefs in the existence of things, such as arising with respect to that which remains devoid of any essential establishment and is beyond all constructions of negation and affirmation. Wishing to dispel these misconceptions, one then makes use of terms such as "absence of arising" and so teaches through superimposition. There is no sincere belief in even the mere marks that negate ultimate arising,

---

63. Nāgārjuna, *Commentary on the Enlightened Mind*, 59.
64. Nāgārjuna, *Rebuttal of Objections*, 28c–d.

constructs, claims, and so forth. Therefore, such negations are not genuine theses. Hence, it should be understood that [the presence of theses concerning ultimate issues] does not contradict the explanation that there are neither positive nor negative theses in terms of the ultimate.

Proving the Thesis

Second, proving the theses includes four discussions. The first of these presents a refutation of the Enumerators' assertion that things such as sound arise as transformations of the primary principle and that these transformations are, therefore, of the same identity as the primary principle.

Production from Self

This assertion will be refuted from (1) the perspective of reasoning based on examination and analysis as well as from (2) the unanalyzed worldly perspective. The first of these two refutations involves (1) demonstrating that the arising of something out of itself is meaningless and (2) that it is absurd. On the first point, it is taught:

> When it has not arisen itself,
> How could arising produce its own nature?
> If it does so having already arisen,
> Having arisen, what is it that is produced?[65]

Therefore, when something is not established itself, it has no essence, just like the utpala flower of the sky. Hence, neither will it be able to produce itself. Something that *is* established, on the other hand, already has its own essence, so its arising would be meaningless. It might be argued: "Even if something's essence is already established, it may still subsequently become actually manifest. Hence, its arising does make sense." Yet this is not the case. The arising of something that is already established in essence is meaningless. If, on the other hand, there is arising in the sense of a conceptually distinguishable manifestation, then it would contradict the position on arising that effects are already present as the identity of the causes.

The second issue has four subdivisions. The first concerns this position's commitment to something contrary to what is widely recognized. If an effect, such as a sprout, were to arise through its identity being established

---

65. *Root of the Middle Way*, VII.13.

within its cause, it would then also follow that its cause, the seed, would perpetually arise with that identity out of its own identity because that also would exist by its own identity. One cannot argue, at this point, that that there is no established entailment because the reason just given is identical to the one given in the context of the result, the sprout. It may then be argued: "These reasons are not identical. Because the effect, the sprout, exists in the seed in a latent form, it can arise in a manifest form. The seed that causes the sprout, on the other hand, is already fully manifest, so its reproduction would be meaningless." If that is so, however, then we may just as well ask how the arising of an effect with a preestablished essence could possibly serve any purpose. If the effect is not established as manifest from the outset, and then subsequently arises with this manifest nature, then why would it not be the case that what arises is an essence that did not previously exist?

Second, this position is in conflict with what is widely recognized. Due to the reasons outlined above, effects such as sprouts could never take place because they are not preceded by the cessation of seeds and other such causes. It cannot be objected that this argument lacks entailment. First, philosophical systems teach that the arising of an effect requires an immediately preceding condition, namely, the cessation of its cause. Second, this would not make sense. If an effect were to occur while its cause is still present, cause and effect would be simultaneous. If this were the case, one could not affect the other, and the effect would end up uncaused.

Third, in this account cause and effect become essentially mixed up. According to those who adhere to this form of causality, the seed that functions as cause and the sprout that results are directly perceived to be different in terms of shape, color, taste, capacity, maturation, and so forth. All of these factors will, however, become indistinguishable because they are essentially the same, as is the case with a conch and its white color. Once again, it cannot be said that no entailment is established since two things that possess different characteristics and conflicting qualities, such as a white garlic seed and a banana palm sprout, cannot possibly be of the same substance.

It might, however, be argued: "Seed and sprout possess conflicting qualities in terms of their shape, and so forth. Yet, although they differ temporarily in this way, their nature is not one of conflicting qualities. Hence, they share the same nature." This, however, is not the case. If these two possessed a nature that was essentially different from their shape and other temporary qualities, we would be able to observe it. Since we cannot observe any such nature, we can conclude that there isn't one. Also, if they are inseparable in essence, their nature must still possess the same conflicting qualities that are present temporarily. Therefore, they cannot feasibly be of one nature. With this reply, we can also reject the position of those who propose that while seed and sprout differ in terms of their color and other qualities, the substance that possesses these qualities is one and the same.

Fourth, it would follow from this position that cause and effect are equivalent in terms of how they appear to the mind. From the perspective of a given mind, neither the seed nor the sprout could appear without the other because they are essentially inseparable, just like the roundness and whiteness of a conch. Since this is invalidated by perception, however, it is untenable. In a granary, for example, seeds may be observed, but not sprouts, while in fields just the opposite occurs. Therefore, cause and effect cannot be essentially the same because they possess conflicting qualities in terms of appearing or not appearing to the perspective of a given mind.

Refutation from the Perspective of the World

Second, the notion that things arise from themselves has no place among the unanalyzed conventions of the world either. The mind of a mundane person who has not engaged in any analysis will notice that, while a cause may have ceased and not be seen any more, its effect *is* seen. On this basis, such a person will not believe these two to be of the same substance. This very line of reasoning is presented in the following verses:

> If something were to arise from itself, no qualitative difference
>   would be achieved at all;
> It does not make sense for something that has already arisen to
>   arise again.
> The idea that what has arisen can do so again
> Entails that the seed would go on arising to the end of existence.
> The arising of sprouts and other such factors would not be found.
> For you, the sprout can have no shape, color, taste, capacity,
>   and maturation
> That are different from those of its agentive cause, the seed.
> If the sprout is nothing other than your seed

Then either the so-called sprout would go unperceived, just like
   the seed,
Or, the seed would be perceived along with its sprout
Since these two are the same. Therefore, this we do not accept.[66]

Along with:

Because they see the effect though its cause has disappeared,
Neither does the world claim, "These two are the same."[67]

This completes the refutation of the notion that things arise from
themselves.

Production from Another

Second, the realists within our own tradition hold that, in terms of the
ultimate, all entities— whether they are associated with the apprehended,
the apprehender, or are nondual—arise from four conditions that are other
than themselves. The Middle Way Autonomists, in contrast, assert that
the apprehended, apprehender, and nondual cognition arise from causes
that are different from themselves at the level of the authentic relative.

Here, all such assertions will be refuted from the perspectives of reasoning and the world. The first involves refuting the notions that (1) cause and
effect are established as different substances and that (2) things arise from
a substance other than their own.

Cause and Effect Are Not Different Substances
Concerning the first, it is taught:

That which is different differs in dependence on something else.
It does not differ without that different thing from which it
   differs.[68]

Hence, Maitreya and Upagupta are labeled as different in dependence
on each other, not because they are different in essence. Therefore, the

66. Candrakīrti, *Entering the Middle Way*, VI.8c–11d.
67. Ibid., VI.12a–b.
68. *Root of the Middle Way*, XIV.5a–b.

resultant entity has not arisen at the time of the cause and is, thus, absent. In the absence of that entity upon which its otherness depends, the cause cannot then be established as other. Thus, it is explained:

> The nature of things is not
> In conditions and so forth.
> If there is no thing itself,
> How could there be anything other?[69]

As well as:

> Sprout and seed are not present at the same time,
> So how could the seed be different when there is nothing to
>   be different from?[70]

It might then be thought: "While an effect does not exist at the time of its cause, a cause can still be classified as different in dependence on an effect that will occur later."

Yet, if an effect exists now, it cannot occur later. If, on the other hand, it does not exist now, then we lack the reference point needed to establish the cause as different in the present. Despite the absence of an effect, we may create one that will occur later as a mental object, and then, on that basis, classify its cause as something different. In that case, however, the basis for the classification is merely nominal. "Otherness," therefore, is just a label and cannot be established within the entity itself.

Things Do Not Arise from Another Substance

The second section refutes this notion (1) by demonstrating its complete absurdity and (2) by means of analysis. The absurd consequence will be ascertained by (1) presenting it and (2) refuting some possible objections. As for the first, if this effect, the sprout, had arisen from a seed that were something other than itself, then a sprout could also arise from what are not its causes, such as fire or charcoal. The reason for this is that [both causes and noncauses] would all be on a par in being different from the sprout. This cannot be asserted because if things could arise in this manner

---

69. Ibid., I.3.
70. Candrakīrti, *Entering the Middle Way*, VI.17a–b.

it would be perceivable. Since no such arising can be observed, however, we can exclude it based on perception. The notion that things can arise from what are not their causes, furthermore, entails either the flaw that they do not arise from what *are* their causes, or, since this would be a negation of causality as such, that they are uncaused.

Second, some may think: "This argument is not conclusive, for while cause and noncause are alike in being something other than the effect, the effect arises based only on the former and not the latter."

Nonetheless, this argument is indeed conclusive. We will show this (1) by means of an argument that turns on the equivalence of identical reasons and (2) by considering the way that the entailment of a single conceptual distinction is equally relevant in the case of "other." As for the first, we shall here (1) inquire into the specific reasons [underlying the notion that cause and noncause are different], (2) refute these reasons, and (3) show how this same critique cannot be leveled at our own presentation of the relative.

In the context of the first, we may recall the following:

> If there is, indeed, a difference,
> Then present an argument for this distinction.[71]

Hence, since cause and noncause are the same in being other, why should the effect, in reality, arise from the former and not from the latter? This is the question under consideration.

Concerning the second issue, we shall demonstrate the inadequacy of replies that appeal to (1) appearance, (2) capacity, and (3) the intrinsic nature.

The Reply by Appeal to Appearance
First, it may be thought: "The reason we can say that cause and noncause differ is that we directly perceive this to be the case."

Indeed, this is how things appear from the perspective of a deluded mind that has not engaged in analysis. Yet once we examine this notion, what is the specific reason that one thing gives rise to the effect whereas the other does not, while both are particularly characterized as "other"? A reply by appealing to perception does not work because something may

---

71. Nāgārjuna, *Rebuttal of Objections*, 2c–d.

appear to arise without objectively doing so. You, the objector, yourself accept this to be the case when it comes to dreams, illusions, and so on. There are also times when arising is not observed, yet its actual occurrence is undeniable. Again, this is what you hold with respect to karmic action and its effects.

It may then be said that the examples of dreams and illusions are not equivalent since production from other is witnessed by undeluded minds. This notion, however, is untenable. All these objects that appear to the mind are the same in that they appear to a mind that has not examined, while upon examination we find them to be nonexistent. Therefore, it is not possible to find any objective demarcation between real and unreal. Hence, there are no grounds for distinguishing deluded minds from those that are not. This completes the explanation of why the first reply is untenable.

The Reply by Appeal to Capacity
Second, it may be thought: "Whether or not something is a cause depends on the presence or absence of capacity."

If this were the case, how could one determine whether or not something has this capacity? As we have already seen, replying that we know this based on whether or not we perceive an effect will not do. This is the very point that the Master makes when he argues:

> It functions as if there were an object;
> Is this not like a problem in a dream?
> When awakening from sleep there is no difference
> In terms of the function being performed.[72]

The Reply by Appeal to the Intrinsic Nature
Third, it may be thought: "Although cause and noncause are alike in being other than the effect, it is [due to] the intrinsic nature, or the greatness of dependent origination, that something either arises or does not."

Now, for something to be the intrinsic nature there cannot be anything that invalidates its status as such. Furthermore, we must also be able to prove that it is, indeed, the intrinsic nature. However, our perception of arising and lack of arising does not prove that these are the intrinsic nature

72. Nāgārjuna, *Commentary on the Enlightened Mind*, 21.

of things, for the same reasons that were stated above. Therefore, there are no reliable means of cognition whatsoever that could establish, as the intrinsic nature of things, that while cause and noncause are equally different from the effect, the latter truly arises based only on its cause. Thus, according to the opponent, cause and noncause, while being equally other, can nevertheless differ in terms of whether or not they are able to produce in reality, or as per their particular characteristics. When we examine why this should be so, however, no one will find any reason.

The Middle Way's Relative Truth and This Problem

Third, we shall now show how this problem does not apply to our version of the relative. It may be argued: "You followers of the Middle Way accept yourselves that, for example, factors that are the same in being actions can nevertheless have definite forms of ripening. In this way, there are many things that you hold to be certain in terms of the relative. Nevertheless, as a consequence of what you have been saying, this is no longer reasonable."

For us, under examination nothing is ascertainable in terms of its particular characteristics, even relatively. From the perspective of a deluded mind that has not engaged in examination, however, matters such as the effects of action appear in a way that is not random. It is from this perspective alone that we speak of, for example, a definite correlation between an action and its effect in terms of the relative.

"Well then," the objector may reply, "while things are the same in being other, this certainty in terms of what arises and what does not is not even relatively supported by any particular characteristics. However, we assert that from the unexamined deluded perspective, there is, in terms of the mere appearance of arising, or lack thereof, nevertheless a certainty that occurs in relative terms."

With this account, however, it is no longer asserted that, in terms of the relative, things arise from what is other than themselves and by virtue of their particular characteristics. In contrast, it is now held that all relative causality involves nothing more than merely apparent arising that occurs to a deluded mind, just like dreams and so on. In other words, this validates our own position. Therefore, whatever phenomena appear relatively may be classified in correspondence with how they appear as certain from the perspective of a deluded mind. For you, on the other hand, analysis leads to certainty in terms of particular characteristics, which we do not accept even in terms of the relative. How, then, could any of the flaws that we have stated ever apply to our own position as well? On this point, it is taught:

> The entities of the dependent nature that you assert
> I do not accept even in the relative.
> Since it is fruitful, I say all this exists though it does not;
> I say what I say from the perspective of the world.[73]

The Entailment of a Single Conceptual Distinction

Second, we will consider the way that the entailment of a single conceptual distinction is equally relevant in the case of "other." It may be thought that the absurd consequence demonstrated earlier lacks entailment because though a sprout is equally different than all three, it will grow only from a seed, not out of fire or charcoal. When this is the case, we may then remind the objectors that all their autonomous arguments will be irrelevant without evidence that features entailment. Hence, we may ask them whether they are in possession of such evidence, and if so, request that it be specified.

In reply, they may say that such evidence is found in statements such as the following: "Wherever we find smoke as such,[74] there is also fire, as is the case with a hearth. Likewise do we find smoke as such on the mountain over there." Yet why would such an argument not be inconclusive? Why could it not be the case that although the two are the same in being smoke as such, only the smoke found at the hearth entails fire, and not the one on the mountain? It may be answered that, because it is established that the smoke as such at the hearth entails fire, it is likewise established that the smoke as such on the mountain entails fire as well since the two, in being smoke as such, are the same conceptual distinction. However, since the otherness as such that is associated with the seed entails the arising of the sprout, its arising would then also be entailed by the otherness as such that is found in fire or charcoal. The conceptual distinction of otherness as such is the same in the two cases. Alternatively, it may be that the otherness as such that is associated with fire and charcoal entails the sprout's not arising. In that case, why would the otherness as such that is associated

---

73. Candrakīrti, *Entering the Middle Way*, VI.81.
74. On the expression "as such," see n. 61.

with the seed not also entail the sprout's not arising since it is the same conceptual distinction, otherness as such? Therefore, it is taught:

> If cause and effect were different,
> Cause and noncause would be equal.[75]

As well as:

> If one thing were to occur based on something else,
> The flames of a fire could give rise to dense darkness.[76]

In the context of a refutation based on this type of examination, it suffices merely to notice the pervasion of the evidence in the concordant factors. It is, therefore, easy to establish entailment with respect to the evidence that appears in this scripture.

In response, it may be thought: "Take a living being as such, a cow, for instance. Since being a cow entails having a hump and dewlap, according to your position, it would then follow that being any living being as such, like a human, would also entail having a hump and dewlap since these would be the same in terms of the conceptual distinction of being living beings as such. This would render all principles of convention impossible. If you reply that this is not entailed, the same would be the case with the argument you yourself advanced."

On this point, it is taught:

> There are no conceptual distinctions of a substance other than the
>   substance itself,
> So how could there be an identical conceptual distinction?
> If there were different substances with the same conceptual
>   distinction,
> Then why should we not accept
> That there is a single universal that is different from its instances?[77]

In this way, we do not maintain that a given unqualified conceptual

---

75. *Root of the Middle Way*, XX.20c–d.
76. Candrakīrti, *Entering the Middle Way*, VI.14a–b.
77. Jayānanda, *Logic Hammer*, 5d–6.

distinction may exist in the exact same form throughout multiple sub-stances. Even if we assumed that there could be such a single conceptual distinction, we would still not accept that the unqualified conceptual dis-tinction that is associated with the example has the same extension as the unqualified conceptual distinction that is associated with the basis for dis-pute. Our position, therefore, is not problematic in the ways you describe. You yourselves do not hold that the unqualified conceptual distinctions that are associated with the example and the basis for dispute are one and the same. However, unless one accepts that the unqualified conceptual distinction of the evidence associated with the example entails the prop-erty of the probandum, and that this is entailed by the unqualified evi-dence associated with the basis for dispute, all autonomous evidence will come to an end. Therefore, our position is established.

Refutation through Analysis

Second, the arising of things from other things will be refuted using analy-sis. The argument here is as follows: If one thing were to arise based on another thing that has ceased, it would imply that the former is uncaused. Yet if the effect were to arise without the cause having ceased, it would mean that the two are simultaneous. It might then be thought: "One can-not claim that an effect arises *without* its cause having ceased. Instead, one must say that it arises *by means of* a cause that has not ceased. Moreover, since the effect is not present at the time of its arising, cause and effect are not simultaneous."

This, however, is untenable. If an effect is absent, there can be no act of arising because the support of that action would be missing. Hence, it would not make sense for an effect to arise. Thus, it is taught:

Since this arising lacks its agent, it makes no sense.[78]

In the same way, cause and effect would end up being simultaneous if the latter were to arise through contact with the former. If there were no contact, on the other hand, there would be no cause when the effect arises, and it would then arise uncaused. It may be thought: "Neither of these two problems is entailed because effects arise due to a partial contact with their causes."

78. Candrakīrti, *Entering the Middle Way*, VI.19d.

However, these faults are unavoidable. Ultimately, the notion that cause and effect have parts that respectively do and do not meet makes no sense. In terms of the relative, the notion of contact would imply simultaneity, while that of lack of contact would mean absence of cause.

It may then be asked: "Well, in that case, how can you account for the arising of things in terms of the relative?"

On this point, it is taught:

> The sprout grows neither from a seed that has ceased
> Nor from one that has not.
> Hence, all arising is said
> To be like an illusion.[79]

Thus, once we analyze in terms of whether or not a cause has ceased, or whether or not there is contact between cause and effect, it becomes clear that even relatively things do not arise in terms of particular characteristics. As is the case with dreams and illusions, things merely seem to arise based on causes and conditions from the perspective of a deluded mind that has not engaged in analysis. This is what we assert.

Refutation from the Perspective of the World

Second, from the perspective of the world as well, things do not arise from what is other than themselves. The mundane mind simply sees effects arising from causes. It does not perceive these causes to be different in substance from their effects. If this were not the case and cause and effect were perceived to be different, worldly people would not think, "I produced this child," although they only supplied a seed, or, "I planted this tree," when they only planted the seed. In such cases, the child and the tree are not conceived of as different from the seeds that cause them, and ordinary worldly minds do think this way. Therefore, the world does not see cause and effect as being different in substance.

It might then be thought: "The mundane mind does, in fact, perceive cause and effect to be different in substance, but of the same continuum. Thus, when people think in the ways you describe, it is in acknowledgment of this continuum."

That account, however, is untenable. As with jujube fruits associated

---

79. Nāgārjuna, *Praise to the Supramundane*, 18.

with multiple containers, one single continuum cannot essentially be inseparable from multiple substances. For these very reasons, it is taught:

> People of the world, having supplied only a seed,
> May say, "I produced this child,"
> Or think, "I planted that tree."
> Hence, arising from other is not the world's opinion either.[80]

Therefore, what we observe is that the mundane mind does not distinguish between self, other, and other such factors. Instead, it simply thinks that effects are due to causes. The Master treats the relative in this way as well:

> That which arises in dependence on something else
> Is not identical with it,
> Nor is it something other.
> Hence, it is neither annihilated nor permanent.[81]

This concludes the explanation of the refutation of the idea that things arise from what is other than themselves.

Things Do Not Arise from Both Themselves and Other Things

Next, the notion that things come about due to both themselves and other things is refuted. This position is taken by those among the Enumerators, who assert a primary principle as well as the Almighty. They explain that resultant things arise from both themselves and something else. Hence, they neither assert that things are exclusively the product of themselves nor that they are due exclusively to something other than themselves. In this way, they believe their position to be free from the problems explained earlier. This position is refuted by means of (1) the arguments that were explained earlier and (2) further arguments not previously supplied. Concerning the first, it is taught:

> Arising due to both is not reasonable either
> Because the flaws just explained would ensue.[82]

---

80. Candrakīrti, *Entering the Middle Way*, VI.32.
81. *Root of the Middle Way*, XVIII.10.
82. Candrakīrti, *Entering the Middle Way*, VI.98a–b.

Hence, because this account involves both the idea that things arise from themselves and that they arise from something else, all the problems that were presented in the respective contexts of these two positions will ensue here as well, without exception.

Regarding the second issue, it is explained:

> If suffering were produced by each of these,
> Then suffering would be the product of both.[83]

Let us imagine that the power to produce were present in both the thing itself as well as something else. If this were the case, then their coming together could also be productive. Yet, as was explained above, neither of these has this capacity. Therefore, just as sesame oil cannot be derived from sand, the coming together of these two will yield nothing.

It may then be objected: "This argument is inconclusive because, for example, the eyes, visual forms, and the other factors that engender visual cognition do not have the power to do so in isolation, yet they do once they assemble."

This, however, is not so. On this point, it is taught:

> So-called continua and assemblies
> Are, like garlands and armies, false.[84]

Hence, since assemblies have no substantial existence, in reality, they lack the capacity to produce. We might then allow that they have this power conventionally, yet, as is the case with the assembly, the eye and each of the other contributing factors would then also be in possession of the mere capacity to produce visual cognition. According to the opponent, however, each of these is powerless, and so this counterargument is not valid.

Causeless Arising

The refutation of causeless arising concerns the Proponents of the Beauty of This Side and the Ritualists. The former believe that mere awareness and the experience of pleasure and pain in the present are not caused by mere awareness and virtuous and nonvirtuous action in previous lives. Rather,

---

83. *Root of the Middle Way*, XII.9a–b.
84. Śāntideva, *Entering the Activity of the Bodhisattvas*, VIII.101.

they hold these simply to be the effects of aggregations of the material elements of this world and the various constellations of favorable and unfavorable conditions. Thus, they do not accept imperceptible causes.

The Ritualists assert the following:

> The sun rising and water falling,
> The pea being round and the thorn long and sharp,
> The color and shape of the peacock—
> All of this is not anyone's design; it occurs by itself.

In this way, they assert that the various forms of sentient life manifest of their own accord, without any causal dependence. Thus, they do not even accept perceptible causes.

To refute these ideas, we will demonstrate the absurd consequences of these positions, namely, that (1) things would no longer occur occasionally, (2) all efforts to cause an effect to occur would be futile, and (3) no apprehended objects could appear to the mind.

The Absurd Consequence That Things Could No Longer Be Occasional
Concerning the first topic, it is taught:

> Since the uncaused does not depend on anything,
> It would be permanently present or absent.[85]

If things were uncaused, they would be entirely independent of all the variations in terms of time, place, and so forth. This would mean that once such a thing had come into being, it would continue to exist everywhere and for all eternity. The rationale, here, is that there could never be a place or time at which something required for the existence of this thing would be lacking. All places and times, therefore, would be indistinguishable from what is held to be the place and time of its manifestation.

On the other hand, if such thing were ever absent at some point, it would follow that it could never manifest anywhere else either because there could never be any place or time at which the factors upon which its existence depends would come together. All places and times would,

---

85. Dharmakīrti, *Commentary on Reliable Means of Cognition*, I.35a–b.

therefore, be identical with what is held to be the place and time of its absence.

This, however, is untenable. It is invalidated by the perception of the world, which sees things only at particular times and places. Therefore, because things are seen only occasionally, it follows that they depend on variations in time and place. Because their features are seen to differ, moreover, it follows that they depend on causes that are responsible for such specific features. In terms of the relative, therefore, it is established that things have causes.

The Absurd Consequence That All Effort Would Be Futile

Second, given that things are uncaused, it would follow that engaging a cause to bring about a particular result, such as doing farm work to create a harvest, would be as futile as trying to grow a sky flower. Perception, however, tells us that such efforts do serve a purpose. This as well establishes that things do have causes. On this point, it is taught:

> If what happens is entirely uncaused,
> Anything can occur anywhere and always.
> The worldly would not, then, for the sake of the fruition,
> Apply hundreds of efforts to things such as seeds.[86]

The Absurd Consequence That Objects Could Not Appear to the Mind

Third, things being uncaused would entail that all objects apprehended by the mind would be as nonappearing as the sky flower. It is taught:

> If the world had no causes, it could not be apprehended,
> Just like the scent and color of the utpala of space,
> Yet the world is apprehended in all its vivid variations.
> Therefore, as is the case with your consciousness, know that the
>   world is due to causes.[87]

It may be objected: "Though not the product of causes, object universals, reflections, the appearance of a double moon, and other such things

---

86. Candrakīrti, *Entering the Middle Way*, VI.99.
87. Ibid., VI.100.

still appear as apprehended objects to those suffering from delusion. Therefore, the absurd consequence as well as its reversal are both not valid."

However, the aforementioned factors appear only when certain conditions are present. Respectively, the mind has to be directed in a certain
way, there has to be a mirror and a face, the sense faculty that is involved
must be defective, and so forth in order for such things to appear. If these
conditions are not met, however, they will not appear. In terms of convention, therefore, all of these have causes.

It may then be thought: "Those conditions simply form the basis for
the occurrence of such deluded forms of perception. The features of the
objects that appear only manifest to a deluded mind. No entity is actually
present. Hence, the examples given above are not the products of causes
and conditions."

Yet this will not do either. These are not the objects of a mind that is
free from delusion, and they are not apprehended as arising due to causes
and conditions by virtue of their own particular characteristics. They are,
however, present as objects apprehended by the deluded mind and, thus,
merely appear to arise in dependence on causes and conditions. Thus, it is
explained:

> A mind that relies on a defective sense faculty
> May see hair tufts due to a visual impairment.
> For that mind, the two are both true,
> And false for one with clear sight.[88]

It is with this in mind that the Master says:

> Apart from what originates dependently,
> There are no phenomena at all.[89]

A sūtra likewise states:

> All known phenomena have causes and conditions;
> None are known that have no causes and conditions.[90]

---

88. Ibid., VI.54.
89. *Root of the Middle Way*, XXIV 19.a–b.
90. From the *Sūtra of the King of Meditative Absorptions*.

This completes the explanation of the way uncaused things are refuted.

As explained earlier, any fifth version of arising is impossible. Therefore, once these four extremes associated with arising have been refuted, it will also have been established that that which originates dependently does not arise by nature. Something unarisen that possesses distinctive properties, such as cessation, is as unintelligible as the notion of a garland of sky flowers. Thus, it has now been perfectly established that, as was argued above, dependent origination is free from the eight mentally constructed extremes.

This Refutation's Immunity to Critique

Third, to show how this approach is immune to critique, we will explain (1) how it does not conflict with scripture and (2) how refuting the four extreme positions on arising does not invalidate arising in terms of the relative.

How the Refutation Does Not Conflict with Scripture

Concerning the first, we may find the following objection: "The position that dependent origination is free from the eight mentally constructed extremes conflicts with the sūtras. They explain that the condition of ignorance gives rise to formation and so on. Thus, they teach that, when it comes to dependent origination, arising and the other factors that you deny do indeed exist."

While it is true that such explanations are given in the sūtras, one also finds statements such as these:

> What arises due to conditions does not arise;
> It lacks the nature of arising.[91]

And:

> All phenomena do not arise and do not cease; by nature, they
> are peace.

One must, therefore, seek out the intent of the sūtras. On this topic, the *Sūtra Taught by Akṣayamati* explains:

---

91. From the *Sūtra Requested by Anavatapta, King of the Nāgas*.

When a sūtra shows how to practice the ultimate, it is of "definitive meaning." When it shows how to practice the relative, it is of "expedient meaning."

In this way, the teachings of the Able One are of both expedient and definitive meaning. Moreover, the meaning of a teaching that expounds arising and other such principles cannot be established as definitive because rational analysis shows that such principles cannot be true in reality. Therefore, when sūtras of expedient meaning teach, for example, the existence of relative arising, in no way does it harm the message of our sūtras of definitive meaning, which teach that dependent origination is ultimately free from arising, ceasing, and all other mental constructs. The *Sūtra of the King of Meditative Absorptions* states:

> The Bliss-Gone One's teaching of emptiness
> Is what distinguishes the sūtras of definitive meaning.
> Teachings about sentient beings, individuals, and persons—
> All such Dharmas are known to be of expedient meaning.

And Candrakīrti explains:

> Those sūtras that explain something other than reality are taught
> To be of expedient meaning and should be relied upon as such.
> Those with the meaning of emptiness are then to be known as
>   definitive.[92]

How the Refutation Does Not Deny Relative Arising

Second, it may be argued: "The refutation of arising in the manner of the four extremes is made with respect to both truths. Since no fifth type of arising is possible, even relative arising would be untenable."

As explained before, an analysis of the four extremes will indeed invalidate arising, even in terms of the relative. Therefore, contrary to what the Autonomists believe, there is nothing that arises by virtue of its particular characteristics. However, when the mind's eye suffers from ignorance, its

---

92. *Entering the Middle Way*, VI.97b–d.

vision becomes distorted, and it then merely appears as though things arise due to causes and conditions. Therefore, so that the flow of conventions will not be interrupted, we refer to that mere appearance using the term "dependent origination." In the words of the noble master Nāgārjuna:

> That suffering is created by itself,
> By something other, by both, or that it is uncaused—
> This is what logicians assert.
> You speak of dependent origination.[93]

Specific Refutation of Arising from Other

Having offered a general presentation of the refutation of arising in terms of the four extremes, the focus turns specifically to a refutation of arising from other. At this point, the Master does not explain the refutation of the other three positions further because their untenability is quite clear and because refuting them as an aside in another context is sufficient. The idea that things arise from other things, however, is somewhat tenable and difficult to refute. This notion, therefore, will now be refuted with respect to both (1) the way it is accepted in treatises and (2) the way it is accepted in the world.

Arising from Other as Accepted in the Treatises

On the first issue, the treatise states:

> *There are four conditions:*
> *Causal, objective, immediately preceding,*
> *And, likewise, the ruling.*
> *There is no fifth condition. [I.2]*

Here, the opposing view is presented first. Members of our own tradition state: "It is indeed reasonable to refute arising in terms of the other three extremes. To refute arising from other, however, is extremely unjustified. In the Abhidharma sūtras, the Transcendent Conqueror himself taught that resultant entities are produced by four conditions and that these four

---

93. Nāgārjuna, *Praise to the Supramundane*, 21.

are something other than their effects. In the context of philosophical tenets, moreover, it is explained that there are six causes and four conditions, although these are not two separate sets. As it is taught:

> The causal condition consists of five causes.
> The mind and mental states that have arisen
> Are the equal and immediately preceding, except for the last.
> The observed are all phenomena,
> And the 'agentive cause' is explained to be the ruling.[94]

Hence, the six causes are included in the four conditions. The *causal condition* includes the five causes that establish the essence of the effect. The occurrence of a sprout or an eye cognition, for example, is due to a causal condition. With the former, this condition is a seed, while with the latter it is the seminal element located in the all-ground that is responsible for that type of cognition. Next, the *observed condition* is an object that makes the mind and mental states take on its own features when observed. *Immediately preceding conditions*, on the other hand, are moments of awareness that arise within a mental continuum. Specifically, this refers to a previous moment of awareness that, in having just ceased to be, accommodates for and produces a subsequent moment of awareness. Finally, anything that makes the arising of an effect possible when present, yet does not belong to these three categories, is known as a *ruling condition* or *agentive cause*. As with the previous conditions, this factor facilitates an effect.

Thus, every factor that facilitates an effect, even if only slightly, is included in these four categories. Since whatever lies outside of these four, such as the Almighty, is not a condition, there is no fifth condition. Hence, all outer and inner entities arise due to these four conditions, which are different from what they produce."

Now, while this has indeed been taught, if we examine this teaching with reasoning, it does not make sense. The meaning it expresses, therefore, is of an expedient nature; it is not definitive. This will be explained by (1) offering a general refutation of the notion that arising is due to conditions that are something other than their effects, (2) refuting the notion that arising is caused by actions that are other than their effects, (3) refut-

---

94. Vasubandhu, *Treasury of Abhidharma*, II.61d–62d.

ing the general rationale for conditions, and (4) specifically refuting the characteristics of each of the four conditions.

Conditions as Something Other Than Their Effects

On the first issue, the treatise states:

> The nature of things is not
> In conditions and so forth.
> If there is no thing itself,
> How could there be anything other? [I.3]

Here, the preposition "in" is applied in the construction of the seventh case, the locative. In the present context, the locative can be understood in a temporal sense, as well as being indicative of a supportive basis. Thus, reflective of the locative's dual significance, this passage refutes the notions that cause and effect are different in substance and that effects arise based on causes.

The first argument goes as follows: As the subject, let us take the nature of sprouts and other such resultant entities. These are not present when the causal seed and conditions such as water and fertilizer remain unchanged, regardless of whether we consider these causal factors individually or collectively. The reason, here, is that such effects will not yet have arisen. If this were not the case, cause and effect would be simultaneous, and the conditions could not, then, have any influence on their effects. Thus, effects would be uncaused. If, when its conditions are present, the resultant entity is not present itself with a nature of its own, how could these conditions ever be something other than their effects? Since there is no point of reference, classifying conditions as different under these circumstances would be similar to having short without long, or a "this side" without any "that side." This point was explained extensively above.

According to the second interpretation, the nature of sprouts and other things is not present in such factors as conditions. Whether we consider causes and conditions individually, as a collection, or in some other way, there is nothing that supports an effect before it has arisen, as if it were a jujube fruit sitting on a plate. If an effect were present in such a way, we would be able to perceive it, yet we do not. Moreover, its arising would then be meaningless. Therefore, if an effect is not itself present in causes and conditions, how could it arise from causal factors that are other than itself. As the saying goes, this would be as impossible "as getting sesame oil from sand." The entailment of this argument is explained in the following stanza:

> *If, without being present there,*
> *It were still to arise from conditions,*
> *Why would it not also arise*
> *From that which is not a condition? [I.12]*

The Sanskrit term *bhava* [that in the third stanza is translated as "thing"] means both "thing" and "element." The first explanation of the argument builds on the former sense of the word, whereas the second employs the latter. The master Bhavya treats the first half of the third stanza as a refutation of arising from self and the second half as a refutation of arising from other.

Arising Caused by Actions That Are Other Than Their Effects

On the second issue, the treatise reads:

> *Actions do not have conditions,*
> *Yet there are no actions without conditions.*
> *Without an action there are no conditions,*
> *Yet no conditions are involved in an action. [I.4]*

The Proponents of Differences of the Listener Vehicle believe that different conditions do not themselves produce effects. Rather, they believe that conditions engender an ontologically separate factor, the action of arising, and it is this that produces an effect. We may then ask whether or not such an action itself has conditions. Let us begin by considering the first option. If an effect has already arisen, an action that produces that effect would be pointless. If the effect has not arisen, however, no action of arising could possibly relate to it, for the effect would, at that point, be as nonexistent as the sky flower. Finally, there is nothing that is "currently arising" apart from what either has or has not arisen, and so we do not find the action of arising in any present process either. Thus, since we will fail to find such an action in any of the three times upon examination, we can conclude that actions do not have conditions.

Now let us consider the alternative. If it were the case that actions had no conditions, actions would be uncaused. Therefore, even from the uncritical perspective that considers merely what seems to be the case, we must agree that there are no actions without conditions. It might then be thought that it is the conditions themselves that produce effects. Yet unless an act of producing is involved, there are no grounds to classify conditions as such, just as one would not apply this term to the sky flower. Hence, it is not the conditions themselves [that produce]. It might then be thought that what determines whether something is produced is the presence of conditions that become involved in a given action. Yet, as explained above, the act of production is nonsensical in relation to what has arisen, what has not arisen, and what is in the process of arising.

The General Rationale for Conditions
On the third topic, the treatise states:

> *They are known as conditions*
> *Because things arise in dependence on them.*
> *Yet as long as nothing arises,*
> *Why would they not be nonconditions? [I.5]*

> *Neither for the nonexistent, nor for the existent,*
> *Could there possibly be conditions.*
> *For the nonexistent, what would be conditioned?*
> *For the existent, what role could conditions play? [I.6]*

It may be thought: "What is the point of all this analysis? Consciousness, sprouts, and other such things arise based on the eye, form, and so forth. In other words, they arise based on the four conditions, as is taught. Indeed, it is because this is the case that the latter are known as "conditions" of the former and referred to as such."

Be that as it may, it has still not been established that effects arise based on these conditions. Think of the time when all the factors conducive to an effect have not yet come together, or when an adverse factor prevents the manifestation of an effect. Thus, so long as an effect has yet to arise, we have no grounds for classifying anything as conditions because our reason for doing so, the act of arising, is absent. How could the four conditions be anything but nonconditions under these circumstances, in the same way that the ear and sound are nonconditions for the production of visual consciousness? Indeed, that is precisely what they are. Moreover, when something is a noncondition for the arising of a certain effect, it cannot reasonably start producing that effect at some point in the future either, just as sand will not suddenly begin to yield sesame oil.

It may then be replied: "Something that is not a condition for the arising of a certain effect to begin with may, due to the influence of another condition, later become a condition that is actually capable of producing it."

However, this additional condition does not start out as the condition for the first condition's becoming actually capable of producing the effect, so it could not reasonably become so later. If one believes that, in order to become a condition, a third condition is required, then that third condition would require a fourth and so on. As the *Commentary* explains, this would entail an infinite regress.

Some[95] may think: "When an effect arises, a certain act, that of production, is present in the condition. It is, therefore, a condition."

Yet, if the act of production is found in the condition at that time, then the act of arising will be present in the effect. If the effect does possess such an act, however, it will be established as an entity, and therefore not require any conditions.

We may examine this same issue in reference to effects. If such conditions were to produce an effect, what they produce must either be something that did not exist before or something that did. In consideration of these two alternatives, the Master presents his own genuine thesis with the statement, "Neither for the nonexistent, nor for the existent, could there possibly be conditions."

To prove this statement, he shows first that the very classification of something as a cause depends on there being an effect. If there is no effect, calling something a cause would be similar to speaking of a son in the absence of a father. In such a case, what would the conditions be the conditions for? The same point is made in the following lines:

> Without the existence of an effect,
> The cause lacks what makes it a cause.

---

95. At this point the Tibetan text contains an annotation that reads: Tsangpa (gtsang pa).

If, on the other hand, an effect were present, like a jujube fruit in a bowl, it would already be established. Since it would not need to be created, what role would conditions have to play?

The Characteristics of the Four Conditions

Fourth, it may be argued: "In any case, the Transcendent Conqueror has taught, for example, that 'the cause is that which effectuates.' In this way, he explained the characteristics of each of the four conditions. Hence, they are existent by nature."

In reply, we may point out that since the given characteristics do not stand to reason, such teachings are not of definitive meaning. Next, to show how their characteristics are unreasonable, we shall consider them individually.

First, the following verses highlight the untenability of the causal condition:

> If no existent, nonexistent, or both existent and nonexistent
> Phenomenon comes into being,
> How can we speak of "effectuating conditions"?
> When this is the case, they do not make sense. [I.7]

If an effect were to come into being, there would also be causal conditions responsible for its occurrence. However, an existent effect does not need to be effectuated, a nonexistent effect cannot be effectuated, and an effect both existent and nonexistent would not only be a contradiction, it would also entail both of the flaws identified in the previous two cases. Hence, without any effectuated effect, how can we speak of "conditions that effectuate the essence of their results"? If there is no such thing as an effectuating condition, it would be unreasonable to insist that causal conditions exist by virtue of their characteristics.

Second, refuting the characteristic of the observed condition, the treatise states:

> It is explained that, with existent phenomena,
> There are no observations whatsoever.
> How could a phenomenon for which there is no observation
> Ever relate to an observation? [I.8]

It is also taught:

> What phenomena possess observations? All phenomena subsumed
> under mind and mental states.[96]

It may be thought that subjective primary minds and subsidiary mental states arise due to conditions in the form of observed objects. Yet, if this were the case, would we conceive of the observed condition in reference to an observer that exists or one that does not? The first idea is refuted by reversing the sequence of the stanza's two halves. Thus, the words "a phenomenon" in the third line present the subject, a resultant mind or mental state that exists. How could such a phenomenon depend upon an observed condition? Without any relation to something observed, it already exists prior to any such condition. Hence, it is explained that this preexistent, observing phenomenon cannot be conditioned by anything that is observed. Therefore, the opponent's teaching that such phenomena have their own observed conditions is nothing but an empty claim.

For the refutation of a nonexistent observer, we follow the actual sequence of the stanza's two halves, yet change the phrase "existent phenomena" in the first line to "nonexistent phenomena." Thus, contrary to what the opponent declares, if a resultant observing phenomenon does not exist, it cannot possibly be conditioned by a given object of observation. In the case of a phenomenon for which there is nothing observed, the observer as such is nonexistent, just like the sky flower. How, then, could it possibly relate to something observed?

The master Bhavya explains this stanza as follows: A phenomenon that already exists as an observer to begin with cannot depend on an observation in any way. Such dependence would be nothing but mere verbiage. Moreover, if this phenomenon, an observer, did not exist, how could there possibly be anything that it observes? Thus, according to this reading, the refutation of observed conditions for existent and nonexistent observers is found in the first and the second halves of the stanza, respectively.

Third, refuting the characteristics of the immediately preceding condition, the treatise states:

---

96. Vasubandhu, *Explanation of the Treasury of Abhidharma*, commentary to II.62c.

If phenomena have not arisen,
Cessation makes no sense.
Hence, an immediately preceding condition is untenable.
If it has ceased, how could it be a condition? [I.9]

Indeed, the immediately preceding condition for a given effect is a cause that ceases immediately before the effect manifests. However, so long as no resultant phenomenon, a sprout, for instance, has arisen, any cessation of a phenomenon that is its cause, such as a seed, would not make sense. Since a cause will not have ceased when its effect has yet to arise, the effect's arising cannot be preceded by the cessation of the cause. Hence, it does not make sense to speak of an immediately preceding condition.

If a cause *were* to cease before its effect had arisen, in having ceased it would have become nonexistent. What kind of condition for the production of a subsequent effect does that then leave us with? Also, since it is by the power of the manifestation of a subsequent effect that a preceding cause comes to an end, what would the condition be for the cause's cessation?

This stanza can be alternatively read as a follow-up to the previous refutations: Since it has been shown that no phenomena arise, there cannot reasonably be any cessation. Hence, the idea of an immediately preceding condition is nonsensical. Even if there were cessation without arising, what conditions could there be for the arising of an effect or the ceasing of a cause?

Fourth, refuting the characteristics of the ruling condition, the treatise states:

Since there is no existence
Of things that have no nature,
Saying, "this occurs because of that"
Would not make any sense. [I.10]

The ruling condition is defined as that which is not any of the other three conditions and yet whose existence contributes to the occurrence of a given effect. This definition, however, is unsound because *being* itself is not established; there is no existence as such. We are justified in saying this because, since all things originate dependently, they have no nature, like reflections in a mirror.

At this point, one might object: "For an opponent who does not accept this absence of nature, such as a realist, your argument will remain unfounded. For those who do, however, merely invalidating nature itself will suffice since this will also serve to invalidate the nature of ruling conditions. In the latter case, offering evidence to support such a claim would be pointless."

As explained earlier, to an opponent for whom the absence of nature is not established, this absence will be proven by presenting dependent origination as evidence. Indeed, when nature as such has been invalidated by this evidence, the idea that being produced by ruling conditions is the nature of things will have been invalidated as well. However, just as one may negate the presence of an aśoka tree by referring to the absence of any tree, using the absence of nature as evidence to refute this convention does not pose a problem.

The unproblematic character of the argument is clarified further by considering how, in this particular context, this functions to disprove the argument advanced by the opposition. Our opponents may say that because the characteristics of ruling conditions do exist, things arise from something other than themselves. In reply, we may say that, for those of us who assert that things have no nature, such characteristics are not established.

The Worldly Notion of Arising from Other

What now follows is a refutation of the worldly notion that things arise from what is other than themselves. Worldly people, as well as certain logicians, form their opinions without basing their views on any philosophical system. "Sprouts, woolen garments, and other such things," they say, "come about due to seeds, earth, yarn, and so on. We can see this for ourselves, just as we see that these causes are something other than what they produce. Therefore, things arise from other things!"

Nevertheless, as is the case with dreams, while this may be the perception of a conventional deluded mind, when we investigate we will find that things do not arise based on other things. To explain further, we shall (1) consider how effects cannot reasonably arise, regardless of whether or not they are present or absent in their conditions, and (2) regardless of whether they are of the nature of their conditions or not. This will then be followed by (3) a conclusion.

On the first issue, the treatise states:

In separate conditions and their gathering,
The effect is entirely absent.
How could something that does not exist in the conditions
Ever arise from them? [I.11]

Let us consider whether effects arise due to their presence or absence in conditions. The first option involves an effect manifesting while having already been present in its conditions. Concerning this view, it may be held that an effect is present in each of its individual conditions. There is, however, no such presence at all. If there were, there would be just as many effects as there are conditions. Moreover, such a presence would have to be observable, yet it is not. Effects are also entirely absent from their conditions en masse. If they do not exist in any of their individual conditions, they cannot exist in their assembly either. Furthermore, if effects were indeed present in a collection of multiple conditions, each of them would individually need to have two aspects, one in which the effect is present and another in which it is not. The effect would then emerge only from those aspects in which it is present, and so a single effect would be the product of a fraction of each condition.

Alternatively, if effects did not exist within their conditions, how could sprouts, woolen garments, and other such effects arise from seeds, yarn, and other conditions? Our position is that they could not, and we prove it by taking as evidence the fact that they do not exist within those conditions, in which case their arising would be as likely as getting sesame oil from sand.

The objection that there is no entailment will be to no avail. If sprouts and woolen garments were to result from conditions, such as seeds and yarn, within which they do not exist, why would they not also arise based on factors that are not conditions, such as fire and grass? Indeed, nonconditions would then produce these effects as well, for they would be the same as conditions in being completely devoid of the effect. This, then, shows the significance of the evidence that we have advanced.

Therefore, the probandum that is entailed by the evidence is established by an equivalence of identical reasons. Should the opponent again call that into question, he or she will be asked to explain why effects truly arise only from their conditions, although these same effects are equally nonexistent in both conditions and nonconditions. Any reply that refers to appearance, capacity, or intrinsic nature will, as explained earlier, be insufficient.

On the second issue, the treatise states:

> *The effect may be of its conditions' nature,*
> *But these conditions have no nature of their own.*
> *How could the effect of that which is not an entity itself*
> *Be of the nature of that which conditions it? [I.13]*

> *Hence, it is not of the nature of its conditions,*
> *Nor of the nature of that which are not its conditions. [I.14a–b]*

Next we shall consider whether or not the effect is of the nature of its conditions. In this context, it may be thought: "The Enumerators hold that sprouts and woolen garments are identical in nature with the seeds and yarn that produce them. The issue of whether or not the effect is present in its conditions is, therefore, irrelevant."

Now, if conditions such as seeds and yarn themselves had their own nature, then their effects could certainly be of that same nature. Conditions, however, do not have any essence or nature of their own. On this point, it is taught:

> Apart from what is composite,
> The mind does not encounter any entity.[97]

Hence, whatever dwells in the center of the ten directions, or in the interim between the past and future, must have multiple parts that face in each direction and that relate to the past and future, respectively. Its nature, then, is compartmentalized; it is a mere imputation based on constituent parts. With this in mind, how might the effect of our subject, that is, conditions, be of the nature of these very same conditions? Indeed, it could not. To prove this, we may present as evidence the fact that conditions are themselves not entities; they lack any established nature. In this sense, they are similar to the son of a barren woman.

---

97. From the *Journey to Laṅkā*.

Again, members of our own tradition may think: "Effects arise from conditions that are of a different nature than their own."

Nonetheless, no effect is of the nature of factors that are not its conditions. That is to say, if sprouts and woolen garments were not of the nature of their conditions, seeds and yarn, these conditions would be of a nature that is contrary [to their effects, as is the case with] fire, grass, and other such factors that are not conditions. Moreover, it would be meaningless for that which is established as having a different nature than its conditions to still depend on them. Hence, effects would end up causeless.

On the third issue, the treatise states:

> *As there is no effect, how could there be*
> *Conditions as well as nonconditions. [I.14c–d]*

At this point, it may be thought: "You just claimed that if an effect arises from conditions within which it is absent, it would also have to arise from what are not its conditions. In other words, you do acknowledge that there are certain things that are conditions and others that are not. It then follows that effects, as counterparts to these conditions, exist as well."

Now, while we do express ourselves in this way, we do so only in consideration of what you yourself accept, or what is agreed upon in the world. Whether effects are believed to be present or absent in their conditions, or whether or not they are believed to be of the nature of their conditions, our investigations have refuted the notion of arising. Therefore, as there is no effect, how could the conditions and nonconditions that it relates to possibly exist?

SUMMARY OF THE CHAPTER'S SIGNIFICANCE

Having offered this explanation of the scripture, this third section presents a summary of its significance. This first chapter refutes the notion that effects arise from something other than themselves. It does so by refuting the ideas that effects arise based on conditions that are other than themselves, that the essence of the effect does or does not exist, that effects are present or absent in their conditions, and that effects are or are not of the nature of their conditions. In emphasizing the refutation of arising from other, this chapter also functions to present a general refutation of all four extreme notions that concern arising.

Thus, explicitly, the present chapter demonstrates how the principle of absence of arising is immune to critique. It performs an existential negation of the constructs of real arising, and establishes that the appearance of dependent origination is of a relative nature. Moreover, since there cannot reasonably be phenomena that do not arise, this chapter also presents an implicit existential negation of the constructs related to the true existence of any phenomenon, establishing their appearance to be relative and illusory. Hence, it serves to engender the insight that is the realization of the two truths exactly as they are.

The same teaching is found in the sūtras. As the *Noble Śālu Sprout Sūtra* states:

> When a seed causes a sprout to manifest, it is not created by itself or by something else. It does not come from both, yet neither is it uncaused. It is not produced by an almighty or by time. It arises, rather, in dependence.

This concludes the explanation of the first chapter, the analysis of conditions, in the *Ornament of Reason*, a commentary on the *Root of the Middle Way*.

CHAPTER TWO

Analysis of Going and Coming

THE ANALYSIS of going and coming will be treated under the same three headings that were used in the previous chapter.

THE CONTEXT OF CHAPTER 2

First we will discuss the chapter's context. Concerning its relation to the profound sūtras, we may consider the following passages. The *Mother of the Victorious Ones* states:

> Form does not come from anywhere or go anywhere, nor does it remain anywhere.

While the *Noble Jewel Mound* states:

> The venerable ones do not proceed anywhere, nor have they arrived from anywhere. The monk Subhūti does not go some- where, and he has not come from anywhere. For this reason, the Transcendent Conqueror has taught the Dharma.

The present chapter employs reasoning to ascertain the meaning of such passages.

As for the chapter's relation to the other chapters, we may see it as a response to the following idea: "By demonstrating that dependent origi- nation does not occur, the analysis of conditions has also implicitly estab- lished that there is no going or otherwise. Nevertheless, the nonexistence of going and coming should be proven explicitly using a form of reasoning that is thoroughly accepted by the opposition."

Hence, this chapter explicitly refutes this concept by undermining the very notion of going and coming.

THE CONTENT OF CHAPTER 2

Second, the explanation of the content will include (1) an elaborate explanation of the reasoning that refutes the act of going and (2) the conclusion that this refutation leads to. The first of these topics covers (1) a refutation of the act of going by analyzing it in terms of the three times, (2) a refutation through a threefold examination of the agent, (3) a refutation of the arguments used to substantiate the act of going, (4) a refutation through examining whether the act of going and its support, that is, the one who goes, are the same or different from one another, and (5) a refutation of the act of going by examining whether it is singular or multiple. The first refutation involves (1) a general refutation of the act of going on the paths of the three times and (2) a specific refutation with respect to going in the present.

Going and the Paths of the Three Times
On the first issue, the treatise states:

> Where there has been going, there is none;
> Where it has yet to occur, there is no going either.
> Aside from what has been traversed and what has not,
> No place where walking occurs can be identified. [II.1]

The act of going is brought about by an agent in relation to an object. Going must, therefore, entail these two. The term "object" refers here to the basis for engaging in the act of going, that is, the path that is traversed. Such a path, moreover, can be one of only three types: It can be one that has already been traversed, one that has yet to be travelled, and one upon which going has manifested and is still occurring.

Now, if going occurs, it must take place on one of these three paths. Yet it cannot occur on a path that has already been traversed because the act has ceased and is absent there. Likewise, going does not take place on a path that has yet to be traversed since the act, having not yet occurred, is also absent there. Finally, going does not occur on a path that is presently being walked upon either. Consider a single walker proceeding along a path. Because having and not having been traversed are mutually exclusive and exhaustive, we will fail to identify, or observe, any path that is presently being traversed aside from where the walker has already gone or has yet to go. Hence, there is no path being traversed in the present aside from these two.

It may be thought, "Indeed, going is over where the walker has already gone, and where he has not yet gone, it is still to come. Nevertheless, we will find the present act of going on the exact location where the individuals feet are currently stepping."

The walker's feet, however, can be broken down into most subtle particles. The particles that lie behind the particles constituting the tip of the toes on the back foot relate to the path that has already been traversed, while the particles located ahead of the particles that make up the heel of the front foot relate to the path that has yet to be covered.

Moreover, even the most subtle particles that make up the feet must themselves be composed of numerous parts. Therefore, as explained before, in a particle that touches the ground, all that lies behind the front of the particle is included in the path that has already been traversed, while what is ahead of the back part of the particle will belong to the path that has yet to come.

The nonexistence of any path upon which walking presently occurs and which is neither that which has already been traversed nor that which has yet to be walked upon is also established in the verses that begin, "Since what is taking birth is already partly born. . . ." In other words, the path that is currently being traversed cannot reasonably be anything other than a part that has already been covered and a part that has yet to come.

Going in the Present

Our discussion of the second issue begins with a presentation of the opposing view:

> *Where there is movement, there is going,*
> *And movement is found where walking takes place,*
> *Not where going has been, nor where it has yet to occur.*
> *Hence, going is found where walking takes place. [II.2]*

Here, the opponent may argue, "Certainly, going does not take place on a path that has already been traversed, nor on one that has yet to come. Nevertheless, going is indeed found where walking presently takes place because that is where movement occurs. What evidence do we have? And to what does this evidence pertain? By 'movement' we understand the action of the legs as they step. 'Going,' on the other hand, refers to the act of leaving behind one location and proceeding to another. Defined in this way, movement entails going, as can be seen when noticing that wherever a walker is in this type of motion, we also observe going.

"The property of the position is established as follows. Generally, mere movement is observed in direct perception. Moreover, such movement is not present on a path that has already been traversed, or on a path that has yet to travelled. In these two cases, movement has already ceased and not yet occurred, respectively. We must, therefore, conclude that it is found exclusively where walking takes place in the present."

It has already been explained that there is no path presently being walked upon other than what was already traversed and what has yet to be travelled. Since the location where walking occurs in the present itself lacks establishment, the subject that is the basis [for this argument] is not established. Nevertheless, let us imagine that there is such a thing as a path where walking takes place in the present. We may then consider the sentence: "Going is found in the part of the path that is presently being traversed, that is the location where walking takes place." What we will notice is that neither the verbal phrase, ["going,"] nor the object phrase, ["where walking takes place,"] can be related to the act of going. This will be shown by demonstrating (1) that if the object phrase refers to the act of going, the verbal phrase is devoid of meaning, (2) if the verbal phrase refers to the act of going, the object phrase is devoid of meaning, and (3) if it is referred to by both, there will be absurd consequences.

The Object Phrase Referring to the Act of Going
On the first issue, the treatise states:

> *Going where walking takes place,*
> *How could that make sense,*
> *When, without going, there cannot reasonably be*
> *Any place where walking takes place? [II.3]*

When an agent of going, such as Devadatta, goes somewhere, there is but a single act of going. The singular nature of the act is shown by the fact that the result, having gone somewhere, is exclusively singular as well. Therefore, though it is meaningful to link this singular act with the object phrase "where walking takes place" and use this expression accordingly, since the act of going is not twofold, the verbal phrase "going" will have become divorced from its referent, the act of going, and so will be rendered meaningless. How, then, could we make sense of the expression, "going is found where walking takes place"? This statement would make as little sense as the statement, "sound is permanent."

"Why," one may wonder, "does the object phrase 'where walking takes place' have to refer to the act of going?"

To explain, consider how one cannot rightly speak of somebody as 'rich' if that person does not possess any wealth. In the same way, speaking of a *place* where walking takes place does not make sense if it is not thereby implied that the *act* of going is present there. To avoid this nonsensical position, the object phrase "where walking takes place" must, therefore, necessarily refer to the act of going. The necessity of this relationship is evident from the fact that if the expression "where walking takes place" is disconnected from the act of going, it will carry no meaning.

The present stanza can also be seen to anticipate the following explanation. Let us consider that the singular act of going is referred to, and expressed by, the verbal phrase "going." When this is the case, the object phrase "where walking takes place" loses its referential connection to the action. Moreover, speaking of a place where walking occurs does not make sense if it does not include a reference to the act of going. Thus, this stanza can also be read as [an explanation of the way] the object phrase is rendered meaningless.

The Verbal Phrase Referring to the Act of Going
On the second issue, the treatise states:

> *For whomever there is going where walking takes place,*
> *It then follows*
> *That there is no going where walking takes place*
> *Because "going is found where walking takes place." [II.4]*

It may be thought: "The aforementioned flaw does not occur when the verbal phrase 'going' refers to the act of going." However, as explained before, there are not two acts of going. For this reason, the object phrase "where walking takes place" will lose the meaning it is meant to convey and the statement "going is found where walking takes place" will then no longer make sense.

The opponent holds that because the statement "where walking takes place" does not imply the act of going, it should be understood purely as a noun phrase. Instead, it is the verbal phrase "going" that refers to the act of walking. For those who take this position, however, it follows that there is no act of going in relation to the object phrase "where walking takes place." How so? Because a) there is only a single act of going and b) it was explained that while the phrase "where walking takes place" should be understood purely as a noun phrase, it is the verbal phrase "going" that refers to the act of going.

This stanza can also be read in accordance with the explanation above,[98] in which case the position under critique claims that the act of going pertains to the place where walking occurs. With this position, the opponent thus holds that the phrase "where walking takes place" indicates the existence of going. For those who take this position, the assertion that the phrase "where walking takes place" refers to the act of going leads to the conclusion that the verbal phrase "going" does not refer to the existence of the act of going. Again, this follows because here it is held that the phrase "where walking takes place" is linked with the act of going. We thus arrive at this interpretation by reading the statement "where walking takes place" in the third line as another way of speaking about going. Seen in this way, this stanza also shows how the verbal phrase ends up being rendered meaningless.

Both Phrases Referring to the Act of Going
On the third issue, the treatise states:

> *If going took place where walking takes place,*
> *It would follow that there are two acts of going:*

---

98. In an apparent error, the Tibetan text here reads "the explanation below" ('og gi bshad pa).

One due to which there is a place with walking
And another that is the going that happens there. [II.5]

When it follows that there are two acts of going,
It follows that there are two agents of going,
Because without something that goes,
It makes no sense for there to be going. [II.6]

One may then object further, "Neither of these problems occurs because both object- and verbal phrase involve the act of going."

If this were the case, both the object phrase "where walking takes place" and the verbal phrase "going" would have a referent. Nevertheless it would, therefore, follow that a single agent of going performs two acts of going. One act qualifies the path that is walked upon, justifying the use of the phrase "where walking takes place" to refer to it. The second is the act of going over that place and proceeding to somewhere else. Thus, we end up with two acts of going. Yet this is unacceptable because if there were two acts of going, there would also be two agents.

We cannot argue that having two actions with a single agent presents no problems. Generally, whenever an action is performed, it is done by an agent and in relation to some object. Hence, there cannot reasonably be any act of going without an agent, that is, without something that goes.

To this, one may respond, "Indeed, if nothing goes, there cannot reasonably be an act of going. However, a single agent performing two actions at the same time is not a contradiction. Take the case of Devadatta, for example. Though he is a single agent, we still observe him performing different actions at the same time, such as looking, speaking, and sitting."

Nevertheless, while a substantially singular agent may simultaneously perform several different actions, we will never observe the simultaneous performance of two actions of the same kind (such as two acts of going). Alternatively, we may say that a substantially singular agent never performs two actions at the same time since there is never more than a single effect, such as having gone to another place. Both of these arguments are excellent.

The *Commentary*[99] explains that the agent is a capacity, not a substance. Hence, when a substantially singular person is engaged in numerous

99. That is, Candrakīrti's *Clear Words*.

actions, such as speaking and sitting, there are an equal number of capacities involved. Therefore, the example of a single agent that simultaneously performs multiple actions is not established. However, on such an explanation, the single substance of the person may well include two capacities for going, and it will then not be contradictory for there to be two acts of going as well. In this way, the point of contention—a single substance of a person that performs two acts of going at the same time—cannot be refuted. The earlier replies, therefore, seem preferable.

Refutation through a Threefold Examination of the Agent

Third is the refutation of going by means of a threefold examination of the agent. This section includes (1) an explanation that going and the agent of going are coextensive, (2) a general refutation of the idea that a third-party person performs the act of going, and (3) a specific refutation of the notion that the agent of going goes.

Going and the Agent of Going Are Coextensive

On the first issue, the treatise states:

> If there is nothing that goes,
> Going makes no sense.
> In the absence of any going,
> How could there be one who goes? [II.7]

As explained before, all acts are performed by agents. Without an agent of going,—something that goes—it makes no sense for there to be an act of going. Likewise, agents are universally classified as such in consideration of the particular acts they perform. Hence, how could there be any agent of going if the act of going to which it owes its very existence is absent? [The agent of going would then be as nonexistent] as space.

The *Commentary*[100] here anticipates the idea that the existence of going is due to the existence of its support, the agent of going. Thus, this stanza is seen as a refutation of the notion that an agent of going can be used to prove the act of going.

---

100. That is, Candrakīrti's *Clear Words.*

A Third Party Does Not Perform the Act of Going

On the second issue, the treatise states:

> One who goes does not go,
> Nor does one who does not go.
> Other than goers and nongoers,
> What third party could be going? [II.8]

Going is entailed by the agent of going. Who, then, is it that goes? Is it one who goes, someone with the activity of going? Or is it one who does not go, someone with no such activity? Or, perhaps, is it a third party that ensues from the negation of the former two? Someone who is already one who goes does not go, for there would then have to be two actions, and there are not two acts of going. Neither does someone who does not go, for such an agent would lack the act of going in the same way that space lacks it. What third party—someone who is not one who goes, and yet not someone who does not go either—could be going? One who goes and one who does not are mutually exclusive and exhaustive, so no third category can be derived from the negation of both.

Those Who Go Do Not Go

One may then respond, "A nongoer does not go, and it is likewise true that no going is performed by some party that is neither someone who goes nor someone who does not. Nevertheless, the one who goes does indeed go."

The refutation of this idea parallels the reasoning demonstrated above. A single agent of going cannot, at a given point in time, perform more than a single act of going. Hence, if the verbal phrase refers to the single act of going, the agent phrase will be rendered meaningless. On the other hand, if the agent phrase refers to it, the verbal phrase loses meaning, and if linked with both, the result is absurdity. In the next section, these three consequences will be examined individually.

Linking Going to the Verbal Phrase

On the first issue, the treatise states:

> When, in the absence of going,
> A goer does not make sense,

The statement "going is engaged in by the one who goes"—
How could that possibly make sense? [II.9]

These lines raise the question of how it could possibly make sense to say that "going is engaged in by the one who goes," indicating that this phrase is entirely nonsensical. Why is it nonsensical? Well, someone who goes, such as Devadatta, does not perform more than a single act of going. If the verbal phrase "going is engaged in" refers to that action, then that phrase is meaningful. However, there are not two actions, and "the one who goes" does not make sense unless it carries a reference to going. The problem, here, is then that the agent phrase ends up losing its meaning. In other words, although the verbal phrase is meaningful in this case, the agent phrase is not. We will, therefore, fail to make sense of the sentence "going is engaged in by the one who goes."

The present stanza can also be seen to indicate what is explained below,[101] arguing that since the term "the one who goes" does not make any sense without an act of going, this part of the sentence must refer to such an act. Yet, as a consequence of making this link, there is no act of going left to be designated by the verbal phrase "going is engaged in." This term ends up being devoid of meaning.

Linking Going to the Agent Phrase
On the second issue, the treatise states:

> *For those who hold that going is engaged in by one who goes*
> *It would then follow that there is*
> *One who goes in the absence of going,*
> *For it is asserted that going is performed by one who goes. [II.10]*

It may be thought that such inconsistencies can be avoided by asserting that the agent phrase refers to the act of going. However, in that case the verbal phrase "going is engaged in" cannot express the meaning it should, that is, the action of going. The phrase "going is engaged in by one who goes" could not, then, reasonably be said to make sense.

---

101. In an apparent error, the Tibetan text here reads "what is explained above" (gong gi bshad pa).

This explanation is given to an opponent who holds that the agent of going is linked with the act of going. Thus, in the sentence "going is engaged in by one who goes," the term "one who goes" applies to the act of going. For this reason, it follows that the word "going" cannot serve to designate the act of going because it is held that the agent phrase "one who goes" is linked with the single act of going, insofar as it expresses that meaning.

Alternatively, this stanza can be seen to indicate the explanation above. According to this reading, the opponent holds that the verbal phrase "going is engaged in" refers to the single act of going. For this position, it follows that the one who goes is unrelated to the act of going because there are not two actions. In this case, "one who goes" is mere verbiage. The assertion, here, is that the verbal phrase "going is engaged in" contains the sense of going. The consequence of this position is that the one who goes has no association with going. Thus, this stanza can also be interpreted to mean that the agent phrase is rendered meaningless.

Linking Going to Both the Agent Phrase and the Verbal Phrase
On the third issue, the treatise states:

> *If going is engaged in by the one who goes,*
> *It follows that there are two acts of going:*
> *One that characterizes the one who goes,*
> *And another going in that capacity. [II.11]*

In response, one may say, "Both of these flaws will be avoided by holding that 'the one who goes' and 'going is engaged in' refer to the act of going."

However, when it is held that both of these elements in the sentence are linked to the act of going, it follows that there are two acts of going. One act of going qualifies Devadatta for the label "the one who goes," and so makes him the agent of that action. The second is the going that he, in that capacity, subsequently performs. Hence, there are two actions here: the going [that characterizes the agent] plus the going that the agent is to perform. This, however, is untenable because if there are two acts of going, there must, as was explained before, also be two individuals that engage in those acts of going.

Refuting the Arguments for the Act of Going
Third, refuting the arguments that are advanced to prove the act of going involves five separate refutations. We will begin by refuting the "initiation" that causes going to occur.

Refuting the Initiation of the Act of Going
Here an idea such as the following is anticipated: "It is certainly in the nature of things that there are acts of going. We can know this from the fact that such acts are initiated. When in this way the initiation of going is used as evidence to prove the existence of going, it is not the case that the property of the position and the entailment are not established. We directly perceive that standing still comes to an end and that is precisely the initiation of going. If going were as nonexistent as a robe made of tortoise hair, it would not make sense for it to be initiated."

Once examined and investigated, however, this argument can be shown to be unestablished. This involves demonstrating that the initiation of going is not established, (1) even if it is accepted that there is an object to which it relates, and (2) that the initiation of going is not established because the object to which it relates is not established.

On the first issue, the treatise states:

> *Going does not begin where it has been,*
> *Nor does it begin where it has yet to occur.*
> *Going does not begin where walking takes place,*
> *So where does going begin? [II.12]*

Let us assume that such a thing as ceasing to stand still and stepping onto the first part of a path, thus initiating the act of going, existed naturally. In terms of where it would take place, the beginning of such an act can be conceived of in only three ways. Going would have to be initiated on a path that has already been tread, on one that has yet to be traversed, or on a path where walking is ongoing in the present.

A path that has already been traversed is not where going begins because it has ceased there. Neither is going initiated on a path that has yet to be traversed, for there, the act of going has not been initiated and is still absent. It is also contradictory for an act of going to commence where walking has yet to occur. Going does not begin on a path where walking takes place in the present either because, as explained before, there is no path upon which there may be walking in the present apart from what has already, or not yet, been tread. If this is where going were initiated, it would also follow that there are two acts of going.

If going does not begin on any of these three paths, where *does* it start? The answer that is implied here is, "nowhere."

On the second issue, the treatise states:

> *Before going has been initiated,*
> *There is no place where walking occurs or has taken place*
> *Upon which going could begin.*
> *And how could there be going where there is none yet? [II.13]*

For going to begin, there must first be a place for it to occur. Before going begins, however, the path that has already been traversed, the one where the act of going has ceased, does not exist. Similarly, there is no path where going takes place in the present either. Since these paths do not exist, going cannot be initiated on them.

"Before going has been initiated," one may object, "there is still a path that has yet to be traversed. That is where going is initiated."

Nevertheless, the initiation of going requires the act of going, and no such act has been initiated on a path that has yet to be traversed. Hence, as going is not occurring there, how could that possibly be the place where it is initiated?

Refuting the Object to Which Going Relates

Second is a refutation of the object that going relates to. On this topic, the treatise states:

> *Since we never witness a beginning of going*
> *How can we conceive of the traversed,*
> *Of what is being traversed,*
> *And what has yet to be traversed? [II.14]*

This stanza anticipates the following objection: "You have not explicitly refuted the existence of the object to which going relates, namely, the paths that are covered in the past, future, and present. Therefore, going by nature does indeed exist because these three paths exist. This argument, moreover, does not lack entailment because the act of going is the cause for the designation of these three paths."

In response, it is shown how the evidence presented in this argument, that is, the natural existence of the three paths, is itself not established. As was explained earlier, the initiation of going can never be witnessed or perceived from the perspective of reason. How, then, can we conceive of a path where the act of going has ceased, that is, a path that has already been traversed? Likewise, how should we conceive of a path where the act of going has not been initiated and which has yet to be traveled? Finally, how may we imagine a path upon which going has occurred and not yet ceased, a path that is being walked upon in the present? Indeed, the implication here is that there is nothing to conceive of in any way at all.

Refutation of the Result, Stopping
Third is a refutation of the result of going, stopping. On this topic, the treatise states:

> Stopping does not occur where walking takes place,
> Where going has been, or where it has yet to occur. [II.17a–b]

"The act of going exists by nature," one may think, "because its result, stopping, exists. Moreover, it is not the case that the property of the position and the entailment are not established. The commencement of standing still is directly perceived, and that commencement is itself the cessation of going. Moreover, the stopping that results cannot occur without its cause, namely, going, just as one who has not observed a pure lifestyle cannot later stop doing so."

Two stanzas below, it is shown how the evidence presented in this argument is not established since once we subject it to analysis we will find that there is no stopping. Stopping does not occur on a path that has already been traversed, or on one that has yet to be traveled. On the first, the act of going has ceased, while on the second it has yet to occur. Stopping does not occur on a path where walking is presently taking place either. Such a path does not exist because we will fail to observe any path where walking occurs in the present apart from what has and has not been traversed. Locating stopping on a path where walking is presently taking place, moreover, would also entail that there are two acts of going: one that is the act of walking along the path and another that is stopping.

Refutation of That Which Counters Going

Fourth, refuting that which counters going, the treatise states:

> *The one who goes does not stand still,*
> *Nor does one who does not go.*
> *Aside from those that do and do not go,*
> *What third party could stand still? [II.15]*

> *In the absence of going,*
> *There cannot reasonably be anyone who goes.*
> *How, then, could it reasonably be said*
> *That it is the one who goes who stands still? [II.16]*

"Standing still counters going," it may be thought, "yet this has not yet been explicitly refuted. Therefore, because something that makes it stop exists, going has a natural existence as well, for something that does not exist cannot be countered, just as the son of the barren woman cannot have an enemy."

In response, it is explained that this evidence is not established. The reason, here, is that when the act of standing still is examined with reference to the three possible types of agent, as was done in an earlier section, the act of standing still will be seen to be nonexistent. The one who goes cannot also be standing still because going and standing still are incompatible. Moreover, someone who is not going cannot not stand still either because there would have to be two acts of standing still were this to take place, and this is not the case. Finally, apart from those who go and those who do not, what third party could stand still? Since being and not being someone who goes are directly contradictory, the existence of a third party that ensues from the negation of the former two is impossible.

One may then object, "While nongoers and third parties do not get to stand still, those who are involved in going do."

Let us explain the contradictory nature of this notion. A sentence such as "x stands here" indicates the presence of the act of standing still. Moreover, it also affirms the absence of going, for the act of going is incompatible with standing still. Therefore, in a situation where the act of going is absent, it would be meaningless to say that there is someone who goes. In such a situation, to speak only of standing still would be meaningful, but the words "the one who goes" would be meaningless. How, then, would we make sense of the sentence, "It is the one who goes who stands still"? Indeed, this statement is nonsensical.

Refuting the Arguments for That Which Counters Going

Fifth is a refutation of the arguments for that which counters going. The treatise states:

> *With going, beginning, and stopping,*
> *The case is the same as with going. [II.17c–d]*

There are three parts here. First, it may be thought that standing still, that which counters going, has a natural existence since its counterpart, going, exists. This idea is shown to be untenable by refuting the argument advanced to support it. In other words, going, as that which counters standing still, is refuted in the same manner as before, in which standing still, as the contrary to going, was refuted. Hence, whereas before it was argued that, "The one who goes does not stand still," the argument now becomes, "The one who stands still does not go, nor does one who does not stand still." In this way, stanzas fifteen and sixteen turn into a refutation of the natural existence of standing still.

Second, these lines also anticipate the notion that standing still, the contrary to going, exists because there is something that causes it, namely, the initiation of standing still. The refutation of this cause, the initiation of standing still, is equivalent to the one applied to the initiation of going. Whereas before it was, "Going does not begin where it has been," we may now read, "Standing still does not begin where it has been." Thus, stanzas twelve through fourteen turn into a refutation of the initiation of standing still, which is what counters going.

Third, one may seek to prove the existence of standing still by arguing: "That which counters going, standing still, has a natural existence because standing still eventually stops."

The refutation of this argument parallels the one explained in relation to the stopping of going. The natural existence of stopping going was refuted by arguing, "Stopping does not occur where walking takes place, where going has been, or where it has yet to occur." Hence, the refutation of what counters standing still now becomes, "Going does not occur where there is standing still, where standing still has been, or where it has yet to occur."

In this way, the very refutations of that which counters going, the initiation that causes going, and the stopping that results also serve as refutations of the same factors in relation to standing still, which is what counters going. Hence, these verses can be read as saying, "With the contrary, beginning, and stopping, the case is the same as with going."

Is Going Identical to or Different from Its Support?

In this fourth section, the refutation of going involves examining whether agent and action are identical or different. The treatise states:

> *The act of going and the one who goes*
> *Cannot rightly be said to be the same.*
> *The act of going and the one who goes*
> *Cannot rightly be said to be different. [II.18]*

> *If that which is the going*
> *Were also the one who goes,*
> *It would follow that agent and act*
> *Would be one and the same. [II.19]*

> *Yet if the going and goer*
> *Are thought to be different,*
> *There could be going without something that goes*
> *And someone who goes in the absence of going. [II.20]*

> *When two things cannot be*
> *Established as identical,*
> *Yet not as different things either,*
> *How can they be established at all? [II.21]*

In the preceding verses, the thesis is presented first. The act of going and its support, the one who goes, cannot rightly be claimed to be identical in essence, yet they cannot rightly be considered essentially different either. Why not? Well, if that which is the act of going were identical with the one who goes, it would universally follow that all agents are essentially the same as their activities. In other words, they would be the same as the actions they perform. The entailment of this argument is ensured by an equivalence of identical reasons. This notion is untenable because, to give one example, a woodcutter would end up being essentially the same as the act of cutting wood. This, however, stands in direct opposition to what we see.

If, on the other hand, the act of going and the one who goes are thought to be essentially different, these two would have to be independent of one another. It would then follow that there can be an act of going without there being any support for it, that is, anyone who goes. Likewise, there could also be someone who goes in the absence of going. However, we do not observe anything of this sort. Thus, since action and agent are mutually dependent, they cannot be established as essentially different.

It might be thought that while the one who goes and the act of going cannot be said to be either identical or different, they nevertheless are existent by nature. Yet that will not do either. As was already explained, when two things, such as the act of going and the one who goes, cannot be established as either the same or different, how can they be existent by nature? The negation of two directly contradictory notions cannot possibly lead to the establishment of a third category.

Is Going Singular or Multiple?

Fifth is a refutation of the act of going by examining whether it is singular or multiple. The treatise states:

> The one who goes does not engage in the going
> That characterizes him as someone who goes,
> Because there is no one who goes before going.
> Someone goes somewhere. [II.22]

> The one who goes does not engage in going other than
> The going that characterizes him as someone who goes,
> The reason being that for a single agent of going,
> It does not make sense for there to be two acts. [II.23]

> Someone who goes does not engage
> In any of the three kinds of going.

Someone who does not go does not engage
In any of the three kinds of going. [II.24]

Someone who does and does not go does not engage
In any of the three kinds of going either. [II.25a–b]

One may then respond, "We may say that 'a speaker utters an expression' or 'an agent performs an action.' Just so, going as well exists as an act that is performed by an agent."

Now, when someone who goes performs the act of going, is this act then the same as the one that characterizes him or her as someone who goes or is it different? First, Devadatta does not engage in the act of going that characterizes him as someone who goes, that is, the going that qualifies him for the label "someone who goes." A potter can make pots because he exists prior to the pot he makes. Likewise, if a given agent of going were to exist prior to the act of going that characterizes him or her as such, then that previously existent individual could perform the act of going to a given location, such as a town or a city. Thus, the fourth line in the stanza shows the argument's reverse entailment. The third line presents the evidence: The agent of going does not exist as an agent of going prior to the act of going that qualifies him or her as such an agent. The implication here is that there cannot be someone who goes independent of the act of going. This way of reversing the last two lines, and so reading them as respectively the reverse entailment and the evidence, is the approach of the *Commentary.*

Secondly, apart from the act of going that characterizes and qualifies Devadatta as someone who goes, that is, the one that shows that he is the agent of that action, there is no other act of going being performed. It does not make sense for there to be two acts of going: one that qualifies a goer such as Devadatta as someone who goes and another going that this goer engages in.

Furthermore, neither does it make sense for someone who goes to engage in the act of going. The reasoning, here, is as follows: Someone who is a goer by virtue of his or her being engaged in the act of going does not engage in any of the three types of going. In other words, this person does not engage in an act of going that is already an action, one that is not yet an action, or one that both is and is not an action. The same is true when we consider someone who does not go, someone not engaged in the act of going. Such a nongoer does not engage in any of these three types of going. Finally, someone who both does and does not go, someone who both is and is not engaged in going, does not engage in any of these three kinds of going either.

In the chapter that analyzes actions and agents, the notions that the act of going is performed by someone who is already someone who goes, by someone who is not, and by someone who both is and is not someone who goes are likewise all refuted. In that chapter, it is argued:

> That which is an agent would have no activity.
> There would also be action without an agent.[102]

Likewise:

> If one that is not an agent performs,
> The agent will lack its cause.[103]

And:

> Since being and not being are incompatible in one thing,
> How could this ever be the case?[104]

The ideas that something that is already an act, something that is not an act, and something that both is and is not an act can be performed are also addressed. Dispensing with these ideas, the text states:

> That which is an action is not performed,
> So the agent would be lacking its action.[105]

and:

---

102. *Root of the Middle Way*, VIII.2a–b.
103. These two lines appear to be based on *Root of the Middle Way*, VIII.3.
104. Ibid., VIII.7c–d.
105. Ibid., VIII.2c–d.

If something that is not an action is performed
The action will lack its cause.[106]

and:

Since being and not being are incompatible in one thing,
How could this ever be the case?[107]

CONCLUSION

This second section relates to the chapter's conclusion. The treatise states:

There is, therefore, no going,
No one who goes, and nothing traversed. [II.25c–d]

Thus, as explained above, once we have investigated the matter with reasoning, we find no act of going, no agent engaging in such an act, and no foundation for the activity (that is, no path that is traversed).

SUMMARY OF THE CHAPTER'S SIGNIFICANCE

Having explained the progression of the text, we may now offer a summary of the third topic: the significance of this chapter. Here, we have seen explicit refutations of the objects of the act of going and coming as they pertain to the three times, of the three categories that pertain to the agent, of the act and its agent being either the same or different, and of the act itself being singular or multiple. As a result, any going and coming that occurs within dependent origination *in reality* has been existentially negated. Similarly, it has also been affirmed that the *appearance* of going and coming pertains to the relative and resembles an illusion. Implicitly, this also serves as an excellent analysis of all active phenomena by considering the objects to which these phenomena relate in terms of the three times.

---

106. These two lines appear to be based on *Root of the Middle Way*, VIII.3.
107. Ibid., VIII.7c–d.

Moreover, a phenomenon without a function is impossible. Thus, we find statements such as the following:

That which does not act is equal to the nonexistent.[108]

As well as:

Apart from what originates dependently,
There are no phenomena at all.[109]

In terms of reality, the present chapter therefore existentially negates all constructs associated with the full range of outer and inner phenomena, while with respect to the relative it establishes illusion-like dependent origination. Thus, as was the case with the previous chapter, it serves to engender an unmistaken insight into the two truths. In the process, it reveals the full significance of the following passage from the *Sūtra Taught by Akṣayamati*:

Venerable Śāriputra, "coming" means assembling, "going" means separating. That which cannot be described as either "assembling" or "separating" knows neither coming nor going. Indeed, this absence of coming and going is the going of the noble ones.

This concludes the explanation of the second chapter, the analysis of going and coming, in the *Ornament of Reason*, a commentary on the *Root of the Middle Way*.

---

108. Āryadeva, *Four Hundred Stanzas*, X.17c.
109. *Root of the Middle Way*, XXIV.19a–b.

CHAPTER THREE

Analysis of the Sense Sources

THIS SECTION demonstrates how dependent origination is devoid of a self in the form of the phenomena that constitute the aggregates, elements, and sense sources. Of these three, the sense sources are analyzed first, and the notion that they have naturally established essences is refuted.

THE CONTEXT OF THE CHAPTER

The treatment of this chapter is also threefold. First, we will consider the chapter's context. With respect to the profound sūtras, this chapter relates to a teaching from the *Mother of the Victorious Ones*, which states, "There is no eye, no ear . . . ." Similarly, the *Noble Sūtra Requested by Upāli* states:

> The eye sees no forms
> And the mind knows no phenomena.
> The supreme truth resides
> Where the world has no access.

And:

> In dependence on light, the eye sees all sorts
> Of attractive and unattractive forms.
> As its seeing is thus dependent,
> The eye never sees any form.

This chapter employs reasoning to ascertain the meaning of such statements.

In terms of its relationship to the other chapters, this analysis can be seen as a response to the following objection: "You may have refuted going, the one who goes, and the path traversed. Nevertheless, the Abhidharma teaches the natural existence of sight, the one who sees, seen objects, and other such factors."

Thus, this chapter serves to refute the natural existence of these factors.

THE CONTENT OF CHAPTER 3

The explanation of the content of this chapter includes (1) a presentation of the opposition's view and (2) a refutation of this view.

THE VIEW OF THE OPPOSITION

The schools of the listeners believe in the natural existence of the external and internal sense sources, such as sight and the seen object. They support this claim by referring to sūtras of Abhidharma that teach:

> *Sight, hearing, smell,*
> *Taste, touch, and cognition—*
> *The experiential domain of these six faculties*
> *Are the objects that are seen and so forth. [III.1]*

Sight refers to the eye faculty, that which sees forms. Some schools hold that the physical faculty is the [actual] observer, while others consider it a contributor to sight The same difference of opinion pertains to the remaining inner sense sources as well.

REFUTATION OF THE OPPOSITION'S VIEW

Second, it will be proven that the aforementioned is an expedient teaching since sight and the rest of the outer and inner sense sources lack natural establishment. This involves (1) a refutation of the natural establishment of sight and (2) an extension of this analysis to other topics. The first of these entails refuting the beliefs that the eye is (1) the one that sees or (2) the producer of sight. The first of these includes (1) a refutation by means of the evidence that the eye does not see itself and (2) a refutation through examining whether the eye is of the nature of sight. The first refutation involves (1) presenting the evidence in a way that establishes the property of the position, (2) demonstrating that this evidence is not inconclusive, and (3) drawing the conclusion.

The Eye's Failure to See Itself
On the first issue, the treatise states:

> *Sight does indeed not see*
> *Its own identity.*
> *How can something that does not see itself*
> *See anything else either?* [III.2]

As indicated in the following verses, the Proponents of Differences believe that the eye faculty with its support, consciousness, is the agent in the seeing of forms:

> The sense faculties with support
> Are the perceivers of visual forms,
> Not the supported consciousness,
> Because no form is seen where there is an obstruction.[110]

The eye faculty that sees, however, does not see its own identity. The reasons for this are that it would be contradictory for something to take itself as an object, and we do not observe any such seeing.

How, then, could the eye faculty see a form or anything else? Indeed, it cannot. The evidence presented here is the fact that the eye does not see itself, as is the case with a vase. The entailment is established by pointing out that since the vase and the eye are the same in not seeing themselves, there is no sound reason why one of them should, in reality, see and the other not. Thus, the entailment is in terms of the previously explained sameness of reason and the entailment of a single conceptual distinction being equally relevant in the case of "other." Some[111] teach that this equals the mind's failure to know anything else unless it knows itself.

110. Vasubandhu, *Treasury of Abhidharma*, I.40.
111. At this point the Tibetan text contains an annotation that reads: Tsangpa (gtsang pa).

The Evidence Is Not Inconclusive
On the second issue, the treatise states:

> *A solid establishment of sight cannot*
> *Be provided through the example of fire.*
> *With what was, has yet to be, and is being traversed*
> *We have replied to that along with sight. [III.3]*

"That something does not see itself does not preclude it from seeing other things," one may object. "Fire, for example, does not burn itself, yet we can see that it burns firewood."

However, the example of fire burning other things without burning itself does not fully establish the idea that sight sees other things without seeing itself. Earlier we refuted the notions of acts of going that occur on paths that have already been traversed, that have yet to be traversed, or that are being traversed in the present. This reasoning has already responded to and refuted the example presented here, namely, fire burning a fuel that is something other than itself.

How about examining the object that the burning relates to, that is, firewood, in terms of the three times? We would then say, "Where there has been burning, there is none." We could also undertake a threefold examination of the fire, the agent of burning, in which case we would say, "One that burns does not burn." These analyses show that fire does not burn something else, that is, firewood. In fact, these analyses do not only respond to and refute this example but also what it represents—the case of sight. We may just as well say, "Where there has been sight, there is none" and "One that sees does not see," thereby examining the place where seeing occurs with reference to the three times and the three types of agent of seeing, respectively. These examinations demonstrate the untenability of the idea that the eye sees forms that are different from itself.

Drawing the Conclusion
On the third issue, the treatise states:

> *When nothing at all is seen,*
> *Neither is there one that sees.*
> *"Sight is what performs seeing,"*
> *How could this be right? [III.4]*

In reading the conclusion, we may reverse the two halves of this stanza. Thus, some might say that since the eye sees forms, it is the one that sees. Yet how could that be right, for when nothing at all is seen, neither is there one that sees.

Is the Eye of the Nature of Seeing?
On the second issue, the treatise states:

> *Sight does not see,*
> *Yet nonsight does not see either. [III.5a–b]*

Furthermore, if the eye is thought to see forms, does it do so by virtue of being intrinsically involved in, and so of the nature of, the act of seeing? Or is the eye something that is related to seeing, yet not itself intrinsically of the nature of sight? That which sees a given form is not an eye with the nature of sight because there are not two acts of seeing. Neither is that which sees an eye that is not of the nature of seeing because such an eye is just as uninvolved in seeing as the fingers are. This stanza should be linked with the conclusion stated above.

Does the Eye Create Seeing?
Second is the refutation of the view that the eye creates seeing. The Followers of Sūtra and others argue that the eye is indeed not that which sees. Rather, they hold that the eye produces seeing and, in that capacity, allows consciousness or the self to become that which sees forms. Here, however, it is shown that, since there is nothing that sees, it does not make sense to speak of the eye as something that creates seeing. This includes (1) a refutation of the proposed agents of seeing by means of the previously explained reasoning, (2) a refutation of these agents through a reasoning not explained before, and (3) a conclusion to the refutation of that which sees.

The Previously Explained Reasoning
On the first issue, the treatise states:

> *Know that sight itself*
> *Also explains the one that sees. [III.5c–d]*

Earlier, the notion that the eye faculty sees form was refuted. It should be understood that the same reasoning also explains the refutation of other agents of seeing, such as consciousness or the self. For example, we may change the wording of the second stanza to the following: "The one that sees does indeed not see its own identity. How can something that does not see itself..." In this way, it becomes a refutation of the positions that hold consciousness or the self to be that which sees forms.

A Reasoning Not Explained Before
On the second issue, the treatise states:

> *Whether seeing is involved or not,*
> *There is nothing that sees.*
> *Without the one that sees,*
> *How could there be something seen and seeing? [III.6]*

If there is something that sees, such as consciousness, does it depend on seeing, or is it independent of it? Something that sees, which involves seeing (that is, depends on seeing), does not exist. The reason for this is as follows:

> How could an entity that is established in dependence
> Depend on something when it is not established?
> If it is said that it depends while established,
> Its dependence does not make any sense.[112]

As will be explained below, either nothing is established, as is the case with the sky flower, or any sense of dependence is lost. Therefore, we may conclude that neither an unestablished nor an established observer can reasonably depend on seeing.

On the other hand, something that sees does not exist without seeing, that is, independently of seeing, because without that we lack the reason for classifying it as such, just as we lack the same reason in the case of a vase.

---

112. *Root of the Middle Way*, X.11.

Conclusion to the Refutation of That Which Sees
On the third issue, the treatise states:

> *As there is nothing to see and no sight,*
> *The four, such as consciousness, do not exist.*
> *How could appropriation and other*
> *Such factors come into existence? [III.7]*

"This project of invalidating all phenomena associated with sight has," it may be objected, "included a refutation of that which sees, but the object and the producer of seeing have not been negated. These do exist."

However, if, as explained before, that which sees does not exist, how could there possibly be any natural establishment of those things that depend on that which sees, such as the seen object and the eye faculty that produces sight? These three are established in mutual dependence. Nevertheless, it may still be thought: "Well, those two have been invalidated. Nevertheless, the *Sūtra on [the Discernment of] Dependent Origination* teaches that consciousness manifests based on the eye and form, just as a child is produced based on its father and mother. Therefore, would not the seen object and the faculty of sight also exist, given that the four effects of these two—consciousness, contact, sensation, and craving—all exist."

As was explained before, neither the form that is the object of sight nor the eye that produces sight exist. It has, therefore, also been established that the stated four effects of these two have no natural existence. However, one may still think, "Be that as it may, factors such as appropriation, becoming, and aging and death are all caused by the aforementioned four factors, and those effects do indeed exist."

Nevertheless, previously we certainly did not say that there is any existence of consciousness and the other factors that are said to cause these effects. When there are no causes, how could something, such as appropriation, possibly manifest as an effect? Indeed, such things are utterly nonexistent!

Extending the Analysis to Other Topics
Extending this analysis to other topics, the treatise states:

> *Hearing, smell,*
> *Taste, touch, and cognition;*

The hearer, the heard, and so forth—
Know that all are explained through sight. [III.8]

Thus, this refutation can be applied equally to all of these elements. We may, for example, just as well say, "Hearing does indeed not hear its own identity."

SUMMARY OF THE CHAPTER'S SIGNIFICANCE

To summarize, in refuting sight, the seen object, and so forth, the present chapter has presented an explicit existential negation of the mental constructs associated with the true reality of the outer and inner sense sources. Likewise, it has affirmed that the appearance of the sense sources is relative and illusion-like. Implicitly, it has presented an existential negation, in terms of the ultimate, of the constructs associated with the full range of active phenomena, as was previously explained. In so doing, it has also affirmed illusion-like dependent origination in terms of the mere relative. The *Sūtra of the King of Meditative Absorptions* discusses this point in the passage that begins:

> Based on the eye and form,
> Visual consciousness arises.

And continuing to the lines:

> Emptiness without any coming and going,
> Like an illusion, this is what the yogin sees.

This concludes the explanation of the third chapter, the analysis of faculties, in the *Ornament of Reason*, a commentary on the *Root of the Middle Way*.

CHAPTER FOUR

Analysis of the Aggregates

THE ANALYSIS of the aggregates will also be treated in three sections, the first of which concerns the context of the chapter.

THE CONTEXT OF CHAPTER 4

The analysis of the aggregates relates to teachings of the profound sūtras, such as the following line from the *Mother of the Victorious Ones*:

Subhūti, form is empty by nature.

And this passage in the *King of Meditative Absorptions*:

The aggregates are devoid of nature; they are emptiness.
Enlightenment is devoid of nature; it is emptiness.
That which experiences is empty of nature as well.
This is known by the wakeful, not by the immature.

It is the significance of such statements that will here be established through reasoning.

As for this chapter's relationship to the other chapters in the text, the analysis of the aggregates can be seen as a reply to an objection such as the following, "Well, you have refuted the outer and inner sense sources, yet the sūtras of Abhidharma still state, 'What are conditioned phenomena? They are the five aggregates.' Hence, this sūtra teaches that the five aggregates exist by nature. Moreover, since the aggregates are included in the sense sources, this means that the sense sources also exist by nature."

This present chapter shows that since the aggregates themselves cannot be established to be existent by nature, the meaning of the aforementioned scripture is expedient.

THE CONTENT OF CHAPTER 4

Second, the explanation of the chapter's content involves (1) refuting the nature of form, (2) extending this analysis to other topics, and (3) subsidiary instructions on superior debate methods.

THE NATURE OF FORM

The first of these includes (1) a refutation of the notion that causal and resultant forms are different from one another by generally acknowledging that since the aggregates are included in the conditioned, they are both cause and effect, (2) a refutation of existent and nonexistent causes and effects, and (3) a refutation of similar and dissimilar causes and effects.

Causal and Resultant Forms Do Not Have Distinct Natures
The first issue has two subdivisions. We begin with the refutation of the notion that resultant forms are something other than causal forms. On this topic, the treatise states:

> *Apart from the cause of form,*
> *Form is not observed. [IV.1a–b]*

> *If there were form apart from its causes,*
> *It would follow that form has no cause.*
> *Yet there are no objects at all*
> *That do not have causes. [IV.2]*

The genuine thesis presented here is as follows. Apart from the causes of form (that is, the causal forms of the four elements), no essentially distinct resultant forms can be observed. Resultant forms, here, are either the ten elemental transformations (the five objects and the five faculties) or, alternately, the same ten elemental transformations plus the category of nonassociated formations posited by certain schools.

To establish the rationale of this thesis, let us consider the view that resultant forms are in fact established as something other than causal forms. If that were the case, they would be independent of causal forms. Being established as something other than causal forms, these resultant forms would be as different from them as a vase is from a woolen blanket.

"Resultant forms *are* different than causal forms," it may then be argued, "but that does not contradict the fact that the former depends on the latter. Likewise, sprouts are different than seeds, and yet they depend on them."

Even if we accept that sprouts depend on seeds in a conventional sense, the two would still not be established as verily different from one another. This conclusion is based on our previous refutation of the belief that effects are different from their causes, a refutation that was undertaken in terms of both of the two truths. Moreover, if cause and effect were established as different from one another, they would also be independent of each other, and if resultant forms were independent of their causes, they would be uncaused. Nevertheless, nowhere, throughout all space and time, does any such thing as an uncaused visual form, or some other uncaused sense object, exist. This we know from the fact that both spatial and temporal restrictions on the occurrence of things can be observed. Hence, the reversal [of this consequence] can be established as follows: Because resultant forms depend on their causes, causal forms, they cannot be established as something other than those causes.

Second is the refutation of causal form being established as something other than resultant form. The treatise states:

> Likewise, aside from so-called form,
> No cause of form can be observed either. [IV.1c–d]

> If, aside from form,
> There were a cause of form,
> There would be a cause with no effect,
> Yet there are no causes without effects. [IV.3]

The genuine thesis presented here is as follows: Aside from so-called resultant forms, we do not perceive any essentially different causes of form, meaning any essentially different causal forms of the four major elements, from the perspective of thorough analysis. The rationale for this thesis becomes evident by considering the belief that there are causes of form that are not themselves resultant forms. If this were the case, these causes would be independent of their effects. The entailment, here, is the same as in the previous section. It is unacceptable for there to be a cause of form independent of form because any identification of something's being a "cause" requires and depends on the presence of an effect. Similarly, any use of the term "father" necessitates a relationship to a child. For this reason, it is concluded that causes that are independent of effects are as nonexistent as the sky flower.

Simply refuting the notion that cause and effect are substantially different from one another is generally insufficient to show that cause and effect are not established by nature. To do that, one would also have to refute the notion that they are substantially identical. In the present context, however, no such refutation is found. This may be because the latter refutation is considered simple or, alternatively, because in this context the tenets of our own tradition are being refuted, and these tenets do not include the misconception that cause and effect are substantially identical.

Existent and Nonexistent Causes and Effects

The second section includes (1) a refutation of the causes of existent and nonexistent effects, (2) a refutation of uncaused effects, and (3) a conclusion. On the first issue, the treatise states:

> *When form exists,*
> *A cause of form does not make sense,*
> *Yet when form does not exist,*
> *A cause of form does not make sense either. [IV.4]*

If there were such a thing as the cause of form, would it then produce an existent or nonexistent resultant form? If the resultant form exists, it would make no sense for it to have a cause. Causes serve to bring their effects into being, so if a given effect is existent, it would be meaningless for it to have a cause. On the other hand, if a given resultant form does not exist, it would not make sense for it to have a cause either. The act of producing cannot be related to something like a sky flower, which does not provide any basis for it. Hence, the nonexistent cannot be created. Moreover, as was explained before, if there is no effect there cannot be any cause either.

On the second issue, the treatise states:

A form without a cause is impossible,
Utterly impossible. [IV.5a–b]

In a similar manner, here it is asked whether resultant forms are held to have existent or nonexistent causes. The first cannot be the case, however, given the previous explanation that there are definitely no causes at the time of their respective effects. How about the second idea? Well, a form that does not have causes makes no sense when examined, yet it does not make sense from an unexamined perspective either because what we see, we see only occasionally.

On the third issue, the treatise states:

Therefore, do not give rise
To any thoughts about form at all. [IV.5c–d]

When we investigate causal and resultant forms, it becomes clear that there are none. The yogin who wishes to recognize reality should, therefore, not give rise to any thought whatsoever about form being a particular way, that it is delightful or repulsive, obstructive or not obstructive, demonstrable or not demonstrable, past or future, blue or yellow, and so on. There is no basis for such distinctions. Hence, thoughts of this kind are similar to concerns about whether a donkey's horn is sharp or blunt. This stanza can also suitably be taken as conclusion to the chapter as a whole.

Similar and Dissimilar Causes and Effects

On the third issue, the treatise states:

It is not right to say
That effects resemble their causes.
It is not right to say
That effects do not resemble their causes. [IV.6]

Here it is asked whether the causes of form produce effects that resemble them. It would not be right to say that effects resemble their causes because the characteristics of the causal forms of the four elements differ from those of the resultant forms of the five faculties and five objects. Thus, [the earth element], for example, is characterized by solidity, whereas the [eye faculty] is a buoyant form that supports eye consciousness. Moreover, the five objects are the objects of distinct faculties. The characteristics of the causal and resultant forms are, thus, as different from each other as existence is from peace. Moreover, we never witness causes and effects that resemble each other in the way that, for example, śālu seeds do when they are present at the same time. Finally, neither is it right to say that resultant forms are produced by causal forms that they do not resemble. With no resemblance, such a situation would be the same as with existence and peace.

EXTENDING THIS ANALYSIS TO OTHER TOPICS

The second issue concerns how we may extend this analysis to other topics. The treatise states:

> *With feeling, identification, formation,*
> *Mind, and all things*
> *The steps are, in all regards,*
> *The same as in the case of form. [IV.7]*

Feeling and the contact that causes it, identification and the consciousness that accompanies it, formation and ignorance, the consciousness of the primary mind versus formation—all of these we may examine to see if they are the same or different. If we do, we will find that neither of these options makes sense. The steps involved in this process will be exactly the same as they were in the case of form. In fact, we may investigate anything, including characteristics and the bearers of characteristics, or wholes and parts, in terms of whether they are the same, different, or otherwise, just as we have done here with the refutation of form. By following the same steps in the same way, we will come to see that none of these options are correct.

SUPERIOR DEBATE METHOD

Third, as an instruction in superior debate method, the treatise states:

When a critique is made using emptiness,
Whatever may be replied
Will not be a reply,
But the same as what is still to be proven. [IV.8]

When an explanation is given using emptiness
Whatever flaws one may find
Will not be found to be flaws,
But the same as what is still to be proven. [IV.9]

The special method for countering the positions of others is to point out that the realist's argument is identical to what has yet to be proven. Espousing emptiness, the representative of the Middle Way may criticize the realist position by asking for the reason that things exist by nature. The realist may then respond that this is because they originate dependently. Yet whatever reply is given will not be a proper one. The reason, here, is that the property of the realist's position (something that is real and dependently originated, or whatever else the attempted argument may have been) as well as the entailment of the evidence (that what appears as dependent origination exists by nature) amounts to what would still need to be proven, namely, that things exist by nature. This necessarily follows because all phenomena are emptiness in precisely the same way that the Middle Way has shown with respect to a given phenomenon.

The superior method for demonstrating the flawlessness of our own position is to show that the flaws found in the Middle Way are inaccurate because they take for granted that which still needs to be proven. When the representative of the Middle Way explains that all phenomena are emptiness, a realist may find flaw with this and object that this would render karmic causality nonexistent. In perceiving such a flaw, however, a genuine problem is not identified. The representative of the Middle Way clearly accepts the consequence that karmic causality lacks nature. The realist then argues that this implies that there cannot be any consequences of karmic acts at the level of the relative either. At this point, however, this argument begs the question by taking for granted that which has yet to be proven. The inconclusive nature of this argument is made explicit by bringing in an example such as illusion.

SUMMARY OF THE CHAPTER'S SIGNIFICANCE

The third section presents a summary of the chapter. This chapter explicitly provides an existential negation of the constructions of ultimate reality that are associated with the five aggregates, while it has affirmed that the aggregates originate dependently in an illusion-like manner in terms of the relative. This has been done by demonstrating that the aggregates are not established when examined, for example, in terms of whether they are the same as or different from their causes.

Implicitly, this chapter presents a refutation of all dependent phenomena because it has been shown that, for example, they are neither identical to, nor different from, that which they depend on. Hence, this chapter has shown that ultimately all phenomena are not established in any way that would accord with the marks of mental constructions. It has likewise been affirmed that relatively phenomena appear in an illusion-like way. This message also accords with the *Sūtra of Instruction to the Listeners*:

> Form is like drifting foam
> And feeling like bubbles in water.
> Identification can be likened to a mirage,
> While formation resembles the plantain,
> And consciousness is like an illusion.
> Thus the Kinsman of the Sun has taught.

This concludes the explanation of the fourth chapter, the analysis of the aggregates, in the *Ornament of Reason*, a commentary on the *Root of the Middle Way*.

CHAPTER FIVE

Analysis of the Elements

THE ANALYSIS of the elements will also be covered in three sections, of which the first concerns the chapter's context.

THE CONTEXT OF CHAPTER 5

In terms of the profound sūtras, this chapter relates to the following passages from the *Mother of the Victorious Ones*:

> The element of earth does not exist.

And:

> How, you may ask, is one to understand earth and the other elements. They should be perfectly understood to be exactly like space.

Likewise, it also relates to this teaching from the *King of Meditative Absorptions*:

> Able One, you have seen that the aggregates are empty,
> Just as you have seen that the elements and sense sources are as well.
> That the city of the faculties is devoid of marks,
> That, Able One, you have likewise seen in full.

Thus, this chapter employs reasoning to prove the significance of such statements, showing how the elements are just as empty of nature as the sources and aggregates.

As for this chapter's relationship to the other chapters in the text, the analysis of the elements can be seen as a response to the following concern: "The sense sources and aggregates have indeed been negated. Nevertheless, in scripture we find the statement, 'Great king, the individual, or person, comes down to six elements.'[113] Thus, the six elements are taught to be the basis for the designation of the person. As these six have not been explicitly refuted, they must have natural existence. Moreover, given that the sense sources and aggregates are contained in the elements, they must exist by nature as well."

To dispel such doubts, this chapter shows that, upon examination, the elements can be seen to be devoid of nature.

THE CONTENT OF CHAPTER 5

Second, the explanation of the content of this chapter involves (1) a refutation of the element of space, (2) extending this analysis to the other elements, and (3) a concluding rebuke of views. The first includes (1) a refutation of the characteristic of space and the bearers of it, (2) a refutation of space as an established entity or nonentity, and (3) a conclusion. Among these three sections, the first presents (1) a refutation of the bearers of the characteristic, (2) a refutation of the characteristic, and (3) a conclusion. The first of these issues includes (1) showing how the characteristic has no reasonable application and (2) that if the characteristic has no application, there cannot be any bearers of it. The first of these two sections refutes the applicability of the characteristic by (1) demonstrating that there is no characteristic prior to its bearer and (2) showing that the characteristic cannot apply to what bears it, to what does not bear it, or to some third category.

There Are No Characteristics Prior to Instances
On the first issue, the treatise states:

> *Before the characteristics of space,*
> *There is no space whatsoever.*

113. From the *Sūtra of the Meeting of Father and Son.*

If it existed before its characteristics,
It would follow that it has no characteristics. [V.1]

Something without characteristics
Does not exist anywhere at all.
Since there is no thing without characteristics,
To what do the characteristics apply? [V.2]

It is taught that "space is nonresistance." In this way, the characteristics of unconditioned space are its not being produced by causes and conditions and its not being tangible as something resistant or obstructive. A characteristic can apply to a bearer if the bearer is there before the characteristic. Yet before the presence of this characteristic, there is no space to be characterized by nonresistance. There is no such thing as a bearer of the characteristic of space that exists prior to its nonresistance. Given that, therefore, there is nothing that can bear it, what then does this characteristic apply to? Similarly, it would not make sense to say of jujubes that they are contained in a jar if there is no such container to begin with.

It may then be thought: "A characteristic and its bearer are not two different substances but essentially the same; they are not a support and something supported in the same way that a container and jujubes are. Therefore, the bearer does not need to precede its characteristics."

Yet this will not do because when two things are essentially the same, one cannot be the support of the other, nor can one take the other as its object.

One may then object that it has not been established that the bearer does not precede its characteristics. Yet if a given space existed as the bearer of its own characteristics prior to the characteristics themselves, then that space would have no characteristics.

This, however, is untenable. Nowhere throughout space and time does there exist a phenomenon or thing that lacks its own characteristics. It is impossible for there to be a phenomenon that lacks the very essence that is the special reason for its being given its name.

Characteristics Do Not Apply to Anything
On the second issue, the treatise states:

Characteristics do not apply to what has them,
Nor do they apply to what does not.
Neither do characteristics apply to something
Other than what does or does not have them. [V.3]

Furthermore, if a given characteristic applies to something, does it apply to something that already has this characteristic, to something that lacks it, or to something other than these two? Characteristics do not apply where they are lacking because, like a donkey horn, that which has no characteristics could not have any characteristics applying to it. Neither do they apply to things that have had them from the beginning because their application would then be both meaningless and endless. Finally, characteristics do not apply to things that neither possess nor lack them. Since possession and lack of possession directly contradict one another, no third category is possible.

If the Characteristic Does Not Apply, There Cannot Be Any Bearers of It

One the second issue, the treatise states:

> *If characteristics have no application,*
> *It makes no sense that there should be bearers of them. [V.4a–b]*

It may be thought: "Although characteristics have no application, space—the bearer of the characteristic—does indeed exist."

Yet if characteristics have no application, as explained before, their bearers do not make sense either because it is the characteristic of the bearers to function as the support for characteristics.

The Refutation of Characteristics

On the second issue, the treatise states:

> *If the bearers of characteristics are unreasonable,*
> *Their characteristics cannot exist either. [V.4c–d]*

One may then object: "While you may have refuted the notion that characteristics apply to their bearers, you have yet to refute the characteristics themselves. Therefore, they do indeed exist." As explained before, the fact that the characteristics do not apply to anything means that space itself—as the bearer, support, or object of these characteristics—cannot reasonably exist either. For that very reason, the characteristics that it bears, supports, or receives cannot exist either, as is the case with the sky flower.

Conclusion

In conclusion to the refutations of the bearer and the characteristic, the treatise states:

> *Therefore, the bearers of characteristics do not exist,*
> *And characteristics themselves have no existence either. [V.5a–b]*

As characteristics do not apply to anything, the bearer of the characteristics of space does not exist. Since nothing bears them, these characteristics themselves do not exist either.

Refuting the Notion That Space Can Be Established to Be an Entity or Nonentity

This second section concerns the refutation of space being an established entity or nonentity. This involves refuting (1) the notion that space is an established entity, (2) the notion that space is an established nonentity, and (3) the subjective apprehension of space.

Refuting Space as an Established Entity

On the first issue, the treatise states:

> *Yet aside from bearers and characteristics*
> *There are no entities. [V.5c–d]*

The Proponents of Differences assert that space is an unconditioned, permanent entity. Space, however, cannot be an entity. As it has no characteristics or bearers of characteristics, space is equal to a sky flower. The property of this position has already been established. The entailment can be seen to be established from the fact that no entity exists aside from bearers and their characteristics. The implicit reason for this is that it is impossible for there to be a phenomenon that has no instances and lacks the very essence that is the reason for its being given its unique name.

Refuting Space as an Established Nonentity
On the second issue, the treatise states:

> *If there is no entity,*
> *Of what would there be no entity? [V.6a–b]*

The Followers of Sūtra teach that space is by nature a nonentity devoid
of efficacy. Arguing against this position, it is said: "In reality, the subject, space, is not established as nonentity either. As was just explained, it
does not exist as an entity, and is, therefore, equal to a rabbit horn. It may
then be objected that this argument lacks entailment because the very fact
that it is not established as an entity establishes it to be a nonentity. Yet
this objection is not reasonable either. That which is to be negated and
the negative property that ensues from the negation depend upon one
another, as do long and short. Therefore, given that there is no entity to be
negated, what would the negative property, nonentity, be a negation of?
Similarly, the child in a dream is not real, and, therefore, its death is not
real either.

The Subjective Apprehension of Space
On the third issue, the treatise states:

> *What entity, nonentity, or otherwise*
> *Would be the knower of entity and nonentity? [V.6c–d]*

It may be thought: "There is a person who examines entities and nonentities, so there must also be entities and nonentities that are examined."

Yet the subject that examines these two does not exist either. If it did,
there would have to be an entity, nonentity, or something other than an
entity or nonentity that knew of and examined entities and nonentities.
Entity and nonentity have, as such, already been universally refuted, and
the third option has also been dismissed because it is impossible to derive
any third category through the negation of two qualities that are directly
contradictory. As a sūtra instructs:

> See the nature of the inner as empty,
> And see that which is outside as empty too.

As for the one who meditates on emptiness——
There is no such meditator at all.

And:

A mind aware of the qualities
Of peace, utter peace, never occurs.
All constructs are the mind's thinking,
So realize that the qualities defy thought.

Conclusion
In conclusion, the treatise states:

Space, therefore, is not an entity, not a nonentity,
Not a bearer of characteristics, not a characteristic. [V.7a–c]

Because no characteristics apply to it, space is not a bearer of characteristics. Since there is no bearer of characteristics, the characteristics of space do not exist either. In the absence of bearer and characteristic, space could not be an entity, and because nothing is negated, space is not a nonentity either.

EXTENDING THIS ANALYSIS TO OTHER TOPICS

Extending this analysis to other topics, the treatise states:

As for the other five elements,
The case is the same as with space. [V.7c–d]

All of the above holds for earth and the rest of the remaining five elements as well. Thus, we may just as well say, "Before the characteristics of earth, there is no earth whatsoever."

A CONCLUDING REBUKE OF VIEWS

Third, in a concluding rebuke of views, the treatise states:

The feebleminded who see
Things in terms of existence and nonexistence
Fail to see what is to be seen—
The peace of complete pacification. [V.8]

The present line of reasoning has established that all outer and inner phenomena are, in reality, devoid of the constructions of characteristics and their bearers and of existent and nonexistent things. Nevertheless, the feebleminded, whose eye of cognition is damaged by ignorance, view the inner and outer entities that constitute the relative in terms of either real existence or complete nonexistence. They thereby fail to see what is to be seen—the ultimate and the natural transcendence of suffering, the peace that is the complete pacification of verbal and mental constructs—just as the blind are unable to see the sun. Therefore, in terms of the relative, they have no chance to achieve either the mere peace of having relinquished the extreme of existence or the nonabiding transcendence of suffering that comes with the relinquishment of both the extremes of existence and peace. Hence, those who pursue the transcendence of suffering should train in the complete separation from existence and nonexistence and all other such extremes, as was previously explained. This is also taught in the *Sūtra of the King of Meditative Absorptions*:

> So-called existence and nonexistence are extremes,
> Just as clean and unclean are dual extremes.
> "Existence" and "nonexistence" are argumentation.
> Clean and unclean are argumentation as well.
> Arguments do not pacify suffering,
> But when arguments disappear, suffering ends.

SUMMARY OF THE CHAPTER'S SIGNIFICANCE

The summary of this chapter's significance can be understood by following the same approach that was used in the previous chapters.

This concludes the explanation of the fifth chapter, the analysis of the elements, in the *Ornament of Reason,* a commentary on the *Root of the Middle Way.*

CHAPTER SIX

Analysis of Desire and the Desirous One

THE SELF of phenomena has now been negated by refuting the essences of the aggregates, elements, and sense sources. The next three analyses are concerned with refuting counterarguments. The first of these, the analysis of desire and the desirous one, serves as a refutation of the nature of the subject associated with these factors or as a refutation of the nature of the resultant affliction. This chapter will also be discussed in three sections.

THE CONTEXT OF CHAPTER 6

The present chapter relates to the profound sūtras by using reasoning to ascertain the meaning of certain teachings, such as the following passage from the *King of Meditative Absorptions*:

> Desire, the object of desire, and the desirous one—these phenomena are not seen or observed in accordance with reality.

The same scripture also teaches:

> Understanding that the essences of desire, anger, conceit, and
>   stupor
> Are produced by thought and mistaken engagements,
> They do not conceive of them and do not separate from desire.
> Such meditators are all things.

As for its relation to the other analyses, the present chapter can be seen as a reply to opinions such as the following: "You have negated the sense sources, aggregates, and elements. Nevertheless, all of these do indeed exist, for within these factors we find subjects that suffer from desire and the other causes of the affliction of action and birth. A sūtra teaches:

> Monks, immature ordinary individuals who are not learned suffer from a continuous fall. As their eyes see forms, they fixate on what they see as a source of pleasure for the mind, thereby creating desire. This, in turn, forms the physical, verbal, and mental actions that arise out of desire.

If objects were as nonexistent as the child of a barren woman, the occurrence of the afflictions would make no sense."

This chapter was composed to show that when the afflictions are themselves subjected to examination, they are seen to be unestablished.

THE CONTENT OF CHAPTER 6

The explanation of this chapter's content includes (1) a refutation of desire and the desirous one and (2) an extension of this analysis to other topics. The first topic contains two further divisions: a refutation of the notion that desire and the desirous one occur (1) in sequence and (2) that they coexist.

The Sequential Manifestation of Desire and the Desirous One
On the first issue, the treatise states:

> *If, before the presence of desire,*
> *The desirous one exists without desire,*
> *Based on that, there would be desire.*
> *When the desirous one exists, so does desire. [VI.1]*

> *Yet if the desirous one does not exist,*
> *How could there possibly be desire?*
> *Given the presence or absence of desire,*
> *This follows also in the case of the desirous one. [VI.2]*

Let us assume that desire, the mental state that takes delight in qualities that are not genuine, has a nature of its own. We may then ask whether its support, the desirous one (that is, the primary consciousness that desires), exists prior to desire or subsequent to it.

With the first alternative, the desirous one would be present in a desireless state prior to the desire. If this were the case, the supportive primary consciousness that is the desirous one would be preestablished, and the supported mental state of desire would then come to exist based on that. Hence, the idea here is that desire is preceded by the desirous one.

Nevertheless, someone without desire cannot possibly be desirous. If this were possible, even a noble foe destroyer could be desirous. Therefore, in the end, the presence of the desirous one entails the presence of desire.

Second, how could there possibly be desire if the one that desires, that is the one that supports this emotion, does not precede it? Likewise, if there is no fruit to support it, there can be no ripening. The idea that the desirous one can exist in the absence of desire is untenable.

In this way, we have noticed that, given either the presence or absence of the desirous one, there can be no desire. Yet the same problems follow if we consider the support, the one that desires, in light of either a preceding presence or absence of the supported desire. Given the preceding presence or absence of desire, it does not make sense that there is something that desires. It may be held that before the presence of the desirous one, desire exists without a desirous one. In that case there could, on that basis, be something that is desirous. Thus, it might be reasonable to claim that desire precedes the desirous one. However, there cannot possibly be any prior existence of desire because without someone who desires there would be no basis for desire. There can likewise be no ripening if there is no fruit that can function as the basis for ripening to begin with.

If the opposite is the case, and there is no desire to begin with, how could there possibly be someone that desires? If it were possible for the desirous one to exist even in the absence of desire, then a noble foe-destroyer could be desirous as well.

The Coexistence of Desire and the Desirous One

As for the second issue, some hold that desire and the desirous one do not occur in sequence. Instead they see them as an instance of the type of causality referred to in this statement:

Those that arise together are the effect of each other.[114]

According to this position, the mind produces a coexistent mental state of desire, which, in turn, by its presence is responsible for the mind being desirous.

The refutation of this position relates to (1) the consequence that these two will then lack mutual dependence and (2) the untenability of identical and different things occurring in coexistence.

The Lack of Mutual Dependence

On the first issue, the treatise states:

> Desire and the desirous one
> Cannot reasonably arise together.
> In this case, desire and the desirous one
> Would not depend on one another. [VI.3]

Desire and the desirous one cannot reasonably coexist. If they did, desire and the desirous one would be as independent of one another as the right and left horns of a cow. Desire and the desirous one are, however, seen to be mutually dependent by nonanalytical direct perception. Therefore, it does not make sense to say that they coexist.

Neither Identical nor Different Things Can Coexist

The second issue involves (1) a general refutation of the coexistence of identical and different things and (2) a specific refutation of the coexistence of different things.

The Coexistence of Identical and Different Things

On the first issue, the treatise states:

> Identical things are not coexistent,
> As nothing is coexistent with itself.
> Yet if they are different,
> How could they be coexistent? [VI.4]

---

114. Vasubandhu, *Treasury of Abhidharma*, II.50b.

If a single thing were coexistent,
This would occur in isolation as well.
If the different were coexistent,
This would occur in isolation as well. [VI.5]

Now, are desire and the desirous one coexistent by virtue of being essentially the same or different? In the first case, these two cannot be coexistent, precisely because they would then be essentially the same. The entailment of this argument holds because coexistence implies that something is present along with something else, yet it is not feasible for something to be together with itself. It may be thought that simultaneity would be feasible in the case of essential sameness and different conceptual distinctions. Yet this will not do because the difference between conceptual distinctions is a conceptual imputation that does not have any bearing on the object.

How about the alternative? Well, if these two were indeed essentially different, how could they possibly be coexistent? The entailment of this argument can be understood from the following: Two things being different precludes their occurrence at the same place and time. No material or mental entity can occupy the same location, or the same continuum, as a second different entity, and time is not something that can be observed apart from the given entities themselves.

These two options can also be refuted by showing the absurd consequences of both positions. If it is held that simultaneity applies to what is essentially one and the same, it would follow that when Devadatta is unaccompanied and all alone, he is nevertheless present together with himself. On the other hand, if the position is that coexistence applies to things that are essentially different, then two different things that have nothing to do with each other—like a horse on a mountain in the east and a cow on a mountain in the west—will still be present together, despite their respective isolation.

The Coexistence of Different Things
The second section shows that (1) desire and the desirous one are not established as different and are, therefore, not coexistent; (2) that if they were different, it would be meaningless to prove their natural existence by referring to coexistence; and (3) if their difference depends on their coexistence, difference and coexistence become mutually dependent.

Nondifference
On the first issue, the treatise states:

> *If they are different and coexistent,*
> *How could desire and the desirous one*
> *Be established as two different things*
> *That would then be present together? [VI.6]*

It may be held that desire and the desirous one are essentially different, yet coexistent, and that, in this way, they are established as different without any mutual dependence. Yet if these two are coexistent, how could desire and the desirous one be established as different from one another in the absence of mutual dependence? Indeed, they cannot. Therefore, they are not coexistent.

The Reference to Coexistence Is Meaningless
On the second issue, the treatise states:

> *If desire and the desirous one*
> *Are established as different,*
> *Then why would you think of them*
> *As being coexistent? [VI.7]*

The opponent might take the position that there cannot be coexistence unless there is difference, and that, therefore, desire and the desirous one are indeed established as distinct without being mutually dependent. But if this were the case, then their nature would be established as such. Why, then, would you think of them as being coexistent in an attempt to prove their natural existence?

It was previously explained that because these two do not occur in sequence, they have no nature. You[115] objected to that explanation, arguing that they do have such natural existence because they are coexistent. You also asserted that these two must be established as independent and different and that they could not be coexistent if this were not the case. Now,

---

115. Even if the opponent is nobody in particular, one may, according to Tibetan debate rhetoric, still use the second person pronoun when addressing a counterposition. Here and elsewhere, we have let this convention be reflected in the translation as well.

given that they are established as distinct, it will also have been established that they exist by nature. Yet you also stated that because they are established as distinct, they are coexistent, and because they are coexistent, they exist by nature. This part of your argument, in which you again refer to simultaneity, serves no purpose in proving their natural establishment.[116]

Mutual Dependence of Difference and Simultaneity
On the third issue, the treatise states:

> *If they are asserted to be coexistent*
> *Because their difference lacks establishment,*
> *Would you also assert their difference*
> *To prove their coexistence? [VI.8]*

> *When things are not established as different,*
> *Neither are they established as coexistent.*
> *When there is a thing that is different,*
> *It may be claimed that it is coexistent. [VI.9]*

A further reply might then be given: "It is not meaningless to speak of coexistence because without it their difference will not be established. Hence, we hold that the coexistence of desire and the desirous one is proof that they are different."

Now, since it is explained that "identical things are not coexistent," there cannot be any coexistence if things are not different. Would you then also assert that their difference proves their coexistence? You would have to, and then the arguments for difference and coexistence would end up being circular. Therefore, when there is a thing that is different, it may be claimed that it is coexistent, yet coexistence cannot be established by recourse to difference because the argument for difference, presupposes, as explained before, the very thing that it is meant to prove, that is, coexistence. In this way, the former is never established prior to the latter. Reference to the essential difference of things can, therefore, not be used to prove that things are coexistent.

---

116. That is, the opponent might as well just say, "Because they are distinct, they are established by nature."

228 ORNAMENT OF REASON

Likewise, recourse to coexistence cannot prove difference either. To demonstrate this point, we may restructure the ninth stanza as follows:

> *When there is a thing that is coexistent,*
> *It may be claimed that it is different.*
> *When things are not established as coexistent,*
> *Neither are they established as different.*

Summary

On the third issue,[117] the treatise states:

> *Therefore, desire and the desirous one*
> *Are not established as coexistent or otherwise. [VI.10a–b]*

As demonstrated above, desire and the desirous one can be shown to be neither coexistent nor otherwise when subjected to examination. We can, therefore, conclude that they have no nature.

Extending This Analysis to Other Topics

Concerning the second issue, the treatise extends this analysis to other topics:

> *As is the case with desire and the desirous one,*
> *No phenomena are established as coexistent or otherwise. [VI.10c–d]*

Desire cannot coexist with its support, the desirous one. Nor can these two be separate. The same holds for the affliction of anger, or any other phenomenon that relates to something else. Anger, for instance, is not established as coexistent with its support, the one who is angry, nor is it otherwise. Hence, all dependently originated phenomena are emptiness by nature, for we can argue the same about all of them. This is demon-

---

117. Perhaps Mabja takes these verses as a summary (don bsdu ba) of the "Refutation of desire and the desirous one." In that case, it would appear that a reference to this section is missing on p. 222, where the primary subsections of the "Refutation of desire and the desirous one" are enumerated. Alternatively, it could be that Mabja reads these lines as the concluding summary of chapter 6 as a whole.

strated about anger in the following line: "If, before the presence of anger, the angry exists without anger, . . ."

This concludes the explanation of the sixth chapter, the analysis of desire and the desirous one, in the *Ornament of Reason*, a commentary on the *Root of the Middle Way*.

CHAPTER SEVEN

Analysis of the Characteristics of the Conditioned

THE ANALYSIS of the characteristics of the conditioned will be covered in three sections, of which the first concerns the chapter's context.

THE CONTEXT OF CHAPTER 7

The present chapter relates to the profound sūtras in that it uses reasoning to ascertain the intent of statements such as the following passage from the *Mother of the Victorious Ones*:

> When the conditioned and the unconditioned, and the qualities of
>   good and evil,
> Have all been demolished through insight, so that not even a par-
>   ticle is observed,
> Within the worlds, they then come to belong to transcendent
>   insight,
> In the same way that space does not abide anywhere at all.

And this excerpt from the *Sūtra of the King of Meditative Absorptions*:

> Phenomena do not arise nor do they cease.
> They do not abide, they are nonabiding, beyond all abiding.
> By nature they are illusory, and always devoid of essence.

As for its relationship to the other chapters in the text, this present chapter can be seen as a response to the following objection: "The aggregates, elements, and sense sources—those phenomena that are of a conditioned nature—do indeed exist, for the *Sūtra of the Great Cloud* teaches:

> Monks, these three are the characteristics of the conditioned.
> Conditioned phenomena can be observed to arise, cease, and
> change from their present state.

These, then, are the characteristics whereby we may know a thing to be
conditioned. Thus, arising, abiding, and cessation exist by nature."

The seventh chapter explains that the purport of such statements is not
definitive. This is done by showing how arising, abiding, and cessation are
not feasible from the perspective of reasoning.

THE CONTENT OF CHAPTER 7

The content of this chapter includes (1) a refutation of the reality of the
characteristics of the conditioned, (2) an explanation of that which is
established thereby, and (3) a rejection of the criticism that this refutation
contradicts scripture.

THE REALITY OF THE
CHARACTERISTICS OF THE CONDITIONED

The first of these includes two further topics: (1) a general refutation of
arising, abiding, and cessation and (2) an individual refutation of each.

A General Refutation of Arising, Abiding, and Cessation
The first refutation involves examining (1) whether or not these three are
conditioned, (2) whether they are separate or united, and (3) whether or
not they themselves have other characteristics.

Are Arising, Abiding, and Cessation Conditioned?
On the first issue, the treatise states:

> *If arising were conditioned,*
> *It would possess these three characteristics.*
> *If arising were unconditioned,*
> *How could it be a characteristic of the conditioned? [VII.1]*

Among the listeners, the Proponents of Differences teach that arising, abiding, and cessation are what characterize a given thing as conditioned and that these characteristics exist separately from that which they characterize. When it is held that the characteristic of arising is essentially different from the thing that bears it and that this characteristic indicates that a thing is conditioned, we may ask whether that characteristic is itself conditioned or unconditioned. If it were conditioned, it would have to itself possess arising and the other two characteristics, just as a vase does. The entailment is present because the opposition itself claims that no conditioned phenomenon fails to arise, abide, and cease. Yet it cannot be accepted that arising itself has these three characteristics because arising would then be a bearer of the characteristics of the conditioned, just as a form is, and it could then no longer be its characteristic. If, on the other hand, arising were unconditioned like space, then how could it be a characteristic of that which is conditioned? The entailment holds here as well because something that remains an impossibility with respect to a given definiendum and a set of bearers cannot possibly be the characteristic of that definiendum and those bearers.

The refutation of the remaining two characteristics becomes explicit by substituting "abiding" and "cessation" for "arising," respectively.

Are the Three Characteristics Separate or United?

On the second issue, the treatise states:

> Arising and the other two are each
> Incapable of characterizing the conditioned.
> But how could they simultaneously
> Come together anywhere? [VII.2]

Are these the characteristics of the conditioned individually or as a group? The first cannot be the case because none of these characteristics can characterize the conditioned on its own. The presence of any one characteristic, unaccompanied by the other two qualities that characterize the conditioned, would make the thing that is characterized unconditioned, unarisen, not present at its own particular time, permanent, and unfit to be an entity. Yet, in the case of the alternative, how could all three be simultaneously present in the same thing? Each functions in a way that is as incompatible with the others, as is the case with light and darkness.

Do the Three Characteristics Themselves Have Characteristics?
The third issue has two elements, the first of which involves two absurd consequences. The treatise states:

> *If arising, abiding, and cessation themselves*
> *Bear further characteristics of the conditioned,*
> *There will be an infinite regress.*
> *Yet if they do not, they are not conditioned. [VII.3]*

What if arising, abiding, and cessation are themselves characterized by arising, abiding and cessation? In that case, these additional characteristics must also have these three characteristics, and there is then an infinite regress. Since no end to the sequence can be established, none of the initial links are established either. However, if arising, abiding, and cessation do not each have their own arising, abiding, and cessation, then they are not conditioned. Not being conditioned, they cannot be the characteristics of the conditioned.

The First Counterargument
The following verses address two different replies to these consequences. The treatise presents the first reply as follows:

> *Due to the arising of arising,*
> *There arises only fundamental arising,*
> *Yet fundamental arising is responsible*
> *For the arising of arising as well. [VII.4]*

Faced with the first consequence, some Sammitīyas respond with the following objection: "The characteristics of arising, abiding, and cessation do have their own characteristic arising, abiding, and cessation. Therefore, the second flaw does not apply. There is no infinite regress either because the characteristics and their subsidiary characteristics characterize and establish each other. Seven phenomena are involved here, namely the bearer of characteristics, the three characteristics, and the three subsidiary characteristics. The arising of arising produces only the fundamental arising. Yet the fundamental arising produces the arising of arising and all the other phenomena except itself. Thus, the arising of arising performs the function of producing arising itself, whereas the fundamental arising is responsible for the production of all the involved phenomena with the exception of arising. Similarly, the abiding of abiding makes the fundamental abiding abide, while the latter provides for the abiding of the other six phenomena. Finally, the cessation of cessation makes fundamental cessation cease, while the latter causes the other six phenomena to cease. Thus, all seven phenomena—the three characteristics, the three subsidiary characteristics, and the bearer of these characteristics—first arise, then abide, and finally cease. This shows that they are conditioned."

In this way, it is held that characteristics and their bearers are different substances that perform independently.

In the Abhidharma, we find the following explanation:

> It is discerned that by including aging there are four characteristics. As these are accompanied by the arising of arising, and so forth, eight phenomena in all apply to one.[118]

Nevertheless, here aging refers to the degeneration of abiding. It is, therefore, included in the latter. The *Commentary*[119] enumerates fifteen phenomena by specifying seven characteristics, seven subsidiary characteristics, plus their bearer, thereby explaining that fourteen phenomena are held to apply to one. This is not explicit in the root text.

Response to the First Counterargument
Next, the objection raised above will be dispensed with by showing that it is a circular argument. This involves (1) explaining how the arising of arising cannot reasonably produce fundamental arising, (2) explaining why fundamental arising cannot reasonably produce the arising of arising, and (3) refuting a further reply to the first two explanations.

The Arising of Arising Cannot Reasonably Produce Fundamental Arising
On the first issue, the treatise states:

> *If your "arising of arising"*
> *Produces fundamental arising,*

---

118. Vasubandhu, *Explanation of the Treasury of Abhidharma*, commentary to II.46.
119. Candrakīrti, *Clear Words*.

How could it do so when not produced
By this "fundamental arising?" [VII.5]

According to your account, the arising of arising produces fundamental arising. Yet how could the subject, your "arising of arising," produce fundamental arising, as it is not present before the latter? The implicit argument is that since the arising of arising depends on fundamental arising, the former cannot be produced prior to the latter.

Fundamental Arising Cannot Reasonably Produce the Arising of Arising
On the second issue, the treatise states:

If the product of this "fundamental arising"
Itself produces fundamental arising,
Then how could fundamental arising produce it,
When it has not been produced by that? [VII.6]

It may be argued: "The flaw presented above is irrelevant because the arising of arising that is produced by fundamental arising in turn produces fundamental arising."

However, how could the subject, your "fundamental arising," produce the arising of arising, given that it is not present before the latter? Fundamental arising itself depends on the arising of arising. Therefore, fundamental arising cannot be produced prior to the arising of arising.

Refutation of a Further Reply
On the third issue, the treatise states:

If that which has not yet arisen
Were capable of production,
Your assertion of production by the currently arising
Would have been acceptable. [VII.7]

It may be replied: "We assert the substantial existence of the three times. Hence, while fundamental arising is not produced by the arising of arising prior to the arising of arising, the future holds a currently arising fundamental arising, and that is what produces the arising of arising. This arising of arising, in turn, makes the fundamental arising that is contained in the future arise in the present."

As was explained above, "That which is currently arising is approaching arising and is, hence, not existent."[120] Thus, that which is currently arising has not yet arisen and, therefore, does not exist. If, generally speaking, something that has not itself arisen, and so does not yet exist, were capable of producing something else, then your "fundamental arising," a not-yet existent thing of the future that nevertheless produces the arising of arising, would be acceptable. Yet just as a barren woman's daughter cannot have any offspring, something that itself has yet to arise and come into existence is incapable of producing something else. It is, therefore, untenable that a currently arising fundamental arising produces the arising of arising.

The same can be said with respect to an arising of arising that is currently arising and contained in the future, thereby giving rise to fundamental arising.

The refutation of the remaining two factors is made explicit in the following ways:

> If your "abiding of abiding"
> Causes fundamental abiding to abide,
> How could it do so when it has not
> Been made to abide by this "fundamental abiding?"

And:

> If your "cessation of cessation"
> Causes fundamental cessation to cease . . .[121]

The Second Counterargument

Next follows the treatment of a second objection to the consequences that were stated in the third stanza. First, the counterargument itself is presented:

---

120. Candrakīrti, *Entering the Middle Way*, VI.19a.
121. Compare with stanza 5 in this chapter.

Just as a light illumines
Both itself and other things,
Birth produces both itself
As well as other things. [VII.8]

This objection goes as follows: "There are no further arising, abiding, and cessation apart from those that are the characteristics of the conditioned. Hence, there is no infinite regress. Moreover, the absurdity of the characteristics becoming unconditioned does not apply either. Consider how a light, being illuminating by nature, can illumine both itself and other things. Performing the act of arising is, similarly, the nature of arising, and so it gives rise to both itself and other conditioned things. The same is the case with abiding, which makes both itself and other things abide, and cessation, which is responsible for the cessation of both itself and other entities."

Response to the Second Objection
Refuting the second objection involves showing that (1) the example is not established and (2) its meaning is unreasonable. The first of these includes refutations by presenting (1) evidence that the entailed is unobservable and (2) an absurd consequence of this position.

Lack of Observation of the Entailed
On the first issue, the treatise states:

Light itself and the place where it is—
Neither of these have any darkness.
What does light illuminate?
Illumination occurs by dispelling darkness. [VII.9]

When light that is currently arising
Does not encounter darkness,
How could the currently arising light
Illuminate the darkness? [VII.10]

If light were to dispel darkness,
Even without encountering it,

Then the one right here would dispel
All the darkness in the world. [VII.11]

Upon investigation, we find that the example, the light that illumines both itself and other things, is not established. How could the subject, the aforementioned light, illumine both itself and other things since it does not dispel darkness in either itself or something else? This evidence, furthermore, is not established because it is impossible to bring light and darkness together in the same place. Therefore, whether we think of the light itself or the place around it, neither of them contains darkness that can be dispelled. It may then be asked why this lack of darkness being dispelled should rule out that the light illuminates. The reason is that the world holds that illumination occurs by the dispelling of darkness.

It may be thought that a light that has already arisen does not dispel darkness, but a light that is currently arising does. Yet this will not do. As was already mentioned, light and darkness cannot be present at the same location and time. The currently arising light, therefore, never encounters the dark. How, then, could it illuminate darkness? Just as light does not dispel darkness in places that are entirely unrelated to it, light does not dispel darkness anywhere.

Someone might then think: "Even if light and darkness do not encounter one another, why would it not still follow that light dispels darkness?"

If this were the case, the subject, the light right here, must then also be able to dispel, for example, the darkness between the continents. In fact, it should be able to dispel all the darkness in the entire world! Just as the light here does not encounter darkness where we are now, it does not encounter darkness in the rest of the world either.

It might then be argued: "How so? Although there is no difference insofar as no encounter takes place, light only dispels darkness in places where the circumstances are right for that to happen. It they are not, darkness will not be dispelled. Hence, there is no problem. The same principle is at work in visual perception. In a suitable location, seeing will occur without the eye faculty actually touching the object that is seen, yet in an unsuitable location, perception will not take place."

Here, neither the example nor the intended meaning is appropriate. Given that no encounter ever takes place, it does not makes sense for there to be differences in terms of certain places being fit for perception and certain instances of darkness being able to be dispelled. When an encounter does not take place due to distance or material obstruction, no perception or illumination can take place. The reason is that the distance or obstruction will have rendered an encounter impossible. If, then, no encounter ever were to take place, there could not be any perception or illumination, even if the place is close by and obstructions are absent.

We have already discussed why objections that appeal to the way things appear will not be sufficient here.

An Absurd Consequence
Second, pointing out the absurd consequence of this position, the treatise states:

> *If light could illumine*
> *Both itself and other things,*
> *Darkness would undoubtedly conceal*
> *Both itself and other things as well. [VII.12]*

If it were the case that, since light illuminates, it could illumine both itself and other things, then darkness, since it conceals, would undoubtedly conceal both itself and other things as well. This position would then imply that darkness would conceal itself and that it would, therefore, be invisible. However, mundane direct perception does see most subtle particles of darkness. It is, therefore, not self-obscuring. Similarly, light does not illuminate both itself and other things. As the *Noble Jewel Mound* teaches:

> If some people light a lamp
> In a house after a very long time,
> The darkness there will not be thinking:
> "I have been here so long, so I won't go away!"
> Once the lamp is lit, even the darkest darkness
> Cannot but disappear.
> Due to the lamp, the dark disappears.
> Both are empty; there is no conceit at all.

The Meaning of the Second Reply Is Unreasonable

Second, it will be shown that the meaning of the example is also untenable. This includes (1) refuting that arising produces itself and (2) refuting that it produces something else.

Arising Does Not Produce Itself

Concerning the first issue, the treatise states:

> When it has not arisen itself,
> How could arising produce its own nature?
> If it does so having already arisen,
> Having arisen, what is it that is produced? [VII.13]

If arising gives rise to itself, does it do so before or after it has arisen? If the first, we may ask how the subject, arising, could give rise to its own nature, given that it has not yet arisen. That which has not arisen is just as devoid of essence as the sky flower. Therefore, it lacks any power to produce itself. Alternatively, if arising produces itself after it has already arisen, then what is it that the subject, arising, produces if it itself has already arisen? That which already exists does not need to be established.

Arising Does Not Produce Anything Else

The second issue refutes this notion by (1) examining the object of arising in terms of the three times and (2) examining whether arising itself has a further arising. The first examination involves (1) a general refutation of arising with respect to the objects of the three times, (2) a specific refutation of arising in the present, and (3) dispensing with the criticism that this is irreconcilable with dependent origination.

General Refutation of Arising in the Three Times

When the act of arising, as a distinct entity, produces a vase or another conditioned phenomenon, does it produce something that has already arisen, something that has yet to arise, or something that is currently arising? In response, the treatise states:

> The arisen, unarisen, and arising
> Is not produced in any way.

This was explained before
By what was, will be, and is being traversed. [VII.14]

As was the case with the earlier refutation of the object that going relates to with reference to the three times, here we may follow the same steps with respect to arising. In the first case, the act of arising is already over, and in the second, it has not yet begun. Similarly, no current arising can be observed to be taking place in the present apart from these two. Thus, all three replies are untenable.

Particular Refutation of Current Arising
The second issue involves (1) showing the nonexistence of current arising by pointing out the lack of a support for the act of arising and (2) refuting an objection to this refutation.
   On the first issue, the treatise states:

When there is arising,
Current arising occurs,
Yet, when there is none, how can you claim
That this current arising is based on arising? [VII.15]

It may be argued: "What arises is not that which has already arisen or what has yet to arise. The current arising arises. It is not that there is no such thing as that which currently arises apart from the former two. The vase is explained to be the object to which the activity of arising relates. Thus, the object possesses the activity of arising and is, thereby, produced by an arising that is an entity other than itself."
   If the act of arising existed, it would, as here suggested, make sense to speak of a "currently arising vase," when a vase would possess that act of arising. However, as it is taught, "When there is nothing that arises, arising does not make sense."[122] In other words, when the vase is currently arising, the vase that should be the support of that activity has not yet arisen. It is, thus, nonexistent. Without any support, there cannot be any supported

122. Candrakīrti, *Entering the Middle Way*, VI.19c.

activity, that is, the arising of a vase. As this is the case, how can a so-called currently arising vase be based on the presence of the act of arising? As the currently arising vase is itself not established, it does not make sense to say that it is produced by an arising that is a different entity.

Refutation of the Objection
On the second issue, the treatise states:

> *If an unarisen entity were to exist somewhere,*
> *Then that could arise.*
> *But, when it does not exist,*
> *What sort of thing could then arise? [VII.17]*

Some may think: "The three times exist substantially. Hence, the arising vase exists as a future entity. As such, it supports the activity of arising, and thus comes to arise as a present entity."

A reply to this notion is provided one stanza later: If an entity, such as a vase, could somehow exist as a future entity without having arisen, then it could serve as the support for the act of arising, and so that thing could come to arise. Yet, since future entities are just as unborn and devoid of identity as the sky flower, what sort of thing could then arise? Indeed, since there is no support for it, the activity of arising cannot apply to anything.

One may then object: "When a vase is currently arising, no vase exists yet. Nevertheless, there is something else that the act of the vase's arising applies to, and on that basis the vase then comes into being."

Yet this is not the case. If the activity of arising is supported by something other than the vase, that which arises could not be the vase.

This Does Not Exclude Dependent Origination
On the third issue, the treatise states:

> *That which originates dependently*
> *Is peace by its very essence.*
> *Arising and the currently arising as well*
> *Are, therefore, peace itself. [VII.16]*

Members of our own tradition may argue: "The Transcendent Conqueror taught:

Here, there is no self or sentient being;
These are phenomena that have causes.

Thus, he has taught that reality consists of mere phenomena; phenomena that are empty of any permanent, singular, and independent self, as otherwise imputed by the extremists; phenomena that originate dependently and are of an impermanent nature. Now, with the pretence of teaching the sublime words of the Buddha, you say things like, 'The arisen, unarisen, and arising do not produce in any way.' Denying dependent origination, the great Mother from whom all the Thus-Gone Ones are born, your teaching is utterly nihilistic."

The reply is as follows: We do indeed refute dependent origination as you think of it, namely, as established by nature. In refuting the natural establishment of dependent origination, we show it to be compelling only so long as one does not examine it. Thus, our explanation clarifies the intent of the sūtras. By making certain statements, such as "Nature cannot reasonably occur due to causes and conditions,"[123] we show that fabrication through causes and conditions is possible where nothing exists by nature, whereas if things existed by nature that would be impossible. Therefore, that which originates dependently is the very essence of peace; it is emptiness. A sūtra teaches:

What arises due to conditions does not arise;
It lacks the nature of arising.
What depends on conditions is taught to be empty.[124]

Likewise:

Mahāmati, it is with their natural nonarising in mind that I explain all phenomena to be empty.[125]

Therefore, both the product, that which arises in the present, and the producer, arising, are by nature peace itself.

123. *Root of the Middle Way*, XV.1.
124. From the *Sūtra Requested by Anavatapta, King of the Nāgas*.
125. From the *Journey to Laṅkā*.

Does Arising Itself Arise?
Second follows a refutation by means of examining whether arising itself has a further arising. The treatise states:

> *If arising gives rise*
> *To the currently arising,*
> *Then what, in turn,*
> *Gives rise to arising? [VII.18]*

> *If arising is due to a separate arising*
> *There will be an infinite regress.*
> *If it arises without arising,*
> *Then so does everything else. [VII. 19]*

According to the objector's position, the currently arising vase is produced by a separate entity, the activity of arising. If this is the case, does this separate entity of arising arise by itself or is it produced by something else? If it is held that arising is produced by another arising, then that arising as well will require its own separate arising. Hence, there will be an infinite regress. If, alternatively, arising arises without any separate arising involved, then the case will be the same with all those things that are reportedly produced by arising. They will also arise without there being any separate entity of arising involved because they too are entities, as is arising.

This refutation of arising by examining whether it is produced by itself or something else can, by replacing terms in the way that was shown earlier, be turned into a refutation of abiding and cessation, in which case one examines whether they abide and cease by themselves or due to the agency of something other than themselves.

Individual Refutations of Arising, Abiding, and Cessation
Having offered a general refutation of the three characteristics of the conditioned, we shall now refute each individually.

Refutation of Arising
First is the refutation of arising, which involves (1) recalling what was previously explained and (2) a reasoning that has not been explained before.

On the first issue, the treatise states:

The existent and nonexistent cannot reasonably arise.
Something that is both
Cannot do so either.
Indeed, this has already been explained. [VII.20]

Here, the message of the sixth and seventh stanzas in the analysis of conditions is to be recalled.

On the second issue, the treatise states:

A thing that is currently ceasing
Cannot reasonably arise.
A thing that is not currently ceasing
Cannot reasonably be a thing. [VII.21]

Is that which arises something that is ceasing from one moment to the next? To answer yes would not make sense because a thing that is currently ceasing cannot also be arising, for these two are incompatible with one another. In addition, something that is currently ceasing is still present and has not yet ceased.

The alternative is not acceptable either. As has been taught:

That which by nature does not cease
Is referred to by the wise as "permanent."[126]

Thus, something that is not in the process of ceasing, and therefore remains for a second moment, would be permanent and unconditioned. Hence, it could not be a [conditioned] thing.

It might be objected: "That does not follow because the thing is not in the process of ceasing from the very beginning. Rather, its cessation only occurs once its continuum comes to an end."

That, however, cannot be maintained. On this point, it is taught:

Abiding is impossible and what does not change
To begin with does not cease in the end.[127]

---

126. Dharmakīrti, *Commentary on Reliable Means of Cognition*, II.204c–d.
127. Āryadeva, *Four Hundred Stanzas*, XI.17b–d convey a similar message but with a somewhat different wording.

Thus, if the thing would not be gone in the next moment, its remaining at a second point in time would make its presence endless. This could not be reconciled with a cessation at the end of a continuum.

Refutation of Abiding

The second issue, the refutation of abiding, covers four points. The first is a refutation of abiding with reference to the refutation of arising.

Given the Absence of Arising, There Is No Abiding

Concerning this first issue, the treatise states:

> What thing abides that does not arise? [VII.22d]

Since the arising of conditioned phenomena has already been refuted, below it is asked what could possibly abide. Nothing at all abides, just as in the case of the sky flower.

Refutation of Abiding with Reference to the Three Times

The second refutation examines abiding in terms of the three times. The treatise states:

> A thing that has abided does not abide,
> A thing that has yet to abide does not abide,
> And no currently abiding thing abides either. [VII.22a–c]

Let us assume that the activity of abiding is responsible, as a distinct entity, for the abiding of a given conditioned thing. Is that which it makes abide then something that has already abided, something that has yet to abide, or something that is currently abiding? Abiding does not make something that has already abided abide because in such a thing the activity of abiding has ceased. Neither does it relate to something that does not yet abide because in such a thing abiding has not yet arisen. Finally, it does not make something that is currently abiding abide either because there are no things that currently abide apart from the two that were just mentioned. Moreover, if the latter were the case, it would also follow that there would be two activities of abiding.

Is What Abides Currently Ceasing?
The third section offers a refutation by examining whether what abides is currently ceasing or not. The treatise states:

> *A thing that is currently ceasing*
> *Cannot reasonably abide.*
> *A thing that is not currently ceasing*
> *Cannot reasonably be a thing. [VII.23]*

> *All things, at all times,*
> *Are subject to aging and death.*
> *What thing then remains*
> *Free from aging and death? [VII.24]*

Is that which abides something that is currently ceasing or something else? It does not make sense for something that is currently ceasing to abide because abiding and ceasing are mutually incompatible. On the other hand, were that which abides not currently ceasing but remaining for a second instant, it would, as explained before, never cease. Therefore, it could not be a functional thing. Thus, the twenty-fourth stanza implies the absolute impossibility of something's remaining for a second instant upon its arising.

One may then object that although substantial things are momentary and, therefore, do not abide, abiding is found in their continua. This, however, is not tenable either. It is not possible to observe any continuum that is essentially different from a momentary substance. And if the two are essentially inseparable, the continuum would be incompatible with abiding, just as the substance is.

Does Abiding Itself Have a Further Abiding?
The fourth refutation examines whether abiding itself has a further abiding. The treatise states:

> *Abiding cannot reasonably abide*
> *Due to itself, nor due to another.*
> *The case was the same with arising,*
> *Which arises neither by itself nor through another. [VII.25]*

248 ORNAMENT OF REASON

If conditioned things are made to abide by a separate entity of abiding, does that abiding then make itself abide, or is there yet another abiding that is responsible? Neither alternative makes sense. In the second case, there would be an infinite regress. Given the first option, it is impossible for something to act on itself. Here the case is the same as that of arising, which, as we have seen, neither arises by itself, nor due to anything else. The first two lines of the nineteenth stanza, the first two lines of the thirteenth stanza, and the last two lines of the nineteenth stanza can, thus, easily be turned into refutations of abiding by saying, "If abiding is due to a separate abiding, there will be an infinite regress," and so on. For these reasons, the *King of Meditative Absorptions* teaches:

> These phenomena do not abide;
> They have no abiding.
> That which does not abide may be spoken of as if it did,
> Yet it has no essence.

Refutation of Cessation
Third is the refutation of impermanence. This has six subsections, the first of which is a refutation with reference to causal arising, which has already been refuted.

Given the Absence of Arising, There Is No Abiding
The treatise states:

> *What thing ceases that did not arise? [VII.26d]*

Below, it is asked what sort of thing could be ceasing, when no thing has arisen. The notion that things arise has already been refuted.

The Refutation of Cessation with Reference to the Three Times
Next is a refutation by examining cessation in terms of the three times. The treatise states:

> *A thing that has ceased does not cease,*
> *A thing that has yet to cease does not cease,*
> *And no currently ceasing thing ceases either. [VII.26a–c]*

A thing that has ceased does not cease, for its act of ceasing is over and, hence, absent. Something that has yet to cease does not cease either. In such a thing, the act of cessation has not yet begun, and a cessation of it would be in conflict with its having yet to cease. Finally, that which is currently ceasing does not cease any more than the previous two, for apart from what has already ceased and what has yet to do so, there cannot possibly be anything that currently ceases. The existence of such a thing would, moreover, also result in there being two activities of cessation.

Is What Ceases Currently Abiding?
The third section presents a refutation by examining whether or not what ceases is currently abiding. The treatise states:

> *A thing that abides*
> *Cannot reasonably cease,*
> *Yet a thing that does not abide*
> *Cannot reasonably cease either. [VII.27]*

It does not make sense for a thing that currently abides to cease, for its abiding is incompatible with ceasing. However, a thing that does not currently abide, a thing without any abiding, cannot cease either because such a thing would be unconditioned. Moreover, a phenomenon that does not abide at its own specific time is impossible.

Is Cessation Due to the Initial State Itself or to Another State?
The fourth subsection is a refutation that considers whether cessation is brought about by the initial state itself or by some other state. The treatise explains:

> *The same state does not*
> *Bring an end to itself,*
> *Nor is it that a different state*
> *Makes the initial one cease. [VII.28]*

> *When no phenomenon's arising*
> *Makes any sense,*
> *No phenomenon's cessation,*
> *Makes any sense either. [VII.29]*

If it is held that an effect follows the cessation of its cause, is the cessation of the causal state then due to that state itself, or is it instead brought about by a different resultant state? The first could not be the case. The causal states of, say, milk or being young, do not bring an end to themselves because nothing can act upon itself. Yet the alternative is not feasible either. It is not the case that a different resultant state, such as curd or being old, brings an end to the causal state of milk and being young. There is no contact between these different states, just as there is no contact between the heat of a kitchen stove and the cold of a snow ball.

It may be argued: "Nevertheless, the causal milk and youth do indeed cease because we observe the arising of the curd and aging that result."

Yet we have already shown how the arising of curd, or any other resultant phenomenon, makes no sense. Thereby, we have also made it clear that milk, or any other causal phenomenon, cannot reasonably cease.

Is That Which Ceases a Thing?
The fifth refutation examines whether or not that which ceases is a thing. The treatise states:

> A thing that exists
> Cannot have a cessation,
> Because the same thing cannot
> Be both thing and no thing. [VII.30]

> A thing that does not exist
> Cannot have a cessation,
> Just as it is impossible
> To cut off a second head. [VII.31]

Is that which ceases a thing? This would not make sense. If the support, the existent thing, is essentially the same as its cessation, which is itself the absence of a thing, the former could not exist as a thing. Likewise, if the property, the nonentity of cessation, is essentially the same as the existent thing that supports it, the former could not be the absence of that thing. Any idea of these two being the same will always be contradictory. Just as something cannot be both light and darkness, it does not make sense for something to be both a thing and no thing.

There cannot be any cessation where no thing exists either. In the absence of a support for it, the cessation would be similar to a painting on space. It would be just as impossible as it is to cut off the second head of a living being that only has one.

Does Cessation Itself Have a Further Cessation?
The sixth refutation examines whether or not cessation itself has a further cessation:

> *Cessation is neither brought about*
> *By itself nor by anything else,*
> *Just as arising is not produced*
> *By itself or something else. [VII.32]*

Let us assume that for each conditioned phenomenon there is a separate entity of cessation that makes the phenomenon cease. Would that cessation then cease by its own nature, or because of some other cessation? Cessation is brought about neither by itself nor by anything else because nothing can act on itself, and if something else were to be involved, there would be an infinite regress. It was explained earlier how arising cannot arise by itself or because of something else. We can, therefore, simply substitute cessation for arising and draw a similar conclusion.

At this point, the *Commentary* explains why the above criticism does not apply equally to cessation as we teach it in terms of the relative. It also presents a refutation of the view that cessation is uncaused and explains why the position that cessation involves a cause is flawless. These explanations are presented lucidly in the *Commentary* itself.

THE ESTABLISHED MEANING

Having refuted the notion that the characteristics of the conditioned are real, the second issue involves presenting the meaning that is established thereby. The treatise states:

> *As arising, abiding, and cessation are not established,*
> *There is nothing that is conditioned.*
> *Since the conditioned lacks any establishment,*
> *How could the unconditioned be established? [VII.33]*

It may be thought: "The three characteristics of the conditioned have indeed been negated, but their bearers, such as forms, sensations, and all other outer and inner entities, do exist."

Yet this is not the case. It was shown earlier how the characteristics in terms of arising, abiding, and ceasing are not established by nature. This also proves that the bearers of these characteristics of the conditioned, such as the things that belong to the aggregate of form, have no nature.

It might then be thought that the unconditioned must exist since it has not been refuted. However, once we examine things in the way described above, we find nothing conditioned. How, then, could the negation of that, the unconditioned, be established? Without anything to be negated, there cannot be any negation. The *King of Meditative Absorptions* explains:

> As neither the conditioned nor the unconditioned have any
> bearing,
> The sage does not conceive of either of these.
> Since in every realm the unconditioned is achieved
> He is always entirely beyond views
> Of the wanderers who [strive to] achieve the unconditioned.

How the Above Refutation Does Not Contradict Scripture

Third, explaining how these negations do not conflict with scripture, the treatise states:

> *Like a dream, like an illusion,*
> *Like a city of scent-eaters—*
> *This is how arising, abiding,*
> *And cessation are taught to be. [VI.34]*

It may be argued: "If, in this way, there were no nature of arising, abiding, and cessation, it would conflict with the following teaching from the *Sūtra of the Great Cloud in Twelve Thousand Stanzas*:

> Monks, the conditioned obviously arises. It likewise obviously
> ceases, and changes from the way it is into something else."

This is indeed taught, but it is not an explanation of the ultimate, definitive meaning. In dreams, things do not arise although they appear to; in an
illusion, there is nothing that abides, although there seems to be; and a city
of scent-eaters contains no things that cease, despite giving that appearance. The arising, abiding, and cessation of conditioned things is taught
to be similar to these. There is, therefore, no contradiction.

Alternatively, each of these three examples is equally applicable to arising, abiding, and cessation: A dream, an illusion, or a city of scent-eaters
does not contain any actual arising, abiding, and cessation, and yet it still
appears to. In the very same way, conditioned things do not have any
objective arising, abiding, or cessation, yet they seem to from the perspective of a mind in delusion.

SUMMARY OF THE CHAPTER'S SIGNIFICANCE

The present chapter has explicitly refuted the ultimate [reality of] both
the conditioned and the unconditioned and has shown that with respect
to the relative, such things are like dreams and illusions. Since there cannot possibly be any phenomenon that is not included in either the conditioned or the unconditioned, this chapter has thus affirmed that, in
reality, all phenomena are of the nature of emptiness, while in terms of the
relative, their appearance is illusion-like. This is also taught in the *King of
Meditative Absorptions*:

> No phenomenon arises or disintegrates;
> There is no death, no transference, and no aging.
> This is what the Lion of Men has taught,
> And in this he has established hundreds of beings.

Likewise:

> The Protector of the World has not taught
> That anything abides or arises.

Aware of this Protector of the World,
Recognize the meditative absorption.

This concludes the explanation of the seventh chapter, the analysis of the conditioned, in the *Ornament of Reason*, a commentary on the *Root of the Middle Way*.

CHAPTER EIGHT

Analysis of Action and Agent

THE ANALYSIS of action and agent is treated in three sections, the first of which addresses the chapter's context.

THE CONTEXT OF CHAPTER 8

The present chapter relates to the profound sūtras, insofar as it employs reasoning to ascertain the meaning of certain teachings, such as the following passage from the *Noble Sūtra on the Ten Grounds*:

> Where ultimately there is no action, no agent can be observed.

As for its relationship to the other chapters of the text, the present analysis is a response to the following notion, "Consciousness, and all other conditioned phenomena that comprise the aggregates, elements, and sense sources, do indeed exist. A sūtra teaches:

> A person who is subject to ignorance creates meritorious, nonmeritorious, and undisturbed formations.[128]

Thus, this statement affirms the existence of actions that function as causes, as well as the agents of such actions. Now, the nonexistent could not be the object of any action or agent, just as a garment made of turtle hair cannot involve an action or agent."

This chapter shows that, when subjected to examination, action and agent will be seen to be devoid of establishment.

---

128. From the *Sālu Sprout*.

THE CONTENT OF CHAPTER 8

Explaining the content of this chapter involves (1) refuting the natural establishment of action and agent, (2) explaining their merely conventional, mutually dependent establishment, and (3) extending this analysis to other topics.

REFUTING THE NATURAL ESTABLISHMENT OF ACTION AND AGENT

As for the first issue, an agent is something that performs an action. In this regard, only three alternatives are possible: something may be involved in the performance of an action, not involved in it, or both involved and not involved. In the first case, we have an agent, in the second we do not, and in the third case, the thing in question both is and is not an agent.

Similarly, an action is something that is performed; it is what an agent carries out. Here, there are also only three alternatives: Something may be performed by an agent, not performed, or both performed and not performed. In the first case, we have an action, in the second we do not, and in the third case, what we are concerned with both is and is not an action.

The refutation of action and agent will be carried out within the framework of these six alternatives. Thus, we will refute (1) actions and agents that are of the same ontological status and (2) actions and agents that are of a different ontological status.

Refuting Agent and Action with the Same Ontological Status

The first includes refutations of (1) the notion that an agent performs an action, (2) the notion that what is not an agent performs what is not an action, and (3) the notion that something that both is and is not an agent performs what both is and is not an action.

An Agent Does Not Perform an Action

On the first issue, the treatise states:

> *That which is an agent does not*
> *Perform something that is an action. [VIII.1a–b]*

Here a genuine thesis is presented as follows: Something that is an agent by virtue of being involved in a given activity does not perform something that qualifies as an action. Presenting the rationale for this statement, the treatise explains:

> *That which is an agent would have no activity.*
> *There would also be action without an agent.*
> *That which is an action is not performed,*
> *So the agent would be lacking its action. [VIII.2]*

If one that is already an agent were to perform an action, as explained earlier, that would require that there are two performances. There will have to be one performance that justifies the agent being referred to as such and, once it is qualified as an agent, there must then be another performance that the agent subsequently carries out. Hence, we may argue: The subject, that which is an actual agent, does not have any activity because there is no performance other than the one that justifies the agent being referred to as such. Thus, since a single agent does not perform two activities, the action ends up having no agent. In other words, the act would be independent of, and not performed by, any agent. Such an act is as impossible as a vase made by the son of a barren woman.

Likewise, if an agent performs something that is already an action, there will have to be two performances, as explained earlier. First, one performance must justify the action's being referred to as such and then, once it has become an action in this way, there must be a second performance that the agent subsequently effectuates. Thus, we may argue: The subject, an action, is not performed by any agent because there is no performance other than the one that justifies its classification as an action. Hence, as there are not two performances, something that is already an action is not performed. This means that the performing agent would end up lacking an action, and an agent that does not depend on or perform an action is impossible, just as it is impossible to have an agent of a deed with immediate consequences if no such deed has been committed.

A Nonagent Does Not Perform a Nonaction
The second issue likewise includes both (1) the thesis and (2) its rationale.

The Thesis
On the first issue, the treatise states:

> *A nonagent does not*
> *Perform a nonaction. [VIII.1c–d]*

A nonagent, that is someone not engaged in any activity, does not perform any action that, in not being performed, is not an action.

The Rationale
The justification of the thesis will be addressed by (1) stating the absurd consequence that action and agent would have no causes and (2) pointing out why this cannot be accepted.

The Absurd Consequence
On the first issue, the treatise states:

> *If a nonagent were to perform*
> *That which is not an action,*
> *The action would have no cause*
> *And the agent would have no cause either. [VIII.3]*

If something that is not yet involved in performing an action, and thus is not yet an agent, were to engage in an activity, there would be no cause for classifying it as an agent. Likewise, if something that is not yet performed by an agent, and therefore is not yet an action, were to be performed, we would have no cause for classifying it as an action. This absence of cause for speaking of both agent and action is entailed because it is the presence of activity that justifies agent and action being classified as such.

Why This Consequence Is Unacceptable
Pointing out the unacceptability of this consequence has two parts.[129] First it will be shown how this consequence entails the nonexistence of cause and effect. The treatise states:

---

129. In an apparent error, the Tibetan text here mentions four parts.

If there is no cause,
Cause and effect become untenable.
Without these, action, agent, and activity
Will all be nonsensical as well. [VIII.4]

If action and so forth are unreasonable,
There can be no Dharma and non-Dharma,
And without Dharma and non-Dharma,
Their effects do not exist either. [VIII.5]

Without such effects, paths to liberation
And to the higher realms do not make sense. [VIII.6a–b]

If one were to accept that conventions have no causes, it would, by the same rationale, become generally unreasonable to think in terms of effects that are produced by causes and causes that generate effects. Accepting that such thinking is unreasonable would entail a universal disappearance of all the conventions associated with action and agent. Without effects and the causes that bring them about, there could not reasonably be any action in the form of the arising of an effect; there could not be an agent that is in control of such an action; and there could not be any object that such an agent relates to, so as to give rise to the manifestation of a result.

To accept that would lead to the collapse of all the conventions that are discussed in the treatises. If action, agent, object, and activity have all become untenable, there could be no Dharma associated with the truly elevated and the definitive good because there would not be any engagement in the ten virtues or any meditation on the absence of self.

Non-Dharma, which is the opposite of these activities, could not exist either. Without Dharma and non-Dharma, it also follows that the effects of these two would be nonexistent. Hence, neither the happiness of the higher realms and liberation, nor the suffering of cyclic existence and the lower realms could exist.

If we were to accept that, it would be meaningless to train on either the transcendent path to liberation or the mundane path to the higher realms, for the effects of Dharma training would be nonexistent. Any such training would, therefore, make no sense.

Second, the treatise points out that this would also entail the disappearance of all worldly conventions:

All activities would indeed
End up entirely meaningless. [VIII.6c–d]

If there were no such things as cause and effect, farming and other mundane activities, which are undertaken with the expectation of a certain result, would be entirely meaningless. Such activities are, however, not entirely futile. Thus, causality is not completely nonexistent.

One That Both Is and Is Not an Agent Does Not Perform Something That Both Is and Is Not an Action

The third issue includes (1) the thesis and (2) its rationale. The treatise states:

> *That which both is and is not an agent*
> *Does not perform something that both is and is not.*
> *Since being and not being are incompatible in one thing,*
> *How could this ever be the case? [VIII.7]*

Something that both is and is not an agent and that, hence, both does and does not perform a given activity does not perform something that both is and is not an action. The reason, here, is that being and not being are mutually incompatible. How, then, could a single thing both be and not be an agent or action? How could the same thing both perform and not perform, or be performed and also not performed?

Refutation of Agent and Action Where the Ontological Status Differs

Having thus refuted agents and actions in pairs with the same ontological status, we will next refute them in pairs where that status differs. Doing so includes (1) pairing a single agent with a single action of different status and (2) treating the agent in relation to two actions that are of a different status.

Single Agent versus Single Action

On the first, the treatise states:

> *One that is an agent does not perform*
> *Something that is not an action,*

Nor does one that is not perform something that is
Because the same flaws would ensue. [VIII.8]

Something that is an agent does not perform a nonaction. Likewise, a nonagent does not perform an action either. Were either of these options to be asserted, the same flaws as we saw above would ensue. If a real agent is asserted, we have the problem shown in the first two verses of the second stanza:

That which is an agent would have no activity.
There would also be action without an agent.

The notion of a nonaction is addressed in the third stanza, where it is explained that such an action has no cause. In the case of a nonagent, the same stanza pointed out that such an agent would be causeless. Finally, it does not make sense for there to be an action that is performed because, as stated in the last line of the second stanza, the agent would be lacking its action.

Single Agent versus Two Actions
The second section is divided into three parts. First, an agent that performs a nonaction, or something that both is and is not an actual action, is refuted. The treatise states:

The agent involved does not
Perform any nonaction,
Or something that both is and is not an action.
The arguments have already been given. [VIII.9]

An agent does not perform any nonaction, or something that both is and is not an action. The arguments that explain this have already been given. The notion of an agent was refuted in the first two lines of the second stanza; the performance of a nonaction was disproved in the third stanza; and something's both being and not being an action was refuted in the last two lines of the seventh stanza by pointing out that it is contradictory to claim that one single thing can be both.

Second, the notion of a nonagent performing an action, or something that both is and is not an action, is refuted. The treatise states:

That which is not an agent
Does not perform any action,
Or something that both is and is not an action.
The arguments have already been given. [VIII.10]

A nonagent does not perform an action or something that both is and is not an action. The reasons for this have already been stated. The third stanza explained that a nonagent will be lacking its cause; the last two verses of the second stanza have made it clear that the performance of an action would result in the agent's lacking its action; and the last two verses of the seventh stanza have called attention to the incompatible natures of being and not being.

Finally, the following stanza negates the notion that something that both is and is not an agent performs an action or a nonaction:

One that both is and is not an agent
Does not perform an action or a nonaction.
Here as well it should be understood
That the arguments have already been given. [VIII.11]

One that both is and is not an agent is not involved in the performance of any action or nonaction. Here as well the reasons that explain this have already been given. The last two verses of the seventh stanza have shown the impossibility of any such agent; the last two verses of the second stanza have stated that the performance of an action would render the agent actionless; and the third stanza has shown that a nonaction has no cause.

With the refutation of these eleven alternatives that relate to action and agent, it should be understood that neither action nor agent is established in the sense of particular characteristics.

As Mere Conventions, Action and Agent Are Established in Mutual Dependence

On the second issue, the treatise states:

Agent comes about in dependence on action,
And action, in turn, in dependence on agent.

Apart from that we do not see
Any cause of their establishment. [VIII.12]

It may be objected: "The Able One taught:

The [consequences of] an individual's actions
Will each be experienced by that same individual.

Now, your arguments go against all such teachings. You have, therefore, fallen prey to a distorted view, a type of nihilism that holds things such as actions and their consequences to be nonexistent."

This, however, is not the case. Let us recall the following statement:

When no thing can be observed,
How could there be a nonthing?[130]

In other words, in reality we do not find any established existence of anything that could be negated, such as actions and their effects. For that reason, we would not even claim that the negative property of mere non-existence, which depends on the negation of things, has any establishment. From the perspective of a relative, deluded consciousness, however, actions and agents are established in mere mutual dependence. Hence, what we assert is the occurrence of the illusion-like, mere conditionality that constitutes dependent origination.

We may consider the statement, "This is the agent of that action." The designation "agent" depends on there being an action, and since that action is precisely that which the agent is performing, the action, in turn, depends on the agent itself as well. Apart from this dependent occurrence of agent and action, upon examination, we see no other cause of their establishment. They are not established by virtue of any particular characteristics. Below, the following question is raised:

If an entity is established in dependence,
And is itself depended on

---

130. Nāgārjuna, *Jewel Garland*, V.98.

By that upon which it depends,
What is established in dependence on what?[131]

Thus, it will be explained that things that are established in mutual dependence do not have any nature.

Extending This Analysis to Other Topics
Third, extending this analysis to other topics, the treatise states:

> *Appropriation should be understood in the same way,*
> *As here action and agent have been excluded.*
> *Agent and action will provide*
> *Understanding of the remaining issues. [VIII.13]*

It has been explained that while action and agent are established in mutual
dependence as mere conventions, they are not naturally established. In the
same manner, appropriation should be understood to be established as
mere convention due to mutual dependencies, and thus not as established
by nature (although only the activity of appropriation is explicitly mentioned, this implies the factors that constitute appropriation, that is, the
appropriated aggregates and the appropriating self). That this is the status
of the appropriated aggregates and the appropriating self follows from the
way that we have excluded any natural establishment of action and agent.

Yet the present reasoning can be extended beyond these two factors.
All remaining things—cause and effect, characteristics and their bearers,
signified and signifier, cognition and objects of cognition, reliable means
of cognition and the objects evaluated thereby, and so forth—all such topics taught in the treatises can be understood in the same way. As conventions, they are established in mutual dependence, yet none of them are
established by nature.

SUMMARY OF THE CHAPTER'S SIGNIFICANCE

Third, to sum up, in terms of the ultimate, the present chapter has provided
an existential negation of the constructs associated with all phenomena.

---

131. *Root of the Middle Way*, X.10.

With respect to the relative, it has also established a dependent origination that is a mere illusion. This is precisely the intent of the following teaching from the *Noble Sūtra Requested by Upāli*:

> I have taught about the horrors of hell,
> And so saddened many thousands of sentient beings.
> Yet beings that die and transfer to terrifying realms of misery,
> Such wandering beings never existed.
> The torturers, brandishing their great swords and arrows,
> Have never had any existence either.
> It is the power of thought that creates the experience
> Of a body within such realms of misery.
> There are no weapons.

This concludes the explanation of the eighth chapter, the analysis of action and agent, in the *Ornament of Reason*, a commentary on the *Root of the Middle Way*.

CHAPTER NINE

Analysis of Prior Existence

HAVING SHOWN that dependent origination is empty of any self in the form of phenomena, it will next be explained how it contains no self in the form of a person. First, the analysis of prior existence refutes the naturally established essence of the person. This chapter will be treated in three sections, the first of which addresses the chapter's context.

THE CONTEXT OF CHAPTER 9

The present chapter relates to the teachings of the profound sūtras. The *Mother of the Victorious Ones*, for example, states, "Form is empty of I and mine." While the *Journey to Laṅkā*, explains:

> This so-called self is a demonic idea;
> From this, views issue forth.
> These conditioned aggregates are empty;
> Here, there is no self and no sentient being.

Thus, all the sūtras teach the complete nonexistence of any subject that is involved in doing or feeling. It is the meaning of that very teaching that the present chapter employs reasoning to ascertain.

As for its relationship to the other chapters of the text, the analysis of prior existence serves as a refutation of an idea such as the following: "It was earlier taught that the appropriated and the one who appropriates have no nature. Yet that is not tenable because the appropriator exists before the appropriated and appropriates in that capacity. Hence, both the appropriator and appropriated exist by nature."

THE CONTENT OF CHAPTER 9

Second, explaining the content of this chapter includes (1) a refutation of the appropriating self, (2) a refutation of what the self appropriates, and (3) the resulting conclusion.

THE APPROPRIATING SELF

The first issue is twofold. The view of the opposition is presented first.

The View of the Opposition
The treatise states:

> *Some assert that sight, hearing, and the rest,*
> *As well as sensation and so forth,*
> *Are in the possession of, and belong to,*
> *Something that precedes them. [IX.1]*

> *If there were no thing,*
> *How could there be sight and so forth?*
> *Hence, prior to these factors,*
> *There is an abiding entity. [IX.2]*

Some of the Saṃmitīyas within our own tradition will object when it is said that:

> Appropriation should be understood in the same way,
> As here action and agent have been excluded.[132]

Thus, they will argue: "That statement is unreasonable. The appropriated includes sight, hearing, and the rest of the six inner sense sources, as well as sensation, contact, volition, and so forth. All of these factors are in the possession of, and appropriated by, something, namely, the person. Moreover, this person, this self that appropriates and possesses all of these, exists prior to them."

---

132. *Root of the Middle Way*, VIII.13a–b.

Explaining their rationale for this position, they will explain: "If the entity of the appropriating self did not exist before that which it appropriates, how could it engage in the causal accumulation of action that is necessary for the resultant appropriation of sight, and so on? Any appropriation would be as impossible as it is to take possession of the wealth that has been gathered by the child of a barren woman. Therefore, prior to the appropriated sight, and so forth, the abiding entity of a self, which is the one that takes possession, must exist."

Refutation

To disprove this view, the following notions are refuted: (1) the appropriator's existence prior to the totality of appropriated factors, (2) its existence prior to each individually, and (3) that there is an appropriator of the causes of sight, and so on.

The Appropriator's Existence Prior to the Totality of the Appropriated Factors

The first section addresses two points. We begin with a refutation that calls attention to the absence of any reason for speaking of a "self."

No Grounds for Speaking of a Self

The treatise states:

> Before sight, hearing, and the rest,
> And before sensation and so on,
> What are your grounds for speaking
> Of that abiding entity's existence? [IX.3]

A sūtra teaches:

> Based on the assembly of its parts
> We can speak of "a chariot."
> Likewise, based on the aggregates
> We speak relatively of "a sentient being."

In general, "the self" is an imputation based on the aggregates. More specifically, the self that sees, for instance, is labeled as such based on there being sight. Now, think of that appropriator, the abiding entity of self, which is held to exist prior to sight, hearing, smell, taste, touch, and cognition; which is held to precede the consciousness of sensation, etc., and be present before contact, sensation, and so forth. When none of these factors yet exist, what grounds are there for speaking of a person? What seeing, or any other phenomenon, is there that could make us conceive of "a seeing subject," etc? Indeed, since there is no seeing, nor any other reason for thinking in terms of a person, we can conclude that a self, such as "someone who sees," is as nonexistent as the child of a barren woman.

Refutation of a Self That Is Independent of the Bases for Imputation
Second, the refutation of a self that is independent of the bases for imputation includes (1) stating an absurd consequence of this position and (2) showing that this consequence is unacceptable.

An Absurd Consequence
On the first issue, the treatise states:

> *If this remains in the absence*
> *Of sight and these other factors,*
> *Then they will undoubtedly be present*
> *Even in the absence of that. [IX.4]*

Why should the self of the appropriator not exist even in the absence of something to appropriate, such as sight? Well, by the same token, sight and whatever else is included in the appropriated aggregates would then undoubtedly be present even if there were no appropriating self.

Why This Consequence Is Unacceptable
Second, a reply is given to the opponent, who at this point accepts the consequence presented above. The treatise states:

> *Something manifests somebody,*
> *And somebody manifests something.*
> *How could somebody exist in the absence of anything?*
> *How could something exist in the absence of anybody? [IX.5]*

In the world, people say things such as, "This is the cause of that, and that is the effect of this." Thus, the cause and effect that they talk about are mutually dependent. One cannot be without the other. Likewise, when it is said that, "This is the appropriator of that," the appropriator is manifested and labeled as such because there is something that is appropriated, such as sight. Likewise, when something is classified as "the appropriation of such and such," it is the presence of the self that appropriates that manifests sight and provides the grounds for it to be labeled as appropriation.

Hence, how could there possibly be somebody, that is, the self of an appropriator, in the complete absence of sight or another factor that is appropriated? The point of reference would be missing. Again, if the point of reference is missing, if there is no appropriating self at all, how could there then be sight or another factor that is appropriated? In either case, it is impossible to have one without the other.

The Appropriator's Existence Prior to the Individual Appropriated Factors

As for the second issue, the treatise states:

> *This is not present before*
> *The totality of sight and so forth.*
> *Yet each factor among sight and the rest*
> *Individually makes it manifest. [IX.6]*

It may be thought: "The self cannot be asserted to exist prior to the totality of appropriated factors, such as sight, because that would lead to the flaws just mentioned. As this is the case, the self cannot exist in such a manner. Nevertheless, as separate instances of sight, hearing, and so forth occur in temporal succession, they each individually serve to make the appropriator manifest and classifiable as such. The flaw of there being no basis for speaking of a self is, therefore, not applicable."

Refutation

The refutation of this account is twofold. First we will show that unless the self is present before all of the factors in their totality, it cannot reasonably exist prior to each of them individually. On this point, the treatise states:

Unless it precedes the totality
Of sight and the rest,
How could it possibly precede
Each of them individually? [IX.7]

If the self is always present before any of the individual occurrences of appropriated factors, it follows that in the end it must be present before their totality. Hence, given that it does not exist before all of these factors collectively, how could it possibly be present before each and every one of them individually? There cannot be any "totality" apart from the full collection of the individual factors, so if the self is present before each single factor, this also means that it exists earlier than them.

The second section refutes this notion by pointing out that neither identical nor distinct appropriators can reasonably exist prior to the individual appropriated factors. The treatise states:

If that which sees were that which hears,
And what hears were that which senses,
This would exist before every one of them,
Yet that does not make sense. [IX.8]

If the seer, the hearer and the one that senses
Were all different from each other,
The hearer could be present at the time of the seer
And there would be multiple selves. [IX.9]

Let us assume that it were possible for a mere self to precede sight and every other appropriated factor, yet without existing prior to their totality. If this were the case, it would still not make sense for the appropriator of, for example, an instance of sight to exist prior to the sight that it appropriates. The appropriator of sight is held to be the self that is involved in sight, and that self is, moreover, identical with the self that engages in hearing and sensation. Thus, a hearer may be present before the presence of sight, but that hearer would be the same as the seer. Therefore, it follows that a given appropriator, such as the seer, would be present before the sight that it appropriates. Such a scenario of a single agent performing a series of distinct actions is, therefore, untenable. The hearer may exist before there is sight, but the seer cannot. It does not make sense that a given appropriator exists before that which it appropriates.

Wishing to avoid the contradictory idea of a single agent performing different successive actions, the opponent may argue that there are different appropriators involved in seeing, hearing, sensing, and so forth. Yet, since these appropriators differ from each other, they will be independent of each other as well. Hence, in the same way that a horse and a cow can be present at the same time because they do not depend on each other, a hearer and any and all of the other agents can then be present at the same time that a seer is present. This conflicts with the opponent's own denial of the six collections being simultaneous. Moreover, accepting such an idea would make one committed to the seer, hearer, and so on all being different selves. This would also conflict with the scriptural statement: "When the world is born, it is one single person that is born."

Refuting the Appropriator of the Causes of Sight, and so Forth
On the third issue, the treatise states:

> Sight, hearing, and the rest,
> As well as sensation and so forth—
> Among the causes from which these emerge,
> There is no existence of that. [IX.10]

It may be thought: "The self exists before the entirety of factors such as sight. It is not the case that we have no basis for designating the self as such because it is taught, 'Due to the conditions of name and form, the six sense sources arise.' Thus, given the causal presence of the forms of the four elements that join with the four names in the subtle embryo, there will also be a presence of the self that appropriates these effects."

Yet we cannot find any appropriating self among the causes from which sight, hearing, and the other internal sense sources, as well as sensation and so forth, emerge. No appropriator exists among the material elements that come together with four names and make up the subtle embryo. As we have seen, the appropriating self cannot be present before the material elements that it appropriates. Hence, given the absence of the appropriator, it does not make sense for there to be any appropriation taking place either.

The Appropriated

Some groups, including the Followers of Sūtra, claim that although there is no self that appropriates, there is still the mere process of the appropriation of sight and so forth. Hence, in the second section, the text offers a refutation of the appropriated. The treatise states:

> Sight, hearing, and the rest,
> As well as sensation and so forth—
> If there is no one to whom these belong,
> Then they do not exist either. [IX.11]

If there were someone who appropriates, there would also be appropriations. Yet it was already shown that there is no such self that appropriates; there is nobody that takes possession of factors such as sight and hearing, or of sensation and so forth. There is no one to whom all these factors belong. This means that there is nobody to accumulate the karmic actions that establish these factors. It also means that the counterpart necessary to designate sight and so forth as appropriations will be absent. None of the appropriated factors can, therefore, have any natural existence either.

Conclusion

Third, in conclusion, the treatise states:

> That which does not exist
> Before, together with, or after sight and the rest
> Will no longer be thought about
> As existent or nonexistent. [IX.12]

The appropriated and the appropriator are, as we have seen, mutually dependent. Therefore, the self of the appropriator does not exist prior to sight and other such factors, for when these do not exist, all reasons for designating a self will be missing as well. Neither does the appropriator coexist with these factors because it has no establishment separate from them. Moreover, if appropriator and appropriated were simultaneous, they would be independent of each other. Finally, the appropriating self does not exist subsequent to factors such as sight either. If the appropriated preceded the appropriator, it would, in the absence of the latter, lack its cause. The same goes for the appropriated: it is not established before, together with, or after the appropriator. Given that the appropriating self and appropriated factors, such as sight, do not exist simultaneously or in succession, what intelligent person would then think that they are established by nature?

Given the above, someone may then ask whether or not we hold the appropriator and appropriated to be nonexistent. Well, as has been taught:

> Here the intent is to negate existence,
> Not to prove nonexistence.[133]

Hence, this has simply been a refutation of the imputations made by others that these things exist by nature. What intelligent person would take this as grounds for believing in the negative formula, "In reality, these have no nature"? When the nature of something is as unobservable as the child of a barren woman, all thoughts of its existence or nonexistence will come to an end.

SUMMARY OF THE CHAPTER'S SIGNIFICANCE

Third, to summarize, the present chapter has explicitly shown that the self and the aggregates are, in reality, free from all mental constructs of existence and nonexistence. It has likewise explained explicitly how, in terms of the relative, they are illusion-like and established in mutual dependence. Hence, the implicit message is that all dependently originated phenomena transcend the extremes of existence and nonexistence in reality and that relatively they are illusion-like. This is also the intent of the *Noble Jewel Mound*, which states:

> "Kāśyapa, "existence" is one extreme and "nonexistence" another. The middle that lies between these two cannot be

---

133. From the *Investigation of the World (Lokaparikṣa)*, a lost text attributed to Nāgārjuna by Bhāvaviveka.

shown or cognized. It does not appear and does not remain. Kāśyapa, on the path of the Middle Way, this is referred to as "discernment."

This concludes the explanation of the ninth chapter, the analysis of prior existence, from the *Ornament of Reason*, a commentary on the *Root of the Middle Way*.

CHAPTER TEN

Analysis of Fire and Fuel

THE ANALYSIS of fire and fuel will be treated in three sections, the first of which addresses the chapter's context.[134]

THE CONTEXT OF CHAPTER 10

First, as for the chapter's context, the analysis of fire and fuel is connected to the profound sūtras, such as the following passage from the *King of Meditative Absorptions*:

> Although ablaze for many hundreds of eons,
> Until now, space has never been burned.
> Once it has been understood that phenomena are equal to space,
> Fire may arise, yet nothing will be burned by it.
>
> If the realms of the Buddhas are ablaze
> And someone prays, "May these fires be pacified,"
> While abiding within meditative absorption,
> The ground may collapse, and yet there will be no change.

The present chapter employs reasoning to ascertain the intent of such teachings.

As for its relation to the other chapters in the text, the present discussion offers a reply to the following objection: "The appropriated aggregates and the appropriating self are mutually dependent, but that does not conflict

---

134. In this chapter the summary appears to be contained in the section on "Extending the Reasoning to Other Topics."

with their natural existence, just as fire and fuel are mutually dependent, but still exist by nature as the object and agent in burning."

Thus, here it will be shown that fire and fuel are not naturally established.

THE CONTENT OF CHAPTER 10

Second, the content of chapter 10 (1) refutes the notion that fire and fuel are established by nature, (2) extends this reasoning to other topics, and (3) offers a concluding rebuke of views.

ARE FIRE AND FUEL ESTABLISHED BY NATURE?

The first issue involves (1) refuting the essences of fire and fuel by examining whether they are the same or different, (2) refuting the arguments that are advanced to support these views, and (3) providing a summary of the meaning of these refutations.

Are Fire and Fuel the Same or Different?

If fire and fuel exist by nature, are they identical or different from each other?

Fire and Fuel Are Not the Same

Refuting the first option, the treatise states:

> *If fuel were the same as fire,*
> *Then agent and object would be the same. [X.1a–b]*

If the fuel that is burned were the same as the fire that burns it, all agents and objects would, by the same token, be identical as well. This, however, cannot be accepted because it is impossible for something to act on itself. If this were the case, it would follow that the potter and his pots, or the woodcutter and his wood, could be essentially the same.

Fire and Fuel Are Not Different

The second option, that fire and fuel are different, will be refuted by pointing out how, as a consequence, (1) fire would be independent of fuel and (2) there would be no contact between the two.

Fire Is Not Independent of Fuel

The first issue involves showing that (1) fire would be observable indepen-dent of fuel, (2) fire would be causeless, and so forth, and (3) that neither of these two consequences can be questioned.

Fire Would Be Observable Independent of Fuel

On the first issue, the treatise states:

> *If fire were different from fuel,*
> *Then it would burn even without it. [X.1c–d]*

If fire were essentially different than fuel, it would occur independent of it. This entailment is valid because when the essential difference of two things, such as a vase and woolen garment, is established, there is no rea-son for them to depend on each other. This has already been decisively explained.

The consequence of fire being independent of fuel is unacceptable because the observation of fire that is independent of fuel would be the observation of a burner where nothing is burnt. Because this is not the case, fire depends on fuel, and because of this dependence, fire cannot be established as something other than fuel.

Fire Would Be Causeless, and so Forth

On the second issue, the treatise states:

> *Fire would burn forever,*
> *It would not arise from what causes it to burn,*
> *Trying to light it would be pointless,*
> *And it would not relate to any object. [X.2]*

> *Because it would not depend on anything else,*
> *It would not arise from what causes it to burn.*
> *Because it would burn eternally,*
> *Lighting it would be pointless. [X.3]*

Furthermore, if fire were something other than fuel, it would not arise from what causes it to burn, that is, fuel. Moreover, it will not be possible to object to this by stating that this is not entailed because if fire is something other than fuel, then it will be as independent of fuel as a pot is of a blanket. Hence, if fire is not dependent on fuel, it follows that its burning cannot arise from that fuel, which is what causes it to burn. Alternatively, this can also be read as an elaborate explanation of the consequence [that was stated in the last two lines of the first stanza].

Were one to accept the consequence that fire does not arise from what causes it to burn, it would also follow that fire burns forever. As is taught:

> Since the uncaused does not depend on anything,
> It would be permanently present or absent.[135]

As stated here, if there were a time when fire did not burn, there could never be any burning later on either because a coming together of factors that fire depends on would be precluded. Likewise, if it burns just once, it would go on burning forever because there would, in the same way, never be any lack of the factors necessary for fire.

Moreover, if this consequence is accepted, a third consequence will follow: any activity that uses fuel to start a fire would then be pointless. Given that fire burns forever, it would be impossible to start or maintain a fire by doing certain things to fuel, such as arranging and igniting it.

Accepting this consequence will lead to a fourth: If doing things to fuel for the sake of fire is futile in this way, there may also be fire in the absence of that object to which fire relates, namely, fuel (the word "either" in the fourth verse of the second stanza indicates the relation [between these four consequences]). This consequence is unacceptable because it is contradictory for there to be something that performs an act of burning without anything being burned, just as there can be no fire that burns the body of the child of a barren woman.

Here, one should also understand the implicit presence of the reversals of these four consequences: There is no fire that does not relate to its object, the fuel that it burns. It is, therefore, meaningful to gather fuel if one wishes to start or maintain a fire. Since such activity does serve a purpose, fire is something that emerges from the cause of burning, that is, fuel. Finally, since it does emerge from its causes, fire is not different than fuel.

---

135. Dharmakīrti, *Commentary on Reliable Means of Cognition*, I.35a–b.

Neither of the Consequences Can Be Questioned
Third, showing how neither of these consequences can be questioned, the treatise states:

> *It may be thought that the fuel*
> *Is that which is burning,*
> *But if that is all that it is,*
> *What is it that burns the fuel? [X.4]*

It was argued that if fire were different from fuel, it would be independent of it. This would mean that a) fire could be observed in the absence of fuel and b) fire would not arise from the fuel that causes it to burn. Faced with these two consequences, someone may object in the following way: "Although fire is something other than fuel, that does not mean that it cannot depend on it. Fuel is precisely that which is in the process of being burned by fire, so fuel depends on fire. Fire, in turn, is precisely that which performs the act of burning the fuel, so it is dependent on fuel as well. Hence, fire and fuel are different from one another, as well as mutually dependent. In this way, they are unlike a vase and a blanket, which are distinct but also independent. For these reasons, neither of the above consequences are applicable."

Such a line of thought would make sense if fire could burn fuel, but this is not feasible. Given the subject, fuel, what fire is it that burns it? Indeed, there is no fire that does so. We argue this by pointing out how fuel was identified as simply that which is in the process of burning. This entails that no fire can burn the fuel because it is impossible to observe any fire that performs the act of burning apart from that which is in the process of burning. The fuel can, therefore, not be burnt because it is impossible for something to act upon itself. For these reasons, it does not work to say that fuel is that which fire is in the process of burning, whereas fire is that which is in the process of burning fuel. The position that these two are both dependent and different then becomes untenable, and so the attempt at blocking these consequences has failed.

There Could Be No Contact between Fire and Fuel
If fire and fuel were distinct, but also dependent, they could not meet at any place or time. Since there could not be any contact between them, fuel could not be burned by fire, and, therefore, it could not be that which fire

is in the process of burning. In this way, the *Commentary* considers the following discussion a refutation of the notion that fuel is that which is in the process of burning.

Alternatively, the arguments below can also be understood as a refutation of fire and fuel being different. Having already refuted that fire and fuel are distinct by pointing to the consequence that they then would be independent of each other, the text can be seen to further refute their distinctness by showing that fire could then not come into contact with fuel.

The discussion of this issue is divided into two sections. First, the consequences are presented. The treatise states:

> *If they are distinct, they do not touch;*
> *If they do not touch, nothing is burned;*
> *If nothing is burned, nothing dies out;*
> *If nothing dies out, it will remain with its mark. [X.5]*

Since fire and fuel are different substances, they cannot meet anywhere in space or time, like light and darkness. Since these two do not come into contact, fire cannot burn fuel, just as we know will be the case when fire and fuel are separated in terms of space or time. Since fire can then not burn any fuel, it is independent of burning fuel. Hence, it will not die out if there is no longer any fuel. Finally, if this is the case, then fire will continue to display its unique marks and characteristics even in the absence of fuel. This, however, is untenable because once its fuel has run out, we no longer observe the heat and burning that are the defining characteristics of fire.

This line of consequences also implies four reversals. Fire does go out when its fuel is gone. Therefore, fuel is burnt by fire, and because fuel is burnt by fire, fire comes into contact with fuel. As this is the case, fire is not different than fuel.

These Consequences Cannot Be Questioned

Second, showing how these consequences are unquestionable, the treatise states:

> *Just as a woman touches a man*
> *And a man touches a woman,*

Fire can be different from fuel,
And yet still touch it. [X.6]

If fire and fuel,
Would exclude each other,
Fire would be different from fuel,
And so fire could touch fuel. [X.7]

It may be thought: "Fire and fuel are different things, but just as a man and a woman can touch each other, the two can still come into contact with one another."

When a man and a woman come together, their contact is between two things that are mutually different *and* independent. If fire and fuel were two different and independent things, this type of contact would be possible, but they are not. There is, therefore, no contact between them.

To elaborate, if fire and fuel were mutually exclusive and independent of each other in the same way that a man and a woman are, then there could also be a time when they came together. Fire could then be something other than fuel and yet still touch it. But since fire and fuel are not established as different and independent things like a man and woman, their meeting is altogether impossible.

Refutation of Arguments

Second, the refutation of the [advanced] arguments is divided into two sections, the first of which is a refutation of dependence.

Are Fuel and Fire Mutually Dependent?

It may be thought: "It may be the case that fire and fuel are not both different and independent. Nevertheless, because they are dependent, they exist by nature. Something nonexistent, like the child of a barren woman, could not possibly depend on something else."

From the unexamined perspective of a deluded mind, there does indeed seem to be dependence. Nevertheless, as in the case of a reflection, such mere appearances do not imply any natural establishment. Moreover, upon examination, we will find that dependence itself is not established. This discussion involves (1) showing why neither sequential nor simultaneous fire and fuel can be dependent, (2) showing why neither established nor unestablished fire and fuel can be dependent, and (3) drawing the conclusion.

Why neither Sequential nor Simultaneous Fire and Fuel
Can Be Dependent
First, refuting the dependence between fire and fuel that occurs in sequence, the treatise states:

> *If fire depends on fuel*
> *And fuel depends on fire,*
> *Of fire and fuel, the two dependents,*
> *Which is established first? [X.8]*

> *If fire depended on fuel,*
> *An established fire would be reestablished,*
> *And fuel would end up*
> *Existing without fire. [X.9]*

We may state that "fire is that which burns fuel," positing fire in dependence on fuel. Having done that, we may in turn present fuel in dependence on fire by saying, "Fuel is that which fire burns." Since fuel, then, is responsible for the establishment of fire, it follows that it will itself have to be established before fire. Yet what fuel could exist prior to fire? If it is not in the process of being consumed by fire, then it is not fuel.

If, alternatively, fuel is established in dependence on fire, then it follows that fire is established first. Yet what kind of fire would that be? Such a fire would have no cause. Therefore, neither fire nor fuel can be established before the other, and this means that neither of them can be established in dependence on the other.

Moreover, if fire depended on fuel, an already established fire would have to be reestablished. This entailment is valid since it does not make sense for fire to depend on something if it is not established, as is the case with the child of a barren woman. This position, moreover, is also unacceptable because fire that is already established does not need to be established by fuel. Hence, since it is already there, its reestablishment by fuel would be pointless.

The position that fire depends on fuel and that an unestablished fire then becomes established is also untenable. The unestablished cannot be established. All of these points are implicit in the first two lines of the ninth stanza.

Also, if fire were established in dependence on fuel, fuel would end up existing without fire. That this is entailed can be seen from the fact that if no fuel is established, fire clearly cannot depend on it, and if fire is established, then it does not need to depend on anything.

Showing why dependence between simultaneous fire and fuel is untenable, the treatise states:

> If an entity is established in dependence,
> And is itself depended on
> By that upon which it depends,
> What is established in dependence on what? [X.10]

It may be thought: "Fire and fuel are not established sequentially. Rather, they are strictly simultaneous and are established in mutual dependence as such. The aforementioned flaw, therefore, does not apply."

This, however, is not acceptable. If the entity of fire is established in dependence on fuel, and if that fuel upon which fire depends in turn depends on fire for its own establishment, then what fire is it that depends, and on what fuel? If fire is established, it does not need to depend on fuel. Alternatively, if fire is not established, it cannot become so by depending on fuel because the fuel itself requires [the establishment of] fire [as a condition for its own establishment].

Likewise, if the entity of fuel is established in dependence on fire, and if the fire that is depended on itself depends on fuel, then what fuel is it that depends, and on what fire? An established fuel does not need to depend on anything else, and if fuel is not established, it cannot be established in dependence on fire because the latter itself requires fuel for its own establishment.

Why neither Established nor Unestablished Fire and Fuel Can Be Dependent
On the second issue, the treatise states:

> How could an entity that is established in dependence
> Depend on something when it is not established?

If it is said that it depends while established,
Its dependence does not make any sense. [X.11]

If is held that the entity of fire is established in dependence on fuel, we may ask whether that which depends on fuel is established or not. If it is not established, how could it depend on anything? Similarly, the horn of a rabbit cannot depend on anything either. Any form of dependence must always involve two things, that which is dependent and that which is depended upon. Unless there is something that depends, it does not make sense to speak of something being depended on.

On the other hand, to claim that an established fire depends on fuel is also untenable, precisely because the fire is already established. This entailment is valid because if something is already established, it follows that it cannot depend on anything because that which is already established cannot be influenced by anything at all.

The same problems ensue if we consider whether an established or unestablished fuel depends on fire.

Drawing the Conclusion
Third, drawing the conclusion, the treatise states:

> *There is no fire that depends on fuel,*
> *There is no fire that does not depend on fuel.*
> *There is no fuel that depends on fire,*
> *There is no fuel that does not depend on fire. [X.12]*

Upon examination, it will be seen that dependence itself is untenable. There is, therefore, no fire that depends on fuel. Is fire then independent of fuel? No, for even in terms of the unexamined conventional perspective there is no fire that does not depend on fuel. Such fire would lack any cause. Likewise, once we investigate, we will find no fuel that depends on fire. Meanwhile, because fuel is precisely that which is burned by fire, there is no fuel that is independent of fire either, even in terms of the unexamined conventional perspective.

Fire and Fuel Cannot Be Established by Perception
Second, refuting the use of perception as proof, the treatise states:

Fire does not come from anything else,
Nor is there any fire in the fuel.
The rest about fuel has been explained
By what was, will be, and is being traversed. [X.13]

It may be thought: "Why should we ponder whether fire and fuel are essentially the same or different? We can directly perceive that fire burns fuel, so these things do exist by nature."

However, this observation is not made by perception that is free from delusion because once we examine, we find that fire is not fit to burn fuel. If fire burns fuel, does it do so having come from something other than the fuel? Or was it already present in the fuel before it began to burn? The first cannot be the case because we cannot observe any fire that emerges from anything other than fuel. Moreover, since there is no fire in the absence of its cause, namely, fuel, fire is not something that somehow comes to fuel. As fire always accompanies fuel, it does not need to be added to fuel, for this would serve no purpose.

The alternative is not acceptable either. Fire is not present in fuel before it starts burning because we do not observe any such presence.

It might then be thought, "Fire is indeed present in fuel from the beginning, but it takes certain conditions, such as a match, to manifest."

This notion is not acceptable either. If the fire's own essence is already established, it need not be made [manifest by conditions], and if it *is* made manifest, this shows that it did not exist earlier. The position that the result is present in the cause is, therefore, indefensible.

The remaining arguments that disprove fire's burning fuel were explained earlier, when it was shown that going cannot be present where it has already taken place, where it has yet to occur, or where it is currently taking place. Thus, it is now easy to alter the previous verse, so that it states, "Where burning has been there is none . . .," and so on.

As we have now seen, there is no such thing as fire that burns fuel. Any perception to the contrary will, hence, be as false as that of fire burning fuel in a dream. In this way, the *Commentary* treats the present stanza as a refutation of the use of perception to prove that fire and fuel are established by nature.

Some hold that the first half of the stanza is a refutation of fire's being based on fuel, and that the latter half is a refutation of the activity of burning fuel.

A Summary of the Meaning of the Refutations

Third, offering a summary, the treatise states:

> *Fuel is not the same as fire,*
> *Nor is there fire apart from fuel.*
> *Fire does not possess fuel.*
> *Fuel is not in fire, nor is fire in fuel. [X.14]*

The preceding reasoning has shown that while fuel is not the same as fire, there is no fire apart from fuel either. This same reasoning also makes it clear that fire cannot possess fuel, regardless of whether such a possession is thought of in terms of fire and fuel being identical or distinct from one another. Moreover, when one thing is supported by another, it follows that the two are distinct. We may, therefore, also conclude that fire does not support fuel, just a fuel does not support fire. Therefore, since fire and fuel are not established in any of these five ways, it has been established that they have no nature.

EXTENDING THE REASONING TO OTHER TOPICS

Second, extending this analysis to other topics, the treatise states:

> *Through the treatment of fire and fuel,*
> *The self and its appropriation,*
> *Along with vases, woolen garments, and so forth,*
> *Have all been explained without exception. [X.15]*

Once we examine fire and fuel with respect to the five positions that are referred to in the fourteenth stanza, we end up not finding anything. The same fivefold analysis can be applied in precisely the same way to the self and what it appropriates, such as the aggregates. We will then notice that the self cannot be identical with the aggregates since this would make object and agent one. Neither can the self be different from the aggregates. If it were, it would have to be observable as such. Moreover, since it would be independent of the causal aggregates, there would be no reason to conceive of any self based on them.

Having refuted the notions that the self and the aggregates are the same or different in this way, we have also excluded the possibilities of the self's possessing the aggregates (either by being identical to or different from them), the self's being the support of the aggregates, and the self's being supported by the aggregates. Yet the fivefold treatment of fire and fuel is applicable not only to the self and the aggregates. It can just as well be applied to vases, garments, and all other such things, for it applies to, and explains, everything that is contained within parts and wholes, causes and effects, or characteristics and the bearers of characteristics.

Therefore, our insight that fire and fuel cannot be established in terms of any of the five positions referred to in the fourteenth stanza is applicable to all dependently originated phenomena. Independent phenomena are, moreover, impossible. Hence, in these five steps, we may examine the relationship between any dependent phenomenon and the things upon which it depends. In the process, the conceptually constructed reality of all dependently originated phenomena will be existentially negated. Likewise, such an examination will, in terms of the relative, also affirm that while these phenomena cannot be said to be either the same or different from each other, they resemble an illusion. This very message is taught in the following passage from a sūtra:

> When the drilling stick, its support,
> And the manual efforts all coincide,
> Fire will occur due to these conditions.
> Having arisen, fire functions and quickly ceases.
>
> "Where did it come from?" or "Where did it go to?"
> What wise person would make such enquiries?
> We may search in all the cardinal and intermediate directions,
> Yet never will we succeed in finding its going or coming.
>
> The aggregates, elements, and sense sources
> Are all empty, without and within.
> All are devoid of self and without support;
> Their reality and characteristics are of the nature of space.[136]

136. From the *Sūtra of the Great Display*.

A Rebuke of Views

Third, in a concluding rebuke of views, the treatise states:

> *Those who teach that self and entities*
> *Are the same or different*
> *I do not consider knowledgeable*
> *About the meaning of the teachings. [X.16]*

While the meaning of dependent origination is established in this manner, some members of our own tradition lack understanding of this most profound principle. In their ignorance, they teach that mutually dependent phenomena—such as the appropriating self and the appropriated aggregates, causes and their effects, wholes and parts, and characteristics and their bearers— are either essentially indistinguishable or essentially distinct. Concerning such individuals, the Master states, "I, Nāgārjuna, do not consider such people knowledgeable about the meaning of the Able One's most profound teaching of dependent origination. The dependent origination that the Buddha teaches cannot be described in terms of identity or difference; it lies beyond both permanence and annihilation." In one of his praises, the Master thus proclaims:

> Wandering beings are like an echo,
> Beyond all sameness and difference,
> They are free from transmigration and destruction.
> This is what you, the irreproachable, comprehended in full.[137]

This concludes the explanation of the tenth chapter, the analysis of fire and fuel, in the *Ornament of Reason*, a commentary on the *Root of the Middle Way*.

---

137. Wording almost identical to Nāgārjuna, *Praise to the Incomparable*, 13.

CHAPTER ELEVEN

Analysis of Beginnings and Ends

THE THREE ISSUES also pertain to the analysis of beginnings and ends.[138] First is the chapter's context.

THE CONTEXT OF CHAPTER 11

First, regarding the chapter's context, the present discussion relates to teachings of the profound sūtras, such as the following passage from the *Noble Jewel Cloud Sūtra*:

> When turning the wheel of Dharma,
> You, Protector, revealed the qualities
> Of the natural transcendence of suffering,
> Primordial peace beyond arising.

The current chapter employs reasoning to ascertain the meaning of such passages, which state that cyclic existence has no nature.

As for its relationship to the other chapters of the text, the present analysis constitutes a reply to the following idea: "The essence of the personal self and its metaphor, fire and fuel, may have been refuted, yet a sūtra teaches:

> Monks, this cycle of birth, aging, and death has no beginning
> and it has no end.

---

138. In this chapter there is no separate, final summary. Instead, the summary appears to be included in the explanation of stanza XI.6.

Thus, since this passage teaches the existence of cyclic existence, we may also infer the existence of the self that cycles through these phases."

As a reply to this view, the present chapter will show that since cyclic existence, when examined, can be seen to be not established, the self that is supposed to cycle through it cannot be established either.

THE CONTENT OF CHAPTER 11

Second, the explanation of the content involves (1) refuting the natural existence of cyclic existence and (2) applying this refutation to other topics.

Is Cyclic Existence Naturally Existent?

The first section includes demonstrations that (1) cyclic existence has no beginning, end, and middle and that (2) birth, on the one hand, and aging and death, on the other, can be neither sequential nor simultaneous.

Cyclic Existence Has No Beginning, End, or Middle
On the first issue, the treatise states:

> *When asked whether any beginning can be seen,*
> *The Able One answered in the negative.*
> *Cyclic existence has no beginning or end;*
> *There is no before and there is no after. [XI.1]*

> *When something has neither beginning nor end,*
> *How could it possibly have a middle? [XI.2a–b]*

If cyclic existence existed by nature, it would need to have a beginning, middle, and end, just like a vase. Yet since cyclic existence does not have a beginning, middle, or end, as is the case with space, it has no natural existence. That is the implicit message of the preceding stanza.

As for the property of this position, it is indeed possible to use reasoning that is accepted by others to prove that cyclic existence has neither of these three. However, first the position will be established for members of our own tradition by means of the Able One's scriptural authority. Hence, when asked whether any beginning of cyclic existence can be seen, the Great Able One, the Buddha, the Transcendent Conqueror, replied in the negative with the following words:

> Those who are obscured by ignorance and bound by craving race around in a circle, bound by the infinite chain of craving. No beginning to this process can be seen.

Likewise, he also said:

> Monks, this cycle of birth, aging, and death has no beginning and no end.

Thus, cyclic existence has no beginning and no end. In other words, there is no before and no after in cyclic existence.

It might be thought that since it has not been refuted, the middle of cyclic existence must still have natural existence. Yet when cyclic existence does not have any beginning or end, as was just explained, how could it possibly have a middle? When those two are not there to begin with, there cannot be anything that lies between them.

Refutation of Sequence and Simultaneity

The second topic is divided into three sections: (1) presentation, (2) explanation, and (3) conclusion.

Presentation

On the first issue, the treatise states:

> *Therefore, cyclic existence cannot*
> *Be either sequential or simultaneous. [XI.2c–d]*

Cyclic existence does not have beginning, end, or middle. Therefore, birth, aging, and death, which constitute the nature of cyclic existence, cannot reasonably occur in sequence or simultaneously. This, in turn, means that cyclic existence has no natural existence.

Explanation

On the second issue, the treatise states:

If birth came first
And aging and death followed later,
There would be birth without aging and death,
As well as birth without anyone having died. [XI.3]

If birth occurred later,
And aging and death before,
How could this causeless aging and death
Happen to someone who was never born? [XI.4]

Birth, aging, and death
Cannot occur simultaneously,
For the one being born would then be dying,
And both would be lacking their cause. [XI.5]

To refute the sequential occurrence of birth, aging, and death, let us first consider the notion of a birth that occurs before aging and death. Thus, the target here is the idea that birth is prior to an aging and death that may be either identical with, or distinct from, the entity of birth. Thus, given the subject, birth, it follows that it can occur without there being any aging and death. Moreover, if birth preceded aging and death, the one who is born would not be someone who has died. These propositions, however, are untenable because they imply that birth is, respectively, permanent and causeless—two qualities that are incompatible with being an entity.

Next is a refutation of the notion that aging and death precede birth. If birth occurred later, preceded by aging and death, then how could aging and death be happening to someone who never was born? Indeed, like a sky flower, aging and death would have no cause.

Finally, it is refuted that birth occurs simultaneously with aging and death. It is impossible for birth to occur at the same time as aging and death in the same time in one thing. As a consequence, if these events occurred simultaneously, the one who is being born would also be dying, and it is impossible to have the two incompatible activities of manifesting and disintegrating occur at the same time in the same thing. Furthermore, if they were simultaneous, birth would be independent of aging and dying, which again would mean that both of these events would be lacking their cause.

Conclusion

Third, in conclusion, the treatise states:

> *As it is impossible for them to occur*
> *In sequence or simultaneously,*
> *Why would anyone think*
> *In terms of birth, aging, and death? [XI.6]*

For the reasons explained above, birth cannot occur sequentially in relation to aging and death, yet neither can the two be simultaneous. Hence, they cannot be observed at all. Why would anyone, then, whether a noble or a childish individual, ever think or speak in terms of there really being, or there really not being, any such things as birth, aging, and death? Indeed, they would not. If they did, they would not make sense.

EXTENDING THIS ANALYSIS TO OTHER TOPICS

Third, extending this insight to other topics, the treatise states:

> *Not only does cyclic existence*
> *Have no beginning,*
> *But also cause and effect,*
> *Characteristics and their bearers, [XI.7]*

> *Feelings and those that feel—*
> *Whatever there may be.*
> *The same applies to all things;*
> *None have a beginning. [XI.8]*

We have examined the birth and the aging and death that pervade cyclic existence and found that they have no beginning and do not coincide. But this is the case not only with this pair. When we examine cause and effect, characteristics and their bearers, feelings and those that feel, cognition and its object of cognition, and so on—whatever there may be—we will find precisely the same. Indeed, all mutually dependent things do not have a beginning (as would be the case if one were established before the other), and yet they do not coexist.

This shows us that, in terms of the ultimate, all dependently established phenomena are emptiness, whereas relatively it is established that they are like an illusion. If cause preceded effect, the basis for designating the cause as such would be missing. If, on the other hand, effects were present before their causes, the essence of the effect would be uncaused. And if cause and effect were simultaneous, they would both be causeless. This [insight] can be applied to all [dependent phenomena]. In the *Sūtra of the King of Meditative Absorptions*, it is taught:

> Phenomena are primordially empty, they have not arrived.
> Not departing or remaining, they know no abiding.
> Their nature is that of illusion, never is there any core.
> Everything is pure, utterly pure, like space.
>
> No end of cyclic existence can be found
> And the beginnings of time are devoid of characteristics.

This concludes the explanation of the eleventh chapter, the analysis of beginnings and ends, in the *Ornament of Reason*, a commentary on the *Root of the Middle Way*.

CHAPTER TWELVE

Analysis of Suffering

THE THREE ISSUES also pertain to the analysis of suffering. First, regarding its context, this chapter relates to the profound sūtras, such as a statement from the *Mother of the Victorious Ones* that proclaims, "There is no suffering!" and the following passage from the *Noble Sūtra on the Ten Grounds*:

> Children of the Victorious Ones, when it is understood that the painful conditioning, with its myriad of problems, is devoid of any essence and has neither arising nor cessation . . .

It is the meaning of such statements that will here be proven through reasoning.

As for its place among the other chapters of the text, the present chapter presents a reply to the following objection: "The personal self may have been refuted. However, in the sūtras it is taught, 'Birth is painful. Sickness, aging, and death are painful.' Likewise, there is mention of 'the aggregates involved in the appropriation of suffering.' Thus, the sūtras teach the existence of the defiling aggregates, the constituents of suffering in its three aspects. Given the existence of suffering, it follows that the person exists as well, for the person is the support of suffering."

Hence, the present analysis will show that, since suffering itself does not arise in any of the four ways, there is no personal self that could serve as the support of suffering.

THE CONTENT OF CHAPTER 12

Second, the explanation of the content of chapter 12 involves (1) stating the assertions of the logicians, (2) refuting these assertions, and (3) extending this analysis to other topics.

The Assertion of the Logicians

On the first issue, the treatise states:

> *Some say that suffering is produced by itself,*
> *By something other, by both,*
> *Or that it arises without a cause. [XII.1a–c]*

If suffering exists by nature, it must arise in one of the four extreme ways. Thus, some of the Enumerators claim that suffering is self-produced, while certain members of our own tradition assert that suffering is produced by something that is other. Those who believe in a primary principle that involves an almighty God hold suffering to be created partly by itself and partly by something else. Finally, the Far Throwers and the Ritualists respectively teach that there are no imperceptible causes of suffering and that suffering has neither imperceptible nor perceptible causes.

Refutation of the Assertions

Second, to refute these assertions, a concise thesis is formed in the following line:

> *Such production is not possible. [XII.1d]*

Suffering cannot feasibly arise, or be produced, in any of the four extreme ways proposed here.

The Reasoning That Refutes the Arising of Suffering

The explanation of the refuting reasoning will cover (1) a refutation of suffering as arising either due to self or other, (2) a refutation of the notion that suffering is created by both self and other, and (3) a refutation of the idea that suffering has no cause.

Suffering Does Not Arise Due to Self or Other

The first includes (1) a refutation of production by self and other with reference to suffering, (2) a refutation of production by self and other with reference to the person, and (3) a refutation of production by something other for the reason that nothing is produced by itself.

Production By Self and Other with Reference to Suffering
The first section is divided into two discussions. We begin by looking at suffering so as to refute that it produces itself. The treatise states:

> *If suffering were produced by itself,*
> *It could not arise in dependence,*
> *Because, based on these aggregates,*
> *Those aggregates arise. [XII.2]*

If these appropriated aggregates of suffering were produced by themselves, they could not arise in dependence on other causes and conditions. This is entailed because if the aggregates are already established, their arising due to causes and conditions would be meaningless. On the other hand, if they are not established, it would follow that there is nothing that can produce them. Yet we perceive that the subsequent aggregates associated with the quality of arising come about based on the earlier aggregates associated with the quality of ceasing. Therefore, it is impossible to accept that suffering arises independently of causes and conditions.

Second, the treatise considers the process of appropriation so as to refute the notion that suffering is produced by something other than itself:

> *If those were something other than these,*
> *And these were something other than those,*
> *Suffering would be produced by something other,*
> *And they would produce something other. [XII.3]*

If the resultant aggregates associated with the quality of arising were substantially different from the causal aggregates associated with the quality of cessation, then the product, suffering, would be produced by something other than itself. Likewise, if the causal aggregates associated with the quality of cessation were substantially different from the resultant aggregates associated with the quality of arising, then the suffering that the causal aggregates produce would be something other than themselves. Yet cause and effect cannot be substantially different because they are not simultaneously present. Also, if two things are established as substantially different, it would be meaningless for one to depend on the other. Hence, these two things could not be cause and effect. Therefore, even if we allow that the causal aggregates associated with cessation produce the resultant aggregates associated with arising, it could still not be the case that the productive cause is different from its effect and that the produced effect is different from its cause. The aggregates of suffering are, therefore, not produced by something other than themselves.

Production by Self and Other with Reference to the Person
The refutation of production by self and other with reference to the person has two parts. First is a refutation of the idea that suffering is produced by a person who is identical with it. The treatise states:

> *If the person itself*
> *Produces suffering,*
> *Then what, apart from suffering,*
> *Is this person who produces suffering? [XII.4]*

It may be thought: "Suffering is not passed from one person to another. Rather, that very person who is designated as such due to the presence of suffering produces the suffering himself or herself. Thus, suffering is self-produced."

This position in unacceptable as well. It may be thought that persons produce their own suffering and that this is the reason for them being designated as persons, but consider the human person who would then be held to be the producer of human suffering. What is that human person, apart from human suffering? Indeed, we will not observe any distinction between that suffering and the person associated with it, and it is impossible for something to act on itself. Therefore, that suffering is not produced by the person.

It may then be thought that the suffering experienced by a god has been created by the person of its previous life as a human, for example. Thus, according to this position, object and agent are distinct. Yet given such a scenario, why would suffering not be produced by a different person? It cannot be argued that while the sufferings of the god and the human in consecutive lifetimes are distinct, the appropriating person is not because it is impossible to show any person that is essentially different than his or her suffering.

The second refutation concerns suffering being produced by a different person. It may be thought: "The human of a past life and the god of a future life are indeed not the same. They are substantially different.

Hence, the human person of the past life accumulates the formations that will produce the suffering of the future god. Having done so, he passes it on to the divine person and this serves as the grounds for designating that person. Thus, suffering is created by a different person."

The refutation of this idea contains two parts, the first of which is concerned with the absence of an appropriator. The treatise states:

> *If suffering comes from a different person,*
> *Then how, when produced by another person,*
> *Could it be given to somebody*
> *Who is something other than suffering? [XII.5]*

It may be believed that the suffering of the god in a future life is produced by a different human person in a previous life. If this is the case, how could the god's suffering, once it has been produced by this other person, be passed on to a divine person who is something other than suffering? We cannot observe any appropriator of suffering apart from the suffering itself. Therefore, suffering does not come from a different person.

Second, considering the absence of a donor, the treatise states:

> *If suffering occurs because of another person,*
> *Then who is this producer,*
> *This other who gives suffering to another,*
> *Yet who is not that very suffering? [XII.6]*

If the suffering of the future god is held to be produced by a different human person, we may ask who this producer is. Who, apart from human suffering, is this other human person who gives suffering to a different divine person? As we cannot observe any human person who is different from human suffering, suffering is not produced by a different person.

Since Suffering Is Not Produced by a Self, It Is Not Produced by Anything Other

Next we will refute the notion that suffering is produced by anything other because it is not self-produced. There are two parts to this, of which the first is a refutation where self and other are understood in terms of the person. The treatise states:

As it cannot be established to be produced by a self,
How could suffering be the product of another?
The suffering produced by the other
Is the product of that other itself. [XII.7]

How could suffering possibly be the product of an "other"? Consider the human being that is substantially identical with [human suffering]. How could it possibly produce the nature of suffering that is associated with someone else, [such as] a god? Indeed, it could not, for since there is no human being that exists as something other than suffering, we cannot establish human suffering as the product of the human person itself. The entailment here is as follows: If one person produces the suffering associated with another individual, the suffering associated with the first person would have to be produced by that person himself or herself. If instead that suffering further depends on yet another person, it turns out to be an illusion-like construction. It is taught:

When the seed of something is false,
How could its arising be true?[139]

Thus, a different person is incapable of producing the nature of suffering. The situation is just as described here:

The vase is established by causes,
And those causes are themselves established by other causes.
How could that which does not establish itself
Succeed in establishing something else?[140]

The second part of the refutation of the notion that suffering is produced by another because suffering is not self-produced considers self and other in terms of the appropriated. The treatise states:

Suffering is not self-produced;
It is not its own product.

139. Nāgārjuna, *Jewel Garland*, I.29.
140. Āryadeva, *Four Hundred Stanzas*, XIV.13.

If the other is not the product of itself,
How could suffering be produced by another? [XII.8]

The human aggregates of suffering that are [held to be] the producer of a suffering that is different from them are not produced by themselves, for it is contradictory for something to relate to itself as an object. Given that they thus are not the products of themselves, we may once more ask how suffering could be produced by something that is other. Consider that which is substantially identical with human suffering. How could that possibly produce the nature of another suffering associated with a god? It could not because the former suffering is not produced by itself. The entailment here can be understood from the one given in the previous section.

Suffering Is Not Produced by Both Self and Other

Having thus refuted the notions that suffering is self-produced or produced by another, it will now be shown how it cannot be produced by both self and other. The treatise states:

If suffering were produced by each of these,
Then suffering would be the product of both. [XII.9a–b]

If suffering were produced by self and other individually, that suffering would be produced by both. Yet it has already been shown that neither self nor other can produce suffering. Therefore, combining these two will not deliver the producer of suffering either, just as it is impossible to extract sesame oil from sand, no matter how much sand you gather.

Suffering Is Not Uncaused

Third, refuting the belief that suffering is uncaused, the treatise states:

Neither produced by self nor other,
How could suffering be uncaused? [XII.9c–d]

Suffering is not produced by self, other, or by both of these combined. How, then, could suffering be uncaused, like the sky flower? If something has no causes, it follows that it cannot appear as an object apprehended by the mind, and it cannot be present only at certain times.

If suffering exists by nature, its arising cannot be conceived of in any other way than these four extremes. Therefore, since it follows that suffering must arise in one of these ways, and because it has now been shown that it does not arise in any of these four ways, it has been established that suffering has no nature. By extension, we can also conclude that there is no person who functions as the support for suffering.

Extending the Reasoning to Other Topics

Extending this analysis to other topics, the treatise states:

> *Not only does suffering*
> *Not exist in any of these four ways,*
> *External entities as well*
> *Do not exist in any of the four ways. [XII.10]*

The suffering that consists of the internal aggregates imbued with consciousness does not exist in any of these four ways. In the same manner, vases and every other external entity do not arise in any of the four ways outlined above either. The preceding discussion applies to all things.

SUMMARY OF THE CHAPTER'S SIGNIFICANCE

Third, as for the summary, the present chapter has existentially negated the mental construction of real arising in relation to all phenomena. Likewise, it has affirmed that the appearance of dependent arising is relative and illusion-like. As the Master himself taught:

> That suffering is created by itself,
> By something other, by both, or that it is uncaused—
> This is what logicians assert.
> You speak of dependent origination.[141]

Similarly, the *King of Meditative Absorptions* explains:

---

141. Nāgārjuna, *Praise to the Supramundane*, 21.

In terms of the relative, the Victorious One teaches the Dharma,
Speaking of the conditioned and the unconditioned in dependence.
In reality, there is no self and no human being.
The characteristics of all wandering beings are like this.

This concludes the twelfth chapter, the analysis of suffering, in the *Ornament of Reason*, a commentary on the *Root of the Middle Way*.

CHAPTER THIRTEEN

Analysis of the Conditioned

ABOVE IT WAS EXPLAINED how dependent origination is devoid of any self in the form of a person. Next it will be shown how dependent origination is empty of the nature of mere things, undifferentiated in terms of phenomena and persons. First is the analysis of the conditioned, which refutes the belief that things have a nature. The three issues pertain to this analysis as well.[142]

THE CONTEXT OF CHAPTER 13

First, concerning the context of chapter thirteen, the present analysis relates to the profound sūtras, such as the following statement from the *King of Meditative Absorptions*:

> In rocky caves, mountains, ravines, and gorges,
> Conditions come together and an echo occurs.
> Understand all conditioned things to be like this.
> Wandering beings are like an illusion, like a mirage.

Similarly:

> Monks, the sacred truth is one; it is the subject that does not deceive, the transcendence of suffering. All conditioned things are deceptive and false subjects.

---

142. In this chapter the concluding summary is not explicit as a separate section of the text.

This chapter employs reasoning to ascertain the meaning of such statements.

As for its relation to the other chapters in the text, the analysis of the conditioned is a follow-up to the analysis of suffering, in which it was refuted that outer and inner phenomena may arise in the manner of one of the four extremes. Thus, while it was established that all phenomena do not arise in reality, arising and other such things appear to those whose perception is distorted by ignorance. It is, therefore, established that conditioned things are deceptive phenomena. Scripture as well teaches that such phenomena are necessarily false. The present chapter was written to demonstrate that very falsity.

THE CONTENT OF CHAPTER 13

Second, the explanation of the content involves (1) using scripture to establish that there is no nature and (2) refuting a different exegesis.

SCRIPTURE TEACHES THE ABSENCE OF NATURE

On the first issue, the treatise states:

> *The Transcendent Conqueror has taught*
> *That all deceptive phenomena are false.*
> *All conditioned phenomena are deceptive,*
> *And, therefore, they are false. [XIII.1]*

> *If a phenomenon that is deceptive is also false,*
> *Then what is it that deceives?*
> *With this, the Transcendent Conqueror*
> *Has fully revealed emptiness. [XIII.2]*

In a sūtra, the Transcendent Conqueror states:

> Monks, any subject that is deceptive and conditioned is also a false.

And elsewhere:

> Likewise, here there is no suchness, no unmistaken suchness.
> Rather, these subjects are deceptive. Illusory and false, these
> subjects fool the immature.

With these words, he teaches that a deceptive phenomenon is also necessarily a false phenomenon.

When we examine all conditioned outer and inner phenomena with the reasonings presented above, true arising and true entities will be invalidated. Still, to those whose vision is distorted by ignorance, these phenomena nevertheless mistakenly appear to be arising and existent things. Hence, it is established that these phenomena are deceptive subjects and that all external and internal conditioned things are, therefore, just as false and essenceless as a person in an illusion.

Secondly, the scriptures do not teach nothingness. Someone might object to the above reading, saying that this is a nihilistic view that denies the existence of all conditioned things. Yet this is not the case. If any subject that is conditioned and deceptive is also false and devoid of nature, then what could be deceptive? What could become nothing or annihilated, given that no object of negation or annihilation can be observed? Hence, it is explained:

> If entity is not established,
> Then neither is nonentity.[143]

And likewise:

> As for that which by nature has no arising,
> How could it possibly last or end?[144]

One may then wonder: "Well, if it is not nothingness, what do these passages teach?"

The Transcendent Conqueror states that all conditioned, deceptive phenomena are also false phenomena. Thereby, he fully reveals that natural

---

143. *Root of the Middle Way*, XV.5a–b.
144. Jñānagarbha, *Commentary on Discerning the Two Truths*, interconnecting verses appearing between stanzas 36 and 37.

emptiness in which all constructed marks, such as negation and affirmation, are entirely absent. On this point, it is taught:

> Recognize that all things
> Are empty of their very essence.
> "Empty" also is empty.
> Thus, there is nothing that is not empty.

And similarly:

> The Dharma has no syllables and yet is taught using syllables.

Refutation of a Different Exegesis

Second, it will be shown that impermanence is not the intent of these scriptural statements.

The View of the Opposition

Presenting the view of the opposition, the treatise states:

> *Things are devoid of essence*
> *Because they are perceived to change.*
> *There are no entities without essence*
> *Because entities possess emptiness.* [XIII.3]
>
> *If there is no essence,*
> *To what does change pertain?* [XIII.4a–b]

Some members of our own tradition do not understand the intent of these teachings to be an existential negation of nature. Instead, they perceive a predicative negation of nature. They explain that, while these passages do negate the permanent entities that are imputed by non-Buddhist schools and childish individuals, they also affirm the presence of mere phenomena that are conditioned and impermanent, in the sense that their substance is momentary and their continua come to an end. This affirmation is implied, they argue, because the presence of such mere phenomena is supported by reasoning.

Contrary to what is imagined by the non-Buddhists, no conditioned outer or inner entity features any essence that is indestructible or that lasts for more than a moment. This is evident, they hold, from the fact that we perceive these entities undergoing change and coming to an end.

Nor is it the case that these things are absolutely devoid of any essence, as the Followers of the Middle Way claim, because it is accepted that they are entities that are qualified by emptiness. Without any essence, they would be no different than a sky flower. If this were the case, what could change pertain to? It could not be located anywhere. Therefore, they claim, things are not devoid of essence.

Disproving the View of the Opposition
Disproving the view of the opposition will include showing that (1) change cannot be used as an argument for the natural existence of mere phenomena and (2) emptiness is not established.

Change Cannot Be Used as an Argument for the Natural Existence of Mere Phenomena
The first section explains that (1) nature and change are contradictory and (2) in reality, change as such has no establishment.

Nature and Change Are Contradictory
On the first issue, the treatise states:

> If there were essences,
> How could there be change? [XIII.4c–d]

If things had a nature or essence, how would they be able to change? Indeed, it follows that it would not be possible for them to turn into something else. This is entailed because when the world speaks of the "nature" of something, then what is meant is something that a given phenomenon unmistakenly has, such as the heat of fire. A given heat or extent of water is essentially produced by causes and conditions; if a fire is "five-tongued," it is classified as such in dependence on other phenomena; and if gold is stained, it is gold that has undergone alteration. Hence, in none of these cases are [we referring to] something that is unmistakably [intrinsic to the thing in question]. Therefore, none of these qualities can be their nature. This, in turn, shows that if things were to exist by nature, that would preclude their undergoing change. Therefore, be aware that since things do appear to change, they are as devoid of nature as an illusory person.

In Reality, Change as Such Has No Establishment
On the second issue, the treatise states:

> *Change is not in that itself,*
> *Nor is it in something else,*
> *Because the young do not age,*
> *And because the aged do not age. [XIII.5]*

> *If that itself changes,*
> *Then milk itself is yogurt.*
> *What, other than milk,*
> *Would turn into yogurt? [XIII.6]*

Change is something that, without analysis, is merely apparent to what the opponent accepts as being direct perception. When the reality of the situation is investigated, however, change is seen to be impossible. That is to say, an initial situation does not itself contain change because change is not possible unless the initial situation is dispensed with. Neither does something other than the original condition contain change. In a situation that is different from the initial one, the change has already taken place. Doing so once more would, therefore, be meaningless.

To give an example, nobody is aged while still being young because these two are mutually incompatible. One may then think that aging occurs once the situation of being young is over. Yet this is not the case either because being aged is precisely what is the case when youth is over. Hence, the aged person does not age either, for such an aging of the one who has already aged would be meaningless.

Similarly, if the earlier situation were itself what changed, it would mean that milk could become yogurt while still remaining milk. On the other hand, if it were something other than the initial situation that undergoes change, it would be something other than milk, such as water, that turns into yoghurt. This, however, is impossible. Discussing this point, the *Noble Sūtra of the Source of Jewels* states:

No phenomenon arises or disintegrates;
There is no death, no transference, and no aging.
This is what the Lion of Men has taught,
And in this he has established hundreds of beings.

Emptiness Is Not Established

Second, showing that emptiness is not established includes (1) refuting the belief that emptiness can withstand analysis and (2) showing how this refutation does not contradict scripture.

Emptiness Cannot Withstand Analysis

On the first issue, the treatise states:

> *If there were a bit of something that is not empty,*
> *There could be a bit something that is empty.*
> *As there is not a bit that is not empty,*
> *How could there be anything that is empty? [XIII.7]*

It is not possible to prove that things truly possess the property of emptiness because there is nothing that is not empty. This argument features entailment because, as was explained above, negative properties and objects of negation are mutually dependent. Therefore, let us imagine that there is some object of negation—a person or phenomenon—that is not empty of real entity. If this were the case, a bit of emptiness, the absence of a true entity in the form of a person or phenomenon, could be present as well.

Earlier refutations, however, have shown that there is nothing whatsoever that without being empty exists as a true entity in the form of a person or phenomenon. How, then, could there be an emptiness, an absence of persons and phenomena that are real entities, since such emptiness is a property that depends on the former objects of negation? Indeed, this is similar to a man in a dream. Since the dream man is not real himself, neither is his death.

The Refutation of Emptiness Does Not Contradict Scripture

On the second issue, the treatise states:

The Victorious Ones have taught emptiness
As a deliverance from all views.
For those whose view is emptiness, they teach,
Nothing can be accomplished. [XIII.8]

Some may argue: "Unlike the teachings of the extremists, the Able One's
sūtras reveal the three gateways to liberation. Your words are a dismissal
of his teaching, a distorted view that denigrates that intrinsic nature of
emptiness, which is established by both scripture and reasoning."

This is not the case. As stated in the *Mother of the Victorious Ones*:

> The bodhisattva may think, "These aggregates are empty,"
> Yet he still engages with marks and has no faith in the abode
>   of the unborn.

Hence, the meaning of emptiness as taught in the profound sūtras transcends empty, not empty, and all other constructs of negandum and negation; it lies beyond all claims. What you understand is the mere property of
the negation of the self of the person and phenomena. This is the absence
of arising as a negative property, or emptiness as an indicative negation.
That I do refute, for it is not the intent of the sūtras.

The Victorious Ones have conquered the enemy, the discards, and have
vanquished those factors that cover and conceal sublime qualities. Having
uprooted the two obscurations, along with the habitual tendencies, they
are Buddhas, Transcendent Conquerors. What they teach is an emptiness
that delivers from all views, all beliefs in properties such as existence, nonexistence, and so forth. The *Noble Jewel Mound* states:

> Kāśyapa, emptiness alone is the deliverance from all views.

And in the *Mother of the Victorious Ones*:

> Engagement with the idea that form is empty, or that it is not
> empty, is still engagement with marks. It is not engagement
> with transcendent insight. When there is no engagement with
> anything at all, it is the engagement with transcendent insight.

People who lack wisdom develop a view that seizes on the marks associated with the negative property "emptiness," or view it as a positive determination. Thus, they cannot free themselves from the fundamental root of all problems, the beliefs in existence, nonexistence, and other such views. Unable to give up these views, they fail to accomplish both liberation from cyclic existence, as well as the nonabiding transcendence of suffering that is confined to neither existence nor peace. This is taught in the sūtras, such as the following passage from the *Noble Jewel Mound*:

> Kāśyapa, I say that the one who observes emptiness, and thus conceives of emptiness, has failed, failed entirely, with respect to these teachings. Having a belief in personal existence that is as solid as the King of Mountains is a minor problem compared to the arrogant view of emptiness. Why is that? Because emptiness is a deliverance from all views. Hence, I say that if the view is exclusively emptiness, then there is no cure.

Subsequently, the Buddha gives the example of the man who is unable to digest the medicine that would otherwise heal him, and therefore does not recover from his disease. In the same manner, while holding the view of emptiness one will be unable to sever the root of all problems by eliminating all views. So long as this is the case, one will be unable to attain mere liberation or accomplish the nonabiding transcendence of suffering because one continues to perceive marks in the very emptiness that is the remedy against all views.

This can also be illustrated as follows. Imagine that someone says, "I have no merchandise," and someone else answers, "Well, then give me that merchandise called 'no'!" Here, the second person takes the word that negates the object of negation, merchandise, to be an affirmation of merchandise. It is, therefore, impossible to make him understand that there is, in fact, no merchandise. This is what the Master has in mind when he states:

> To conquer all thoughts,
> You taught the elixir of emptiness.
> For those who grasp even at that,
> You show your contempt.[145]

145. Nāgārjuna, *Praise to the Supramundane*, 23.

This concludes the explanation of the thirteenth chapter, the analysis of the conditioned, in the *Ornament of Reason*, a commentary on the *Root of the Middle Way*.

CHAPTER FOURTEEN

Analysis of Contact

THE THREE ISSUES pertain to the analysis of contact as well.[146] First is the chapter's context.

THE CONTEXT OF CHAPTER 14

The present chapter relates to the profound sūtras, such as the following teachings from the *King of Meditative Absorptions*:

> Based on the eye and form,
> Visual consciousness arises.
> Yet the eye is not based on the form,
> Nor has the eye gone out to the form.
>
> These selfless and repulsive phenomena
> Are still spoken of as "self" and "delightful."
> This misconception where there is nothing,
> Is that from which visual consciousness occurs.

Thus, the sūtras teach that the contact between factors like a faculty, object, and consciousness is devoid of nature. It is the meaning of such teachings that the present chapter employs reasoning to ascertain.

Concerning its relationship to the other chapters, the analysis of contact forms a reply to the following objection: "The analysis of the conditioned

---

146. In this chapter the concluding summary is not explicit as a separate section of the text.

contained a refutation of the nature of things, but things do indeed exist by nature. In the sūtras, we find statements such as:

> The visual consciousness arises based on the eye and form.

And:

> Contact comes about due to the coming together of three factors. Contact is accompanied by sensation.

As well as:

> The two phenomena, sensation and identification, involve contact. It is not the case that there is no contact.

Thus, it is taught that conditioned phenomena are in contact.

There cannot be any contact between things that are nonexistent, just as the sons and daughters of barren women cannot meet." The present chapter demonstrates that the meaning of such scriptural statements is expedient and that there is no nature of contact.

EXPLANATION OF THE CONTENT

Second, the explanation of the content of this chapter includes (1) a presentation of the thesis that there is no contact between conditioned phenomena, (2) an explanation of the rationale for this thesis, and (3) a conclusion.

The Thesis of No Contact

On the first issue, the treatise states:

> *The seen, sight, and the seer*
> *Do not, either in pairs*
> *Or as a group,*
> *Ever come into contact. [XIV.1]*

The same goes for desire, the desirous one,
And the object of desire, the other afflictions,
The remaining sense sources,
And for all such triads. [XIV.2]

The seen form, the eye that is the faculty of sight, and the visual consciousness that sees do not meet in pairs. That is to say, there is no contact
between eye and form, eye and consciousness, or consciousness and form.
Yet neither do all three of them contact each other simultaneously. The
same goes for desire, the desirous primary consciousness that is the support
for desire, and the attractive object of desire. They do not meet in pairs, or
all together at once. The same also holds for the other afflictions—anger
and stupor—as well as the ear and the rest of the six sense sources. None of
the factors in these triads that we may thus distinguish, such as anger, the
angry consciousness, and the object of anger, or the heard, hearing, and
hearer, ever come into contact, neither in pairs nor in groups of three.

THE RATIONALE

The second issue will be covered by showing (1) the absence of contact due
to lack of difference and (2) the infeasibility of contact whether things are
the same or distinct.

The Absence of Contact Due to a Lack of Difference
The first of these includes (1) a presentation of the evidence by demonstrating a reverse entailment, (2) the application of the evidence to all phenomena, and (3) the establishment of the evidence.

Presentation of the Evidence
On the first issue, the treatise states:

Contact occurs between different things,
So because the seen and so forth
Do not exist as different things,
They do not come into contact. [XIV.3]

If different things were to come into contact with each other, their contact
would entail their being of different substance. In the case of things such

as the seen object, sight, and the seer, there are, however, no such substantial differences present that would otherwise have been entailed by their contact, and so the entailing contact can be precluded.

Application of the Evidence to All Phenomena

On the second issue, the treatise states:

> It is not only the seen and the rest
> That do not differ from each other;
> Wherever there is coexistence
> There cannot reasonably be difference. [XIV.4]

Lack of difference does not preclude contact only in cases where things are causally related or mutually dependent, as is the case with seen objects and sight. Upon investigation, it becomes clear that wherever there is coexistence—as there may be, for example, with a vase and a blanket—there cannot reasonably be any substantial difference. Hence, things that coexist can never contact one another.

Establishment of the Evidence

The third issue includes (1) explaining that things that are mutually dependent cannot reasonably be different, (2) showing that the universal "difference" has no establishment, and (3) drawing the conclusion.

Things That Are Mutually Dependent Cannot Reasonably Be Different

On the first issue, the treatise states:

> That which is different differs in dependence on something else.
> It does not differ without that different thing from which it differs.
> Where something depends on something else,
> The two cannot reasonably be different. [XIV.5]

> If the different differed from something different,
> It would be different even without anything different.
> But nothing differs without something different,
> And, hence, this is not the case. [XIV.6]

In the world, vases and other such things are labeled "different" in dependence on something else, such as a blanket, from which it differs. Without
a referent from which it differs, there is no basis for applying the term
"different" to a vase. This is how things are perceived and accepted in the
world.

Therefore, a vase that is held to be different in relation to a blanket
cannot reasonably be different from the blanket because it is dependent
on it. That is the implicit argument here. The entailment of this argument
can be stated as follows: When something is different in dependence on
something else, then the former cannot in reality, or by nature, be different
from the latter. As is the case with seeds and sprouts, and long and short,
the position that these two are different is untenable.

It may be thought: "The difference of the vase is not independent of
the blanket. But what is the problem with saying that the vase really, or by
nature, differs from the blanket while depending on it?"

If the vase and the blanket were established as different by nature, their
mutual dependence would be meaningless. Take the subject, the vase that
is different. Because the vase is different by its own nature, it would follow
that it is different also in the absence of anything different from it, such as
the blanket. Just as the vase can be present in the absence of the blanket
because its essence does not depend on the it, [the vase would, if it were
different by its own nature, be different even in the absence of anything
else].

That cannot be accepted, however, because from a worldly point of view,
we can see that unless there is something from which it differs, such as the
blanket, the vase cannot exist as, or be established as, different. Hence,
there is no such thing as natural difference.

The Universal "Difference" Has No Establishment
On the second issue, the treatise states:

> *Difference does not exist in the different,*
> *Nor does it exist in what is not different. [XIV.7a–b]*

It may be argued: "For other groups, the convention 'different' is not
applied in dependence on other things. Rather, it is applied in relation to
the universal 'difference.'"

This account might work if there were such a thing as the universal "difference," but no such universal is established. The universal cannot apply to instances that are already established as different because the universal "difference" is conceived of to provide establishment for the convention of difference. Hence, it would be meaningless for the universal difference to apply to such instances. On the other hand, it cannot be present anywhere other than in those instances either because the universal "sameness," with which it is incompatible, would be present in such other places. Finally, being and not being an instance of difference are directly contradictory qualities. Therefore, there cannot be any third category of things apart from these two. Hence, as it cannot be found anywhere else either, the universal quality of difference is an impossibility.

Drawing the Conclusion
On the third issue, the treatise states:

> *As difference as such does not exist,*
> *Nothing is different and nothing is the same. [XIV.7c–d]*

It has been shown that the universal quality of difference, the reason for classifying things as instances of difference, does not exist. Hence, there are no instances of difference, and no instances of sameness either.

Whether They Are Different or the Same, Things Cannot Be in Contact

Having thus refuted contact with reference to the lack of difference, next a second refutation is presented that refutes contact between things that may be different or the same. The treatise states:

> *Nothing comes into contact with itself,*
> *Nor do different things come into contact. [XIV.8a–b]*

If contact between phenomena is something that exists by it is own nature, we may ask whether such contact occurs between things that are essentially the same or things that are different? In the first case, there cannot be any contact for there would not be two things that could contact one another. Nor is contact possible in the second case because, as was already explained, things that are different cannot exist at the same place and time.

CONCLUSION TO THE CHAPTER

Third, in conclusion, the treatise states:

> *Contacting, contacted, and contactor*
> *Do not exist either. [XIV.8c–d]*

Given the above, there is no act of contacting currently being carried out, no act of contact that is already finished, and there is no contactor, no agent who is in charge of such an activity.

This concludes the explanation of the fourteenth chapter, the analysis of contact, in the *Ornament of Reason*, a commentary on the *Root of the Middle Way*.

CHAPTER FIFTEEN

Analysis of Nature

THE THREE ISSUES pertain to the analysis of nature as well.[147]

THE CONTEXT OF CHAPTER 15

First, concerning its context, the present chapter relates to the profound sūtras, including the following passage from the *Journey to Laṅkā*:

> Those who suffer from distorted vision
> May erroneously perceive hairs.
> Similarly, this thought of a thing
> Is an erroneous imputation of the childish.
> There is no nature, no awareness,
> No all-ground, and no nonthing.
> These are the imputations
> Of childish, unwholesome, corpselike logicians.

The present chapter employs reasoning to ascertain the meaning of teachings such as the one found here, as well as the fourfold summary of emptiness—the emptiness of entity, emptiness of nonentity, emptiness of nature, and emptiness of other-nature—that appears in the *Mother of the Victorious Ones*.

As for its relationship to the other chapters of the text, the analysis of nature replies to this objection: "The notion that things have an essential nature has been negated. Likewise, the idea that contact can be used as proof that there are essential natures has also been refuted. Still, outer

---

147. In this chapter the concluding summary is not explicit as a separate section of the text.

entities such as sprouts and inner entities such as karmic formations do indeed exist by nature because they arise in dependence on causes and conditions, such as seeds, ignorance, and so forth."

The present chapter will argue that while the evidence advanced in that objection is not established in reality, the very fact that conventionally things arise in dependence on causes and conditions itself shows that they resemble an illusion and have no nature.

THE CONTENT OF CHAPTER 15

Second, the explanation of the content of this chapter covers (1) a refutation of the mental constructs of the four extremes, (2) a concluding rebuke of views, and (3) instructions on applying one's mind to the Middle Way.

THE FOUR EXTREMES

The first includes refutations of (1) nature and other-nature[148] and (2) entity and nonentity.

The first of these issues will be treated sequentially, beginning with the refutation of nature. This refutation involves negating the notions that nature (1) originates dependently and (2) undergoes change.

Does Nature Originate Dependently?
The first of these issues will take the form of a demonstration of the entailment found in the argument: "outer and inner things have no nature because they originate dependently, just like an illusion." This will be done in two sections. First, we will show that it is pointless for nature to arise due to causes and conditions.

It Is Pointless for Nature to Arise Due to Causes and Conditions
The treatise states:

---

148. According to Abhidharma thought, things that can be analyzed into constituent parts do not possess a nature of their own. Rather, since their being is due to the nature of their constituents, the constructed nature of such composites is termed "other-nature" (Skt. parabhāva, Tib. gzhan gyi dngos po).

> *Nature cannot reasonably occur*
> *Due to causes and conditions. [XV.1a–b]*

According to the Proponents of Differences, a nature that exists in the future comes about in the present based on causes and conditions. Yet a nature that exists in the future cannot reasonably arise due to causes and conditions because such a nature would already exist, just like things that exist in the present.

Nature and Dependent Origination Are Incompatible

Second, it will be shown that nature and arising due to causes and conditions are incompatible. It may be thought that no fault is incurred by the Followers of Sūtra and Mind Only Proponents who assert that nature does not exist before it arises due to causes and conditions. The refutation of this idea involves (1) stating an absurd consequence, (2) showing why the consequence cannot be accepted, and (3) presenting our own approach in terms of the conventional.

An Absurd Consequence

On the first issue, the treatise states:

> *A nature that arises due to causes and conditions*
> *Would be a nature that is produced. [XV.1c–d]*

It follows from the opponent's idea that nature is a product because it is produced by causes and conditions, just as a vase is.

Why This Consequence Cannot Be Accepted

On the second issue, the treatise states:

> *"A nature that is produced,"*
> *How could that be right? [XV.2a–b]*

If one believes this to be the case, we may ask the following: How could this so-called produced nature be possible? In the world, people speak of a thing's "nature" with reference to something that is essential to the thing in question, as when heat is considered to be the nature of fire. This nature or essence cannot be removed and, by being intrinsic, ensures that the entity that possesses it is not mistaken for anything else.

Thus, nature must be something such as the heat of fire or the fluidity of water, something that does not arise due to contact with other causes and conditions, and which is, thus, not fabricated. For example, if water is hot, or earth is moist, then that is the result of its contact with other causes and conditions. Such qualities can be removed, they are not intrinsic, and will hence not ensure that the entity in question is not mistaken for something else. Such qualities cannot, hence, be natural for the given thing.

Now, as this is the case, heat cannot be the nature of fire either because just like the heat of water it is the product of causes and conditions. This argument, moreover, does not lack establishment because fire is produced by tinder and other such factors, and there is no fire that is essentially different from heat.

It may be argued: "While fire and heat are produced by causes and conditions, the heat of fire is not, as is the case with the heat of water, the result of causes and conditions other than itself."

Yet this idea is untenable because it is precisely such things as tinder that produce the heat of fire. The fact that it is accepted in the world that heat is the nature of fire does not show any flaw in our argument because we do not deny that this is what the world accepts. Rather, we state that this cannot reasonably be the nature of fire in reality, and the world is no authority when it comes to the issue of reality.

Conventional Presentation of Our Own Approach
On the third issue, the treatise states:

> *The natural is not fabricated,*
> *And does not depend on anything else. [XV.2c–d]*

Some may wonder: "Heat appears to be the nature of fire, but the apparent nature of things is not their real nature. Like reflections and other such phenomena, that which appears to be natural from the perspective of a deluded mind is essentially false. What, then, might the real nature of things be?"

A sūtra declares:

> What can be heard and taught
> About phenomena that are letterless?
> Aside from superimposition, there are no letters.
> That, however, is still heard and taught.

Thus, since the real nature of phenomena is not established as an object of speech and mind, it cannot be shown in terms of any essence of its own. Yet those who are to be influenced can still realize the unmistaken nature of things, within which none of the constructed marks remain in any way at all. To facilitate this realization, there is a teaching that uses conventional superimposition to explain the characteristics of the true nature of phenomena, the object of undefiled wakefulness. The true nature of things possesses three qualities: a) It is not produced by causes and conditions, b) it is independent of any other phenomena in the form of conventional designators, and c) it does not change into anything else. Throughout the three times, this is the unmistakable innate essence.

Concerning the bearer of these characteristics, it is taught:

> Whether or not the Thus-Gone Ones appear, this intrinsic nature
>   of phenomena thoroughly remains.

Thus, the bearer of the characteristic of the true nature is phenomena's natural emptiness, which is not established in the manner of any of the marks of mental construction, such as negation and affirmation, and which is the object of the noble ones' nonconceptual wakefulness during equipoise. It is taught:

> Phenomena's nature is not produced and not created. Thus, it is not
>   created by the listeners.

In other words, all phenomena are primordially emptiness. It is not that they are made emptiness by something else. Thus:

> Recognize that all things
> Are empty of their very essence.
> "Empty" also is empty.
> Thus, there is nothing that is not empty.

Hence, each and every phenomenon is even empty of its own nature. If phenomena could be said to be empty of *p*, but not of *q*, their emptiness would be dependent on extrinsic designators. Yet emptiness cannot be qualified in this way. Emptiness, moreover, does not turn into anything else, neither in a next moment nor at the end of a continuum. [The emptiness that is the real nature of things] thus possesses the three characteristics that were outlined above. It is in consideration of this that the *Mother of the Victorious Ones* teaches:

> Form is empty of form. Why? Because that is its nature.

While the Master himself explains:

> Just as heat is the nature of fire
> And sweetness the nature of molasses
> Emptiness is held to be
> The nature of all phenomena.

This explanation does not conflict with the earlier statement that phenomena are empty of their own nature. In reality, all phenomena are without any established nature whatsoever. When it is said that "their nature is emptiness," it simply demonstrates this using a superimposition. It is not meant as a claim that there are cognizable qualities such as existence or nonexistence.

Can the Natural Change?
The refutation of a nature that changes involves (1) presenting an absurd consequence, (2) demonstrating its entailment, and (3) showing that the refutation of nature is indisputable.

An Absurd Consequence
On the first issue, the treatise states the following some verses below:

> *If something is existent by nature,*
> *It would never become nonexistent. [XV.8a–b]*

If things such as the heat of fire existed by nature, they would never become nonexistent.

The Entailment of the Consequence
On the second issue, the treatise states:

> *A nature that undergoes change*
> *Would never make any sense. [XV.8c–d]*

It cannot be argued that the stated consequence lacks entailment. Just as in the case of the nonresistance of space, a nature that changes would never make any sense. As explained above, the nature of a given entity cannot be removed and, by being intrinsic, ensures that the entity in question is not mistaken for anything else. Hence, if a quality undergoes change, as is the case with the heat of water or the five-tongued design of a fire, then it cannot constitute the nature of the entity in question.

Yet it cannot be asserted [that things do not change] because, from the unexamined perspective of the inference and direct perception that is accepted by the opponent, it is observed that continua come to an end and that substances change from one moment to the next. It must, hence, be understood that things are subject to change, like illusory people, and that, therefore, they do not have any nature.

The Refutation of Nature Is Indisputable
On the third issue, the treatise states:

> *If no nature exists,*
> *To what does change pertain?*
> *Even if nature exists,*
> *To what could change pertain? [XV.9]*

It may be argued: "If things did not have any nature, they would be like sky flowers. If this were the case, to what would change pertain? It follows that there would be nothing that changes. Hence, because there is change, nature exists."

Since change has already been refuted, it is not something that is established by nature. Absence of nature, moreover, does not exclude the appearance of change, as in the case of illusory people. Let us neverthe-less assume that this is not so and that instead, as the opponent wants it, things exist by nature. To what, we may ask, could change then pertain? Indeed, as in the case of the nonresistant quality of space, change would not be feasible. Whatever appears to change is devoid of nature, and the appearance of change, hence, cannot serve as evidence when arguing that nature exists.

Other-Nature
Second, refuting other-nature, the treatise states:

> *If nature does not exist,*
> *How could there be other-nature?*
> *It is the nature of other-nature*
> *That is identified as "other-nature." [XV.3]*

It may be thought: "Since things do not possess any nature, what they do possess is other-nature."

The notion that all outer and inner entities possess nature has already been refuted. Hence, how could they possibly have an other-nature? The entailment of this argument is as follows. A nature such as heat may be considered an other-nature in relation to another nature, such as fluidity. In this way, "other-nature" is identified as a particular type of nature that is distinguished from another type of nature. Hence, other-nature entails nature.

Entity and Nonentity
Second, the refutation of entity and nonentity involves (1) a refutation using reasoning and (2) a refutation based on scripture. First, entity will be refuted based on reasoning.

Refutation by Means of Reasoning
The treatise states:

> *Apart from nature and other-nature,*
> *What entity could there possibly be?*
> *If there were nature and other-nature,*
> *Entities would be established. [XV.4]*

It may be thought: "Nature and other-nature may have been refuted, yet mere entities have not. Therefore, they exist."

Since nature and other-nature entail [the presence of an entity], if they existed, the entailed entity as such would also be established. The notion that phenomena have a nature or other-nature, however, has already been refuted. Given that both of these are not established, it follows that mere entities are as nonexistent as the sky flower. This is the argument that the present stanza implies.

Its entailment is made explicit in the verses, "Apart from nature and other-nature, what entity could there possibly be?" This question points to the fact that, with respect to the basis, an entity, nature and other-nature are directly contradictory notions.

Second, refuting nonentity, the treatise states:

> *If entity is not established,*
> *Then neither is nonentity.*
> *It is the transformation of entity*
> *That people call nonentity. [XV.5]*

It may be thought: "Indeed, entities do not exist. Yet nonentities do, for they have not been refuted."

It was shown above that, having been refuted with respect to all outer and inner phenomena, entities are not established. As this is the case, it follows that nonentities are not established either. It cannot be maintained that this argument lacks entailment because in the world it is with reference to the transformation of an entity, meaning the disintegration or negation of that entity, that people speak of "nonentity." In other words, negation depends on there being an object of negation.

Refutation by Means of Scripture

Second is a refutation by means of a scriptural statement of definitive meaning. The treatise states:

> *The Transcendent Conqueror,*
> *With knowledge of both entities and nonentities,*
> *Refuted, in his* Instructions to Kātāyana,
> *Both existence and nonexistence. [XV.7]*

As we have seen, the views of nature and other-nature, and of entity and nonentity, are in conflict with reason. Such views, therefore, do not genuinely apply to reality. The Transcendent Conqueror, as a trustworthy and authoritative individual who knows the nature of entities and nonentities precisely and without error, has also refuted the views of both existence and nonexistence for the sake of his disciples who desire liberation. In his *Instructions to Kātāyana*, a scripture that is accepted by all Buddhist schools, he states the following:

> Kātāyana, in this world, beings are, for the most part, attached to existence and nonexistence. Therefore, they are born, grow old, fall sick, and die; they are tormented, cry out in lamentation, and suffer; they are distressed, disturbed, and do not achieve complete liberation.

A Concluding Rebuke of Views

Having thus refuted the mental constructs of the four extremes, what follows is a rebuke of the views associated with these four. The treatise states:

> *Those who believe in nature or other-nature,*
> *In entity or nonentity,*
> *Fail to see reality*
> *Within the teachings of the Buddha. [XV.6]*

Reasoning and scripture have established that, in reality, phenomena are devoid of nature, other-nature, entity, and nonentity. Yet for the realists in our own tradition, the mind's eye is impaired by the distortions of ignorance. This causes them to mistakenly believe that nature pertains to form that is fit to be form, feeling in the sense of sensation, consciousness that is the cognition of individual objects, and so on. They then subscribe to other-nature by holding that, "form, mind, and mental states are different." Some hold that present form, mind, and mental states are all entities, whereas others claim that this is only the case with respect to the latter two categories. Some assert the insubstantiality of the past and the future, imperceptible forms, and nonassociated formations. Others maintain that the apprehended and that which apprehends are both nonentities. Holding such views, they fail to accurately and unerringly see the previously explained reality of dependent origination within the teaching of the Buddha.

Instructions on Applying the Mind to the Middle Way

Third, as instructions for giving up extreme views and applying one's mind to the Middle Way, the treatise states:

> *"Existence" is apprehension of permanence,*
> *"Nonexistence" a view of annihilation.*
> *The wise, therefore, ought not to adhere*
> *To either existence or nonexistence. [XV.10]*

> *That which exists by nature*
> *Is not nonexistent—this is permanence.*
> *"It existed before, but now it does not"—*
> *That implies annihilation. [XV.11]*

The wise ought not adhere to the views of existence and nonexistence that are held by the members of our own tradition, the reason being that neither existence nor nonexistence has any bearing on the nature of objects of cognition. Believing in "existence" is an apprehension of permanence, whereas apprehending "nonexistence" is a view of annihilation. Both of these views go against the teachings of the Able One; they are the cause of cyclic existence and the lower realms. For this reason, they are extremely unreasonable.

To explain further, mere existence does not entail permanence, but you [Buddhist realists] claim that certain outer and inner things exist by nature. Such things could not ever become nonexistent and would have to be permanent. Likewise, mere nonexistence does not entail annihilation, but you say that suffering and its causes exist naturally before, meaning at the time of cyclic existence, and then later, upon the transcendence of suffering, they become nonexistent. That implies annihilation. A sūtra proclaims:

> If phenomena had any nature,
> Then the Victors and the listeners would know it.
> Solid phenomena do not attain the transcendence of suffering.
> The wise would never become free of mental construction.[149]

---

149. From the *Sūtra of the Elephant's Strength*.

Likewise:

> Transcendent Conqueror, the one who teaches that desire, anger, and stupor are initially fully present and then later become nonentities is indeed a nihilist.[150]

Those who wish for true liberation must, therefore, realize that so long as the views of existence and nonexistence go on manifesting, cyclic existence will continue. With this realization, they should dispel those two views and train genuinely upon the path of the Middle Way.

This concludes the explanation of the fifteenth chapter, the analysis of nature, in the *Ornament of Reason,* a commentary on the *Root of the Middle Way.*

---

150. From the *Journey to Laṅkā.*

CHAPTER SIXTEEN

Analysis of Bondage and Liberation

THE THREE ISSUES pertain to the analysis of bondage and liberation as well.[151]

THE CONTEXT OF CHAPTER 16

First, regarding its context, the present chapter's relationship to the profound sūtras can be seen in the following statement from the *Mother of the Victorious Ones*:

> Cyclic existence is like a dream and an illusion, passing beyond suffering is like a dream and an illusion.

The *King of Meditative Absorptions* likewise explains:

> The nonexistence of the transcendence of suffering
> Is what the Protector of the World has taught as the transcendence of suffering.
> Knots tied on space
> Are untied by space itself.

Thus, the sūtras teach the natural emptiness of existence and peace. It is the meaning of this teaching that is here established by means of reasoning.

As for its relationship to the other chapters in the text, the present dis-

---

151. In this chapter the concluding summary is not explicit as a separate section of the text.

cussion presents a reply to the following objection: "The nature of things has been refuted, but things do indeed exist because cyclic existence exists. Something that does not exist cannot be cyclic existence, just like the son of a barren woman."

In response to such an objection, the present chapter shows that cyclic existence is itself devoid of nature.

THE CONTENT OF CHAPTER 16

Second, the explanation of this chapter's content includes: (1) a refutation of the nature of cyclic existence and transcendence, (2) a refutation of bondage and liberation, and (3) a rebuttal of the criticism that such refutations render aspiring to the fruition and applying oneself to the causal path meaningless. The first issue has two subdivisions, of which the first is the refutation of cyclic existence. This topic contains, in turn, a refutation of the cycling of (1) appropriated aggregates and (2) an appropriating person.

The Cycling of the Aggregates
The treatise states:

> If it is claimed that formations cycle,
> They cannot do so if permanent,
> Nor can they if impermanent. [XVI.1a–c]

If cyclic existence is held to exist by nature, we may ask whether it is the appropriated aggregates or the appropriating person that cycles. To such a question the members of our own tradition may reply that what cycles are the appropriated formations of the aggregates. In that case, we may further enquire whether these aggregates are permanent, in the sense of remaining from one instant to another, or whether they are impermanent and disintegrate moment by moment.

If permanent, they could not cycle because that which is permanent and unchanging cannot participate in the act of cycling, which involves a temporal transition. Moreover, one cannot object that, while the stages in this process may differ, their nature remains permanent because no nature can be observed that is essentially distinct from these various stages. In addition, if they are essentially inseparable, the nature would be imperma-nent and composite, just as the stages are.

In the case of the second option, impermanence in the sense of momen-tary disintegration, there could be no cycling either. In such a scenario, everything would disintegrate for there would not be anything that could remain from one stage into another. Neither can it be maintained that while the impermanent substances that are the formations do not them-selves cycle, the unbroken continuum of sequential instants of causality does. First, there can be no cycling even if one asserts a continuum. Sec-ond, continua themselves are not established.

Let us consider the first of these two points. The instants in which a cause ceases and an effect arises do, as was already explained, cease with-out there being any coming and going. Hence, they cannot accommodate any cycling. Moreover, no continuum can be observed that is essentially different than the causal and resultant instants. Thus, given their essen-tial inseparability, a continuum cannot involve any coming or going, in exactly the same way that this is not possible with substances.

A continuum, furthermore, is composed of the three times, but since past and future formations have, respectively, ceased and not yet arisen, they cannot be involved in any cycling. Since the present instant remains in between past and future instants, it must have parts that are related to the past and future. Thus, since those parts then end up *being* past and future, we are unable to find any moment that is present upon examina-tion. Hence, no cycling is possible in a present instant either.

It may be thought that the very arising of a subsequent instant of for-mation itself implies the cycling of a previous formation. Now, that could be the case if the previous and subsequent instants of formation were the same. Yet these two are not the same because (1) they are cause and effect, (2) they are related to multiple moments of time, and (3) their qualities are incompatible, in the sense that, respectively, they have and have not disintegrated and have and have not arisen. Therefore, just as the cycling of an ordinary person cannot prevent a noble individual from transcend-ing suffering, how could the arising of one instant of formation imply the cycling of another distinct instant of formation?

Second, upon examination, continua themselves are not established and, therefore, cannot reasonably cycle. There are no established continua because no subsequent resultant instant can arise from a previous causal instant that has already ceased, one that has not yet ceased, or one that is in the process of ceasing. In the first case, the arising of the subsequent instant of formation has already occurred. In the second case, it has not yet occurred. Finally, there is nothing that is "in the process of ceasing" that is different from both having and not having ceased.

The Cycling of the Person

Second, the refutation of the cycling of an appropriating person involves refuting (1) the cycling of a person that is independent of the aggregates and substantially existent and (2) the cycling of a person who is dependent on the aggregates and whose existence is an imputation.

The Cycling of an Independent and Substantial Person

On the first issue, the treatise states:

> In the case of sentient beings, the steps are the same. [XVI.1d]

Members of other traditions hold that what cycles is a self, or a sentient being, which is independent of the aggregates and substantially existent. The steps that show such a position to be untenable are the very same as those that pointed out the flaws in the belief that permanent or impermanent formations cycle. Hence, there cannot be any cyclic existence for this kind of sentient being either.

The Cycling of a Dependent and Imputed Person

The second issue involves showing that cyclic existence is untenable since (1) the one that cycles is itself not established and (2) there is no appropriation.

The Establishment of the One That Cycles

On the first issue, the treatise states:

> It might be said that the person cycles,
> But when we search the aggregates, elements, and sense sources,
> Using the five steps and there is nothing,
> What is it, then, that cycles? [XVI.2]

Certain members of our own tradition may say: "The above critique applies only if the nature of the person can be stated. Yet the one that cycles is ineffable. Such a person cannot be said to be one with or separate from the aggregates, or permanent or impermanent. Thus, the inconsistencies stated above are not relevant."

Yet when we search for the person among the aggregates, elements, and sense sources that form the basis for imputation in five steps, we will come up with nothing. These five steps involve inquiring whether this self is 1) identical with these factors, 2) distinct from them, 3) in possession of them, 4) the support for them, or 5) supported by them. As we will find no person, who is it, then, that cycles? When the one that is supposed to cycle is as nonexistent as the child of a barren woman, there can be no cyclic existence at all.

Appropriation
On the second issue, the treatise states:

> *If there is cycling from appropriation to appropriation,*
> *Then there cannot be any becoming.*
> *Without becoming there can be no appropriation,*
> *So what kind of cycling is this? [XVI.3]*

Even if we assume the existence of the self, we may still ask, for example, whether the cycling from human appropriation to the appropriation of a god occurs with or without the former appropriation having been relinquished. If the prior appropriation has not been relinquished, the appropriation of a god would then take place while human appropriation is still occurring. This would mean that there could be two appropriations for a single person at a single point in time. Since there would be two appropriations, there would also have to be two imputed selves, one for each appropriation. Hence, the problems that result from this position are that cyclic existence would end up having a beginning and being uncaused.

In the second scenario, the relinquishment of human appropriation would take place prior to the appropriation of the god. If this were the case, there could not be any aggregates of becoming in the gap between the human and the divine states. Given the absence of both becoming and the appropriated aggregates, there would then be no basis for the imputation of the self. What kind of self could there then be? As there would not be any self that cycles, what would be doing the cycling? Alternatively, since the self would not exist, what act of cycling would it engage in? Indeed, there could be no such activity. The expression "what kind of cycling" can thus be seen to criticize the notions of both the self that cycles and the activity of cycling.

One may then object: "In the gap between a human and divine existence, there is an appropriation associated with the intermediate state. Hence, these problems are not relevant."

Yet this idea is also untenable for the same problem will be found once we ask whether or not the appropriation of the intermediate state occurs after the appropriation of the human state has ended.

The Transcendence of Suffering

On the second issue, the treatise states:

> *Formations that transcend suffering*
> *Do not make sense in any way.*
> *Sentient beings that transcend suffering*
> *Do not make sense in any way either. [XVI.4]*

Some may think: "While cyclic existence may have been refuted in this way, the transcendence of suffering exists because it has not been explicitly refuted and because scripture speaks of it."

Whether we associate it with the appropriations or that which appropriates, the transcendence of suffering is also an untenable principle. If there is such a thing as the transcendence of suffering, does it then pertain to the appropriated aggregates or to the appropriating self?

In the first case, the transcendence of suffering would not make any sense, regardless of whether we associate it with something permanent or something that is impermanent. The permanent does not change and could not, therefore, be related to any process of eliminating flaws or acquiring positive qualities. The impermanent, on the other hand, ceases from one moment to the next. Therefore, it too is incapable of participating in any such activities.

The transcendence of suffering does not make any sense in relation to sentient beings either, regardless of whether they are held to be permanent or impermanent. Finally, an ineffable person could not achieve any transcendence of suffering. To begin with, the existence of such a person is itself untenable. Moreover, if it continued to exist once suffering has been transcended, it would be permanent, while if it did not, it would be impermanent. This idea, therefore, has the same flaws that were stated above. For this reason, the *Mother of the Victorious Ones* teaches:

> Venerable Subhūti, the transcendence of suffering is also like a
> dream and an illusion.

While the *King of Meditative Absorptions* proclaims:

> An ultimate truth that is like a dream,
> The transcendence of suffering with its dreamlike nature—
> The wise one who engages them as such
> Is taught to possess the supreme mental vow.

BONDAGE AND LIBERATION

Second, bondage and liberation are refuted (1) in general and (2) individually.

General Refutation

On the first issue, the treatise states:

> *Formations that are subject to arising and ceasing*
> *Are not bound and will not be freed.*
> *As before, sentient beings as well*
> *Are not bound and will not be freed. [XVI.5]*

One may object: "Cyclic existence and the transcendence of suffering may have been refuted, yet being bound by the chains of affliction and being liberation from them does indeed occur. Hence, the nature of things exists."

Nevertheless, we can analyze bondage and liberation in the same manner as before with respect to the appropriated and that which appropriates. Neither of these options makes sense. The appropriated formations cannot be bound by action and affliction, and they cannot be freed from them either because these formations are subject to arising and ceasing from one moment to the next. The entailment here is as follows: Simultaneous factors cannot relate to each other as object and agent. Hence, formations cannot be bound or released when they arise, while in the second moment, they cannot be bound or freed either since they will already have ceased.

As was the case before with the formations, the appropriating self, or sentient being, cannot be bound or freed either. If such a self were impermanent, the same flaws as before would apply, and if the self were permanent, it would not make sense for it to be involved in the activity of being bound or freed.

Individual Refutations

The second issue is twofold. First, the refutation of bondage involves showing that (1) bondage cannot occur whether appropriation is present or absent, (2) there is no bondage prior to that which is bound, and (3) the activity of binding is refuted through an examination of the three times.

Bondage Cannot Occur Whether Appropriation Is Present or Absent

On the first issue, the treatise states:

> If bondage is due to appropriation,
> Since nothing is bound in the presence of appropriation,
> And there is no bondage in the absence of appropriation,
> When, then, is it that bondage occurs? [XVI.6]

Let us assume that appropriations, such as desire, bind either the appropriated formations or the appropriating person. Would something then be bound in the presence of appropriation, or rather in its absence? Something for which there is already appropriation cannot be bound because such binding would be meaningless. Neither can something for which appropriation is absent be bound since bondage and the absence of appropriation are mutually incompatible. The Thus-Gone, for example, cannot be bound. When, then, could there be any bondage? Since the presence and absence of appropriation are mutually contradictory, no third option is open.

There Is No Bondage Prior to That Which Is Bound

On the second issue, the treatise states:

> If the bond existed prior to the bound,
> There could be bondage, yet it does not. [XVI.7a–b]

Furthermore, if there are iron chains to begin with, they can be used to bind Devadatta. Similarly, bondage could occur if desire and other such bonds were present prior to that which is bound, whether it be the formations or a person. Yet these bonds do not exist prior to what they bind because in the absence of something bound, there is no basis for them. Moreover, if bondage were already established before that which is bound, its subsequent relation to the bound would serve no purpose.

The Act of Binding in Terms of the Three Times
On the third issue, the treatise states:

> *The rest has already been explained*
> *By what was, will be, and is being traversed. [XVI.7c–d]*

It should be understood that the remaining elements in the critique of bondage have already been addressed in the refutation of the act of going with reference to what was, will be, and is currently being traversed. Thus, with the proper changes, we easily arrive at the statement, "Where there has been bondage, there is none."

Liberation

Second, refuting liberation, the treatise states:

> *That which is bound is not freed,*
> *Yet the unbound is not freed either.*
> *If the bound were being liberated,*
> *Bondage and liberation would be simultaneous. [XVI.8]*

It may be thought: "Since the sūtras teach the means for liberation, liberation must exist. Given the existence of liberation, bondage must exist as well."

Once one examines this issue, it will be seen that there is no liberation. If liberation takes place, does it occur to that which is bound or to something that is not bound? That which is bound is not freed because the act of binding is incompatible with that of freeing.

One may think: "It is precisely that which is bound that is subsequently liberated through skillful means."

Yet, while it is contradictory to claim that liberation occurs in a situation where there is still bondage, it would be meaningless for liberation to occur once that situation is over. The latter also implies that liberation would still have to be achieved even if the state of bondage has ended. Hence, these two are mutually dependent.

The unbound is not freed either. Since the unbound has already been freed, its being freed again would be meaningless.

Finally, it may be thought that, while the bound is not liberated, it is something that is in the process of being freed that is liberated. In this case, bondage and liberation would be simultaneous, so this does not make sense either. Since binding and freeing are incompatible activities, their occurring at the same time is as impossible as having light and darkness at the same place and time. For this very reason, the *Mother of the Victorious Ones* proclaims:

> Form is not bound and not liberated.

Rebuttal of Criticism

The third section contains a rebuttal of the criticism that the refutation of existence and peace renders aspiring to the fruition and applying oneself to the causal path meaningless. The treatise states:

> *"Without appropriation, I shall transcend suffering;*
> *The transcendence of suffering, that shall be mine!"*
> *Those who grasp in this way*
> *Are engaged in severe appropriation. [XVI.9]*

> *Where the transcendence of suffering is not produced*
> *And cyclic existence is not dispelled,*
> *How to conceive of cyclic existence,*
> *And how of the transcendence of suffering? [XVI.10]*

The members of the schools of the listeners may object: "Perceiving cyclic existence as a wasteland plagued by hundreds of sufferings, we yearningly wonder, 'When will I cross over that which can barely be traversed, and succeed in transcending suffering? When shall the transcendence of suffering be mine?' Hence, with a tremendous aspiration to relinquish existence and cultivate transcendence, we follow spiritual teachers, practice generosity and discipline, and engage in study, reflection, and meditation, thereby applying ourselves to the task of relinquishing existence and achieving peace. Yet, if there were no cyclic existence and no transcendence of suffering, this entire pursuit would be futile!"

Indeed, this is futile. In reality, there is nothing to relinquish or cultivate with respect to all phenomena, nor is there anything that can be established as "I" or "mine." Hence, one might mistakenly think, "Without appropriation, I shall transcend suffering; the transcendence of suffering, that shall be mine!" Yet this type of grasping is the view of the transitory collection and, hence, severe engagement in appropriation. All the various disputes motivated by such a view will do nothing but prevent the transcendence of suffering that takes place in terms of the relative. On this point, it is taught:

> Affliction is explained to be concomitant with grasping.

Thus, it is taught that as long as a focal point is maintained, there will be no liberation from relative cyclic existence.

One may wonder: "How, then, can I transcend suffering?"

In ultimate reality, the basic space of phenomena, there are no new qualities associated with a "transcendence of suffering" to produce, nor are there any old flaws related to a so-called cyclic existence to be dispelled. Existence and peace are equality, primordially beyond arising. How, then, could we conceive of a cyclic existence to be relinquished or a transcendence of suffering to be adopted, given that both the objects of relinquishment and of cultivation lack establishment? With this insight, one will be liberated from relative cyclic existence. The Master himself teaches:

> Here there is nothing whatsoever to exclude,
> And not a bit to maintain.
> Look, genuinely into the genuine—
> When the genuine is seen, there is total liberation.[152]

While the *Noble Sūtra on the Taming of the Demons* explains:

---

152. Nāgārjuna, *Heart of Dependent Origination*, 7.

Likewise, those who are liberated are simply those who completely understand inauthentic identifications. Apart from that, there is no liberation from anything at all. It is the complete understanding of this that is referred to as "liberation."

This concludes the explanation of the sixteenth chapter, the analysis of bondage and liberation, in the *Ornament of Reason,* a commentary on the *Root of the Middle Way.*

CHAPTER SEVENTEEN

Analysis of Action and Its Results

ALSO THE ANALYSIS of action and its results is treated in terms of three issues. First, regarding its context, the present chapter is related to the profound sūtras that teach that action and its results are devoid of nature. The *Sūtra on Transference of Existence,* for example, proclaims:

> Great king, death and transference are empty of death and transference, birth is empty of birth, action is empty of action, and the result of action is empty of the result of action.

Here, the meaning of such statements is established by means of reasoning.

As for its relationship to the other chapters of the text, the present analysis responds to the following notion: "Even though cyclic existence may have been refuted, it does indeed exist. A sūtra teaches:

> I myself will experience
> The results of my own actions.

Thus, the relationship between action and its consequences is a fact. Let us imagine that there is no cyclic existence, in the sense of either the formations or the person coming into this life, and from here passing on to a future life. If this were the case, the results of actions committed in the past could not be experienced in this life, and the results of what was done in this life could not be experienced in the future. Moreover, we do not observe the ripening of a delightful or unpleasant result at the time when the virtuous or nonvirtuous karmic action is carried out."

The present chapter is presented to explain that actions and their results are themselves devoid of nature.

THE CONTENT OF CHAPTER 17

Explaining the content will address (1) objections to this presentation and (2) replies to these objections.

OBJECTIONS

The first includes (1) setting forth the nature of action and its result and (2) showing that the presentations are not flawed by permanence and annihilation.

The Nature of Action and Its Result

The first section includes (1) the divisions of action and (2) the effects of action.

The Divisions of Action

The first of these issues is again divided in three sections, of which the first presents a concise classification.

Concise Classification

The treatise states:

> Restraining oneself properly,
> Helping others, and a loving mind—
> These are Dharma, seeds that bear fruit
> Both here and hereafter. [XVII.1]

Actions are classified as either virtuous or nonvirtuous based on whether or not their ripening will be pleasant. Virtuous actions can be divided further with reference to the following three mental states: 1) Proper restraint from killing and the other misdeeds of body, speech, and mind with respect to oneself (that is, the identity that is imputed based on the aggregates); 2) training in the four means of magnetizing, the means for protecting against fear, and other such factors in order to actively help others; and 3) a loving mind that is intent on freeing others from suffering and wanting them to be happy. These three types of mind are Dharma, in the sense that they keep and protect one from falling into the lower realms. As such, they constitute seeds that will bear the fruits of pleasant karmic ripening in both this life and in lives hereafter.

"Seeds" are distinguished from cooperating conditions in that the former are factors that facilitate a specific effect or serve to produce their effect's essence. Cooperating conditions, on the other hand, are those factors that facilitate a general effect or serve to produce distinct properties .

Nonvirtuous actions are the opposite of the above. Hence, a mind that is inclined toward flawed conduct of body, speech, or mind, and a mind that is actively engaged in such conduct, is classified as non-Dharma. These types of mind result in seeds that will produce unpleasant fruits in both this life and lives hereafter.

Expanded Classification
Elaborating on this classification, the treatise states:

> *The Supreme Sage has taught*
> *That action is volition and the willed.*
> *The subdivisions of these actions*
> *Are set forth in great detail. [XVII.2]*

> *That which is taught as "actions of volition"*
> *Is asserted to be mental,*
> *While the so-called intended actions*
> *Are physical and verbal. [XVII.3]*

The Buddha is supreme among those noble sages who have realized the ultimate. He taught that the aforementioned virtuous and nonvirtuous actions can be further divided into actions that are volition and those that are willed. The subdivisions of these two actions have been set forth in great detail. Those that are taught to be "actions of volition" are asserted to be mental in the sense that they are completed simply by arising in, or occurring to, the mind. So-called willed actions, on the other hand, are classified as physical and verbal. They occur in body and speech and are completed by being physically or verbally performed subsequent to the mind's willing. Thus, actions as well are classified in terms of body, speech, and mind.

The Classification Expanded Further
Third, further expanding this classification, the treatise states:

Speech and movement;
Imperceptible nonabstinence
And imperceptible abstinence—
These are similarly asserted. [XVII.4]

The merit that arises from enjoyment
And the demerit, in a similar manner,
Along with volition—
These seven principles are held to be action. [XVII.5]

When the classification is further expanded, we arrive at seven principles. First, there are the two perceptible actions that take the form of virtuous or nonvirtuous verbal actions and movements of the body. Next is the so-called imperceptible nonabstinence that is associated with not giving up nonvirtues such as killing. Whether or not one was born into a community where nonvirtuous actions, such as killing, theft, and robbery, are the norm, nonabstinence will occur whenever one is capable of performing a negative act and then accepts it as part of one's general conduct. Once it has arisen, this nonabstinence will continuously engender evil, even when one no longer actively pursues the particular nonvirtuous course of action due to, for example, insanity. A vow, on the other hand, is the imperceptible abstinence from flawed conduct, such as killing. A vow arises when, in the presence of a preceptor, disciples, and so forth, one completes the perceptible verbal and physical acts that are associated with pledging to refrain from killing and the like. Once arisen, a vow will continue to bring forth virtue, even if there is a lack of the causes for remaining fully committed to it, as may be the case with insanity, for instance. As is the case with perceptible actions, imperceptible actions are asserted to be either virtuous or nonvirtuous. These two types of action are termed "imperceptible" because, although they pertain to the aggregate of form and create a continuous stream of either virtue or nonvirtue, they cannot be perceived by others.

When enjoyments are offered to the Sangha, for example, their partaking of the offerings will engender merit in the donor's stream of being. Alternatively, building a temple where living beings are killed will mean that demerit is created in the builder's stream of being for as long as the devotees there engage in killing. Thus, there are two further types of action: meritorious actions that arise from enjoyments and demeritorious actions that arise from enjoyments. By finally adding the aforementioned action of volition to these six willed actions, we arrive at an enumeration of seven principles. These are asserted to be bearers of the characteristics of action.

The Effects of Action
Second, on the effects of action, the treatise states below:

> The ten avenues of wholesome action
> Are the means for performing Dharma.
> Here and hereafter, the fruits of Dharma
> Are the five sense pleasures. [XVII.11]

The seven types of action mentioned above include the ten avenues of wholesome action. These avenues are the means for performing Dharma through the completion of the actions associated with the three virtuous mind-sets that were explained above, or with these ten virtues. The fruits of the Dharma that are accomplished in this way will manifest both in this and other lives as beautiful visual forms and the like, that is, as the five sense pleasures. The effects of non-Dharma, on the other hand, are just the opposite.

How This Account Is Not Flawed by Permanence or Annihilation
The second issue relates to the criticism that actions would end up permanent or annihilated. This section includes (1) stating the criticism and (2) presenting replies to this criticism.

The Criticism
On the first issue, the treatise states:

> If an action would remain until ripening,
> Then it would be permanent.
> If it ceases, then having ceased,
> How could it produce an effect? [XVII.6]

If these karmic actions remain until the time of their ripening, they would be permanent. Yet if they do not remain but instead cease, then having ceased, how could they give rise to effects? The effects of such actions would be as unfeasible as sprouts emerging from burnt seeds. These actions would have ceased to be.

Replies to the Criticism
The second issue includes (1) a reply by appealing to a concordance between cause and effect, (2) a refutation of that reply, and (3) a reply by asserting the substance of nondissipation. The first section contains an account of how the Followers of Sūtra, a school of the listener tradition, show examples to demonstrate the irrelevance of the aforementioned criticism. This will include their explanation of (1) how causes produce their effects and (2) how this does not imply either permanence or annihilation.

The Sūtra Followers' Account of Karmic Causality
On the first issue, the treatise states:

> *The continuum of the sprout and so forth*
> *Manifests from the seed,*
> *Due to which the fruit comes about;*
> *Without the seed, it would not arise. [XVII.7]*

In the external world, the continuum that consists of sprout, leaf, stem, and other such factors manifests from a seed. It is because of this resultant continuum based on the seed that finally a harvest of fruit manifests. Without the prior existence of the seed, the sprout and other aspects of the continuum would not arise, and there would then not be any harvest of fruit as a result either. Thus, this concomitance shows that these things are causally related.

How Permanence and Annihilation Are Avoided
On the second issue, the treatise states:

> *The continuum arises from the seed,*
> *And from the continuum comes the fruit.*
> *Therefore, the seed precedes the fruit.*
> *Hence, there is no annihilation or permanence. [XVII.8]*

> *That which is the continuum of mind*
> *Manifests from the mind,*

And from that emerges the effect.
Without this mind, it would not occur. [XVII.9]

The continuum arises from the mind,
And from the continuum comes the effect.
Therefore, the action precedes the effect
And there is no annihilation or permanence. [XVII.10]

If the seed did not cease, there would be the flaw of permanence. On the other hand, if it were to cease without having caused the production of a continuum, the consequence would be annihilation. Yet the seed precedes the fruit and ceases before it. Therefore, there is no permanence. Moreover, as explained before, the seed becomes the cause for the production of the sprout and other aspects of the continuum before ceasing. The resultant harvest emerges from that continuum. There is, therefore, no annihilation either.

The understanding derived from this example can then be applied to show how karmic actions produce their effect, and how the presence of the effect depends entirely on the prior presence of an action. The mental continuum that is conjoined with the formation of virtuous or nonvirtuous volitions manifests from the initial mind that is conjoined with virtue or nonvirtue. From that continuum, the effects of pleasant or unpleasant ripening emerge. Were it not for the initial mind conjoined with virtue or nonvirtue, neither the continuum nor the effect would occur.

This, then, is how permanence and annihilation are avoided. Permanence would be the case if the volition that forms the action would not cease, while annihilation would occur if it were to cease without having caused the continuum's production. Nevertheless, as explained before, the virtuous or nonvirtuous volitions that form actions precede their effects and cease before them. Hence, there is no permanence. Moreover, as they cease, the volitions become the causes for the arising of a continuum. Thus, as the initial mind conjoined with virtuous or nonvirtuous volition gives rise to its continuum, and as the pleasant and unpleasant effects emerge from that continuum, there is no annihilation either.

How the Proponents of Differences Refute This
Second, showing how this account is refuted by the Proponents of Differences, the treatise states:

When it comes to this account,
There are numerous and significant flaws.
Hence, this account
Is untenable here. [XVII.12]

The account that was presented above holds that a mind infused with either virtue or nonvirtue gives rise to a continuum that is of the same character as itself, which, in turn, subsequently leads to the manifestation of the effect, likening this process to the development of a sprout and so on. This account, however, involves numerous and significant flaws. Consider the virtuous, nonvirtuous, and neutral mind-sets; those associated with the desire realm, the form realm, and the formless realm; with defilement and nondefilement; and with being a god and being human. These minds would then all produce exclusively the mental continuum of whatever is characteristic of themselves, whether that be virtue, nonvirtue, and so on. If this were the case, a virtuous continuum could not, for example, be replaced by a nonvirtuous mind-set. Hence, this account seriously contradicts what we see to be the case. Accordingly, here in the context of karmic causality, it is not reasonable to argue that since the essence of an action has ceased, there is no permanence and that because a continuum that is of a similar kind has been produced, there is no annihilation.

The Account of the Proponents of Differences
Well, what response is given to the argument that action ends up either permanent or annihilated? The Proponents of Differences respond by asserting the substance of nondissipation. Their account includes (1) a presentation, (2) an explanation, and (3) a conclusion.

Presentation
For the first, the treatise states:

The account given by the Buddhas,
The self-realized buddhas, and the listeners
Is the one that is tenable here.
That, then, shall be set forth. [XVII.13]

The scriptures of the Buddhas, self-realized buddhas, and listeners present an account that is supported by reasoning and that is tenable here in the context of karmic causality. Hence, it shall be set forth.

Explanation
Second, the elaborate explanation of the position of the Proponents of Differences has nine subdivisions. The first is a presentation of the essence of nondissipation using an example.

The Essence of Nondissipation Shown through an Example
The treatise states:

> *Nondissipation resembles a promissory note.*
> *The action then is the debt. [XVII.14a–b]*

Though a loan may have been spent, because of the promissory note, the capital that was loaned must be returned with interest to the creditor at some point. Thus, the creditor's capital will not be lost. Likewise, when a virtuous or nonvirtuous action occurs, a phenomenon referred to as the "nondissipation" of that action will be present in the agent's stream of being. This nonassociated formation pertains to the category of attainment and is a different phenomenon than the action itself. Resembling the loan, the action ceases as soon as it has occurred and is, for that reason, not permanent. Yet, in the same way that a spent loan must be paid back with interest at some point because of the promissory note, the nondissipation of the action will ensure that its expanded effect will follow at some point, although it has itself ceased. Therefore, the action is not annihilated either.

The Divisions of Nondissipation
Second, presenting the divisions of nondissipation, the treatise states:

> *It is fourfold with reference to the realms [XVII.14c]*

Nondissipation is fourfold, for there is a particular type associated with the desire realm, the form realm, the formless realm, and the undefiling realm.

The Nature of Nondissipation
Third, on the nature of nondissipation, the treatise states:

> *And its nature is neutral. [XVII.14d]*

Nondissipation cannot be understood to be either virtuous or nonvirtuous. It is, therefore, of a neutral nature. If the nondissipation of a virtuous
action were also virtuous, this would mean that for someone whose fundamental virtues have been severed, all the nondissipation of virtue would
be gone as well. This, in turn, would mean that that person would not
experience the pleasant effects of whatever virtuous acts he or she committed in the past. Likewise, if the nondissipation of a nonvirtuous action
were itself nonvirtuous, all the nondissipation of nonvirtue would have
disappeared in the case of someone who has achieved freedom from the
desire that characterizes the desire realm. Such a person would, then, not
have to experience the effects of nonvirtuous actions done in the past.

The Relinquishment of Nondissipation
The fourth issue concerns the classification of nondissipation as a discard.
The treatise states:

> *It is not eliminated by elimination,*
> *Yet it is eliminated through cultivation. [XVII.15a–b]*

It is taught that:

> For those who have seen the truth, there is no impelling.[153]

Hence, reaching the path of seeing means that there will be no engagement in any of the actions that impel ordinary individuals to a rebirth
in the three realms. Nevertheless, such impelling actions were accumulated while the individual was an ordinary being and, generally speaking,
the nondissipations associated with virtuous and nonvirtuous actions
are not eliminated by the attainment of the path of seeing. Hence,

---

153. From Vasubandhu, *Commentary on the Sūtra on the Discernment of Dependent
Origination.*

nondissipation is not eliminated through the elimination of discards that takes place when the intrinsic nature is seen.

It is, however, eliminated through the path of cultivation. From the lesser of the lesser stages through the greater of the greater stages of the path of cultivation, the nondissipation that is responsible for the experience of action ripening within the three realms is gradually eliminated. The process begins with the elimination of the greater of the greater nondissipations and culminates in the disappearance of the lesser of the lesser ones. The word "yet" in the beginning of the second line makes the message similar to the following:

> For them there are no afflictions,
> Yet they perceive the force of action.[154]

In other words, noble foe-destroyers have eliminated all the afflictions that are associated with the three realms and that are to be discarded on the path of cultivation. Yet until they have gone beyond the three realms, they will possess the supportive aggregates and will experience the effects of the virtuous and nonvirtuous actions they engaged in the past. Therefore, they also possess the nondissipation associated with those actions. This nondissipation will be eliminated once they transcend the three realms.

The Rationale
Fifth, on the rationale for the above classification, the treatise states below:

> *If it were eliminated by elimination*
> *Or destroyed by a transference of action,*
> *Various flaws would ensue,*
> *Such as the destruction of action. [XVII.16]*

What if the nondissipation of actions were eliminated along with the actions themselves, or if nondissipation were eliminated by eliminating the factors that are discarded through seeing? What if the continuity of nondissipation associated with an action were destroyed by the transference of action that takes place when shifting from one type of action to

---

154. Śāntideva, *Entering the Activity of the Bodhisattvas*, IX.45c–d.

another? Such scenarios would mean the destruction of the effects of the actions of both noble and ordinary beings because the causes of such effects would be missing. Moreover, it would then be possible to encounter the effects of actions that one had not performed, while the effects of what one has, in fact, done would be lost. All such flaws would ensue from these positions.

The Qualities of Nondissipation
Sixth, on the qualities of nondissipation, the treatise states:

> *Therefore, it is due to nondissipation*
> *That the effects of action are produced. [XVII.15c–d]*

The discards through seeing are, hence, eliminated without nondissipation being eliminated. Although an action ceases, the continuity of its nondissipation will not be destroyed. In this way, it is due to the nondissipation of past virtuous and nonvirtuous actions that noble and ordinary individuals experience the pleasant and unpleasant effects of their actions.

The Arising of Nondissipation
The seventh issue is the arising of nondissipation. First, its arising in this life will be addressed. The treatise states:

> *During the present life it arises*
> *Separately with each instance*
> *Of the two types of action,*
> *Remaining even after the ripening. [XVII.18]*

During the present life, a separate nondissipation arises with every instance of defiling or undefiling action. The action and its nondissipation are substantially different from one another. Nondissipation will, moreover, remain even after it has effectuated a karmic ripening. Yet, just like a promissory note that has been annulled subsequent to the return of a relevant loan, it will no longer be capable of engendering ripening.

The Arising of Nondissipation at the Time of Linking
Next, on the arising of nondissipation at the time of the linking between two lives, the treatise states:

All those associated with realm-specific actions,
Whether congruent or incongruent,
Manifest as only one
When linking takes place. [XVII.17]

Actions that are realm specific (in the sense that their ripening will be experienced in the same realm as the one in which they are performed) may be congruent or an incongruent blend of virtue and nonvirtue. The substantial nondissipation associated with each such action will remain assembled as a multiplicity during the present life. Yet, when one life is linked with another life within the desire, form, or formless realm, all such realm-specific actions will no longer be multiple and instead manifest as a single substance of nondissipation only.

Although the actions may be congruent, actions that are not realm specific, and so are to be experienced in a different realm, will nevertheless not turn into the same single nondissipation.[155]

The Cessation of Nondissipation
Eighth, on the cessation of nondissipation, the treatise states:

It ceases at transference
To the fruition or at death. [XVII.19a–b]

Nondissipation ceases during the gradual process of transference into the four fruitions of virtuous training. How this takes place was explained earlier in the context of the second verse of the fifteenth stanza. Nondissipation also ceases at the point of death. This is to be understood in terms of the cessation of the multiplicity of substances at the time of linking with another life and the subsequent arising of one great nondissipation, as was explained in the seventeenth stanza.

Concise Classification of Nondissipation
Ninth, classifying nondissipation concisely, the treatise states:

155. In an apparent error, the Tibetan text does here not contain any negation, and instead reads, "nevertheless turn into the same single nondissipation" (kyang chud mi za ba gcig tu 'gyur ro).

It should be understood that it is divided
In terms of the defiling and undefiling. [XVII.19c–d]

It should be understood that the defiling and the undefiling constitute a concise classification of nondissipation.

Conclusion
Third, in conclusion the treatise states:

Emptiness and absence of annihilation,
Cyclic existence and absence of permanence—
The phenomenon of nondissipation
Is the teaching of the Buddha. [XVII.20]

Action ceases as soon as it has arisen. Hence, it is empty of any permanent entity and is, thus, not permanent. Nevertheless, it is not annihilated either, because, as it is taught:

The action of corporeal beings does not dissipate,
Even in a hundred eons.[156]

Thus, it is explained that although an action itself ceases, its nondissipation brings about a karmic effect, making all these myriad forms of cyclic existence possible.

This concludes the presentation of the opponents' objections.

REPLIES TO THE OBJECTIONS

In reply to the above, it will be explained that since action and its effect have no nature, the cyclic existence that supports them has no existence either. This includes explaining (1) why there are no flaws in terms of permanence and annihilation, given that action has no nature, (2) the refutation of nature, and (3) how action and its results can be set forth conventionally using examples, although they have no nature.

---

156. From the *Minor Precepts of the Vinaya*.

Without Nature, There Are No Flaws of Permanence and Annihilation

On the first issue, the treatise states:

> *Why does action not arise?*
> *Because it has no nature.*
> *Because it does not arise,*
> *Action does not dissipate. [XVII.21]*

All these attempts at explaining action as beyond permanence and annihilation are like working to restore a city of scent-eaters, or a dream city. They are pointless endeavors. If action were to arise by nature, it would have to either remain or perish, thus resulting in the flaws of permanence and annihilation. Yet given that action does not, in reality, arise, it is neither permanent nor annihilated, like the child of a barren woman. And why would this be the case? Since action has no nature, it does not arise in reality.

At this point, one may then wonder: "If this is the case, why do the sūtras teach:

> The action of corporeal beings does not dissipate,
> Even in a hundred eons.
> When the right time and conditions come together,
> It ripens into its result.[157]

Indeed, what you say contradicts this teaching."

This, however, is not the case. What this sūtra points out is that, since action does not arise in reality, there is nothing that could dissipate. On this point, it has been taught:

> Because it does not cease by nature,
> The capacity is still present, without any all-ground.[158]

Thus, because action does not arise by nature, it does not cease by nature either. Moreover, since this does not conflict with the conventional

---

157. From the *Minor Precepts of the Vinaya.*
158. Candrakīrti, *Entering the Middle Way*, VI.39a–b.

manifestation of the effects of action, it is taught that action does not dissipate.

The Nature of Action

The second section includes (1) a criticism and (2) a refutation of arguments. The first of these includes two further sections: (1) setting forth the consequence of action's becoming permanent and (2) showing how accepting this consequence cannot be accepted.

The Consequence of Action's Becoming Permanent

On the first issue, the treatise states:

> *If action had a nature,*
> *It would, undoubtedly, be permanent. [XVII.22a–b]*

It was objected that the evidence, action's having no nature, lacks establishment. Yet if action had a nature, it would, undoubtedly, be permanent. Its permanence would be entailed because, as has already been explained, "A nature that undergoes change would never make any sense."[159]

How the Consequence Is Unacceptable

The second involves demonstrating (1) the consequence that action would be uncreated and (2) the consequence that ripening would occur ad infinitum.

The Consequence That Action Would Be Uncreated

On the first issue, the treatise states:

> *Action would not be created*
> *Because the permanent cannot be active. [XVII.22c–d]*

For those who believe action to be permanent, action would be as uncreated as space. This is entailed because something permanent cannot participate in any activity. If actions were permanent, they could not change from their previous state of existence or nonexistence. The position that

---

159. *Root of the Middle Way*, XV.8c–d.

action is uncreated conflicts with both (1) scripture and (2) worldly consensus. On the first issue, the treatise states:

> *If action were uncreated, there would be fear*
> *Of encountering that which had not been done.*
> *A lack of pure conduct*
> *Would follow as a flaw as well. [XVII.23]*

> *The distinction between virtuous persons and sinners*
> *Would no longer make sense. [XVII.24c–d]*

Given that their effects would still have to be experienced, if actions were believed to be uncreated, one would have to fear encountering the effects of actions that one did not commit, such as those with immediate effects. Moreover, spiritual practitioners who do not engage in impure conduct could still be stained by lack of pure conduct. Thus, the lack of pure conduct also follows as a flaw of the assertion that action is not created.

Likewise, as pointed out in the next stanza, people who engage exclusively in either virtue or evil could not reasonably be spoken of as "virtuous" or "sinners." Indeed, they could not be distinguished at all because each would be subject to either the virtue or sin that they themselves did not commit.

On the second issue, the treatise states:

> *Undoubtedly, this would*
> *Contradict all conventions. [XVII.24a–b]*

Any activity that is done with the expectation of a certain result, such as tilling a field, would be pointless if this were the case. In the end, this would undoubtedly contradict all the world's conventions as well. For example, since effects would be present without having been created, telling someone, "make a vase," would be pointless.

The Consequence That Ripening Would Occur ad Infinitum

On the second consequence, the treatise states:

> *The ripening that has already ripened*
> *Would go on ripening again and again.*

For if it possessed a nature,
Action would remain present. [XVII.25]

As explained above, if action had a nature, it would remain continuously present. If we accept that, even actions that have already ripened would continue to ripen as if they had not yet done so, due to the fact that past actions would still be present. Indeed, they would go on ripening again and again.

Refutation of Arguments
Second, the refutation of the arguments in favor of naturally existent actions has three subdivisions. First is the refutation of the causal afflictions.

The Causal Afflictions
The treatise states:

> *Action is constituted by the afflictions,*
> *But the afflictions are not real.*
> *If afflictions are not real,*
> *How could action be so? [XVII.26]*

It may be thought: "Action exists by nature. It is taught that 'ignorance serves as the circumstance for formation, grasping serves as the circumstance for becoming,' and so on. Hence, since the afflictions that cause it exist, action exists as well."

The afflictions, however, are not real because they originate dependently and they disintegrate and come to an end. If the afflictions are not real, how could action be real? Its lack of reality is entailed because if, as stated, action is constituted by the afflictions, that is, if it arises in dependence on the afflictions, we may conclude:

> When the seed of something is false,
> How could its arising be true?[160]

---

160. Nāgārjuna, *Jewel Garland*, I.29.

The Resultant Body
Second is a refutation of the resultant body. The treatise states:

> *Action and affliction are taught*
> *To be conditions for the body.*
> *If action and affliction are empty,*
> *Then what can be said of the body? [XVII.27]*

It might be argued: "Action and affliction exist by nature because we observe their effect, namely, the body."

If this were the case, what kind of nature could we ascribe to this subject, the body? Since they have already been refuted, action and affliction are devoid of nature. The entailment of this argument becomes evident by considering that the sūtras teach action and affliction to be the conditions for the body.

The Resultant Consumer
Third is a refutation of the consumer that results from action. The treatise states:

> *The consumer is that being*
> *Who is obscured by ignorance and has craving.*
> *This being is not different from the agent,*
> *Yet neither are these two identical. [XVII.28]*

> *Because action does not arise*
> *Based on conditions*
> *Or based on nonconditions,*
> *There is no agent either. [XVII.29]*

> *If there is no action and no agent,*
> *How could there be a result produced by action?*
> *If there is no result,*
> *How could there be a consumer? [XVII.30]*

It might be argued: "Action exists by nature because its effect, the consumer, exists. A sūtra teaches:

Sentient beings obscured by ignorance
Are tied by the bonds of existence.

Thus, the consumer is the being in whom ignorance obscures the eye of genuine insight, thereby preventing the vision of the path to peace, and who has craving. As is taught:

I myself will experience
The results of my own actions.

Hence, the consumer is not substantially different from the agent that engaged in actions in the past. Yet it is not identical with the agent either, because if this were the case, it would be permanent and, thus, incapable of performing a function. Therefore, the consumer defies description, and by that token action exists as well."

Yet the consumer itself lacks natural establishment. As this has already been refuted in the analysis of conditions and the analysis of action and agent, neither conditions nor nonconditions can produce actions. There is, therefore, no agent of action either. If neither action nor agent exist, how could there possibly be any result produced by action? And when there is no result, how could there possibly be any consumer of that? In other words, how could there be someone who experiences the result?

How Action Can Be Set Forth Conventionally Although It Has No Nature

Third, showing how action can be set forth conventionally although it has no nature, the treatise states:

The Teacher, in a perfect miracle,
Creates emanations,
And these emanations again
Create further emanations. [XVII.31]

Likewise, the act performed by the agent
Resembles an emanation,
Just as when one emanation
Gives rise to another. [XVII.32]

Affliction, action, the body,
The agent, and the result
Are all like a city of scent-eaters,
Like an illusion, and like a dream. [XVII.33]

It may be thought: "The sūtras explain the relationship between action and its effects, teaching that 'I myself will experience the results of my own actions.' Yet all of this has been refuted here. Hence, this view is a mistaken denial of the consequences of our actions; it is nihilism."

This is not the case. Indeed, we have refuted that any of this possesses a nature, but we have not proved that it is nonexistent in a conventional sense. Neither is it the case that if something lacks nature, it cannot reasonably function at the level of convention. Let us use an example that is accepted by the treatises. The Teacher, the Buddha, the Transcendent Conqueror, creates emanations. These emanations are created in a perfect miracle where one emanation gives rise to a second, the second creates a third, and so forth. Likewise, although the agent has no nature, it is still able to act in terms of convention. Thus, the agent resembles an emanation. Although the act has no nature, it can still be carried out conventionally, just as when one emanation gives rise to another. The same point can be made by means of an example that is in line with worldly consensus. Afflictions such as desire; the virtuous, nonvirtuous, or immovable actions that are motivated by affliction; their resulting physical support (that is, the body); the ineffable self that is the agent of the karmic act; and the ripened, ruled, and concordant effects that are the results of affliction and action—none of this has any nature, and yet conventionally it originates in dependence. It all appears in the same way as a city of scent-eaters, like an illusion and like a dream.

SUMMARY OF THE CHAPTER'S SIGNIFICANCE

In this way, the present chapter offers an existential refutation of the belief that such things as actions and their results have an ultimate nature. Likewise, it has established that, in terms of the relative, they originate in dependence, resembling emanations, and so on. *The King of Meditative Absorptions* explains:

When the Bliss-Gone One offers advice,
Then, he, the Protector and Victor,
Out of love for the wayfaring people, produces emanations,
And they too teach the excellent Dharma of the Buddha.

As this is heard by thousands of living beings,
They come to aspire to the Buddha's supreme wakefulness,
Wondering, "When shall I attain such wakefulness?"
Knowing their wishes, the Victor thus grants his prophesy

Furthermore:

A city of scent-eaters may appear,
Yet without existing anywhere in the ten directions, nor anywhere
    else.
There is nothing to it but a name.
It is, in this way, that the Thus-Gone sees this world.

This concludes the explanation of the seventeenth chapter, the analysis of
actions and their results, in the *Ornament of Reason,* a commentary on the
Root of the Middle Way.

CHAPTER EIGHTEEN

Analysis of Self and Phenomena

THE THREE ISSUES pertain to the analysis of self and phenomena as well.[161]

THE CONTEXT OF CHAPTER 18

In terms of context, the present chapter relates to the profound sūtras, such as the following passage from the *Mother of the Victorious Ones*:

> Form is empty of self and of that which belongs to the self.

The *Journey to Laṅkā* similarly states:

> This so-called self is a demonic idea;
> From this, views issue forth.
> These conditioned aggregates are empty;
> Here, there is no self and no sentient being.

Thus, the sūtras teach that the aggregates are devoid of any nature in terms of both the self and that which belongs to the self. This chapter employs reasoning to ascertain the meaning of such teachings.

As for its relationship to the other analyses in the text, the present chapter presents a reply to the following question: "Nothing is as it appears. Hence, the afflictions, actions, the body, and so forth are not real. They are similar to, for example, a city of scent-eaters. While they do not exist in

---

161. In this chapter the concluding summary is not explicit as a separate section of the text.

reality, they mistakenly appear to exist from the perspective of the childish. What, then, is the real condition of phenomena? How is it realized? What are the means for gaining access to it? And what are the results of realization?"

In response to these questions, the analysis of self and phenomena will explain how outer and inner things are not genuinely established. For this reason, the objects of the apprehension of a self and something that belongs it, that is, the aggregates associated with "I" and "mine," are pacified from the beginning. When, through genuine insight, one observes neither the self nor something that belongs to it, all apprehensions of persons and phenomena with respect to outer and inner phenomena will be exhausted.

When one inquires, "What are these aggregates associated with 'I' and 'mine'?" and unerringly uses reason to examine this issue, what happens is as described here:

> Once the object of examination is examined thoroughly,
> Examination itself is found to be baseless.
> Being baseless, it does not occur.
> This as well is taught to be the transcendence of suffering.[162]

What this passage points out is that, from the perspective of rational examination, the aggregates associated with "I" and "mine" are not observed, and there is no apprehension of a self or something that belongs to it. When such apprehension is exhausted, affliction and action cease, the result of which is the complete pacification of the cycle of birth and death, thereby bringing the attainment of the transcendence of suffering.

THE CONTENT OF CHAPTER 18

The meaning of this chapter's content will be explained in terms of (1) how to access reality, (2) the nature of reality, and (3) the results of realization. The first of these involves (1) refuting the notions of "I" and "mine," (2) the effect of this refutation, and (3) showing that this refutation does

---

162. Śāntideva, *Entering the Activity of the Bodhisattvas*, IX.110.

not contradict scripture. The first topic includes (1) a refutation of the appropriating self by showing that it is neither identical to, nor different from, the appropriated aggregates and (2) explaining how the appropriated aggregates that belong to the self are refuted thereby.

The Self Is neither Identical to nor Different from the Aggregates
On the first issue, the treatise states:

> If the self were the aggregates,
> It would arise and cease.
> If it were different from the aggregates,
> It would have none of their characteristics. [XVIII.1]

Is the appropriating self essentially the same as, or different from, the appropriated aggregates? If identical with the aggregates, the self would arise and cease, and it would be a composite of multiple factors. This follows because, if this were the case, the self would be essentially inseparable from the impermanent and multiple aggregates. The self being impermanent and multiple is unacceptable to non-Buddhist schools because it contradicts their claim that the self is permanent and singular. It cannot be accepted by the Buddhist schools either because something momentary cannot provide the common foundation for both the agent of karmic actions and the one that experiences their results. This would render the principle of karmic causality untenable.

A multiplicity of selves would also contradict Buddhist scripture, which states, "When the world is born, it is one single person that is born." Similarly, *Entering the Middle Way* presents an elaborate refutation of those Buddhist schools that hold the self to be essentially the same as the aggregates:

> If the self were the aggregates, it would be many
> Because the aggregates are multiple.
> The self would be substantial, and as the view of self
> Would then apply to substance, it would not be mistaken.
>
> At the transcendence of suffering, the self would certainly be
>   annihilated,
> And before that, the momentary arising and ceasing

Could not involve any agent, so consequences would be utterly
    nonexistent;
What was accumulated by one would be consumed by another.[163]

Our present treatise further explains:

The appropriated is not the self,
For it arises and disintegrates.
How could the appropriated
Ever be the appropriator?[164]

Yet, what if the self were essentially distinct from the aggregates? On this
topic, scripture states:

What is the conditioned? It is the five aggregates.

Hence, if the self were essentially different from the aggregates, it would be
devoid of the arising, remaining, and ceasing that characterizes the conditioned. It would then not be feasible for the self to be a functional thing.

Alternatively, it may be explained that since the self would lack all of
the individual characteristics of the aggregates, such as being suited to be
form, it would have to be observable via different characteristics and with
a different essence. A self that has a different essence than the aggregates
is, however, unobservable. Hence, it does not exist.

In this context, it should be understood that the refutation of a self that
is identical to or distinct from the aggregates implicitly refutes also the
beliefs in a self that supports the aggregates, that is supported by them, or
that possesses them.

The Entailed Refutation of the Appropriated Aggregates

On the second issue, the treatise states:

When the self does not exist,
How could that which belongs to it? [XVIII.2a–b]

---

163. Candrakīrti, *Entering the Middle Way*, VI.127–28.
164. *Root of the Middle Way*, XXVII.6.

When the self that is the agent of causal karmic actions and the appropriator of the resultant aggregates does not exist, how could the effect of karmic actions, the appropriated aggregates that belong to the self, possibly
have any natural existence? Without an agent there cannot be any action,
and if there is no appropriator, there cannot be anything appropriated.

The Effect of These Refutations

Second, the effect of these refutations involves (1) explaining how subjective grasping is renounced, (2) dispensing with objections to this
refutation, and (3) showing how the cessation of grasping brings about
liberation.

How Subjective Grasping Is Renounced

On the first issue, the treatise states:

> Due to the pacification of self and that which belongs to it,
> The belief in an "I" and a "mine" will cease. [XVIII.2c–d]

The yogin observes neither an appropriating self nor any appropriated
aggregates, being aware of their natural pacification. The belief in an "I"
and of aggregates that are "mine" is, therefore, absent and does not occur,
just as knowing a mirage to be devoid of water will make the mind stop
thinking that there is water.

The Renunciation of Grasping Is Indisputable

On the second issue, the treatise states:

> The one who does not grasp at "I" or "mine"
> Does not exist either.
> The one who sees what lacks the grasping of "I" and "mine,"
> That one does not see. [XVIII.3]

It may be thought: "Since the yogin who does not grasp at "I" and "mine"
exists, the self and that which belongs to it must exist as well."

The yogin for whom there is no apprehension of "I" and "mine" does
not have any natural existence either. The mere notions of self and aggregates have already been refuted, and there cannot possibly be any yogin
who is not included in either of these two principles. The yogin who is

free from these two types of grasping is, hence, not established. Therefore, it must be understood that if someone sees, or perceives there to be, an entity that is the yogin for whom grasping "I" and "mine" are absent, then that person is not seeing reality. As the *Sūtra on the King of Meditative Absorptions* instructs:

> See that the identity of the inner is empty.
> See that the external is empty as well.
> The one that meditates on emptiness —
> No such thing exists either.

The Cessation of Grasping Brings Liberation

On the third issue, the treatise states:

> *When the sense of "I" and "mine" that is based*
> *On the inner and outer is exhausted,*
> *Appropriation comes to an end.*
> *As that is exhausted, so is birth. [XVIII.4]*

> *Liberation follows from the exhaustion of action and affliction.*
> *Action and affliction are due to thought,*
> *And thoughts proliferate due to mental construction.*
> *They are brought to an end by emptiness. [XVIII.5]*

The grasping sense of "I" and "mine" is based on the inner aggregates that are imbued with consciousness and the outer aggregates that are not. The exhaustion of this fixation brings an end to the fourfold grasping: grasping in terms of desire, view, the supremacy of view and discipline, and the doctrine of self. The exhaustion of these four causal graspings brings an end to becoming, which, in turn, brings an end to future rebirths as well. Hence, it should be understood that the attainment of liberation and the transcendence of suffering follow from the exhaustion of action and affliction.

What is it, then, that brings an end to action and affliction? Well, action and affliction cease once their causes cease. As was already explained, action and affliction are caused by incorrect thinking, apprehending a self and something that belongs to it, and so on. These thoughts, in turn, are due to mental construction.

The term "mental construction" translates the Sanskrit *prapañca*. This term has several meanings, but in the present context it refers to the mental constructs that are associated with the apprehension of marks. Thus, it implies the mental construction of something that cognizes and something that is cognized; that which is signified and that which signifies; and so forth. All such proliferating constructs stem from a construction of marks to which the mind has been accustomed since beginningless time. By familiarizing oneself with the view that sees the natural emptiness of all the constructed phenomena related to mind and cognized objects, all this is brought to an end. When mental constructs cease, the incorrect thinking that they produce is brought to an end; when incorrect thinking ceases, affliction ends; when afflictions cease, action ends; and the cessation of action means the end of birth.

The Refutation of I and Mine Does Not Contradict Scripture

On the third issue, the treatise states:

> "Self" is stated
> And also "no self" is taught.
> The Buddhas even teach that there is neither
> Self nor absence of self. [XVIII.6]

Some may wonder why the absence of self and that which belongs to it would not contradict certain teachings, such as the following:

> The self is its own protector.
> Who else could provide protection?
> It is by taming the self that the wise
> Attain the higher realms.[165]

And this:

> Black and white deeds are not destroyed;
> The self must experience what it itself brought about.[166]

---

165. *Verses of Dharma (Dhammapada)*, XII.4.
166. From the *King of Meditative Absorptions*.

Nevertheless, while there are indeed such statements, it is also taught that:

> Here, there is no self and no sentient being;
> These phenomena have causes.[167]

And can it be denied that scripture also states:

> All phenomena are empty of self.

Therefore, we must seek the underlying intent of such teachings. When exploring them, we notice that the Buddhas have stated that there is a "self." Yet such statements are generally directed toward inferior individuals that are to be influenced, such as the Far-Throwers. Such people deny karmic causality, arguing that this is impossible given the absence of a self. Cyclic existence is also impossible, they claim, because there is nobody who enters this life from a past existence, and no one who leaves it to proceed to a future life. Given the relative existence of the self that is imputed based on mere phenomena, the Buddhas have said that the self exists to care for such people, who as a result of their denial are prone to fall into the lower realms.

Those to be influenced who are of moderate capacity hold a rigid view of the self. Based on that view, they believe that actions lead to karmic consequences, and for that reason, they avoid doing what is nonvirtuous. Given the merely relative presence of the property that is the negation of truth, the Buddhas also teach that there is no true self, so as to help these people loosen their view of the transitory collection and connect them with the transcendence of suffering.

Among those to be influenced there are also some who are of the highest capacity. These individuals trust in the relative existence of karmic causality and hold the view of the absence of true self. To enable such individuals to give up apprehending the marks associated with negative properties, the Buddhas teach that, in reality, there is neither a self that is to be negated, nor any type of negation or absence of such a self either.

Our position, therefore, is not contradicted by scripture, nor does it

---

167. From the *Minor Precepts of the Vinaya.*

imply that the scriptures contradict each other. Indeed, there are no such flaws. The *Noble Jewel Mound Sūtra* explains:

> Kāśyapa, "self" is one extreme. "No self" is another extreme. The middle that lies between these two extremes cannot be taught.

Alternatively, the sixth stanza of this chapter can be read as follows. The Enumerators and other groups posit the existence of the self because they believe that karmic causality would not be feasible based on momentary formations. The Far-Throwers teach that there is no self because they do not observe a self that participates in cyclic existence. The Buddhas, who see reality without error, teach that there is no self or absence of self as imagined by these groups.

Of these two readings, the former is better.

The Nature of Reality

The second issue concerns the nature of reality. This will be treated with respect to (1) the ultimate and (2) the relative. The first issue will include explaining (1) how the ultimate cannot be taught in terms of an essence of its own, (2) how the ultimate is taught by means of superimposition, and (3) the characteristics of that teaching.

How the Ultimate Cannot Be Taught in Terms of an Essence of Its Own
On the first issue, the treatise states:

> *The expressible is annulled*
> *Because the domain of the mind is annulled.*
> *The intrinsic nature, unarisen and unceasing,*
> *Equals the transcendence of suffering. [XVIII.7]*

It may be thought: "If neither self nor absence of self can be taught with respect to reality, then what *can* be taught?"

If anything could be said about ultimate reality, then that would be taught. But since all that can be expressed concerning the ultimate using linguistic concepts has been annulled, nothing whatsoever is taught. What does this mean? Well, if the ultimate were accessible to the mind, there would be reasons based on which one could refer to it through superimposition. But the entire domain of the mind, all the mind's observations, are annulled when it comes to the ultimate. Applying names to it by means of superimposition is, therefore, impossible.

Why is it that the domain of the mind is annulled? The suchness of phenomena's intrinsic nature is primordially unborn and unceasing. It is, therefore, equal to the transcendence of suffering, free from all adventitious stains. Essentially, it is primordial peace in all regards. Hence, there is nothing there that could possibly present itself to the mind.

The present stanza can also be seen as a reply to a question regarding the way that mental constructs are "brought to an end by emptiness," as was stated above. One may wonder: "How does seeing them as emptiness make mental constructs cease?" Emptiness transcends all that can be expressed and conceived of. All verbal and conceptual constructs, therefore, cease by the very understanding that this is its nature.

The stanza can also be seen as a response to the following question: "It was taught that reality is, with respect to all inner and outer things, the primordial pacification of the self and that which belongs to it. If so, is it then possible to express or conceive of reality in some way or another?"

The reply to this query proceeds in a similar manner to the previous response, by stating that reality transcends that which is expressible and so forth. For these reasons, the Master explains:

> Complete pacification of all observations,
> The complete pacification of constructs, peace —
> Nowhere did the Buddha teach
> Any Dharma to anyone at all.[168]

How the Ultimate Is Taught by Means of Superimposition

On the second issue, the treatise states:

> *Everything is real and unreal,*
> *Real and indeed not real,*
> *Not unreal and not real—*
> *That is the thorough teaching of the Buddha. [XVIII.8]*

168. *Root of the Middle Way*, XXV.24.

It may be argued: "The ultimate truth transcends the objects of word and thought. Nevertheless, unless a teaching is given by means of superimposition in terms of the relative, those who are to be influenced will not be able to realize its nature. Moreover, unless they gain this realization, they will not be able to attain any of the three types of transcendence of suffering. Such a teaching by means of superimposition is, therefore, necessary."

Thus, the present stanza addresses the issue of using superimposition as a skillful way to teach. Generally, to instill faith in novice disciples, the Buddhas first take the mundane and childish perspective into account, teaching that the inner and outer entities that make up the world and its inhabitants are all real. Later, to help those to be influenced give up attachment to such entities, the Buddhas consider the perspective of the mind of a noble one that involves appearance, teaching that such things are unreal. To ensure that these two perspectives are not seen as contradictory, and to avoid the one-sided extremes of existence and nonexistence, they also teach their conventional reality in combination with their ultimate lack of reality. Thus, they teach both reality and the lack of reality. Finally, the most gifted among those to be influenced must succeed in eliminating the subtle obscuration as well, which is nothing but the view that the negative property, lack of reality, is ultimate. To ensure that these disciples eliminate this obscuration, the Buddhas teach in a way that considers the equipoise of the noble ones, explaining that, while all of these things are not real, they are not unreal either. Thus, they teach freedom from all the constructs associated with an affirmed or negated self. Hence, the teaching of the Buddhas accords with those who are to be influenced. As it gradually guides disciples along the path to the nonabiding transcendence of suffering, this teaching is thorough. For this reason, the master Āryadeva states:

> Existence, nonexistence, existence and nonexistence,
> And neither existence nor nonexistence—all this is taught.
> Does it not always depend on the character of the disease
> What will be spoken of as "medicine"? [169]

169. Āryadeva, *Four Hundred Stanzas*, VIII.20.

The Characteristics of the Ultimate Teaching
On the third issue, the treatise states:

> *Not known by anything else, peace,*
> *Not constructed through constructs,*
> *Absence of concepts, and absence of a different meaning—*
> *These are the characteristics of reality. [XVIII.9]*

One may ask: "What are the characteristics of ultimate reality?"

It has already been explained that, if examined with respect to its nature, the essence of the ultimate, or the bearer of its characteristics, transcends the realm of speech and mind. It is, therefore, also taught that since there is nothing to support the characteristics of ultimate reality, there are no characteristics either. Still, just as its essence is taught by means of superimposition, the characteristics of ultimate reality must be explained by way of superimposition as well. Above, the characteristics of reality were, therefore, taught in terms of the exclusion of that which does not accord with reality. What follows here is a presentation of characteristics that is meant to dispel misunderstanding.

Awareness of the ultimate occurs through individual self-awareness within the equipoise of the noble ones, by way of nothing being seen at all. Anything else—such as language, argumentation, examples, and the other factors that serve as means for realization among the childish individuals obscured by ignorance—cannot make it known exactly as it is, by way of nothing being seen at all. Next, reality is peace because from the beginning it has no essential establishment whatsoever. It is not a construct of language for reality is not a linguistically constructed meaning, nor is it something that can be conceived of and expressed. Likewise, concepts cannot capture reality in any way for it transcends the domain of the mind. Finally, reality does not constitute any different meaning because dissimilar instances have no place within the basic field of phenomena to which all phenomena belong. These five properties are explained to be the characteristics of reality. As can be seen from the following citations, they are also taught in the sūtras:

> The suchness of all phenomena is to be realized by means of the wakefulness of individual self-awareness by wise and intelligent noble beings. It is not the domain of logicians.

Turning the wheel of Dharma,
You teach primordial peace and nonarising,
The natural transcendence of suffering;
Protector, these are the qualities you reveal.[170]

Within the ultimate truth there are no movements of the mind,
    much less syllables.[171]

Son of gods, the ultimate must not be taken to be absolutely
    unarisen and treated as something different from all phenomena.

The present stanza can also be read as a sequence of explanations. The ultimate cannot be known by any other means, such as language and argumentation, because it is not constructed by means of verbal or mental constructs. In other words, it is not an object of word and thought because thought cannot conceive of it by way of any name or category. The reason for this is that, in essence, the ultimate has been peace from the very beginning. It is not established as anything whatsoever. There is, therefore, nothing that could present itself to the mind. Hence, we may recall the following statement:

Within the intrinsic nature that is not established as anything at all,
How could there be two, three, and so forth?[172]

Therefore, as there are no separate divisions, the ultimate is not any different meaning.

The Nature of the Relative

Second, concerning the nature, or characteristics, of relative reality, the treatise states:

That which arises in dependence on something else
Is not identical with it,

---

170. From the *Jewel Cloud.*
171. From the *Sūtra Taught by Akṣayamati.*
172. Dīpaṅkaraśrījñāna, *Accessing the Two Truths,* 4c–d.

Nor is it something other.
Hence, it is neither annihilated nor permanent. [XVIII.10]

The Buddhas, protectors of the world,
Grant the elixir of teaching
Without sameness or difference of meaning,
Without annihilation and without permanence. [XVIII.11]

As was explained earlier, the relative is characterized by being true as the object of a conventional, deluded cognition that has not engaged in examination. The bearers of this characteristic, that is, the relative essences, consist of all dependently originated phenomena. Thus, this as well is the path of the Middle Way that is free from the two extremes.

When an effect arises in dependence on a cause in this way, the effect is not substantially identical with its cause because nothing can act on itself. The cause is, therefore, not permanent, as it would be if it were still present at the time of its effect. Nor is the effect substantially distinct from its cause because in that case it would not be dependent on it. Therefore, the cause has not been annihilated either, in the sense of having become nonexistent at the time of its effect.

The Buddhas are the protectors of the world, saving it from the myriads of miserable states that comprise existence and peace. Their teaching of dependent origination and natural nonarising is an elixir that forever eliminates birth, aging, sickness, and death. As was just explained, this teaching of the Buddhas does not consider cause and effect to be either the same or different, and so it does not imply either permanence or annihilation.

It has also been argued that the first stanza explains how relative dependent origination avoids permanence and annihilation, whereas the second stanza shows the ultimate's natural emptiness to be free from permanence and annihilation.

The Results of Realization

On the third issue, the treatise states:

Where a perfect Buddha has not appeared
And the listeners have disappeared,

The wakefulness of self-realized buddhas
Will, in the absence of a teacher, arise in full. [XVIII.12]

One may ask: "What are the results of the exact realization of these two truths?"

Those who possess the potential of a listener will, through study, reflection, and meditation, gradually apply them themselves to the ultimate existential negation of all phenomena and to relative illusion-like dependent origination. As they partake of the elixir of the three accumulations of discipline, meditative absorption, and insight in this way, they bring an end to the causal afflictions of the three realms. Either in that life, or otherwise in a subsequent one, they will effortlessly achieve the transcendence of suffering that is the exhaustion of birth, aging, and death. As Āryadeva explains:

> Even if insight into reality does not
> Bring the transcendence of suffering in that very life,
> One will definitely achieve it without effort in future lives
> In accordance with karmic action.[173]

Those who possess the potential for self-realized buddhahood can be of sharp, moderate, or dull faculties. By means of such faculties, they progressively engage in study, reflection, and meditation, giving rise to wakefulness as a result. The latter occurs in a realm that is empty, devoid of perfect Buddhas, and in which the listeners are absent. The time when their wakefulness arises differs depending on the capacity of the practitioner. For those of sharp faculties, it occurs on the stage of heat; in the case of medium level faculties, it takes place on the stage of acceptance; and for those of dull faculties, it happens on the path of cultivation. Whichever happens to be the case, the arising of this wakefulness occurs without any condition in the form of a spiritual teacher being present and relied on in that life. Rather, it takes place by the power of having become accustomed to virtue in the past, as well as having made aspirations. As a result of this wakefulness, they actualize the knowledge of exhaustion and of nonarising. In the end, both the listeners and self-realized buddhas must achieve the nonabiding transcendence of suffering, just like the offspring of the

---

173. Āryadeva, *Four Hundred Stanzas*, VIII.22.

victors. The following account is, therefore, applicable to the listeners and self-realized buddhas as well.

Those who have the potential for the Great Vehicle gather the accumulation of wakefulness by familiarizing themselves, ultimately, with phenomena's existential negation. Relatively, they gather the accumulation of merit by embracing [their virtuous acts] with the relative enlightened mind, relying on illusion-like dependent origination. As they gather these two accumulations, they achieve a transcendence of suffering in which there is, respectively, no abidance in existence or peace.

Becoming accustomed to the unerring realization of the meaning of the two truths, the three classes thus temporarily arrive at their individual levels of enlightenment. In the end, however, they all accomplish unsurpassed enlightenment. Therefore, as it is so deeply meaningful, it is appropriate for intelligent individuals to pursue this realization without any concern for life and limb, just like the bodhisattva Sadāprarudita.

This concludes the explanation of the eighteenth chapter, the analysis of self and phenomena, in the *Ornament of Reason,* a commentary on the *Root of the Middle Way.*

CHAPTER NINETEEN

Analysis of Time

NEXT IT WILL be shown that dependent origination is empty of time. Doing so involves refuting (1) the essence of time and (2) the arguments in favor of time. The first topic is contained in the analysis of time, which, like the other analyses, is treated in terms of the three issues.[174]

THE CONTEXT OF CHAPTER 19

First, regarding the chapter's context, the analysis of time is related to the profound sūtras, such as the following teachings from the *Mother of the Victorious Ones*:

> Form should not be qualified as past, future, or present, because the past, future, and present do not exist themselves.

This chapter employs reasoning to ascertain such claims that the three times have no nature.

As for its relation to the other analyses, the present chapter presents a reply to an argument such as this: "The nature of things may have been negated, but so far time has not. Time is mentioned in the sūtras, so it must exist. Given the existence of time, entities must exist as well because they are the reason that time is posited. The three times are posited with reference to things that have ceased, not yet arisen, and arisen but not ceased, respectively."

---

174. In this chapter, the concluding summary appears to be included in the explanation of the fourth stanza.

The present analysis will show that, since time itself does not exist, the entities that are the cause for time being posited do not exist either.

THE CONTENT OF CHAPTER 19

The explanation of the meaning of this chapter's content includes (1) showing the natural existence of time to be flawed and (2) refuting the arguments for time's natural existence. The first issue further includes (1) a refutation of present and future time and (2) extending the refutation to other topics. The first of these will be treated by (1) refuting dependence on the past, (2) refuting the absence of such dependence, and (3) drawing a conclusion.

Refutation of Dependence on the Past
On the first issue, the treatise states:

> *If the present and the future*
> *Depend on the past,*
> *The present and the future*
> *Exist in the past. [XIX.1]*

> *If the present and the future*
> *Do not exist in the past,*
> *How can the present and future*
> *Be dependent on it? [XIX.2]*

If the present and future exist by nature, do they depend on the past or not? If this question is answered in the affirmative, it will be argued that they must also exist in the past. Let us consider this argument's reverse entailment: If something is nonexistent in something else, then the former cannot depend on the latter, as is the case with sesame oil and sand. It might be objected that this argument is inconclusive because two incompatible qualities can be absent from each other, yet still be established in mutual dependence, as is the case with light and darkness. This objection does not hold, however, because two such qualities are not, in reality, established as incompatible in dependence on each other. If they were, nobody could avoid the consequence that they would then also exist in each other. If the consequence of the present's and future's existing in the past is accepted, these two must also be accepted as past, and then there would be no present and no future. If this were the case, the past would itself end up being nonexistent because it owes its establishment to the present and future.

Wishing to avoid these flaws, one might say that present and future do not exist in the past. But, in that case, they cannot depend on it. When that which depends is present, that upon which it depends would be absent, and when the basis for dependence exists, the dependent would be nonexistent. Indeed, such dependence is not feasible.

Lack of Dependence on the Past

On the second issue, the treatise states:

> *If the two do not depend on the past,*
> *Then they are not established. [XIX.3a–b]*

Certain followers of non-Buddhist schools teach:

> Time matures the elements.
> Time brings people together.
> Time puts to sleep and wakens.
> Escaping time is extremely difficult.

According to these schools, time is a permanent substance. Thus, both the present and the future exist independently of the past. Yet present and future are not established independently of the past because the two are explained, directly and indirectly, in terms of being subsequent to the past.

Drawing a Conclusion

On the third issue, the treatise states:

> *The present and future*
> *Therefore, do not exist. [XIX.3c–d]*

Because they can be established neither in dependence on, nor independently of, the past, the present and future do not possess any natural existence.

Extending the Reasoning to Other Topics
Second, extending this analysis to other topics, the treatise states:

> By these very same steps, the other two,
> The supreme, the middling, and the inferior, and so forth;
> As well as singularity and so on
> Can also be understood. [XIX.4]

The very same steps that have here shown that the present and future are not established, whether or not they depend on the past, can just as well be applied to the other two combinations. In other words, with the appropriate changes, they can be used to show that there is no establishment for the past and the future, whether or not they depend on the present, and that the present and the past lack establishment, whether or not they are dependent on the future. Thus, we easily arrive at the statement, "If the past and the future depend on the present, the past and the future exist in the present," as well as, "If the past and the present depend on the future, the past and the present exist in the future."

Upon examination, we find that the three times do not exist, whether they are considered mutually dependent or independent of each other. The same insight can be gained with respect to any other set of three mutually dependent things, such as the supreme, the middling, and the inferior; birth, remaining, and ceasing; the desire, form, and formless realms; training, nontraining, and neither of these; the old, the young, and the middle-aged. As indicated by the words "singularity, and so on," the same holds when we examine the singular, pairs, triads, groups, and so forth. All combinations are seen to be unestablished, whether the individual factors are treated as interdependent or self-sufficient. It should, therefore, be understood that they are all devoid of nature.

Hence, the present chapter has explained that, while there cannot possibly be any phenomenon that does not originate dependently, we may test any dependent origination with respect to the presence or absence of dependence. Doing so, we will never find anything established. Ultimately, this chapter has thus offered an existential negation of the mental constructs associated with all phenomena, while relatively, it has established that phenomena resemble illusions.

THE ARGUMENTS FOR TIME

Second, refuting the arguments for time involves refuting time with reference to (1) extent and (2) entities.

With Reference to Extent

On the first issue, the treatise states:

> *A time that does not endure is not apprehended.*
> *Since a time apprehended as enduring*
> *Does not exist, how can one speak*
> *Of a time that is not apprehended? [XIX.5]*

It may be argued: "Time does indeed exist by nature because it has extent. Time is taught to extend from instants and moments up to eons. Something nonexistent, like the horn of a rabbit, could not have extent."

Nevertheless, temporal extent throughout instants and so forth is not naturally established. Does time extend from one moment to another or not? If it does not endure in the next moment, time cannot be apprehended as an extent of instants and so on precisely because it does not last. This is entailed because in the present instant itself there is no basis for measurement, and it was claimed that time does not endure into any subsequent instant. Measuring an extent has, therefore, become impossible.

Alternatively, it may be argued that time endures. If there were time that endures, it could be measured as the extent of instants and so on. Yet since a time apprehended as an enduring extent does not exist, how can it be measured and referred to as an extent of instants and so forth? Indeed, it is as impossible as measuring the child of a barren woman.

Why does enduring time not exist? Well, if time were distinct from entities, it would be observable as such from the perspective of mundane direct perception. The very fact that such a separate time is not observed, therefore, disproves its existence. Moreover, momentary entities are established by conventional inference. [From the perspective of such an inference,] in the end, entities that are of a momentary nature are all that is apprehended and observed. Hence, there is no enduring time.

With Reference to Entities

On the second issue, the treatise states:

> *If time is based on entities,*
> *And there are none, how could there be time?*
> *When there are no entities at all,*
> *How could there be any time? [XIX.6]*

Members of our own tradition may argue: "There is no time that endures separately from momentary entities. Still, because of those entities, there is also time. Time is conceived of based on entities, and because of them we speak of it being naturally existent. Otherwise, how could there possibly be time without entities? Indeed, there is no such thing."

The bases, entities, have already been negated. Hence, there are no entities at all. How, then, could there possibly be any natural existence of time, which is conceived of based on them? This is no different than conceiving of the sharpness of a donkey horn. For this reason, the sūtras teach that time is not naturally established. With respect to the present, they teach:

> If phenomena had any nature,
> Then the victors and the listeners would know it.
> Solid phenomena do not attain the transcendence of suffering.
> The wise would never become free of mental construction.[175]

And on the past:

> Hundreds of thousands of teachings may be given,
> And hundreds of thousands of Buddhas may convene;
> Yet phenomena and syllables still do not end.
> Since they never arose, they do not end.[176]

And concerning the future:

> At a time when the Thus-Gone Ones appear,
> A victor known as Maitreya will come,

175. From the *Sūtra of the Elephant's Strength.*
176. From the *King of Meditative Absorptions.*

And the ground will be spread with gold.
How could there be any time for such events?[177]

This concludes the explanation of the nineteenth chapter, the analysis of time, in the *Ornament of Reason,* a commentary on the *Root of the Middle Way*.

---

177. From the *Jewel Mound*.

CHAPTER TWENTY

Analysis of the Assembly

THE REFUTATION of the arguments for time is contained in two chapters, the first of which is the analysis of the assembly. This chapter, which refutes the assertion that time is a cooperating condition in the production of effects, is treated in terms of the three issues as well.[178]

THE CONTEXT OF CHAPTER 20

In terms of context, the relationship between the analysis of the assembly and the profound sūtras can be appreciated from the following passage from the *Noble [Sūtra of] the Great Display*:

> Based on the lips, the throat, and the palate,
> The sounds of syllables emerge from movements of the tongue.
> Yet this is not done by the throat and not by the palate;
> The syllables are not observed in any of these alone.
>
> Based on their assembly, speech emerges
> Due to the mental consciousness.
> Yet mind and speech are invisible and intangible,
> Observable neither within nor without.
>
> When the arising and cessation of speech, voice, language, and tone
> Are examined by the wise,

---

178. In this chapter the traditional concluding summary appears to be identical with the "Conclusion" that ends the section on "The Content of Chapter 20."

All speech is seen to be like an echo,
Momentary and devoid of essence.

Here, reasoning is used to ascertain the meaning of such accounts of
the lack of natural existence with respect to that which arises due to an
assembly.

As for its relation to the other analyses, members of our own tradition
may argue: "Time was refuted, but it still exists by nature. Sprouts and
other external things arise only at particular times. For example, in the
spring, the inner ripening of karmic results also depends on time. On this
point, it is taught:

The action of corporeal beings does not dissipate,
Even in a hundred eons.
When the right time and conditions come together,
It ripens into its result.[179]

Hence, time exists because it is a cooperating condition in the production
of outer and inner effects. Something nonexistent, like a sky flower, cannot be a condition."

In response to this objection, the present chapter will explain how time
cannot reasonably be a condition for effects because, upon examination,
they themselves are found not to arise.

THE CONTENT OF CHAPTER 20

Second, the explanation of the content includes (1) a refutation of the
notion that production occurs due to an assembly of causes and conditions, (2) a refutation of the belief that production occurs due to a cause,
and (3) a conclusion to the refutations. The first issue includes a refutation
of arising effects by considering (1) the effect and (2) the cause. The first
of these is again divided into refutations that pertain to effects that arise
based on assemblies that (1) precede their effects, (2) are simultaneous
with them, and (3) are subsequent to them.

---

179. From the *Minor Precepts of the Vinaya*.

Effects That Arise Based on a Previous Causal Assembly

On the first issue, the treatise states:

> *If effects are produced by an assembly*
> *Of causes and conditions*
> *And are present in those assemblies,*
> *How could they be produced by those assemblies? [XX.1]*

> *If effects are produced by the very assembly*
> *Of causes and conditions,*
> *And are not present in those assemblies,*
> *How could they be produced by those assemblies? [XX.2]*

> *If effects are present in the assemblies*
> *Of their causes and conditions,*
> *They should be perceptible in those assemblies,*
> *And yet they are not perceptible in those assemblies. [XX.3]*

> *If effects are not present in the assemblies*
> *Of their causes and conditions,*
> *Then the causes and conditions*
> *Equal what are not causes and conditions. [XX.4]*

If a previous assembly of causes and conditions produces an effect, we may ask whether that effect is something that was itself present or absent within that prior assembly. If the first is the case, how could the effect be produced by the assembly, given that it already exists? The argument's entailment can be seen from the fact that it is meaningless for something that is already present to arise.

In the case of the alternative, how could an assembly of causes and conditions produce an effect that is absent within it? Since the effect is non-existent within the assembly, its production would be similar to sesame oil being derived from an assembly of sand grains. This argument's entailment can be seen by considering how the production of something nonexistent is impossible. Indeed, this would be utterly absurd.

Moreover, if, along the lines of the first option, an effect were present in the assembly that causes it, then we would be able to apprehend it there. It follows that the effect would be observable in the assembly, and since it cannot be observed there, we can conclude that it is not present there. If, on the other hand, an effect is not present in the assembly of its causes and conditions, it follows that this set of causes and conditions is equal to those factors that are not its causes or conditions since the effect is equally absent within them. Therefore, such an assembly cannot produce an effect. Here, the entailment can be appreciated from the explanations of the argument from identical reasons and the way that the entailment of a single conceptual distinction is equally relevant in the case of "other." These were supplied [in the commentary on chapter one].

Effects Arising Based on a Simultaneous Causal Assembly

On the second issue, the treatise states:

> If effects arise together
> With their assemblies,
> The producer and produced
> Will then be simultaneous. [XX.7]

It may be argued: "An effect arises from the assembly of its causes and conditions that is simultaneous with it, as when a lamp produces light."

Hence, two stanzas below, it is explained that if an effect arises together with the assembly of its causes and conditions in this way, this implies that the producer and the produced are present at the same time. Such a simultaneity cannot be established, however, because the establishment of the producer excludes the establishment of the produced, and vice versa.

Effects Arising Based on a Subsequent Causal Assembly

On the third issue, the treatise states:

> If effects arise
> Before their assemblies,
> The absence of causes and conditions
> Implies that effects are uncaused. [XX.8]

Certain Proponents of Differences may say: "Prior to the assembly of the causes and conditions, the effect is something that exists in the future. The assembly functions to make this future effect arise in the present."

If the essence of the effect has arisen before the assembly of its causes and conditions in this way, however, the effect that exists in the future would be causeless because it would exist independently of its causes and conditions.

In Consideration of the Causal Assembly

The second section refutes production by an assembly by considering the causes of production. Further below, the treatise states:

> *If the assembly of causes and conditions*
> *Does not itself*
> *Produce its own identity,*
> *How could it produce an effect? [XX.23]*

How could the subject, the assembly of causes and conditions, produce the effect in reality? Nothing can be an agent for itself. Therefore, the assembly does not produce its own identity. It is, thus, similar to space. The argument's entailment is as follows: Since the assembly is not produced by itself but, rather, in dependence on other things, it cannot have a nature of its own. Lacking a nature of its own it will, as was shown in the analysis of suffering, be unable to produce the nature of its effect.

PRODUCTION BY A CAUSE

Second is the refutation of production by a cause. Some may argue: "An effect is actually not produced by the assembly of its causes and conditions. The producer is the cause, and the role of the assembly of conditions is to contribute to it."

The refutation of this idea is divided into ten sections. First, it will be shown that, whether or not it is supplied to the effect, a cause cannot produce anything.

Whether or Not It Is Supplied to the Effect, a Cause Cannot Produce Anything

The treatise states:

> *If the cause ceases to be*
> *Having been supplied to its effect,*

> *It follows that the cause has two identities,*
> *One supplied and another that ceases. [XX.5]*

> *If a cause ceases to be*
> *Without having been supplied to its effect,*
> *The effects that arise when it has ceased*
> *Do not have any cause. [XX.6]*

It is taught:

> As a cause transforms,
> It becomes the cause of something else.[180]

Hence, for the arising of an effect to take place, its cause must have ceased. We may then ask if a cause ceases, having supplied the agentive cause, which is the quality that enables the effect's arising, to its effect or without having supplied the effect with this quality? If the first is the case, and the cause ceases, having passed the agentive cause on to its effect, it follows that the cause possesses two identities because one causal identity ceases whereas another one is supplied. In other words, the cause is half permanent and half impermanent, and it is impossible for the same substance to be both. This idea is, therefore, untenable.

If the second option were the case, the full identity of the cause would then cease without the agentive cause having been supplied to its effect. This, in turn, would mean that the effect is causeless because it arises after its cause has ceased.

Effects Are Not Produced by Identical Causes

Second, refuting the notion that effects are produced by causes that are not different from them, the treatise states:

> *If a cause ceases,*
> *Yet is transferred to its effect,*
> *It follows that a cause already arisen*
> *Would arise once more. [XX.9]*

180. Āryadeva, *Four Hundred Stanzas*, IX.9a–b.

It may be argued: "The aforementioned criticism would be relevant if cause and effect were substantially different, but they are not. As the causal state ceases, it is the cause itself that abides as the identity of the effect."

If, in this way, that which is the nature of the causal state becomes the resultant state by ceasing, it would be as though we were dealing with one actor who keeps putting on different costumes. In this way, the nature of a cause is fully transferred into all other contexts. It follows from this assertion that causes are permanent, in which case they could not be functional things. It is also a consequence of this position that arising as such would become meaningless because it would mean that the same cause that had already arisen once would later arise again.

It may be objected: "Arising is not meaningless because that which arises is not the identity of the previously arisen cause. Rather, it is the identity of the subsequently arisen effect."

This objection, however, is not valid either. First, according to the opponent's assertion, cause and effect are of the same nature. Their difference, therefore, is purely nominal. Second, even if there are different situations, the nature of that which participates in such situations cannot differ throughout them.

Causes Can Produce neither a Present nor an Absent Effect

Third, showing that causes can produce neither effects that have arisen, nor those that have not, the treatise states:

> How could that which has ceased and disappeared
> Be the producer of an arisen effect?
> An enduring cause that is connected to its effect,
> How could that produce it? [XX.10]

> If cause and effect are not connected,
> What effect would then be produced? [XX.11a–b]

Do causes produce effects that have already arisen, or those that have yet to arise? If the first is proposed, we may then ask whether or not an effect's cause has already ceased. If it has, if the cause has disappeared and become nothing, how could it then be the producer of the arisen effect? A cause that has ceased and become nonexistent does not have the power

398 ORNAMENT OF REASON

to produce an effect. Moreover, the arising of an arisen effect would also be meaningless.

If, alternatively, the cause has not ceased but remains in a state of being connected to the presently arisen effect, how could it be the effect's producer? Having undergone no change, it lacks the quality of being a contributor to an effect, which is what characterizes causes. Furthermore, the arising of an already arisen effect is also meaningless.

If, on the other hand, the cause is thought of as producing an effect that has not yet arisen, there cannot be any connection between cause and effect. What sort of effect could then be produced? It would be nothing at all. Otherwise, since all things would then be equally unrelated, any given cause could give rise to anything.

Causes Do Not Produce Seen or Unseen Effects
Fourth, showing that causes cannot produce effects that are seen or unseen, the treatise states:

> Whether seen or unseen by the cause,
> No effect is produced. [XX.11c–d]

Would an effect be produced by a cause that sees it, or a cause that does not see it? The first cannot be because a nonexistent cause could not see, and if a cause already exists, its arising would be meaningless. On the other hand, it would be absurd for a produced effect to be unseen. The cause's product would then be whatever it does not see.

Causes Cannot Contact or Fail to Contact Their Effects
Fifth, regardless of whether or not the two come into contact, causes cannot produce effects. The treatise states:

> A past effect is never in contact
> With a cause that has passed,
> Nor with one that has not arisen,
> Or one that has already arisen. [XX.12]

> An effect that has arisen
> Is never in contact

With a cause that has not arisen,
That has passed, or that has arisen. [XX.13]

An effect that has not arisen
Is never in contact
With a cause that has arisen,
Has not arisen, or that has passed. [XX.14]

If there is no contact,
How could a cause produce its effect?
Even if there is contact,
How could a cause produce its effect? [XX.15]

Moreover, do causes produce their effects while being in contact with them, or not? The first option is not possible because a) contact as such is impossible and b) even if there were contact, there could not be any production. Let us consider the first of these two problems. If there were contact between cause and effect, there might be something produced and something that produces, but no such contact exists. Whether we consider a past, future, or present effect, there cannot be any contact with a cause that is either past, future, or present.

This will be shown in three steps. First, a past effect cannot be in contact with a past, future, or present cause. Any such relationship between a past effect and a cause that has passed, not yet arisen, or already arisen is impossible. In the first case, both cause and effect have passed and ceased to be. In the second, both are nonexistent, with one having ceased and the other not yet arisen, in addition to being separated in time. In the third case, the two are not present at the same time, and the effect is nonexistent.

Second, a present effect cannot be in contact with a future, past, or present cause. There is never any meeting between a presently arisen effect and a cause that has yet to arise, that has passed, or that is arising in the present. In the first case, the two are separated in time, and the cause is nonexistent, having not yet arisen. In the second, they are again temporally separated, while the cause has passed and is, therefore, nonexistent. In the third case, the two are simultaneous. They could not, therefore, be cause and effect, and any sense of contact and dependence would be lost as well.

Third, a future effect cannot come into contact with a cause that belongs to any of the three times either. A future effect never comes into contact with a cause that has arisen, has not yet arisen, or has passed. In the first case, cause and effect are separated in time, and the effect, not having arisen, is nonexistent. In the second, both have yet to occur and are, for that reason, nonexistent. In the third case, the two occur at different times and are nonexistent.

Although this enquiry enables us to see that there is no such contact, let us nevertheless assume that contact is indeed possible, as in the second half of stanza fifteen. In other words, even if there were contact, how could a cause produce an effect? It would not make sense for it to do so because when two things are simultaneous, one cannot produce the other.

Finally, what if we then say, as in the first half of stanza fifteen, that causes produce effects without being in contact with them? Well, if this were the case, how would a cause produce its effect? Any given thing could then produce whatever it is not in contact with. Also, based on such a theory, effects would end up causeless.

Causes Cannot Produce Anything, Whether Empty or Not Empty of Their Effects

Sixth, causes cannot produce anything, whether they are empty or not empty of their effects. The treatise states:

> *If empty of an effect,*
> *How can a cause produce its effect?*
> *If not empty of an effect,*
> *How can a cause produce its effect? [XX.16]*

Do causes produce their effects while being empty of them? If this were the case, how could they possibly do so? Just as those factors that are not causes, a cause would, in this way, be devoid of its effect. It could, therefore, not produce it. On the other hand, how could a cause produce an effect if it were *not* empty of it? Like jujubes in a jar, the effect would already be present within it, in which case its production would be meaningless.

Neither Empty nor Nonempty Effects Can Arise

Seventh, whether or not they themselves are empty, effects cannot arise. The treatise states:

An effect that is not empty does not arise.
An effect that is not empty does not cease.
It follows that what is not empty
Has not ceased and has not arisen. [XX.17]

How can the empty arise?
How can the empty cease?
It follows that the empty
Has not ceased and not arisen. [XX.18]

We may also ask whether the arising effect is itself something that is empty of nature. If it is, then how can such an effect, being devoid of nature, actually arise? Moreover, how can this empty effect actually cease? Arising and ceasing would be as impossible as the sky flower because there would be no basis for them. Moreover, effects that are empty of nature themselves have no support in the first place. Hence, it also follows that, in reality, they neither cease nor arise. As is taught:

In short, only that which is empty
Arises from empty phenomena.[181]

And:

Everything is possible
For those for whom emptiness is possible.[182]

Thus, here it is explained that conventional arising and ceasing are feasible given their empty nature. Hence, these scriptural statements do not contradict the above.

If it is held that the arising effect is not empty, we may recall the previous statement that, "Nature cannot reasonably occur due to causes and conditions."[183] Likewise, it was also shown that "a nature that undergoes change would never make any sense."[184] Thus, effects that are not empty

181. Nāgārjuna, *Heart of Dependent Origination*, 3c–d.
182. *Root of the Middle Way*, XXIV.14.
183. Ibid., XV.1a–b.
184. Ibid., XV.8c–d.

but naturally existent do not arise, just as that which is not empty, and hence existent by nature, does not cease. Why is that? Because it follows that such a thing has not ceased and that nothing has caused it to arise.

Effects Are Not Produced by Identical or Different Causes

Eighth, effects are produced neither by causes that are identical to them, nor by those that are different. The treatise states:

> *Cause and effect being identical*
> *Will never make sense.*
> *Cause and effect being different*
> *Will never make sense. [XX.19]*

> *If cause and effect were identical,*
> *Produced and producer would be the same.*
> *If cause and effect were different,*
> *Cause and noncause would be equal. [XX.20]*

Are effects produced by causes that are essentially distinct from them, or are cause and effect indistinguishable? The cause and the effect's being essentially the same will never make sense; nor will it ever make sense to say that cause and effect are essentially different. This is the Master's genuine thesis.

The reasoning, here, is as follows. If the conventions of cause and effect were the very same substance, this would mean that the produced and that which produces it are the same identical substance. This, however, is unacceptable because nothing can be its own object. This account of cause and effect would also make father and son, the eye and eye consciousness, and other such pairs essentially the same. Alternatively, if cause and effect were different substances, noncauses would be able to produce the same effects that causes do.

Similarly, if noncauses were not able to produce them, these effects could not be produced by their causes either. This follows from the fact that this idea puts cause and noncause on an equal footing. It has already been explained how, with respect to the unqualified single conceptual distinction of otherness, it is impossible to make any distinction in terms of what is and is not produced in reality.

Neither Existent nor Nonexistent Results Are Produced

Ninth, neither existent nor nonexistent results are produced. The treatise states:

> *If an effect is existent by nature,*
> *Then what could its cause produce?*
> *If an effect is nonexistent by nature,*
> *Then what could its cause produce? [XX.21]*

If it is in the nature of things that causes produce effects, are the produced effects essentially existent or nonexistent? If they exist by nature, what would it be that causes produce? Indeed, production would be meaningless; as has already been explained, something created by a cause cannot be natural.

Next, if results are nonexistent by nature, what, really, could causes produce? The basis for production would be absent. Hence, the product would be similar to the sky flower.

Some might call the latter argument into question, stating that a reflection, which is devoid of nature, can still be causally produced. Yet this objection does not hold because such an example shows precisely the absence of real production; it has not been refuted that, conventionally speaking, something devoid of nature can be causally produced.

Causality Is Not Natural

Tenth, subsequent to these refutations follows a conclusion regarding causality's proven lack of nature. The treatise states:

> *If it does not produce any effect,*
> *The cause does not make sense.*
> *If the cause does not make sense,*
> *Of what, then, is the effect? [XX.22]*

Now, if they do not produce any effects, causes do not make any sense because they are classified as such precisely because they produce effects. At this point, it would also be unreasonable to think that while causes are nonexistent, effects still exist. As explained above, if a cause does not exist, of what cause is the effect the effect? Both its essence and the positing of the term depend on there being a cause. Hence, if there is no cause, there cannot possibly be any effect.

Conclusion

Third, concluding the discussion, the treatise states:

> *Therefore, nothing is produced by an assembly,*
> *And yet there is no effect made by anything else.*
> *When no effect exists,*
> *How can there be an assembly of conditions? [XX.24]*

It has been shown that an assembly cannot produce an effect that precedes, follows, or is simultaneous with it. It was also pointed out that since an assembly cannot engender itself, it cannot produce an effect. Therefore, there is no effect that is produced by an assembly.

Nevertheless, the notion that effects can be the product of a mere cause that is not an assembly of causes and conditions has been refuted as well. Hence, no such effect can be established.

Finally, it cannot be maintained that causes exist despite there not being any effects. In the absence of effects, how could there be an assembly of conditions, or any cause at all? Indeed, the rationale for positing them would be absent.

This concludes the explanation of the twentieth chapter, the analysis of the assembly, in the *Ornament of Reason,* a commentary on the *Root of the Middle Way.*

CHAPTER TWENTY-ONE

Analysis of Arising and Disintegration

THE SECOND CHAPTER devoted to the refutation of the arguments for time is the analysis of arising and disintegration. This chapter, which refutes the idea that time is the cause of arising and disintegration, is likewise treated in terms of the three issues.

THE CONTEXT OF CHAPTER 21

First, in terms of context, this chapter relates to the profound sūtras, as indicated by the following passage from the *Mother of the Victorious Ones*:

> Arising and disintegration cannot be seen to accord with reality.

And this quotation from the *King of Meditative Absorption*:

> No phenomenon arises or disintegrates;
> There is no death, no transference, and no aging.
> This is what the Lion of Men has taught,
> And in this he has established hundreds of beings.

Here, reasoning will be used to ascertain the meaning of such teachings on the absence of arising and disintegration.

As for its place among the other analyses, the present chapter can be seen as a response to the following objection from a non-Buddhist: "Although time was indeed refuted here, it does exist by nature because time is what causes the arising and disintegration of external and internal things. There may be an assembly of other conditions, but unless certain temporal changes take place, no arising or disintegration will be observed. Something nonexistent, like the horn of a rabbit, could not be the cause of arising and disintegration."

Thus, it is held that time is a distinct, permanent, and substantially existent factor that causes the arising and disintegration of things. In reply, it will be shown that because arising and disintegration are themselves nonexistent, time cannot be established as their cause.

THE CONTENT OF CHAPTER 21

Second, the explanation of this chapter's content is divided into two sections: (1) a statement of flaws and (2) a refutation of arguments. The first issue presents refutations that involve (1) testing for coexistence and absence of coexistence, (2) considering that which has ceased and that which has not ceased, (3) considering the absence of support, (4) considering the empty and not empty, and (5) testing for sameness and difference. The first topic includes (1) a statement of the thesis, (2) an account of its rationale, and (3) a summary.

The Thesis
On the first issue, the treatise states:

> Disintegration occurs neither apart from
> Nor together with arising.
> Arising occurs neither apart from
> Nor together with disintegration. [XXI.1]

If arising and disintegration were to exist by nature, each would have to be present either separately or together with the other. Yet, upon examination, it will be seen that disintegration does not occur apart from or together with arising, nor does arising occur apart from or together with disintegration.

The Rationale of the Thesis
As for the second issue, the treatise states:

Disintegration without arising,
How could this occur?
There would be dying without birth.
Without arising, there is no disintegration. [XXI.2]

Disintegration together with arising
How could this occur?
Death does not take place
At the very same time as birth. [XXI.3]

Arising without disintegration,
How could this occur?
It is not that things
Ever lack impermanence. [XXI.4]

Arising together with disintegration,
How could this occur?
Birth does not occur
At the very same time as death. [XXI.5]

First, the belief that disintegration can occur without arising is refuted. Disintegration without arising, how could this occur? If this were to happen, it should be possible for something to disintegrate without having arisen, and vice versa. Or, if we think of particular instances of arising and disintegration, there should be sentient beings that die without having been born. Such consequences cannot be accepted, however, because this is not how we see things and because it renders disintegration uncaused. Therefore, the conclusion, by way reversing the consequential argument, is stated in the words, "Without arising, there is no disintegration."

Next is the refutation of the notion that disintegration occurs together with arising. Disintegration together with arising, how could this occur? If this were to happen, a single entity could die at the same time that it is born. Yet that is not how it is because the functions of death and birth are as incompatible as light and darkness.

Following this is a refutation of the idea that arising occurs without disintegration. How could the subject, arising, exist without disintegration, given that it is an entity and, as such, is similar to a stroke of lightning? The entailment of this argument can be seen from the fact that there will never be an entity that is not impermanent. If something were, by its nature, capable of remaining from one moment to another, rather than disintegrating, [its self-perpetuation] could never be stopped. Thus, it would never come to an end. This, however, runs counter to what we see. Also, something permanent and unchanging would not be capable of performing a function, neither gradually nor instantaneously.

Finally, the assertion of the coexistence of arising and disintegration is refuted. How could arising and disintegration occur together? If they did, a single person's birth and death would happen at the same time. This is not the case, however, for birth and death function in ways that are as incompatible as light and darkness.

Summary
Third, as a summary, the treatise states:

> When two things are neither
> Established as coexistent,
> Nor as not coexistent,
> How can they be established? [XXI.6]

When arising and disintegration are neither established as coexistent nor as not coexistent, how can they be established? Indeed, they would then be similar to the right and left horns of a rabbit. [Their complete lack of establishment] follows from the fact that coexistent and not coexistent are directly contradictory.

It might then be thought: "Arising and disintegration still exist, but in such a way that they cannot be said to be identical or distinct."

However, precisely because arising and disintegration do not exist as either of these two directly contradictory qualities, it has already been established that they are completely devoid of nature.

The Ceased and Not Ceased
On the second issue, the treatise states:

> There is no arising of the ceased,
> Nor is there arising of the not ceased.

There is no disintegration of the ceased,
Nor is there disintegration of the not ceased. [XXI.7]

If arising and disintegration exist, do they pertain to something that has ceased or to something that has not? There is no arising of that which was previously present, but which has now ceased because arising and cessation are incompatible qualities and also because that which has ceased cannot provide any support for arising. Neither is there any arising of that which has not ceased, whether we think of the latter as an existential or a predicative negation of cessation. In the first case, "the not ceased" is essentially nonexistence, just like the horn of a donkey. If "the not ceased" is taken as a predicative negation, then that which has not ceased is something that already exists.

Likewise, there is no disintegration of that which previously existed but which has now ceased because such a thing has already disintegrated, and there is an absence of a support for arising. And again, whether "the not ceased" is understood as an existential or a predicative negation of cessation, it cannot involve any arising. In the former case, the not ceased equals essential nonexistence and in the latter, it is something that is incompatible with disintegration.

The Absence of Support

On the third issue, the treatise states:

Where there is no thing,
There is no arising and no disintegration.
Without arising and disintegration,
There is no thing. [XXI.8]

When things themselves do not exist, their supported properties of arising and disintegration are as nonexistent as the braided hair of a frog. And why would things be nonexistent? Because arising and disintegration have already been refuted. Without arising and disintegration, there cannot be any things. In other words, there cannot be any bearers of these characteristics. Given the nonexistence of these properties, that which is entailed by arising and disintegration must be equally nonexistent.

The *Commentary* treats this stanza as a reply to an objection that claims that arising and disintegration must exist, given the existence of their support, things. It thus explains that this evidence, [existent things,] is not established.

The Empty and Not Empty

On the fourth issue, the treatise states:

> *With respect to the empty,*
> *Arising and disintegration make no sense.*
> *With respect to the not empty,*
> *Arising and disintegration make no sense either. [XXI.9]*

Are arising and disintegration empty of nature? If they are, real arising and disintegration do not make sense, for arising and disintegration would then have no support, and thus be similar to the sky flower. Alternatively, if they are not empty of nature, arising and disintegration do not make sense either. As was explained earlier, that which is not empty of nature cannot be altered or undergo any change due to causes and conditions.

Sameness and Difference

On the fifth issue, the treatise states:

> *Arising and disintegration*
> *Do not make sense if the same.*
> *Arising and disintegration*
> *Do not make sense if different. [XXI.10]*

If there is arising and disintegration, are they essentially the same or different? Arising and disintegration do not make sense if they are essentially identical because they are as incompatible as light and darkness. Nor do they make sense if they are essentially distinct because arising would then end up permanent, and disintegration would have no cause. As neither of these can be mistaken for the other, the two are mutually dependent.

REFUTATION OF ARGUMENTS

Second is a refutation of the arguments [advanced to prove the existence of arising and disintegration]. First, the notion that arising and cessation are established by perception will be refuted.

Arising and Disintegration Are Not Established by Perception

On the first issue, the treatise states:

> *If you think,*
> *"I see arising and disintegration,"*
> *Then know that what you see*
> *Is due to ignorance. [XXI.11]*

It may be thought: "Why all this detailed analysis? Arising and disintegration are directly perceived by everyone, including cowherds, so they exist by nature."

Those who think this should understand that what everyone, the cowherd included, sees is similar to a city of scent-eaters and other such examples. While there are no truly existent things, our ignorance makes it seem as if there are. This, however, does not prove their true existence.

Arising and Disintegration Are Not Established by Inference

Second, it will be explained that arising and disintegration cannot be established by inference. Some may argue: "Arising and disintegration exist because the thing that functions as their support exists."

In reply, it will be shown that the evidence in this argument, a thing, is tantamount to what has yet to be established. This reply will take the form of a refutation (1) with reference to the absence of production and (2) by means of an absurd consequence. The first topic begins with a refutation of the notions that production is due to either things or nonthings.

Neither Things nor Nonthings Are Productive

The treatise states:

> *Things do not arise from things.*
> *Things do not arise from nonthings.*
> *Nonthings do not arise from nonthings.*
> *Nonthings do not arise from things. [XXI.12]*

If things exist by nature, are they produced by things or nonthings? One thing is not produced by another thing because [the resultant thing would then] be simultaneous with a cause that has not yet transformed, in which case the effect could not be influenced by it. Also, since the effect is an existent thing in this scenario, its production would be meaningless. Things are not produced by nonthings either because a nonthing possesses no productive capacity.

Likewise, if we assume that certain nonthings exist, we may then ask whether such nonthings are produced by things or nonthings. A nonthing cannot be the product of a nonthing because the resultant nonthing would be indistinguishable from the causal one. Moreover, a cause that is a nonthing would also be powerless. Finally, a nonthing cannot be the product of a thing because nonthing and thing are incompatible. If effects could arise out of something with which they are incompatible, a lamp would also be able to emit darkness.

The Sanskrit term *bhava,* [which is here translated as "thing,"] can also mean arising. With this in mind, the stanza can also be read as a denial of arising and disintegration by arguing that neither of these factors is produced by things or nonthings.

Neither Self nor Other Is Productive
Next is a refutation of the idea that production is due to self or other. The treatise states:

> *Things do not arise from themselves*
> *Nor from something other than themselves.*
> *When nothing arises from either self or other,*
> *How could there be arising? [XXI.13]*

A thing cannot be produced by itself because its absence would then entail the absence of that which produces it as well. Its presence, on the other hand, would contradict its being a product. A thing cannot be produced by something other than itself either because, whether or not that other thing has ceased, production will remain impossible. Finally, when both of these two options have been dismissed individually, it is clear that a thing cannot be produced by their combination either. When this is the case, how could there be any production, given that uncaused production is an extremely unreasonable idea?

An Absurd Consequence
The second issue includes (1) a statement of the absurd consequence and (2) a refutation of the defense.

The Consequence
On the first issue, the treatise states:

> *If the existence of things is claimed,*
> *Views of permanence and annihilation follow*
> *Because these things must then*
> *Be permanent or annihilated. [XXI.14]*

When members of our own tradition claim that things exist, they contradict the words of the Able One. Moreover, this will lead to the views of permanence and annihilation, the sources of all flaws. The reason here is that these things must be permanent if they are not destroyed from one point in time to the next, while if they are destroyed, and thus impermanent, it follows that they are annihilated.

Refutation of the Defense of Existent Things
Second is the refutation of the defense of this position. First the defense itself is presented.

The Defense
The treatise states:

> *Although the existence of things is claimed,*
> *Permanence and annihilation do not follow*
> *Because existence is the continuum of effects and causes*
> *That arise and disintegrate. [XXI.15]*

It may be argued: "Although we claim that things exist, this does not entail permanence and annihilation. As past causes disintegrate, future effects arise in the unbroken continuum that constitutes cyclic existence. Since causes cease while effects arise in such a continuum, there is, respectively, no sense of either permanence or annihilation."

Refutation of the Defense
The refutation of this defense includes demonstrating (1) the consequences of permanence and annihilation even if a continuum is claimed and (2) the inescapable flaws of permanence and annihilation since the continuum itself is not established. The first issue is divided into two sections. First we will consider the consequence of permanence.

Permanence as a Consequence
Below, the treatise states:

> *If things have an essential nature,*
> *They cannot reasonably become nonexistent. [XXI.17a–b]*

If causal things exist by their essential nature, they cannot reasonably disintegrate and become nonthings. Hence, they would be permanent.

Annihilation as a Consequence
Annihilation also follows from this belief. Here, it will be shown that (1) the causal substance is annihilated in the context of existence, whereas (2) the resultant continuum is annihilated in the context of peace.

The Causal Substance Is Annihilated
On the first issue, the treatise states:

> *If a continuum of arising and ceasing*
> *Causes and effects constitutes existence,*
> *That which is destroyed does not arise again*
> *And so causes are annihilated. [XXI.16]*

If existence is an unbroken continuum of causes and effects that arise and cease, it follows that the substances that make up these causes are annihilated because, once they have disintegrated, they do not arise again.

The Resultant Continuum Is Annihilated
On the second issue, the treatise states:

> *When suffering is transcended there is annihilation,*
> *For the continuum of existence is then entirely pacified. [XXI.17c–d]*

When suffering is transcended, things would definitely be annihilated because the continuum that, as was claimed before, is the reason that things are not annihilated would be entirely pacified at that point.

It might then be asked: "Why would you followers of the Middle Way not face the same flaws?"

Indeed, we do not because arising does not ultimately take place;

because, in terms of the relative, cause and effect are not said to be either identical or distinct; and because, in terms of the relative fabrication through causes and conditions, the word "annihilation" does not apply to a pacification in the sense of an annulment of the cause . Therefore, know that there are no flaws of permanence and annihilation with respect to either of the two truths.

The Continuum Itself Is Not Established
On the second issue, the treatise states:

> *If the last ceases,*
> *The first existence does not make sense.*
> *When the last does not cease,*
> *The first existence does not make sense. [XXI.18]*

> *If the last is in the process of ceasing*
> *While the first arises,*
> *There is one that is ceasing*
> *And another that arises. [XXI.19]*

> *Hence, it does not make sense either*
> *For ceasing and arising to occur together.*
> *Could the aggregates with which one dies*
> *Be the ones with which one is born as well? [XXI.20]*

> *Therefore, nowhere in the three times,*
> *Could there reasonably be any continuum of existence.*
> *How could something outside of the three times*
> *Be the continuum of existence? [XXI.21]*

Given that the continuum of existence exists by nature, we may look closer at the connecting point between the present and future lives. At this point, does the first moment of existence of the future life arise after, before, or at the same time as the cessation of the last moment of existence in the present life? If it arises after the last existence (that is the cause) has ceased, the arising of the first moment of existence in the next life (that is the result) does not makes sense because this would be like a sprout growing from a burnt seed, or something arising without a cause.

If the resultant first existence arises without the causal last existence having ceased, its arising does not make sense either, for this would mean that there were two existences for the same one person. That, in turn, would imply the arising of an extra sentient being that did not exist before, and so the original person would be permanent while the new one would be uncaused.

Finally, if the resultant first existence arises while the causal last existence is in the process of ceasing, then there is one existence that performs the activity of arising while another performs that of ceasing. Thus, there would be two existences for a single person. It might be thought that this flaw can be avoided by considering the existence that is ceasing and the existence that is arising to be essentially the same. But having both the ceasing and the arising existence take place at the same time in this way does not make sense either. Could the very substance of the dying aggregates also be that which is born? This would be an extreme contradiction. The word "either" [in the first line of the twentieth verse] recalls that it is not reasonable for arising and ceasing to take place separately.

Therefore, nowhere in the three times—as they relate to the causal last existence's having ceased, not having ceased, and being in the process of ceasing—could there be any arising of a resultant first moment of existence. Therefore, the continuum of existence does not make sense because how could something that, when examined, is seen not to exist anywhere in the three times possibly be the continuum of existence? When investigated, the continuum of existence is, thus, itself devoid of establishment.

SUMMARY OF THE CHAPTER'S SIGNIFICANCE

With respect to the ultimate, the present chapter has offered an existential negation of the constructs associated with dependently originated phenomena as entailed by the presence of arising and disintegration. With respect to the relative, it has proven that these phenomena are false and resemble illusions. As taught in the *Sūtra of the King of Meditative Absorptions*:

> The three realms are like a dream, they have no core.
> Rapidly disintegrating and impermanent, they resemble an illusion.

There is no coming, nor any going away from here.
The continua are always empty and devoid of marks.

And likewise:

Being born and dying,
And yet not being born or dying—
The one who comprehends this
Has no difficulty in discovering this meditative absorption.

This concludes the explanation of the twenty-first chapter, the analysis of arising and disintegration, in the *Ornament of Reason*, a commentary on the *Root of the Middle Way*.

CHAPTER TWENTY-TWO

Analysis of the Thus-Gone

IN THIS SECTION, it will be explained that dependent origination is empty of the continuum of existence. This will be done in two chapters, the first of which is the analysis of the Thus-Gone, the result of this continuum. This chapter, which refutes the natural establishment of the Thus-Gone, is treated in terms of the three issues as well.[185]

THE CONTEXT OF CHAPTER 22

First, in terms of context, the present chapter's relationship to the profound sūtras is evident from the following citations. The *Mother of the Victorious Ones* proclaims:

> Even the truly and completely Enlightened One is like a dream, like an illusion.

And in the *King of Meditative Absorptions*:

> When the Thus-Gone cannot even be observed as the body of qualities,
> Why mention that he cannot be observed as the body of form.
> Phenomena, always unarisen, are the Thus-Gone.
> All phenomena are like the Bliss-Gone-One.
> Those of childish intellect grasp at marks,
> And thus, within the worlds, relate to phenomena that do not exist.

---

185. In this chapter the concluding summary is not explicit as a separate section of the text.

Here, the meaning of such statements that describe the final fruition, the Thus-Gone One, as being devoid of nature will be proven through reasoning.

As for its relation to the other chapters, the present analysis replies to an objection such as this: "Though the continuum of existence was refuted, it still exists. Having gathered the accumulations over three incalculable eons, for example, the Thus-Gone achieves omniscient wakefulness and so realizes the real nature of all phenomena, just as it is. The Thus-Gone is the effect of the continuum of existence. Therefore, given his existence, the continuum exists as well."

In response, it is stated that, contrary to what the opponent believes, the Thus-Gone is himself not established by nature. Thus, his cause, the continuum of existence, is not established in this way either.

THE CONTENT OF CHAPTER 22

Second, the explanation of this chapter's content involves (1) refuting the notion that the Thus-Gone is established by nature, (2) establishing that he is, therefore, beyond all beliefs, and (3) extending this analysis to other topics. The first issue includes (1) showing that the appropriating person who is the Thus-Gone lacks establishment, (2) showing that the aggregates that are appropriated by him lack establishment, and (3) drawing a conclusion. The first of these will include refuting (1) the substantial existence and (2) the nominal existence of the person by pointing out that the person does not exist in relation to the appropriated in any of the five ways.

The Thus-Gone Is Not Substantially Existent
On the first issue, the treatise states:

> He is not the aggregates, nor is he different from them.
> He is not in them, nor are they in him.
> Neither does the Thus-Gone possess the aggregates.
> Who, then, is the Thus-Gone? [XXII.1]

If the appropriating person who is the Thus-Gone exists by nature, we may ask whether he is identical with or different from that which is appropriated (whether that be the five aggregates of discipline and so forth that constitute the ground of Buddhahood, or the five aggregates of form and so on). We may likewise ask whether this appropriator is the support for the appropriated or the appropriated supports him. Finally, we may also enquire as to whether the appropriator possesses that which is appropriated. Indeed, one of these five options would have to be the case.

The Thus-Gone is not of the essence of the aggregates because he would then arise and disintegrate, he would be multiple, and the object and agent in the act of appropriation would be the same. Neither is the Thus-Gone essentially different from the aggregates because no Thus-Gone can be observed separate from them. Moreover, if they were distinct in this manner, he would be independent of the aggregates, and there would then be no reason to associate him with them. Likewise, the Thus-Gone does not support the aggregates, nor are they present as a support for him. Indeed, this is impossible, given that these two are not different from each other. Finally, the Thus-Gone does not possess the aggregates because he is not established as identical with or distinct from them. When we undertake this fivefold analysis with respect to the appropriated, which is the basis for the designation of the Thus-Gone, we fail to find him. Who then is the Thus-Gone? He lacks all natural establishment.

The Thus-Gone Is Not Nominally Existent

Concerning the second issue, the Sammitīyas may now argue: "Indeed, neither of these five options are applicable, for they entail the aforementioned flaws. Yet, in dependence on the aggregates, a Thus-Gone who can neither be described as identical with nor different from these aggregates does exist in reality as a designation."

The refutation of this idea will be carried out by showing that no such nominally designated Thus-Gone is established because (1) there is no basis for this designation, (2) he cannot be established as either a self-entity or as an entity that is of another nature, and (3) there is no appropriation.

There Is No Basis for the Designation

The first issue is treated further below. The treatise states:

> When examined in the five ways,
> He exists neither as identical nor different.

How, then, could a Thus-Gone who does not exist like that
Be spoken of by virtue of appropriation? [XXII.8]

As explained above, the Thus-Gone is neither identical with nor different from the aggregates. This further implies that he cannot support, be supported by, or be in possession of the aggregates. How could one, upon this fivefold examination, speak of a Thus-Gone who does not exist in any of these ways as being involved in appropriation in reality? Indeed, there is as little basis for such a proposition as there is for saying that a donkey's horn is sharp.

The Thus-Gone Is neither a Self-Entity nor of the Nature of Other
The second issue is divided into three parts: (1) a presentation, (2) an explanation, and (3) a conclusion.

Presentation
On the first issue, the treatise states:

If the Buddha exists dependent on the aggregates,
And thus not by his own nature,
How could that which does not exist in terms of its own nature
Exist through the nature of another? [XXII.2]

If the Buddha is designated as such in dependence on the aggregates, he does not exist by his own nature, and so resembles a reflection. How could such a Thus-Gone, who in terms of his own nature is as nonexistent as the child of a barren woman, possibly obtain any natural existence in reliance on the nature of something else, that is, the aggregates? As was explained earlier, that which is fabricated by causes and conditions cannot be natural.

Explanation
In the second section, first the notion of self-entity will be refuted.

The Thus-Gone Is Not a Self-Sufficient Entity
The treatise states:

> *That which depends on the nature of another*
> *Cannot reasonably have an identity of its own.*
> *How could something lacking an identity*
> *Turn out to be the Thus-Gone? [XXII.3]*

That which is spoken of in dependence on the nature of something else cannot reasonably possess any natural identity of its own, as is the case with a reflection. How could something that lacks a natural identity be, in reality, the Thus-Gone? Something like that could not be the Thus-Gone, the one who has traversed the unmistaken path.

The Thus-Gone Is Not an Entity in Dependence on Other
Second, refuting the belief in an entity that is established as the nature of other, the treatise states:

> *If he does not exist by his own nature,*
> *How could there be the nature of something else? [XXII.4a–b]*

If the Thus-Gone himself does not exist by nature, how could there be any aggregates that, in dependence on him, could be considered to be of the nature of something else? As there are no "other" entities, there cannot be a Thus-Gone who exists in relation to such things either.

Conclusion
On the third issue, the treatise states:

> *Apart from what is of the nature of self and other,*
> *What sort of Thus-Gone could there be? [XXII.4c–d]*

Since he is not established on his own or with respect to other things, what sort of Thus-Gone could possibly exist? It would have to be someone who is neither related to himself nor to anything other than himself. Indeed, there is no such Thus-Gone.

There Is No Appropriation
The third issue includes showing that (1) prior to the appropriated, the appropriator does not exist, (2) there could be no appropriation by an appropriator who has no prior existence, (3) without an appropriation

there cannot be something appropriated, and (4) there is no appropriator without appropriation.

There Is No Appropriator Prior to the Appropriated
On the first issue, the treatise states:

> *If, independent of the aggregates,*
> *There were a Thus-Gone,*
> *Then he could now rely on the aggregates*
> *And, based on them, become that. [XXII.5]*

> *Yet, independent of the aggregates,*
> *There is no Thus-Gone at all. [XXII.6a–b]*

When Devadatta exists before his wealth, he can subsequently take possession of it. Likewise, if there were some sort of appropriator, a Thus-Gone, prior to and independent of the aggregates that are composed of the ground of enlightenment, then he could subsequently rely on those aggregates and become their appropriator. Thus, based on his having appropriated those aggregates, he would have become qualified for the title "Thus-Gone." Yet, upon examination, we find that, independent of and prior to the aggregates of the ground of Buddhahood, there is no Thus-Gone at all. Since there is no thing that could receive that title, he is no different than the child of a barren woman.

Without a Preceding Appropriator There Cannot Be Appropriation.
On the second issue, the treatise states:

> *When there is no one who exists independently,*
> *How could there be any appropriation? [XXII.6c–d]*

Hence, when there is no Thus-Gone whose presence precedes and is independent of the aggregates, how could any appropriation of the aggregates be undertaken by him? Similarly, if Devadatta does not exist before his relation to wealth, he cannot take possession of it.

Without Appropriation There Cannot Be Something Appropriated
On the third issue, the treatise states:

Without any appropriation,
There cannot be something appropriated. [XXII.7a–b]

Since the appropriator has no prior existence, no appropriation takes place. As this is the case, the aggregates cannot be something that is appropriated.

Without Something Appropriated There Cannot Be an Appropriator
On the fourth issue, the treatise states:

Not involved in appropriation—
Such a Thus-Gone does not exist at all. [XXII.7c–d]

There is no Thus-Gone who is not involved in the appropriation of aggregates.

The Aggregates Appropriated by the Thus-Gone Are Not Established

That which is appropriated
Does not exist by its own nature.
That which does not exist by itself,
Can definitely not exist due to other things. [XXII.9]

Not only is the Thus-Gone, the person who is the appropriator, nonexistent, that which is appropriated by him, the aggregates of Buddhahood, do not exist either because they occur due to causes and conditions, and because they are dependent on their appropriator. It might be thought that the aggregates do exist, but as a result of other things, such as the causes and conditions from which they are different, or a distinct appropriator. Yet that which is nonexistent in and of itself can definitely not obtain any natural existence in reliance on something else, such as causes and conditions or an appropriator. As was already explained, that which is fabricated and partakes of a relationship of mutual dependence cannot exist by nature.

Conclusion

Third, as a common conclusion to the refutations of the appropriator and the appropriated, the treatise states:

> *Thus, the appropriated and the appropriator*
> *Are empty in all regards.*
> *Given their emptiness, how to speak*
> *Of an empty Thus-Gone? [XXII.10]*

The appropriated and the appropriator are, in this way, empty in all regards. How can we then speak of any reality with respect to a Thus-Gone, who thus is empty and depends on empty appropriations?

THE TRANSCENDENCE OF ALL BELIEFS

The second section discusses how the Thus-Gone transcends all beliefs. One may object: "Giving up other teachers, we go for refuge in the Thus-Gone, and so pursue liberation. You, on the other hand, negate this, the foremost among all sources of refuge. Destroying all hope for liberation, you develop a distorted view of denial."

In response, it will be shown that (1) the reality of the Thus-Gone is beyond all mental and verbal constructs and (2) it is a flaw to apprehend it as confined to such constructs.

The Reality of the Thus-Gone Is Beyond All Constructs

On the first issue, the treatise states:

> *Do not say "empty,"*
> *And do not say "not empty" either.*
> *Do not say "both" and do not say "neither."*
> *These are to be stated for the sake of designation. [XXII.11]*

> *Permanence, impermanence, and the other two—*
> *How could they pertain to this peace?*
> *Limited, limitless, and the other two—*
> *How could they pertain to this peace? [XXII.12]*

One seized by the dense fixation
That the Thus-Gone exists
Will think that, upon his transcendence,
The Thus-Gone no longer exists. [XXII.13]

As for a Buddha empty of nature,
To declare that, upon transcendence,
He exists or does not exist
Would not make any sense. [XXII.14]

The one who made the aforementioned objection may have gone to the Able One for refuge and be in pursuit of liberation. Nevertheless, this individual is unable to accept the unmistaken path to liberation, the path that is revealed by the teaching that no self exists, neither in the form of a person nor as a phenomenon. On this point, it is taught:

> Venerable Subhūti, the Buddha is also like a dream, like an illusion. The qualities of the Buddha are like a dream and like an illusion as well.

Thus, the sūtras teach the existential negation of all constructs associated with the body of qualities, the field free from all adventitious stains. Likewise, they explain the appearance of form bodies that are delusions; illusory objects that are experienced by disciples with pure karma and accomplish their welfare. What we have done here is to duly acknowledge the meaning of that teaching. There is, therefore, nothing reproachable in the above. This is not a denigration.

We have, however, pointed out that the self and the aggregates, as conceived of by the opponent, are devoid of any nature. Therefore, one should not say that the Thus-Gone is, in reality, empty, nor should one claim that he is not. One ought not say that he is both empty and not empty, nor hold that he is neither. And yet, all of these four statements are still to be applied in terms of the expedient meaning, as conventional superimpositions that can guide those to be influenced toward reality. The purpose and intent with respect to that type of teaching has already been explained in the analysis of self and phenomena.

The analysis of the person and the aggregates associated with the Thus-Gone also serves as a refutation of persons and aggregates in relation to sentient beings. The present examination, therefore, equally shows the untenability of all fourteen indeterminate views. It might be believed that the self or the aggregates existed in the past, that they did not exist in the past, that they both did and did not, or that neither of these was the case. Or it may be thought that they are somehow permanent, impermanent, and so on. Yet how could this be the case within this natural peace? In other words, how could this be the case with respect to a Thus-Gone in whom both self and aggregates are primordially pacified, in whom there are no such things? Indeed, it cannot.

It might likewise be thought that the self or the aggregates will be present again in the future, that they will not, that they both will and will not, or that neither is the case. Self and aggregates may thus be thought to be limited, limitless, both, or neither. Yet, how could any of these pertain to this natural pacification of self and aggregates? How could this be the case with respect to a Thus-Gone in whom both have been pacified from the beginning, in whom there is neither self nor aggregates? Indeed, it cannot.

The same goes for the third tetralemma, the four beliefs that concern whether the Thus-Gone exists subsequent to his passing. These four are also irrelevant. When he appears, one might mistakenly think that the Thus-Gone exists. Yet the one who apprehends in this way has been overcome by a vast and dense darkness that obscures the path of transcendence, the witnessing of reality. Such a person will also develop the mistaken thought that, upon his transcendence, the continuum of the Thus-Gone who was present before has now come to an end and no longer exists.

Alternatively, the meaning of the twelfth stanza can be appreciated by reformulating it like this: "One seized by the dense fixation that the Thus-Gone exists will think that, upon his transcendence, the Thus-Gone exists or does not exist."

As explained above, the Buddha is empty of nature from the very moment he appears. It would not make sense to think that, upon transcendence, this Buddha exists as an entity, that he has disintegrated and become nothing, that he both does and does not exist, or that he neither exists nor does not exist. None of these notions would be entertained, just as one does not conceive of the form of a design made of space. Moreover, none of these ideas could pertain or be established with respect to a Thus-Gone who is natural pacification. These issues are, therefore, not determined, as is the case with questions concerning the complexion of the child of a barren woman.

The Flaws of Construction

On the second issue, the treatise states:

> *Those who create constructs about the Buddha,*
> *Who is beyond construction and without exhaustion,*
> *Are thereby damaged by their constructs;*
> *They fail to see the Thus-Gone. [XXII.15]*

The Buddha is beyond all objects of verbal and conceptual construction. He is not even established as something other than these; the Buddha is not the exhaustion, or cessation, of constructs that were there before and that have now come to an end. People may mistakenly think of the Buddha as empty or not empty, permanent or impermanent, omniscient or not omniscient, and so on, yet the mental eye of those who create such verbal and mental constructs is damaged by their own constructions. Therefore, they all fail to see and attain that which they talk of—the Thus-Gone's profound, vast, and perfect qualities. The *Noble Vajra Cutter* teaches:

> Those who see me as form,
> Or know me as sound,
> Have entered mistaken abandonment.
> Such beings do not see me.
>
> Behold the Buddhas as the intrinsic nature;
> All the guides are the body of qualities.
> The intrinsic nature is not an object of the mind;
> It cannot be cognized.

EXTENDING THIS ANALYSIS TO OTHER TOPICS

Third, extending this analysis to other topics, the treatise states:

> *That which is the nature of the Thus-Gone*
> *Is also the nature of this world.*
> *There is no nature of the Thus-Gone.*
> *There is no nature of the world. [XXII.16]*

It has been explained that all persons and phenomena associated with the Thus-Gone are empty of nature. Thereby, it has also been shown that persons and phenomena as related to sentient beings are void. The same holds for the world that is their environment. Therefore, that which is the ultimate nature of the Thus-Gone is also the nature of this world, meaning both beings and their environment. Ultimately, the Thus-Gone has no natural establishment whatsoever, and that which, in perfect accordance with their wishes, appears to the deluded perception of disciples with pure karmic backgrounds is indeed established to be false and like an illusion. Ultimately, this world of sentient beings and their environment has no established nature at all. Its appearing, as it does to a deluded perspective, is established to be false and resembling an illusion. The *Sūtra of the Ornament of Wisdom Light* teaches:

> Phenomena, always unarisen, are the Thus-Gone.
> All phenomena are like the Thus-Gone.
> Those of childish intellect grasp at marks,
> And thus, within the worlds, perpetually relate to nonexistent
>   phenomena.

While Āryadeva explains:

> While the Buddha is not born,
> Aspirations that are causally linked
> Make his magical appearances manifest.

And:

> The emptiness of one
> Is the emptiness of all.[186]

This concludes the explanation of the twenty-second chapter, the analysis of the Thus-Gone, in the *Ornament of Reason*, a commentary on the *Root of the Middle Way*.

---

186. Āryadeva, *Four Hundred Stanzas*, VIII.16c–d.

Analysis of Error

SECOND, THE NOTION that affliction is what causes the continuum of existence will be refuted through the analysis of error. The three issues pertain to this chapter as well.

THE CONTEXT OF CHAPTER 23

First, we will discuss the chapter's context. Its relation to the profound sūtras can be found here, in the *Mother of the Victorious Ones*:

> Desire, anger, and stupor are pure by nature.

And in the *King of Meditative Absorptions*:

> Those knowing the essence of desire, anger, stupor, and pride
> To be the product of thought and mistaken engagement,
> Do not relate to marks and do not become free from attachment.
> Everything is the support of such meditators.

The meaning of the sūtra's teaching that there is no nature of affliction will here be established through reasoning.

Next, as for the chapter's relation to the other analyses, the present discussion can be seen as a reply to the following objection: "The Thus-Gone, as the result of the continuum of existence, may have been refuted. Nevertheless, there is such a continuum, for it is taught:

> As a condition, ignorance creates formation. This, in turn is the condition for consciousness.

As well as:

> The condition of craving engenders becoming, and that condition
> leads to birth.

Thus, the continuum exists because affliction, its primary cause, exists."

This chapter was composed to explain that affliction as such lacks establishment.

THE CONTENT OF CHAPTER 23

Second, the explanation of the chapter's content includes refutations of (1) affliction itself and (2) its proof, the pursuit of the method that eliminates affliction. The first section covers (1) a general refutation of the three poisonous afflictions and (2) individual refutations of these three. The first refutation presents the following evidence: (1) dependent origination, (2) absence of support, (3) lack of cause, and (4) nonobservation.

The Afflictions Originate Dependently
On the first issue, the treatise states:

> *It is taught that desire, anger, and stupor*
> *Originate in dependence on thought.*
> *Their arising depends*
> *On the attractive, unattractive, and mistaken. [XXIII.1]*

> *That which originates in dependence*
> *On the attractive, unattractive, and mistaken*
> *Cannot be due to its own nature.*
> *Hence, the afflictions are not real. [XXIII.2]*

The evidence, [that the three afflictions arise in dependence on thought,] can indeed be established through numerous types of conventional perception and inference. Nevertheless, in the present context, it is established for those of our own tradition by referring to the Able One's statements. The Transcendent Conqueror taught that the primary afflictions—desire, anger, and stupor—all originate in dependence on thought, the mind's apprehension of things. Thus, he states:

> Desire, I know your root;
> You arise from thought.
> I do not conceive of you,
> So, for me, you do not arise.

It is also specified that these three afflictions arise in dependence on objects with features that are, respectively, attractive, unattractive, and mistaken (in the sense of being contrary to fact). In other words, it is explained that the three afflictions originate in dependence on a subject that apprehends things in these three ways. Moreover, the features of the objects are also set forth by thought. For this reason, their origination is, in the end, established as being due to thought as well.

Now, because they arise in dependence on features of objects that are attractive, unattractive, or mistaken—or because they arise in dependence on a subject that apprehends in these three ways—the three afflictions cannot be due to their own nature. Hence, because they do not exist by their own nature, these afflictions are not real. They are not natural. The entailment of this argument has already been elaborately explained in the analysis of nature and the analysis of fire and fuel. While the former showed that the natural cannot be altered and originate in dependence, the latter explained that what originates in dependence cannot be natural.

The Absence of Support
We begin the treatment of the second issue with a general presentation.

General Presentation
One stanza below, the treatise states:

> The one to which the afflictions belong
> Is not in any way established.
> When they do not pertain to anything at all,
> The afflictions cannot exist in any way either. [XXIII.4]

As is the case with a painting on a wall or the ripening of a fruit, the afflictions must relate to some support. Yet no supportive basis to which the afflictions belong can be established in any way. There is no support other than the self or the mind, and both of these have no natural establishment. Therefore, when there is no support at all to which they could pertain, then the supported, the afflictions, cannot exist by nature either, like the afflictions of the child of a barren woman.

One may then wonder: "Why would these two supports not be established?"

What follows is a proof through reasoning. First is a refutation of the self being the support.

Refutation of the Self as Support
The treatise states:

> *The existence or nonexistence of the self*
> *Is not established in any way.*
> *How can the existence or nonexistence*
> *Of the afflictions be established without it? [XXIII.3]*

Upon examination, we find that both the existence of a self in the form of a person, as well as the nonexistence, or negation, of such a self, cannot be established in any way. Both have already been refuted. It was, for example, explained:

> That which does not exist
> Before, together with, or after sight and the rest
> Will no longer be thought about
> As existent or nonexistent.[187]

Thus, given that their support is absent, how could the existence, or the negation of the existence, of the supported afflictions be established in any way?

Refutation of the Mind as Support
Second follows a refutation of the notion that the mind is the support of the afflictions. Sūtra Followers and Proponents of Mind Only will argue: "While it is indeed true that there is no support in the form of a self,

187. *Root of the Middle Way*, IX.12.

434 ORNAMENT OF REASON

the arising of afflictions is supported by the afflicted mind. Moreover, the mind arises together with the afflictions, for it is said, 'Those that arise together are the effect of each other.'[188]

The refutation of this idea will be explained by showing (1) how a support in the form of the afflicted mind cannot be established since it does not relate to the afflictions in any of the five ways and (2) how, as an aside, the afflictions are not established either since they do not relate to the afflicted in any of the five ways.

The Mind Does Not Relate to the Afflictions
On the first issue, the treatise states:

> As in the case of the view of one's body,
> The afflicted is absent in the afflictions in five ways. [XXIII.5c–d]

The view of self can be based on the aggregates of one's body, yet the self that is believed in does not exist in relation to the physical aggregates in any of the five ways. The same holds for the mind that is afflicted and the afflictions that afflict it: The afflicted mind (1) is not identical with the afflictions, (2) is not different from them, (3) does not support them, (4) is not supported by them, and (5) does not possess the afflictions. If they were identical, object and agent would be the same, and if they were different, the afflicted mind could be present in the absence of afflictions. If this were the case, a foe-destroyer's mind could be afflicted. Moreover, since they are not established as essentially different, they cannot reasonably relate to each other as support and something supported. Finally, because they are neither identical nor different, it does not make sense to speak of possession, either in the sense of identity or as a relationship between different things.

The Afflictions Do Not Relate to the Mind
On the second issue, the treatise states:

> As in the case of the view regarding one's body,
> The afflictions are absent in the afflicted in five ways. [XXIII.5a–b]

---

188. Vasubandhu, *Treasury of Abhidharma*, II.50b.

The view of the self may be based on the physical aggregates, yet no such self exists with respect to the aggregates in any of the five ways. In the same way, the afflictions that afflict the mind do not exist in relation to the afflicted mind in any of these five ways either—not by being identical with it, different from it, possessing it, supporting it, or being supported by it. In the first case, object and agent would be the same, and in the second there could be afflictions without something that is afflicted, in which case there would be affliction without any support. The third option is impossible given that afflictions and mind are neither identical nor different, and the fourth and fifth must be excluded because the two are not essentially different.

The Lack of Cause
On the third issue, the treatise states:

> If the attractive, unattractive, and mistaken
> Are not due to their own nature,
> Then what are those afflictions that depend
> On the attractive, unattractive, and mistaken? [XXIII.6]

As explained above, these afflictions originate in dependence on the attractive, unattractive, and mistaken. Yet because they originate dependently, and because they cease and become nothing, the attractive, unattractive, and mistaken do not exist by their own nature. What, then, are those afflictions that depend on the attractive, unattractive, and mistaken as their causes? As it is taught:

> When the seed of something is false,
> How could its arising be true?[189]

Hence, as they arise from false causes, the afflictions do not exist by nature.

Nonobservation as Evidence
On the fourth issue, the treatise states:

---

189. Nāgārjuna, *Jewel Garland*, I.29.

> *Form, sound, taste, tactility, smell,*
> *And phenomena—these six*
> *Are believed to be the bases*
> *For desire, anger, and stupor. [XXIII.7]*

> *Form, sound, taste, tactility, smell,*
> *And phenomena are all without exception*
> *Like a city of scent-eaters,*
> *Like an optical illusion, like a dream. [XXIII.8]*

It might be argued that the afflictions can be established by virtue of the existence of their bases, or foci. Indeed, some may believe that form, sound, taste, tactility, smell, and phenomena are the bases for desire, anger, and stupor. Nevertheless, form, sound, taste, tactility, smell, and phenomena are all, without exception, merely imaginary and devoid of reality. The afflictions that have such focal points are, therefore, also without any nature, like afflictions that focus on the child of a barren woman.

One may then wonder: "How can they appear if they have no nature?"

Like a city of scent-eaters, an optical illusion, or a dream, they appear the way they do to the deluded mind. They are, therefore, false and have no nature.

Individual Refutations of the Three Poisonous Afflictions

Next, the refutations of the individual afflictions include (1) a refutation of desire and anger and (2) a refutation of stupor. The first of these includes (1) a refutation of the cause, the attractive and the unattractive and (2) an invalidation of the result. The first of these sections is again divided into refutations with reference to (1) the false character of the support and (2) their mutual dependence.

The False Character of the Support
On the first issue, the treatise states:

> *They resemble an illusory person*
> *And are similar to reflections.*
> *How could there be any real element*
> *Of the attractive or unattractive in them? [XXIII.9]*

Form and the other [purported] supports [for the arising of affliction] are false and have no nature. In this way, they resemble an illusory person or a reflection. How could they contain any actual element, any real thing (since both "element" and "thing" are among the meanings of the Sanskrit *bhava*), that has attractive or unattractive features? Indeed, there are no real attractive or unattractive entities.

Mutual Dependence
As for the second issue, first the attractive will be refuted.

Refutation of the Attractive
The treatise states:

> *The unattractive upon which*
> *The designation "attractive" depends*
> *Does not exist independently of the attractive.*
> *Hence, the attractive does not make sense. [XXIII.10]*

Let us assume that there are things, such as a silver vase, that are attractive in every way. Would this vase then be attractive independent of things that are unattractive? This could not be because it would then remain attractive when compared to a vase of gold. If the alternative is the case, its being attractive is dependent on there being something unattractive, perhaps a copper vase. Yet the unattractive copper vase, upon which the silver vase's designation, or classification, as "attractive" depends, does not exist independently of the attractive silver vase itself. If the copper vase were by nature unattractive, it would also be unattractive in comparison to a clay vase. Hence, because that upon which it depends is not established prior to itself, a dependent attractiveness does not make any sense either.

Refutation of the Unattractive
Second, refuting the unattractive, the treatise states:

> *The attractive upon which*
> *The designation "unattractive" depends*
> *Does not exist independently of the unattractive.*
> *Hence, the unattractive does not make sense. [XXIII.11]*

If there are unattractive things, such as a copper vase, is the existence of these things independent of things that are attractive or dependent on them? Unattractive things are not independently unattractive, for then the copper vase would still be unattractive when compared to a clay vase. If, however, the opposite is the case, then the attractive silver vase, for example, upon which the copper vase's designation and classification as "unattractive" depends, does itself not exist independently of the unattractive copper vase either. If it were attractive by its very essence, its being compared to a gold vase would make no difference. Hence, because the attractiveness upon which it depends is not established prior to itself, a dependent unattractiveness does not make any sense either.

Invalidation of the Result
On the second issue, the treatise states:

> *When there is nothing attractive,*
> *How could there possibly be desire?*
> *When there is nothing unattractive,*
> *How could there possibly be anger? [XXIII.12]*

When, in this way, there are no attractive objects, how could there possibly be any natural existence of desire, which is a result of such objects? Likewise, when its cause, the unattractive, does not exist, how could there possibly be any real occurrence of the resultant anger?

Refutation of Stupor
Next, stupor will be refuted by showing that its cause, error, lacks establishment. This includes (1) a refutation of the mistaken and (2) the result of this refutation. The first section itself includes (1) a refutation of the distinction between the mistaken and the unmistaken and (2) a refutation of the person involved in the apprehension of these. The first of these will show that (1) the mistaken and the unmistaken are equally devoid of objective establishment, (2) whether objective or not, the mistaken and the unmistaken are equal, and (3) even mere apprehension is not established. The first of these issues will explain that (1) if error occurs when apprehending in a way that is contrary to the way things are, apprehending

things to be permanent cannot be in error and (2) if error occurs when the apprehension does not accord with fact, apprehending things to be impermanent cannot be correct.

Apprehending Permanence Would Not Be in Error
On the first issue, the treatise states:

> *If thinking the impermanent*
> *To be permanent is an error,*
> *Then why, since the empty is not impermanent,*
> *Would that thought be in error? [XXIII.13]*

Generally, the five aggregates may be seen to be *impermanent* since they disintegrate from one moment to the next; *painful*, as they are injured by that very impermanence; *unclean*, since the body is full of the thirty-two unclean substances; and *selfless*, because the aggregates are empty of a self, whether such a self is thought to be identical with or different from them. One might, therefore, argue that thinking these aggregates to be *permanent, delightful, clean*, and *associated with a self* is in error.

On that argument, would the term "error," then be applicable because the aggregates are apprehended to be permanent and so forth, while in fact they are impermanent, painful, and so on? Or, alternatively, would it be an error to think of them as permanent and so on because they are in fact not permanent and so on? If our criterion for classifying the thought of permanence as error is of the first kind, that is, if the error is in terms of thinking the impermanent to be permanent, we may consider the reverse entailment, and so ask why apprehending the subject, the aggregates, as permanent would be an error. Indeed, it would not be an error because the aggregates that are empty by nature do not feature any actual impermanence. By substitution, we can make the same argument with respect to the remaining three thoughts. Thus, for example, we get:

> If thinking the painful
> To be delightful is in error,
> Then why, since the empty is not painful,
> Would that thought be in error?

Apprehending Impermanence Is Not Correct
On the second issue, the treatise states:

> *If thinking that which is not permanent*
> *To be permanent is an error,*
> *Then why would thinking the empty*
> *To be impermanent not also be in error? [XXIII.14]*

If the criterion for error is of the second kind, apprehending permanence would then be wrong because the object of our concern does not contain anything permanent. With this understanding of error, we may then consider the genuine pervasion, and so ask why thinking the subject, the aggregates, to be impermanent would not also be a mistake. Indeed, it would be a mistake because the naturally empty aggregates do not feature any of the impermanence that is ascribed to them either. Again, the same is applicable to the remaining three thoughts. Thus, for example, we get:

> If thinking that which is not delightful
> To be delightful is in error,
> Then why would thinking the empty
> To be painful not also be in error?

If these arguments are accepted, nothing is correct. Since error is dependent on the correct, there can then not be any error either.

Whether Objective or Not, the Mistaken and Unmistaken Are Equal
Further below, the treatise discusses the second issue:

> *If there is a self, something clean,*
> *Something permanent, and something delightful,*
> *The apprehending of self, clean, permanent, and delightful*
> *Are not mistakes. [XXIII.21]*

> *If there is no self, nothing clean,*
> *Nothing permanent, and nothing delightful,*
> *There cannot be any absence of self, anything unclean,*
> *impermanent, and painful. [XXIII.22]*

If, in relation to the aggregates, there is a self, something clean, something permanent, and something delightful, then neither the objects that are apprehended as having these features, nor the mind that apprehends the objects accordingly, can be considered mistaken and counterfactual.

The alternative to this is that there is no self, nothing clean, nothing permanent, and nothing delightful with respect to the aggregates, or the cognized objects. Yet not only would there then be an absence of these four, the negative qualities of their negation—absence of self, unclean, impermanent, and painful—would then also be nonexistent. Thus, the full set of eight qualities will be mistaken. If this is accepted, there is nothing that is correct, and since the mistaken depends on the correct, there is then nothing that is mistaken either. Hence, it is established that there can be neither any features of mistaken objects, nor any thoughts of a subject that is mistaken.

Even Mere Apprehension Is Not Established
On the third issue, the treatise states:

> *The means for apprehending, the apprehension,*
> *That which apprehends, and what is apprehended*
> *Are all completely pacified.*
> *Hence, there is no apprehending. [XXIII.15]*

It may be objected: "Mistaken and unmistaken apprehension may have been refuted, but the mere act of apprehending has not. Therefore, apprehension exists. This, in turn, means that those factors that establish the existence of apprehension—agent, action, and object—exist as well. Our position is, therefore, established."

This is not so. The means for apprehending, such as mistaken judgments; the act of apprehending; the self, or the mind, that apprehends; and the objects that are apprehended thereby, such as form—all of these have been proven to be false through the general refutation of arising in the analysis of conditions. They have also been refuted individually. Thus, we may recall the thirteenth, third, fifth, and eighth stanzas of the present chapter, respectively. Hence, since all of these are completely pacified, there is no such thing as mere apprehension either. In turn, it is then established that there are no mistaken or unmistaken ways of apprehending.

Refutation of the Apprehending Person
The second issue will include (1) a general refutation of the person as a mistaken or unmistaken apprehender and (2) a specific refutation of the person whose apprehension is mistaken.

General Refutation
On the first issue, the treatise states:

> *Given that there is neither mistaken*
> *Nor unmistaken apprehension,*
> *Who could be in error?*
> *Who could be correct? [XXIII.16]*

It may be thought: "The mistaken and the unmistaken do exist because there is a person who has these qualities, or who may apprehend in such ways."

Yet this objection does not hold either. The nonexistence of mere apprehension precludes the existence of mistaken and unmistaken ways of apprehending. Therefore, what person could be in error, and who is the person that is correct? There cannot be anyone to whom such qualities pertain.

Specific Refutation of the Person Whose Apprehension Is Mistaken
The second issue will be covered by showing (1) the impossibility of a mistaken person with reference to the three types of support and (2) its lack of arising in any of the three ways.

The Three Types of Support
On the first issue, the treatise states:

> *The mistaken cannot*
> *Become mistaken,*
> *Nor can the unmistaken*
> *Become mistaken. [XXIII.17]*

> *That which is becoming mistaken*
> *Cannot become mistaken either.*

Where is error possible?
Investigate that. [XXIII.18]

Moreover, becoming mistaken is not possible with respect to an object, or for a support, that is mistaken because becoming mistaken has already been completed there, and because such mistakenness would be nonsensical. Nor are mistakes possible where there is no error because mistakes have yet to occur there, and being and not being mistaken are, moreover, contradictory. Finally, mistakes are also impossible with respect to that which is becoming mistaken because there is no "that which is becoming mistaken" apart from that which either is or is not mistaken. Such a thing could not involve two actions either. Therefore, with respect to which object, or for what support (that is, for what person) is error possible? Let us investigate that with an honest mind. We shall then see that there is nothing that could be in error.

The Absence of Arising in Any of the Three Ways
On the second issue, the treatise states:

> *Since they have not arisen,*
> *How could there be errors?*
> *Given that no error has occurred,*
> *How could there be one that is mistaken? [XXIII.19]*

> *Things do not arise from themselves,*
> *Nor do they arise from anything else.*
> *As things do not arise from self and other either,*
> *How could there be one that is mistaken? [XXIII.20]*

Also, how could there be errors, when none have arisen? Given that there are no errors because no error has occurred, how could there be one that is in error? It may be objected that the absence of arising of error has not been proven. Yet, as it is taught:

> Things do not arise from themselves
> Nor do they arise from anything else.
> As things do not arise from self and other either,
> How could there be one that is mistaken?

The meaning of this statement has already been explained.

The Results of Refutation
In this way, error has been refuted. Third follows a treatment of the results of this refutation, this examination of error. The treatise states:

> *As error in this way ceases,*
> *Ignorance comes to an end.*
> *As ignorance ceases,*
> *Formations and so forth end. [XXIII.23]*

When examined in this way, error cannot be found. Hence, the relative erroneous apprehension ceases. Thereby, its result, ignorance, comes to an end relatively as well. As causal ignorance ceases, its results end as well. Hence, all that pertains to the relative accumulation of suffering that we have been immersed in since beginningless time—from formation up to and including aging and death—is brought to an end without exception. This, therefore, is deeply significant.

REFUTATION OF AN ARGUMENT

Subsequent to the refutation of the afflictions, it is refuted that the remedy, the pursuit of the means for eliminating the afflictions, can serve as a proof for the existence of afflictions. The treatise states:

> *If someone's afflictions*
> *Are existent by nature,*
> *How can they be eliminated?*
> *Who can eliminate the existent? [XXIII.24]*

> *If someone's afflictions*
> *Are nonexistent by nature,*
> *How can they be eliminated?*
> *Who can eliminate the nonexistent? [XXIII.25]*

It may be argued: "The remedy that eliminates ignorance and other such factors does exist. Therefore, the afflictions exist as well. Something like the sprout of a sky mango cannot be eliminated by a remedy."

Nevertheless, upon examination we will see that there is no such thing as elimination by means of a remedy either. If this were to take place, would it relate to something existent or to something nonexistent? If a person's desire and other afflictions were existent by nature, how could they be eliminated? It is entailed that they could not because who can eliminate something that exists by nature? That is just as impossible as the elimination of the nonresistant quality of space.

Next, if somebody's desire and other afflictions were nonexistent by nature, how could they be eliminated in reality? It is entailed that they could not be eliminated because who can eliminate that which by nature is nonexistent? Like the coolness of fire, what by nature is nonexistent does not need to be eliminated.

It might then be argued: "The aforementioned examination leads to the statement, 'As error in this way ceases, ignorance comes to an end.' If the afflictions cannot be eliminated, as just argued, why would this statement not now have been contradicted?"

Although they have no nature, adventitious stains that resemble a tarnish on gold can, from the unexamined perspective, be eliminated by a remedy. Therefore, there is no such contradiction. If one is imprisoned in a dream, one will be freed by understanding that it is not true. Similarly, understanding that both discard and remedy have no existence is itself the remedy that eliminates the relative afflictions. A sūtra explains:

> Ignorance and all that arises by this condition
> Never know any existence.
> Ignorance and the world of ignorance do not exist;
> For this reason, have I spoken of ignorance.

And likewise:

> Mañjuśrī, stupor is perfect freedom. Therefore, it is termed "stupor."

Also the Master himself teaches:

> Here there is nothing whatsoever to exclude,
> And not a bit to maintain.

Look, genuinely into the genuine—
When the genuine is seen, there is total liberation.[190]

This concludes the explanation of the twenty-third chapter, the analysis of error, in the *Ornament of Reason,* a commentary on the *Root of the Middle Way.*

---

190. Nāgārjuna, *Heart of Dependent Origination,* 7.

CHAPTER TWENTY-FOUR

Analysis of the Noble Truths

SHOWING THE NATURE of dependent origination to be emptiness includes two chapters, of which the first is the analysis of the noble truths. The three issues pertain to this chapter as well.

THE CONTEXT OF CHAPTER 24

First, as for the chapter's context, its relation to the teaching of the profound sūtras can be seen from the following statement from the *Mother of the Victorious Ones*:

> There is no suffering, origin, cessation, or path.

Elsewhere, a sūtra teaches:

> Monks, the sacred truth is one; it is the subject that does not
> deceive, the transcendence of suffering.

Thus, the sūtras teach that the four truths have no nature. The meaning of such teachings will here be established through reasoning.

As for its relation to the other analyses in the text, the present chapter was composed to avert the following criticism: "If all phenomena are emptiness, it follows that the four noble truths and other such principles are nonexistent as well."

THE CONTENT OF CHAPTER 24

Second, the explanation of this chapter's content includes (1) an objection and (2) a reply. The objection is presented in five sections, of which the first sets forth the consequence that the topics to be understood, the four noble truths, would become untrue.

The Four Truths Would Become Untrue
The treatise states:

> *If all of this were empty,*
> *Nothing would arise or be destroyed.*
> *For you it follows that*
> *There are no four noble truths. [XXIV.1]*

Here the opponent argues: "If all outer and inner things were the essence of emptiness, everything would be just like space. Nothing could then arise and develop, just as nothing could be destroyed. Given this complete nonexistence, it would follow that, for the proponent of emptiness, there are no four noble truths either.

"The aggregates produced by past actions and afflictions are constantly injured by the three forms of suffering associated with suffering, change, and formation, and so they do not befit the noble. For this reason, and because this painful nature of the aggregates is a truth from the perspective of the noble ones who have abandoned error, the aggregates are referred to as 'the noble truth of suffering.'

"Thus," the opponent argues, "the truth of suffering is something that by nature arises and disintegrates. There could not, therefore, be any such thing according to your position. Moreover, if there is no resultant suffering there could not be any causal action and affliction either, and so there could not be any origin of suffering. In turn, this means that there could not be any cessation of suffering and its causes, nor could there be a path that leads to this cessation. In other words, the eightfold noble path and so forth would be nonexistent as well."

The Four Types of Wakefulness Would Become Nonexistent
The second section sets forth the consequence that the four types of path wakefulness, as associated with the subject, would become nonexistent. The treatise states:

Since there are no four noble truths,
Complete understanding and elimination,
As well as familiarization and actualization,
Do not make any sense. [XXIV.2]

If, in this way, there are no four noble truths, the complete understanding of suffering through its qualities of impermanence, and so forth, the elimination of the origin of suffering, familiarization with the path, and the actualization of the cessation will not make any sense either.

The Three Jewels Would Become Nonexistent
The third issue is the consequence that the resultant three jewels would become nonexistent. First it is argued that there would be no Sangha.

There Would Be No Sangha
The treatise states:

Without these,
The four fruitions do not exist either.
Without fruition, there is no one abiding in that,
Nor anyone who has gained entry. [XXIV.3]

If the eight persons do not exist,
Then there is no Sangha. [XXIV.4a–b]

Since there is no understanding of suffering and so forth, there cannot be any cultivation of the path, nor any attainment that results from this cultivation. The subtle developers that are to be eliminated through seeing can then not be overcome. Likewise, there could be no elimination of the sets of nine greater, middling, and lesser subtle developers that pertain to each of the nine levels of the three realms and that are eliminated through cultivation. Thus, the four fruitions associated with the stream-enterer, once-returner, nonreturner, and foe-destroyer cannot exist either. None of these four fruitions would be possible because they ensue from the elimination of those subtle developers. The fruition of the stream-enterer involves the elimination of subtle developers [up to] the lesser of the middling factors associated with the experience of the realm of desire. The fruition of the foe-destroyer's stage ensues finally from the elimination of the lesser of the lesser afflictions that are associated with the summit of existence.

If none of these fruitions exist, there cannot be anyone who, on the paths of liberation, abides within the fruitions of having eliminated that which is to be eliminated. Nor can there be anyone who has gained entry into any of these four fruitions. In other words, there cannot be anyone who abides in their causes, the paths of no impediment and the preparatory stages.

We may here elaborate slightly on the meaning of the above. The Abhidharma teaches:

> Fifteen instants are the seeing of that which was not seen.
> Hence, these are the path of seeing.
> The sixteenth is the abidance within its fruition.[191]

Thus, according to the approach of the Lesser Vehicle, sixteen instants arise in succession. These instants are related to the understanding of the properties of the four truths. They are, thus, enumerated as instants of the acceptance of understanding, understanding, the acceptance of subsequent understanding, and subsequent understanding with respect to the properties of each of the four truths. The first fifteen instants constitute the entry into the first fruition, and the sixteenth is the abidance within that.

Let us consider each of them individually. The first is *acceptance of the understanding of the properties of suffering.* Here, one observes the truth of suffering as it pertains to the realm of desire. Doing so, one sees it as characterized by *impermanence*, since [the aggregates] disintegrate from one moment to the next; *suffering*, because of the injuries that are sustained; *emptiness*, since no extraneous self is involved; and *absence of self*, because the essence [of the aggregates] does not constitute a self. This understanding eliminates a set of ten subtle developers that are associated with realm of desire.

These are referred to as "discards through seeing suffering." There is one such discard for each of the following ten afflictions: the view of the transitory collection, extreme views, distorted views, belief in the supremacy of one's view, belief in the supremacy of one's discipline and ritual, desire,

---

191. Vasubandhu, *Treasury of Abhidharma*, VI.28c–d.

anger, pride, ignorance, and doubt. Thus, the acceptance of the understanding of the properties of suffering is the path without impediment that pertains to the elimination of these ten.

Next, the *understanding of the properties of suffering* is the path of liberation upon which the aforementioned ten subtle developers have been eliminated by these very observations. Among these ten, there are five that are direct mistaken engagements with the truth of suffering, four that are mistaken engagements with error, and one that is a mistaken engagement due to error. The first category includes ignorance, doubt, view of the transient collection, extreme view, and distorted view. Ignorance is the lack of understanding of the characteristic impermanence and other features that pertain to the five aggregates of the truth of suffering. Doubt is to harbor uncertainty about these characteristics. The view of the transitory collection is to regard the aggregates as if they included a self and something that belongs to it, while in fact they are devoid of these two. Extreme view is to regard the identity of the aggregates as construed by the view of the transitory collection, and so believe that the self is either permanent or annihilated. Distorted view is to denigrate the truth of suffering, denying the existence of karmic consequences and so forth even in terms of the relative. Respectively, these afflictions are direct mistaken engagements by virtue of not realizing, harboring doubts about, and misunderstanding the characteristics of the truth of suffering. Each of these afflictions is caused by the previous factor.

The category of mistaken engagement with error includes belief in the supremacy of view, belief in the supremacy of discipline and ritual, desire, and pride. All of these are mistaken engagements with the previous three views. Thus, belief in the supremacy of view is when, contrary to what is the case, these three are seen as the foremost and supreme teachings that are in accord with the actual nature of things. Likewise, whereas the causes of purification and liberation cannot be found in these three views, belief in the supremacy of discipline and ritual is when it is thought that, in fact, those three views contain such causes. As for desire and pride, the attachment to objects and the pride that ensues from that are both mistaken engagements that relate directly to the aggregates, yet such desire and pride is to be eliminated through the path of cultivation. In the present context, attachment refers to difficulty in renouncing these views, whereas pride is the arrogance that ensues from them. Thus, these two afflictions are mistaken engagement with error.

Finally, anger is mistaken engagement that is due to error. Though anger at an object is direct mistaken engagement, such anger is eliminated on the path of cultivation. In the present context, anger is of the type that specifically arises due to the three views mentioned above. It is the particular aggression that arises with respect to other views, once the above views have been assumed to be supreme or the cause of purification and liberation.

Taking into account the enmity that is directed toward the Dharma, there may as well be anger as a mistaken engagement that relates directly to the path and cessation. While in the two higher realms there is no anger, the other afflictions can be present in the same way as already described.

Acceptance of the subsequent understanding of suffering is the path without impediment upon which the eighteen subtle developers that are associated with the two higher realms are eliminated. On this path, one observes the truth of suffering of the two higher realms in terms of the features of impermanence and so forth. There is a set of nine subtle developers for each of these two realms. With the exception that anger, which is absent in the higher realms, is not among them, the eliminated afflictions are otherwise the same as before.

Subsequent understanding of suffering is then the path of liberation upon which the aforementioned observations have eliminated these eighteen subtle developers.

Next are the four types of wakefulness that relate to the truth of the origin. *Acceptance of the understanding of the properties of the origin* is when one observes the truth of the origin that pertains to the realm of desire, and so sees that it displays the following features: *cause,* since what one perceives are the seeds that produce suffering; *origination,* because this production is manifold; *full arising,* as the production is intense; and *condition,* since the production is continuous. It is taught that as for suffering and the others:

There are respectively ten, seven, seven, and eight.[192]

Thus, there are seven subtle developers that are eliminated through seeing the intrinsic nature of the origin in the context of the realm of desire. These seven afflictions are the above set of ten, minus the view of the tran-

192. Vasubandhu, *Treasury of Abhidharma,* V.4a.

sitory collection, extreme views, and the belief in the supremacy of discipline and ritual. Acceptance of the understanding of the properties of the origin constitutes the path without impediment upon which these seven are eliminated.

Understanding of the properties of the origin is the path of liberation upon which the seven have been eliminated by means of the described observations.

Acceptance of the subsequent understanding of the origin is when the same observations are made with respect to the truth of the origin as it pertains to the form and formless realms. This a path without impediment upon which one eliminates six subtle developers for each of the two higher realms. These six are the same as the seven referred to above, with the exception that there is no anger associated with the higher realms. In sum, there are, thus, twelve subtle developers associated with the higher realms that are eliminated through seeing the intrinsic nature of the origin.

Subsequent understanding of the origin is then the path of liberation upon which these twelve have been eliminated by means of the aforementioned observations.

What follows are the four types of wakefulness related to cessation. *Acceptance of the understanding of the properties of cessation* observes the cessation of suffering in the context of the realm of desire in terms of the following features: *cessation*, as afflictions cease; *peace*, as the fire of the afflictions is extinguished; *excellence*, since the blemish of the origin is absent; and *definitive emergence*, since this emerges as the source of permanent benefit. *Acceptance of the understanding of the properties of cessation* is a path without impediment that eliminates seven subtle developers associated with the realm of desire. These seven afflictions discarded through seeing the intrinsic nature of cessation are of the same kind as those eliminated through seeing the origin of suffering in the desire realm.

Understanding of the properties of cessation is the path of liberation upon which these seven have been eliminated by the above observations.

Acceptance of the subsequent understanding of cessation is when the cessation of suffering in the two higher realms is observed in terms of the aforementioned features. Thus, this constitutes the path without impediment that eliminates twelve subtle developers—six for each of the realms—that are associated with the experience of the form and formless realms. Except for the absence of anger, the eliminated afflictions are here the same as before.

Subsequent understanding of cessation is the path of liberation upon which the described observations have eliminated these twelve.

Finally, four types of wakefulness that are associated with the path will manifest. *Acceptance of the understanding of the properties of the path* occurs by observing the path that ends suffering within the desire realm in terms of the following features: *path*, since this leads to the city of liberation; *practice*, because through it the mind is freed from error; *reason*, since this remedies affliction; and *the granting of definitive emergence*, because it grants the definitive emergence of the source of lasting benefit. The observation of these features constitutes a path without impediment upon which eight subtle developers are eliminated. These eight afflictions—the ones that are eliminated through seeing the intrinsic nature of the path in relation to the desire realm—consist of the same as before, with the addition of the belief in the supremacy of discipline and ritual.

Understanding of the properties of the path is then the path of liberation upon which these eight have been eliminated by means of the aforementioned observations.

Acceptance of the subsequent understanding of the path is the path without impediment upon which the path that ends suffering within the two higher realms is observed in terms of the aforementioned features. This perception of the intrinsic nature of the path causes the elimination of fourteen subtle developers, seven for each of the realms. These afflictions are of the same type as before, with the exception that in the higher realms there is no anger to be eliminated. These fifteen instants[193] of wakefulness are known as "the path of seeing," and because one enters in order to actualize the fruition of a noble stream-enterer, this is also referred to as the stage of "entry" into that.

The sixteenth instant is the *subsequent understanding of the path*, the wakefulness that is the path of liberation upon which the previous observations have eliminated the aforementioned fourteen subtle developers. Abidance within the fruition of a stream-enterer begins with this moment, and it continues through the elimination of the fifth discard by means of cultivation that is associated with the realm of desire. This is the stage of the attainment of the eightfold cognition within the elimination of the complete set of the aforementioned eighty-eight subtle developers that are

---

193. In an apparent error, the Tibetan text here reads, "the fifteenth instant" (skad cig bco lnga pa de).

to be discarded through seeing. These eighty-eight discards are all ways of relating to the truths by means of imputation. This is why they are eliminated, independent of any process of familiarization, precisely through the perception of the intrinsic nature of the truths. This, in turn, is the reason that they are classified as "discards through seeing." These do not just consist of temporary thought patterns that are due to the influence of negative company and destructive philosophical systems. They also include mental states that are associated with such thought patterns, as well as some that are their seeds.

According to the Abhidharma of the Great Vehicle, there are, as is the case in the context of seeing the truth of suffering, also twenty-eight subtle developers to be eliminated through seeing each of the remaining three truths. Thus, a total of 112 discards through seeing are identified. The truths of the origin, cessation, and path are, respectively, seen to be the causal five aggregates, the intrinsic nature free from any number of stains, and the insight that realizes the intrinsic nature, including the aggregates that belong to the same collection. Each one of the four truths is, hence, mistakenly engaged with by means of the ten afflictions associated with the experience of the desire realm, as well as nine further afflictions for each of the two higher realms.

Here, in the context of the Lesser Vehicle, the truth of the origin is considered action and affliction, cessation is the cessation of the continuum of the aggregates, and the paths of seeing and cultivation are the path. These truths, therefore, cannot be mistakenly engaged through the view of the transitory collection or through extreme views. They cannot be so engaged because, while the view of the transitory collection consists of apprehending the aggregates to be a self and something that belongs to it, none of these [three truths] are exactly the characteristics of the five aggregates, and extreme views will follow [only] where there is a presence of the view of the transient collection. It is also explained that since the perception of the empty and selfless features of the truth of suffering are incompatible with the aforementioned two views and the belief in the supremacy of discipline and ritual, these three afflictions are eliminated through the perception of that truth. But since cause and the other features that pertain to the remaining three truths are not incompatible with these three afflictions, the perception of these truths does not eliminate them. As for the specific belief in the supremacy of discipline and ritual, this affliction is incompatible with the perception of the path and the other features that pertain to the truth of the path. Hence, it is classified as a discard through seeing the truth of the path.

The Great Vehicle, on the other hand, explains that cause and the other features of the truths of the origin, cessation, and path are all seen to resemble an illusion. The perception of the intrinsic nature of these truths is, therefore, equally incompatible with the view of the transitory collection, extreme views, and belief in the supremacy of discipline and ritual. Hence, these three afflictions are eliminated by the perception of those three truths as well.

Further afflictions are eliminated through cultivation. According to the Lesser Vehicle, there are four such discards through cultivation that are associated with the experience of the realm of desire. These are innate desire, anger, pride, and ignorance. With the exception of anger being absent, a similar set of emotions is associated with the experience of both the form and formless realms. Thus, there are ten subtle developers in all that are discarded through cultivation.

These ten are then further understood in relation to nine levels: (1) the unsettled mind of the desire realm, (2–5) the four levels of concentration, and (6–9) the four levels of the formless realm. For each of these nine levels, nine stages are further distinguished with reference to nine levels of affliction, beginning with the greater of the greater afflictions, and continuing through to the lesser of the lesser ones. Thus, by multiplication, we arrive at eighty-one [levels of affliction that are to be eliminated in the context of the path of cultivation].

Entry into the fruition of a once-returner is when the first five [of the nine levels of] affliction that are associated with the desire realm have been exhausted, and one thus abides on the preparatory stage and the path without impediment that are associated with the elimination of the sixth such discard. Abidance within the fruition of a once-returner begins when abiding within the wakefulness that is the path of liberation upon which all six have been eliminated. This stage continues through the elimination of the eighth such affliction associated with the desire realm. The once-returner is so called because of not having to return again to the world of humans or gods within the desire realm. Having been born there, the once-returner will then either attain the transcendence of suffering in that same life, or otherwise in a future existence. Thus, it is taught:

The one who has conquered through the fifth
Has entered into the second.[194]

As well as:

The one who has exhausted the sixth
Has become a once-returner.[195]

Moreover:

The exhaustion of eight flaws
Is entry into the third fruition,
The path without impediment that relates to the ninth.
The exhaustion of nine is the nonreturner.[196]

Thus, one who is entering into [the fruition of] a nonreturner abides on the preparatory stage, or on the path without impediment, upon which the ninth affliction of the desire realm is being relinquished, the first eight having already been exhausted. The nonreturner's abiding in the fruition begins with the path of liberation, where this ninth affliction has been eliminated, and continues through the elimination of the eighth affliction associated with the summit of existence. A nonreturner does not return to the realm of desire but will attain the transcendence of suffering either in the [last existence within that realm] or in a future life. Further, it is taught:

The exhaustion of eight obstacles related to the summit of existence
Is entry into the foe-destroyer.
The one who has exhausted nine is a foe-destroyer.[197]

Hence, entry into the [fruition of] a foe-destroyer takes place when the eighth affliction related to the summit of existence has been exhausted and one abides on the preparatory stage and the path without impediment as

194. Vasubandhu, *Treasury of Abhidharma*, VI.35a–b.
195. Ibid., VI.35c–d.
196. Ibid., VI.36.
197. Ibid., VI.44a–c.

associated with the elimination of the ninth. Abidance within the fruition of a foe-destroyer is the abidance within the wakefulness of the path
of liberation upon which that ninth affliction has been eliminated. The
Sanskrit *arhat* means "destroyer of the enemy" as well as "worthy." Hence,
the foe-destroyer is the one for whom the afflictions of the three realms,
the enemies that rob the bliss of transcendence away, have been conquered
or, alternately, one who is a true object of offering, worthy of the worship
of gods, humans, and so forth.

The eight persons described here have all actualized the Dharma of realization. They are, therefore, unswerving in the face of demons, as well as
suited to be objects of veneration. They constitute the Sangha. Hence, it
is argued, without these eight persons, there would not be any Sangha. A
sūtra, for example, teaches:

> They are revered by Indra,
> Royal ruler of the gods,
> And by successful beings involved in agriculture,
> The faithful who wish for merit and happiness,
> All those who continuously engender
> The merit that arises from substance.
> They are explained to be, for them,
> A field that when offered to
> Yields vast and most excellent results.
> They possess awareness and its supports,
> And are the objects of worship, the great Sangha
> Of the four that have gained entry
> And the four that abide in fruition.

According to the Great Vehicle, the afflictions eliminated through cultivation consist of innate ignorance, the view of the transitory collection,
extreme views, desire, pride, and anger. The last of these is found only in
the unsettled mind of the desire realm. It is, thus, absent from all eight levels of equipoise. Anger is, therefore, not distinguishable with reference to
the levels, and so only a single ninefold set of greater, middling, and lesser
afflictions obtains for that affliction. Each of the other five afflictions has
a distinct type for each of the nine levels (the unsettled mind of the desire
realm, the four levels of concentration, and the four levels of the formless
realm). Each of these nine is again divided into nine by enumerating the

greater of the greater afflictions, and so forth, through to the lesser of the lesser ones. Thus, there are eighty-one types for each of these five afflictions, leading to a total of number of 414 discards through cultivation.

Nevertheless, in the present context of the Lesser Vehicle, the view of the transitory collection and extreme views are not held to be included among the discards through cultivation. The reason for this is that the Lesser Vehicle does not accept any all-ground. Without the all-ground, there is no defiled mental cognition that observes it. This, in turn, means that there are no innate views—neither the view of the transitory collection that accompanies the defiled mental cognition, nor the extreme views that follow from the view of the transitory collection.

There Would Be No Dharma

The next consequence is the absence of the Dharma. The treatise states:

> Because there are no noble truths,
> There is no sacred Dharma. [XXIV.4c–d]

The nonexistence of the noble truths also entails the nonexistence of the sacred Dharma, that is, the Dharma that sacred and noble individuals engage in, or which is sacred and supreme among all that is Dharma. The Dharma of realization is freedom from attachment and that which leads to this freedom, that is, the cause and effect of complete purification. The Dharma of scripture, in turn, consists of the excellent discourses that reveal the former. Yet neither of these two aspects of the sacred Dharma can exist if there are no noble truths.

There Would Be No Buddha

There would be no Buddha either. The treatise states:

> If there is no Dharma and no Sangha,
> How could there be any Buddha? [XXIV.5a–b]

In this way, if there is no Dharma in the form of a path to be practiced, and no Sangha in the form of individuals who practice it, how could there be a result of these two? How could there be a Buddha? Generally, if the Dharma exists, one can pursue it in the correct way and eventually comprehend it fully and completely. Likewise, with the presence of the Sangha, one can accumulate merit by making offerings to its members, venerating them, and taking refuge in them, whereas by following their teachings one can accumulate wakefulness. In this way, the presence of the Dharma and Sangha makes the gradual transformation into a Buddha possible.

Alternatively, the verses can be seen to be stating that Buddhahood follows from the correct pursuit of the Dharma by those members of the Sangha that were referred to above. If the verses are understood in accordance with the intermediate teachings of the Common Vehicle, the term "Sangha" will refer to the bodhisattvas that abide on the ten grounds. In that case, it becomes extremely clear that the absence of Buddhas would follow as a consequence.

Summary

Summarizing these three consequences, the treatise states:

> *This teaching of emptiness*
> *Invalidates the three jewels. [XXIV.5c–d]*

The three jewels are held to display five qualities that resemble a jewel. Thus, it is explained:

> Because they are rare, faultless,
> Powerful, ornaments of the world,
> And because they are supreme . . .[198]

It is also taught that they resemble a jewel in being rare and greatly beneficial. The verses above argue that teaching all phenomena to be empty invalidates the three jewels since they are included under "all phenomena." Thus, the teaching of emptiness renders these three jewels nonexistent.

Actions Would Have No Consequences

Fourth, showing how actions would not have any consequences, the treatise states:

> *Likewise, the existence of results,*
> *Non-Dharma and Dharma, [XXIV.6a–b]*

---

198. Maitreya, *Supreme Continuity*, I.22a–c.

The teaching that "everything is emptiness" also invalidates non-Dharma, such as the ten nonvirtues, and the Dharma associated with the higher realms, such as the ten virtues. Because they are also included in "everything," the teaching of universal emptiness invalidates these principles, as well as the existence of their painful and pleasant results.

There Would Be No Mundane Convention

Fifth, setting forth the consequence that mundane conventions would be nonexistent, the treatise states:

> *And all the conventions of the world*
> *Would likewise be invalidated thereby. [XXIV.6c–d]*

When it is said that that "everything is empty," this also includes form, sensation, and so forth, as well as other conventions of the world, such as "make this," "stay there," and so forth. Hence, all mundane conventions are invalidated as well. The claim that all phenomena are emptiness is, therefore, unreasonable.

THE REPLY

Subsequent to these objections follows the reply. This takes the form of a description of (1) the reasons for the opponent's objections, (2) the way the position of the Middle Way does not incur the perceived flaws, and (3) the supremacy of Middle Way realization.

The Reasons for the Opponent's Objections

On the first issue, the treatise states:

> *To explain, you have not understood*
> *The purpose of emptiness,*
> *Emptiness itself, or its meaning.*
> *Therefore this is damaging to you. [XXIV.7]*

The opponent has not understood what the approach of the Middle Way really is, which is why this criticism is presented. The stated flaws, therefore, are not damaging to the Middle Way.

How, then, is it that these flaws do not apply? If all phenomena are empty of nature, it follows that none of them exists ultimately. Yet it does not follow that they do not exist even relatively. As has been stated:

> We do not explain
> Without accepting convention.[199]

Thus, the meaning of emptiness is not that nothing exists at all, even conventionally. The opponent, however, apprehends marks of a negation in relation to the meaning of emptiness, or understands it to imply that there is nothing at all, even in terms of convention.

The purpose of the teaching and realization of emptiness is the attainment of the transcendence of suffering through the exhaustion of all mental constructs. The characteristics, or essence, of emptiness is the freedom, in reality, from all constructions of existence and nonexistence, while its meaning, that is, that which the term "emptiness" explains and applies to, is dependent origination. Failing to understand all of this, the opponent proclaims that the teaching of emptiness is flawed, in that it renders everything nonexistent even at the level of convention. The perception of such flaws and damages, however, is the result of the opponent's own mistaken concepts.

Why These Flaws Are Not Applicable to the Middle Way
The second section (1) sets forth the approach of the Middle Way, (2) shows how it is free from flaws thereby, and (3) explains why denying the Middle Way would be a mistake. The first of these points will address (1) the topics to be understood as taught by the Victorious One, (2) the flaws that occur when one fails to comprehend these, and (3) the conclusion.

The Topics to Be Understood as Taught by the Victorious One
On the first issue, the treatise states:

> *The Dharma taught by the Buddhas*
> *Is genuinely based on the two truths:*
> *The relative truth of the world*
> *And the truth of the ultimate meaning. [XXIV.8]*

199. Nāgārjuna, *Rebuttal of Objections*, 28c–d.

All of the teachings given by the Buddhas are genuinely, or definitively, based on the two truths: the relative truth and ultimate truth. As implied by the Sanskrit term, *samvṛtisatya,* the relative truth of the world is characterized by being something that obscures the perception of reality, and so is true as the object of a conventional, deluded mind. All cognizable, expressible, and measurable phenomena are, thus, the bearers of this characteristic of the relative truth. The ultimate truth is characterized by being true as the object of an ultimate mind and rational cognition. That which bears this characteristic is, thus, all phenomena, which, as the object of such a mind, do not abide as per any of the marks of constructed negation or affirmation.

The Flaws of Failing to Comprehend the Two Truths
The second issue as well is divided into three sections, the first of which explains the general flaw that follows from a lack of insight into the division of the two truths.

The General Flaw of Not Understanding This Division
On the first issue, the treatise states:

> *Those who do not understand*
> *The distinction between these two truths,*
> *Fail to comprehend the profound reality*
> *Of the Buddha's teaching. [XXIV.9]*

From the perspective of the two minds referred to above, there is, respectively, appearance and the complete lack of any established nature. The division into two truths, thus, depends on these two mental perspectives. Those who do not understand this classification will harbor one-sided beliefs about existence and nonexistence. Hence, they will fail to comprehend the profound reality that is revealed by the Buddha, the natural emptiness of dependent origination, free from all one-sided extremes of existence and nonexistence.

Without Realization of the Ultimate, There Is No Liberation
On the particular flaw of failing to gain liberation because of not realizing the ultimate, the treatise states:

Without relying on convention,
The ultimate cannot be shown.
Without realizing the ultimate,
Suffering cannot be transcended. [XXIV.10]

It might be objected: "If, in this way, the ultimate is beyond all that can be spoken and conceived of, then the relative, deluded appearances of the aggregates and other such factors are all to be abandoned. Yet the Buddha has nevertheless taught the existence of such things. Why would he do that?"

Indeed, this objection is correct, but unless one relies on convention, it will not be possible to realize the ultimate. And unless that is realized, there will be no attainment of peace. Thus, just as one who wishes for water needs a vessel, it is indeed necessary to teach the relative for there to be a realization of the ultimate. Without relying on convention, moreover, the ultimate cannot be taught by any means, such as language and signs, because the essence of the ultimate itself lies beyond the sphere of language and mind. Moreover, unless the ultimate is taught through language and signs, the attachment to some sort of ultimate properties cannot be stopped, and so one will not be able to realize it through an existential negation of all mental constructs. Finally, unless one realizes the ultimate truth, as it pertains to all phenomena, by means of an existential negation of mental constructs, suffering cannot be transcended with the elimination of all adventitious stains.

Misunderstanding Emptiness Has Disastrous Consequences
The treatise states:

When viewing emptiness incorrectly,
Those with little insight will be ruined,
As when a snake is caught in the wrong way,
Or a knowledge mantra is used incorrectly. [XXIV.11]

Feebleminded individuals who misunderstand emptiness will be ruined within cyclic existence and the lower realms. Unless the principles of these two truths are acknowledged, the teaching of emptiness will make those with little insight believe either that emptiness means even conventional nonexistence, or otherwise that nonexistence is the real condition. When emptiness is viewed incorrectly in either of these ways, they will be ruined within cyclic existence and the lower realms.

Those whose misunderstanding is of the first kind will adhere either to a literal understanding of emptiness or abandon the teaching. When emptiness is taken in a literal sense, one develops a distorted view that depreciates karmic consequences even at the level of the relative. Hence, one will go to the lower realms. As the Master himself explains:

> As they misunderstand this Dharma,
> Those who lack learning will let it go to waste.
> Thus, they sink into the filth
> Of the view of nonexistence.[200]

For others, the same misunderstanding will not lead to a denial [of karmic causality], but rather to thoughts of the following kind: "I can observe all these phenomena, so how could they be emptiness? Emptiness is not the Dharma; it is not the teaching of our Teacher."

In abandoning this principle, such people commit the act of discarding the Dharma and will go to the lower realms as a result. Hence, we find the following statement:

> Otherwise, misunderstanding this Dharma,
> Fools who pride themselves on learning
> Will abandon it and so, corrupted,
> Fall head first into the hell of incessant pain.[201]

With the second type of misunderstanding, one believes that the real condition is one of nonexistence. This is similar to taking medicine that, because one cannot digest it, turns into a poison. Emptiness is the remedy of all views, and yet here one develops a view about it, taking it to be a mark. Hence, it becomes impossible to separate from all views, and so attain peace. This was explained earlier in the treatise:

> The Victorious Ones have taught emptiness
> As a deliverance from all views.

200. Nāgārjuna, *Jewel Garland*, II.19.
201. Ibid., II.20.

For those whose view is emptiness, they say,
Nothing can be accomplished.[202]

It might then be thought: "That which is beneficial when understood correctly may indeed not be beneficial when misunderstood, but why would such misunderstanding bring ruin and destruction?"

For example, if one catches a snake or a nāga in the prescribed way, one can thereby acquire great wealth. But if, lacking the instructions, one catches it the wrong way, one will not only miss out on the riches but also contract leprosy. Likewise, if one uses black magic or knowledge mantras in accordance with certain instructions, one's enemies will be crushed and one will oneself be granted attainments. But if one does not know these instructions and uses the spell incorrectly, it is oneself who will be crushed. Hence, misunderstanding can be disastrous.

Conclusion
Third, in conclusion, the treatise states:

> *Hence, knowing that the depth of this Dharma*
> *Would be hard for the feebleminded to understand,*
> *The realized mind of the Able One*
> *Turned entirely away from teaching the Dharma. [XXIV.12]*

The meaning of emptiness is profound and hard to realize. Disciples of inferior capacity will misunderstand it, and when they do, the negative consequences are severe. Hence, knowing that the depth of the Dharma of emptiness would be hard to understand for the feebleminded, the realized mind of the Able One turned entirely away from teaching the Dharma. Thus, he spoke:

> Profound, peaceful, stainless, luminous, and unconditioned
> Is this nectarlike Dharma I have found.
> Since if I teach it, no one will understand,
> I shall remain silent in the forest.[203]

---

202. *Root of the Middle Way*, XIII.8.
203. From the *Sūtra of the Great Display*.

How the Middle Way Is Free of Flaws

Having set forth the approach of the Middle Way, it will next be shown that the Middle Way does not incur any flaw. This will include (1) showing that the basis for the flaws is not accepted, (2) presenting the bases for flaws and benefits, and (3) showing how the criticism is, therefore, unreasonable.

The Basis for the Flaws Is Not Accepted by the Middle Way

On the first issue, the treatise states:

> *The flaws that ensue in consequence*
> *Are not reasonable with respect to emptiness.*
> *Hence, your discarding emptiness*
> *Is not reasonable to me. [XXIV.13]*

The opponent presented flaws in the form of the conventional nonexistence of the four noble truths and so on, which were supposed to follow as consequences of the teaching of emptiness. None of these flaws, however, are reasonable, or applicable, with respect to the natural emptiness that is taught by proponents of the Middle Way. The opponent, on the other hand, discards this emptiness, for he thinks of emptiness as implying either that nonexistence is real, or otherwise that nothing exists, even conventionally. That, the Master says, "is not reasonable to me," because that sort of emptiness is not what he accepts.

The Bases for Flaws and Benefits

On the second issue, the treatise states:

> *Everything is possible*
> *For those for whom emptiness is possible.*
> *Nothing is possible*
> *For those for whom emptiness is impossible. [XXIV.14]*

> *That which originates in dependence*
> *Is taught to be emptiness.*
> *This itself is dependent imputation*
> *And so the path of the Middle Way. [XXIV.18]*

> *Apart from what originates dependently,*
> *There are no phenomena at all.*
> *Therefore, apart from emptiness,*
> *There are no phenomena at all. [XXIV.19]*

For the one for whom emptiness is possible, all conventional principles, such as those pertaining to the four noble truths, will be possible as well. Below it is then explained how that which originates in dependence is devoid of nature and, therefore, emptiness. A sūtra teaches:

All phenomena are empty, in the sense that they have no nature.

And likewise:

> What arises due to conditions does not arise;
> It lacks the nature of arising.
> What depends on conditions is taught to be empty;
> Mindful is the one who knows emptiness.[204]

Natural emptiness is itself a conventional imputation based on causes and conditions. Hence, this illusion-like dependent origination, or the absence of nature that is its intrinsic nature, is itself the path of the Middle Way beyond all extremes. Therefore, upon examination, one will see that there is nothing that is not the path of the Middle Way, the reason being that conventionally there are no phenomena at all that are not dependent origination. This, in turn, entails that, in reality, there are no phenomena whatsoever that are not emptiness.

As this is the case, conventional dependent origination is possible for those for whom natural emptiness is possible. All the [principles] mentioned above, from the noble truths to mundane conventions, will then be just as feasible since they are included within dependent origination. Yet for the one for whom emptiness is not possible, that is, the one for whom there is a nature, dependent origination is not possible either. Hence, everything that falls under the category of dependent origination, such as the noble truths and mundane convention, becomes impossible as well.

204. From the *Sūtra Requested by Anavatapta, King of the Nāgas.*

The Unreasonable Nature of the Criticism
On the third issue, the treatise states:

> *All your own faults*
> *You project onto me,*
> *As if, while riding your horse,*
> *You had forgotten all about it.* [XXIV.15]

Here, the Master explains, "You proponents of nature project all your own problems with the four noble truths onto me, the advocate of the completely flawless position of natureless dependent origination. This is comparable to a situation where a distracted person forgets the very horse he or she is riding, and so accuses someone else of having stolen it. While you yourselves ride the horses of error, you argue in distraction that they belong to others, and while you yourselves assert dependent origination— that is the nature of, or that that which is entailed by, emptiness—you distractedly object that emptiness does not make sense.

Why Denying the Middle Way Would Be a Mistake
Third, it is explained why denying the Middle Way is a mistake. One may wonder: "What are the flaws of others that are wrongly attributed to the Middle Way proponents?"

The reply to this question will be given in six sections, of which the first concerns the consequence that causality becomes nonexistent.

The Consequence That Causality Becomes Nonexistent
The treatise states:

> *If you view things*
> *As existent by nature,*
> *Then for you there are*
> *No causes and conditions.* [XXIV.16]

> *Effect and cause;*
> *Agent, means, and action;*
> *Arising, cessation, and result—*
> *These are invalidated as well.* [XXIV.17]

If you deny that all phenomena are empty and instead view things as existent by nature, this means that for you outer and inner things do not have any causes and conditions. This is entailed because it has already been explained that nature could not meaningfully arise based on causes and conditions and that being produced is incompatible with being existent by nature. If you accept that there are no causes and conditions, it follows that vases and other such things, which are effects produced by causes and conditions, cannot exist either. Causal objects such as clay, the potter who is the agent capable of undertaking the action [of producing the vase], the means employed by the potter, such as his wheel, the action that is the arising of the resultant vase, and the phenomena that are associated with this result—all such things would then be nonexistent too. There could be no arising of the vase, no end to its existence, and no containing of water as the result of there being a vase. All of this is invalidated as well.

The Four Truths Would Be Untrue
Second, showing that the topics to be understood would become untrue, the treatise states:

> *If all of this were not empty,*
> *Nothing would arise or be destroyed.*
> *For you it follows that*
> *There are no four noble truths. [XXIV.20]*

> *As it would not originate dependently,*
> *How could there be suffering?*
> *The teaching that the impermanent is suffering*
> *Cannot be relevant where nature exists. [XXIV.21]*

> *Given natural existence,*
> *What could originate?*
> *Hence, for those who deny emptiness,*
> *There cannot be any origin. [XXIV.22]*

> *If suffering exists by nature,*
> *There can be no cessation.*

As it would remain completely,
Cessation would be invalidated. [XXIV.23]

If there were a nature of the path,
It could not reasonably be cultivated.
If the path is to be cultivated,
Then this nature of yours does not exist. [XXIV.24]

If there is neither suffering
Nor its origin and cessation,
What cessation of suffering
Do you assert is achieved by the path? [XXIV.25]

If all these outer and inner things were not empty and instead possessed a nature, they could neither be produced nor undergo change. Hence, nothing would arise and nothing would be destroyed. The four noble truths entail arising and destruction. Therefore, for you who assert that things are not empty of nature, it follows that none of the aforementioned four noble truths have any existence.

To elaborate, where there is nature, there cannot be production and dependent origination. Hence, since it could not originate dependently, how could there possibly be any suffering, how could there be any aggregates produced by past actions and afflictions? A sūtra teaches:

> That which is impermanent is suffering.

Yet this would be impossible for that which exists by nature because nature is incompatible with change, just like nonresistant space.

Moreover, given the natural existence of suffering, what causally conditioned suffering could possibly originate? There could not be any arising of suffering based on causes. Therefore, for those who assert natural existence and deny emptiness, there cannot be any origin, any cause of suffering.

Moreover, if suffering existed by nature, there could be no cessation either. This is entailed because that which is truly natural must remain completely, just like the nonresistance of space. A denial of emptiness is, therefore, also a denial of cessation.

Finally, if there were a nature of the path from the beginning, the path could not reasonably be cultivated and developed in a sequential manner. Hence, since it is taught that the path is to be cultivated, the notion that the path has a nature can be dismissed. If you accept that the path is something to be cultivated, then the nature that you talk about does not exist because production is incompatible with nature.

Likewise, if nature exists there can be no suffering, no origin, and no cessation. What path is it, then, that you assert to be the means for eliminating suffering and its origin, and for achieving cessation? Since there is no cessation of suffering, there cannot be a path that allows one to achieve it either.

The Subject of the Path Would Be Nonexistent
Third, showing that there would be no subject of the path, the treatise states:

> *If complete understanding*
> *Were absent by nature,*
> *How could complete understanding occur?*
> *Does nature not remain? [XXIV.26]*

> *The same with your elimination,*
> *Actualization, familiarization,*
> *Cultivation, and four fruitions—*
> *They are as impossible as complete understanding. [XXIV.27]*

> *Since they retain their own nature,*
> *How could fruitions that are*
> *By nature unachieved*
> *Ever be achieved? [XXIV.28]*

The nature of the complete understanding of suffering would not need to be understood. If complete understanding were absent by nature, how could it occur at a later point in time? The impossibility of complete understanding taking place would be entailed, for would the natural not remain? Indeed, it must.

The same goes for the opponent's positions on the elimination of the origin, the actualization of the cessation, the familiarization with the path, and the four fruitions of the cultivation—they too are as impossible as complete understanding. Since elimination and these other factors would not exist to begin with, they could not reasonably come to exist at some subsequent time either because the natural cannot be changed.

If the nature of something is not there to begin with, it is utterly impossible for it to come about later. Moreover, how could the nature of the four fruitions, which to begin with are unachieved by nature, ever be achieved? Their remaining unachieved would be entailed, as is shown with the words, "Since they retain their own nature."

The Three Jewels Would Become Nonexistent
Fourth, showing how the resultant three jewels would be nonexistent, the treatise states:

> *Without fruition, there is no one abiding in it,*
> *Nor anyone who has gained entry.*
> *If the eight persons do not exist,*
> *Then there is no Sangha. [XXIV.29]*

> *Because there are no noble truths,*
> *There is no Dharma either.*
> *If there are no Dharma and Sangha,*
> *How could there be any Buddha? [XXIV.30]*

> *For you it follows that the Buddha*
> *Does not depend on enlightenment.*
> *For you it follows that enlightenment*
> *Does not depend on the Buddha. [XXIV.31]*

> *For you, the one who by nature is no Buddha*
> *May pursue the conduct of enlightenment*
> *In order to attain enlightenment,*
> *Yet all such efforts will be in vain. [XXIV.32]*

The verses in the twenty-ninth and thirtieth stanzas show, respectively, how the Sangha, Dharma, and Buddha would end up being nonexistent. These three consequences are to be understood in the same way as explained above [in XXIV.3c–5b].

Furthermore, for the opponent, the Buddha, understood as the person that supports enlightenment, exists by nature. Therefore, it follows that this Buddha does not depend on that which is the cause of him being designated as such, that is, the enlightenment of omniscient wakefulness. For the opponent, it equally follows that enlightenment, the omniscient wakefulness that is supported by the Buddha and the cause of him being designated as such, does not depend on the Buddha, that is, the supportive person or that which is defined by enlightenment.

Moreover, it would be unnecessary for someone who is a Buddha by nature to make any efforts on the path. Hence, that person who, according to the opponent, by nature is *not* a Buddha may diligently apply himself or herself to the conduct of enlightenment in pursuit of enlightenment, yet no enlightenment will ever be achieved. Why? Because nothing can annul this person's not being a Buddha by nature.

No Cause and Effect of Actions

Fifth, showing how it would not make sense for actions to have consequences, the treatise states:

> *Nobody would ever perform*
> *Dharma or non-Dharma.*
> *What can be done to the not empty?*
> *There can be no action in relation to nature. [XXIV.33]*

> *In the absence of Dharma and non-Dharma,*
> *For you, there are still effects.*
> *Effects caused by Dharma and non-Dharma*
> *For you, do not exist. [XXIV.34]*

> *If, for you, there are effects*
> *That arise from Dharma and non-Dharma,*
> *Why, then, would these effects*
> *Of Dharma and non-Dharma not be empty? [XXIV.35]*

No one would ever engage in Dharmic or non-Dharmic causes if they existed by nature. This is entailed because what can be done in relation to that which is not empty? Indeed, nature and fabrication are irreconcilable. Hence, there can be no action in relation to nature.

Take also the subject, the pleasant and unpleasant effects of Dharma and non-Dharma. It follows that, for the opponent, these effects may be present even without there being any Dharma and non-Dharma because they exist by nature. Should the opponents accept this consequence, they will be reminded that for them such a consequence is unacceptable. If the effects of Dharma and non-Dharma could arise without there being any Dharma and non-Dharma, the latter two would have become meaningless. These effects, moreover, could not manifest only at certain times.

It may then be argued: "The results, pleasure and pain, exist by nature. Yet this does not mean that there is no Dharma or non-Dharma because these factors are the causes that produce pleasure and pain."

Yet if the opponent asserts that there are effects caused by Dharma and non-Dharma, why would such effects, since they arise based on Dharma and non-Dharma, not then be of an empty nature? That their emptiness is entailed has already been explained more than once.

Conventions Would Not Make Any Sense
Sixth, showing how neither mundane nor transcendent conventions would make any sense, the treatise states:

> *The one who denies*
> *The emptiness of dependent origination*
> *Will, likewise, be denying*
> *All conventions of the world. [XXIV.36]*

> *A denial of emptiness*
> *Will preclude all action.*
> *There will be actions without initiation,*
> *As well as agents without anything done. [XXIV.37]*

> *If beings had any nature,*
> *They would not be born or die.*
> *Indeed, they would remain immutable*
> *And would not know a variety of states. [XXIV.38]*

> *Were it not for emptiness,*
> *The unattained could not be attained,*
> *There would be no liberation from suffering,*
> *And no elimination of action and affliction. [XXIV.39]*

First, it is shown how mundane conventions would become untenable. For those who deny emptiness by asserting natural existence, there cannot reasonably be any fabrication and dependent origination. Moreover, since worldly conventions like "go!" and "stay!" are included in dependent origination, these would be rendered nonsensical. Indeed, the denial of emptiness is also the denial of all mundane conventions.

If emptiness is denied and one asserts the existence of nature, it will also follow that no agent could ever perform any action. Since actions would exist by nature, they would not depend on being initiated by agents, and they could then take place without there being anything that performs them. Likewise, if the agents existed by nature, they would not depend on actions and there could then be agents that perform no action at all. We do not observe any such action or agent, however. Therefore, we can conclude that these two are mutually dependent and, hence, similar to reflections. If they possessed a nature, neither action nor agent would make any sense.

Furthermore, if there were a nature of wandering beings, they would not arise and cease from one moment to the next. Instead, they would remain immutable by virtue of their nature. If this is accepted, however, it will follow that these beings would not know different states, and yet we see that they do indeed participate in different situations. Hence, since they do not remain immutable, but arise and cease, we can conclude that wandering beings have no nature. A sūtra teaches:

> If there were a bit that is not empty,
> The Victorious One would not declare or teach anything.
> Everything would remain immutable as it is,
> Without developing or decaying.[205]

Second, it is explained how transcendent conventions would not make any sense either. If there were no emptiness and things existed by their own natures, all fruitions, from that of the stream-enterer up to a Buddha's, could not first be unattained and then later attained. Similarly, the resultant liberation from suffering without any remainder of the aggregates could not be something that goes from not having to having occurred. Since the causal action and affliction could not first exist and then later

---

205. From the *Sūtra of the Elephant's Strength*.

be eliminated, there could not be any transcendence of suffering with remainder either.

The Supremacy of Middle Way Realization

Third, expressing the supremacy of Middle Way realization, the treatise states:

> *The one who sees*
> *Dependent origination*
> *Sees suffering, its origin,*
> *Cessation, and the path. [XXIV.40]*

The existence of nature would render everything impossible. The one who sees the meaning of emptiness, free from all mental constructions of truth, to be conventionally dependent origination is, therefore, also the one who sees the essential reality of the truths of suffering, its origin, its cessation, and the path.

SUMMARY OF THE CHAPTER'S SIGNIFICANCE

In terms of the ultimate, the present chapter has existentially negated all constructions of truth with respect to all phenomena, including the four truths. As for the relative, it has established that these all appear dependently, just like an illusion. The *Noble Sūtra That Shows the Nonarising of All Phenomena* teaches:

> The one who sees the nonarising of all phenomena has complete understanding of suffering. The one who sees the nonexistence of all phenomena has eliminated the origin. The one who sees all phenomena as total transcendence of suffering has actualized the cessation. The one who sees all phenomena as not being things has cultivated the path.

This concludes the explanation of the twenty-fourth chapter, the analysis of the noble truths, in the *Ornament of Reason*, a commentary on the *Root of the Middle Way*.

CHAPTER TWENTY-FIVE

Analysis of the Transcendence of Suffering

THREE ISSUES also pertain to the analysis of the transcendence of suffering.[206]

THE CONTEXT OF CHAPTER 25

First, regarding the chapter's context, the present analysis relates to the profound sūtras, such as the following teaching from the *Mother of the Victorious Ones*:

The transcendence of suffering is also like a dream, like an illusion.

And in the *King of Meditative Absorptions*:

The nonexistence of the transcendence of suffering
Is what the Protector of the World has taught as the transcendence
of suffering.
Knots tied on space
Are untied by space itself.

Here, the meaning of such teachings that declare the transcendence of suffering to be nonexistent will be ascertained through reasoning.

As for its relation to the other analyses, the present chapter can be seen as a reply to the following objection: "If all phenomena are emptiness in this way, there cannot be any elimination of suffering or cessation

206. In this chapter, the concluding summary is included in the explanation of stanza 24.

of the aggregates' continuity. Transcendence of suffering with or without remainder will then have become impossible."

Thus, the present analysis was composed to explain that the term "transcendence of suffering" refers to the natural purity that, in reality, pertains to all phenomena. There is no transcendence of suffering in the sense of an elimination of certain discards by means of a remedy.

THE CONTENT OF CHAPTER 25

Second, the explanation of the chapter's content contains (1) an objection and (2) a reply.

OBJECTION

Expressing the objection, the treatise states:

> *If all of this were empty,*
> *Nothing would arise or be destroyed.*
> *Which elimination and cessation is it*
> *That you assert leads to the transcendence of suffering? [XXV.1]*

Here it is objected: "If all these outer and inner things were essentially empty, their distinctive arising and cessation would be nonexistent as well. Since both the afflictions and their remedy necessarily entail arising and cessation, what afflictions would it be that are eliminated by the remedy, undefiling wakefulness? Furthermore, how would the cessation of the continuity of the aggregates that results from this elimination take place? Indeed, to say that the transcendence of suffering with and without remainder ensues from this elimination and cessation, respectively, would make no sense."

REPLY

The subsequent reply goes to show that while this problem (1) is relevant for the opponent, it (2) does not pertain to the follower of the Middle Way.

The Flaw Is Incurred by the Opponent

Making the first of these two points, the treatise states:

> *If all of this were not empty,*
> *Nothing would arise or be destroyed.*
> *Which elimination and cessation is it*
> *That you assert leads to the transcendence of suffering? [XXV.2]*

If all these things were not empty and instead possessed a nature, they could neither arise nor disintegrate because nature is incompatible with fabrication and change. How could you then assert the elimination of afflictions and cessation of aggregates that bring about, respectively, the transcendence of suffering with and without remainder? Indeed, any such assertion would be entirely inappropriate. As explained in the *Noble Sūtra of the Elephant's Strength*:

> If phenomena had any nature,
> Then the victors and the listeners would know it.
> Solid phenomena do not attain the transcendence of suffering.
> The wise would never become free of mental construction.

The Critique Does Not Pertain to the Follower of the Middle Way

The second issue involves (1) stating that the transcendence of suffering is the intrinsic nature, primordially free from extremes, (2) proving that this is so, and (3) deflecting the objection that it would then be meaningless to teach the Dharma.

Transcendence of Suffering Is the Intrinsic Nature

On the first issue, the treatise states:

> *No elimination and no attainment,*
> *No annihilation and no permanence,*
> *No cessation and no arising—*
> *This is termed the transcendence of suffering. [XXV.3]*

Some may ask: "Why would you adherents of the Middle Way not incur the same flaw?"

Well, we do not assert that, in reality, there is a transcendence of suffering in the sense of an elimination of certain discards by means of a remedy. What we term "the transcendence of suffering" is the absence of the things that you imagine. For us, the transcendence of suffering is the absence of any elimination of phenomena pertaining to thorough affliction, as well as the absence of any attainment that is the result of complete purification. It involves no annihilation of a previously existing continuum of the self or the aggregates, nor any permanence in the sense of a future existence of such a continuum. There is no momentary cessation of an essence that existed before, nor any arising of something that did not exist earlier. That which is free from these six mentally constructed extremes is what is termed "the transcendence of suffering."

It might here be objected: "Various other distinctions in the form of negative properties are equally possible with respect to the transcendence of suffering. Yet if the properties above are then just examples, the full set would be unnecessary."

This criticism, however, is unfounded. The set of precisely these six distinctive, negative properties is presented to counter the mistaken ideas that Buddhists and non-Buddhists have developed with respect to the transcendence of suffering. Notions of an elimination of flaws and the attainment of good qualities are common to both Buddhists and non-Buddhists. Far Throwers and Followers of Sūtra believe in the annihilation of a previously existent continuum of the self and the aggregates, respectively. Enumerators and Proponents of Differences conceive of permanence in the sense of a subsequent existence of, respectively, the self and the entity of separation. Finally, Mind Only proponents believe that once all the deluded appearances and concepts associated with dualistic perception have been exhausted, the substance of self-awareness exists as an essence that momentarily arises and ceases. These misconceptions are thus perfectly countered by the six distinctions mentioned above.

It might also be argued: "Indeed, the transcendence of suffering does not itself contain any causal afflictions or resultant aggregates. Yet such factors are still naturally existent during the preceding time of cyclic existence. The transcendence of suffering is thus to be understood as the peace that ensues from their exhaustion."

Yet this will not do because what exists by nature to begin with cannot later be made nonexistent. As the Master himself states:

The Great Vehicle teaches the absence of arising,
While for others emptiness is exhaustion.
Exhaustion and nonarising are actually the same;
Hence, do be patient.[207]

While a sūtra teaches:

Within the transcendence of suffering, there are no existent
     phenomena.
In it, there are no phenomena; they never existed.
When conceiving and experiencing in terms of "existence" and
     "nonexistence"
Suffering will not be thoroughly pacified.[208]

Proving That the Transcendence of Suffering Is the Intrinsic Nature

The treatment of the second issue involves (1) refuting the four extremes
with respect to the transcendence of suffering, (2) showing that a Buddha
who has realized this is not established in the manner of the four extremes,
and (3) the ensuing conclusion. The first of these contains refutations of
the notions that (1) the transcendence of suffering is an established entity
or nonentity, (2) it is both, and (3) it is neither of these two. The first
section (1) refutes these two options one by one and (2) refutes them
simultaneously.

The Transcendence of Suffering Is Not an Established Entity

The Proponents of Differences assert the transcendence of suffering to be
an unconditioned permanent entity that brings about the definitive cessation of affliction and suffering as if it were a dam that blocks a stream.
There are three steps to the refutation of this idea. First, showing how such
an understanding would mean that the transcendence of suffering would
involve aging and death, the treatise states:

Now, the transcendence of suffering is not an entity,
For it would then be characterized by aging and death.

---

207. Nāgārjuna, *Jewel Garland*, IV.86.
208. From the *King of Meditative Absorptions*.

There is no entity that is free
From aging and death. [XXV.4]

In the first line, the Master presents his genuine thesis, stating that the transcendence of suffering is not, as the opponent imagines, an entity. It could not be so, for if it were, it would have to be characterized by aging and death, and then it could not be the transcendence of suffering, nor could it be unconditioned. It will not be possible to here object that this is not entailed because there is no functional entity that, while free from aging and death, is unconditioned and permanent like space.

The Transcendence of Suffering Would Be Conditioned
Showing that the transcendence of suffering would end up conditioned, the treatise states:

If the transcendence of suffering were an entity,
The transcendence of suffering would be conditioned.
An entity that is not conditioned
Does not exist anywhere at all. [XXV.5]

If the transcendence of suffering were an entity, it would be, in essence, the product of causes and conditions, which would contradict the claim that it is unconditioned and permanent. Its being conditioned is entailed because nowhere in space or time is there an entity that is not conditioned. This can be concluded from our perception of entities as being confined to particular times and locations.

The Transcendence of Suffering Would Be Dependently Originated
Showing that the transcendence of suffering would originate dependently, the treatise states:

If the transcendence of suffering were an entity,
Why would it not be dependent?
An entity that is not dependent
Does not exist at all. [XXV.6]

Moreover, if the transcendence of suffering were an entity, why would it not be something that is dependent on other designators? Indeed, just as long depends on short, the transcendence of suffering would be dependent on other designators. It could not, therefore, be established by nature. This is indeed entailed. Since entity and nonentity must be set forth in mutual dependence, there is no entity at all that does not depend on other designators.

The Transcendence of Suffering Is Not a Nonentity
Secondly, the Followers of Sūtra assert a transcendence of suffering that is the exhaustion of previously existent entities and which, as such, is a nonentity. The refutation of this idea begins by showing how, given the nonexistence of the negated, there can be no nonentity. The treatise states:

> *If the transcendence of suffering is not an entity,*
> *How could it be a nonentity?*
> *When the transcendence of suffering is not an entity,*
> *Neither is it a nonentity. [XXV.7]*

Given that the transcendence of suffering is not an entity, since this has already been refuted, how could it feasibly be a nonentity? That it could not is entailed because negations depend on there being something negated. Hence, for those who take the position that the transcendence of suffering is not an entity, it cannot be a nonentity either.

The Transcendence of Suffering Would Be Dependently Originated
Showing how the transcendence of suffering would originate dependently, the treatise states:

> *If the transcendence of suffering is not an entity,*
> *Why would it not be dependent?*
> *Indeed, there is no nonentity at all*
> *That is not dependent. [XXV.8]*

Likewise, if the transcendence of suffering is not an entity, but a nonentity, why would it not be dependently originated, either in the sense of being essentially a product of causes and conditions, or in terms of being dependent on other designators? Indeed, it is entailed that the transcendence of suffering would be dependently originated. First, it is taught that "the condition of birth gives rise to aging and death." Therefore, the nonentity that is the impermanence of an entity's disintegration arises based on that entity. Moreover, the convention of "nonentity" is dependent on that which is negated, that is, entity. Hence, there is no nonentity at all that is neither essentially dependent on causes and conditions, nor dependent on other designators.

Simultaneous Refutation

The second section consists of refutations that simultaneously negate [both the transcendence of suffering as an entity and as a nonentity]. Setting forth such a refutation by means of reasoning, the treatise states:

> Entities that come and go
> Are dependent and caused.
> Their being independent and not caused
> Is taught to be the transcendence of suffering. [XXV.9]

It may be asked: "Well then, what is the transcendence of suffering?"

The entities of self and the aggregates that come into this life from a past one, and go from here to a future life, do so in terms of a dependence on previous designators (just as long depends on short and vice versa) and being caused by previous essences (just as the light that emerges from a lamp). When those entities are independent of previous designators and are no longer being caused by previous essences at some point in the future, they will not come and go. It is this that the Able One has taught to be the transcendence of suffering. Hence, it is explained that this mere absence of a further migration of the person and the aggregates cannot feasibly be an entity or a nonentity.

Thus, while this stanza can be read as an explanation that the conventional transcendence of suffering is the exhaustion of adventitious stains, the Commentary explains it along the following lines: The transcendence of suffering is taught to be the nonmigration that is independent of past designators and not caused by past essences. Hence, this natural nonmigration of self and the aggregates cannot reasonably be an entity or a nonentity.

The stanza can also be understood as follows: It may be thought that it is the aggregates that undergo cyclic existence, coming and going in dependence on the succession of previous aggregates, or it may be held that it is the person who cycles, being caused to come and go by the aggregates. In the first case, the transcendence of suffering is taught to be a nonmigration, where there is no longer any dependence on previous aggregates. In the second case, the transcendence of suffering is when the person no longer migrates, not being caused to do so by the aggregates. Therefore, such a nonmigration cannot be an entity or a nonentity. This interpretation is also found in the *Commentary*, with the exception that the nonmigration is there seen as primordial.

Refutation by Means of Scripture

Presenting a simultaneous refutation by means of scripture, the treatise states:

> *The Teacher has declared*
> *The abandonment of arising and disintegration.*
> *Thus, it makes sense that the transcendence of suffering*
> *Is not an entity or a nonentity. [XXV.10]*

Let us assume that the transcendence of suffering were either an entity or a nonentity. The views that there are, respectively, either the arising of an entity or the nonentity of disintegration would then be views that accord with the way the transcendence of suffering actually is. If this were the case, such views would not need to be abandoned.

The Teacher has, however, declared:

> Monks, some strive to definitively emerge from existence through entry or disintegration. Such people suffer from a great lack of understanding.

Thus, he has stated that those views that see the transcendence of suffering in terms of arising and entity, or disintegration and nonentity, must be abandoned. Accordingly, since these views are not in harmony with the transcendence of suffering, it makes sense that the latter is not an entity or a nonentity.

Transcendence of Suffering Is Not Both Entity and Nonentity

Some believe the transcendence of suffering to be the absence of affliction and arising, which is intrinsically and essentially existent. Hence, they hold it to be both entity and nonentity. The refutation of this view begins with a demonstration of the absurdity of this position:

> *If the transcendence of suffering*
> *Were both entity and nonentity,*
> *Entity and nonentity would be liberation,*
> *Yet this does not make sense. [XXV.11]*

What if the transcendence of suffering were both entity and nonentity by nature? By the same token, it would then have to be the case that entities and nonentities, whatever they may be, were all liberation. Sentient beings would then all be effortlessly liberated. Yet since it does not make sense for entity and nonentity to be liberation, the transcendence of suffering is not of the nature of entity and nonentity.

The Transcendence of Suffering Would Be Dependently Originated
Showing how the transcendence of suffering would turn out to be dependently originated, the treatise states:

> *If the transcendence of suffering*
> *Were both entity and nonentity,*
> *The transcendence of suffering would not be independent,*
> *Because these two are dependent. [XXV.12]*

Also, if the transcendence of suffering were both entity and nonentity, it would not be independent of other designators. Instead, it would be reliant on other phenomena. That this is entailed can be seen from the way that entity and nonentity are mutually dependent.

Refutation by Reference to the Transcendence of Suffering Being
Unconditioned
Refuting that the transcendence of suffering is both entity and nonentity by referring to its being unconditioned, the treatise states:

> *How could the transcendence of suffering*
> *Be both entity and nonentity?*
> *The transcendence of suffering is unconditioned,*
> *Entity and nonentity are conditioned. [XXV.13]*

> *How could the transcendence of suffering*
> *Possess both entity and nonentity?*
> *These two cannot coexist,*
> *Just like light and darkness. [XXV.14]*

How could the transcendence of suffering be both entity and nonentity, given that the transcendence of suffering is unconditioned? While an entity is the product of causes and conditions, the nonentity of disintegration is a condition for arising. Thus, they are both conditioned. This, then, shows the argument's reverse entailment.

It may then be argued: "Entity and nonentity do not constitute the nature of the transcendence of suffering. The latter, however, possesses the former two." Yet how could the transcendence of suffering possess both entity and nonentity? Just like light and darkness, these two are mutually incompatible and, therefore, could not coexist in a single substance, which in this case would be the transcendence of suffering.

The Transcendence of Suffering Is Not neither Entity nor Nonentity

Third, the refutation of the assertion that the transcendence of suffering is neither an entity nor a nonentity includes: (1) presenting the criticism and (2) refuting the arguments.

The Criticism

As for the first, the treatise states:

> *The teaching that the transcendence of suffering*
> *Is neither entity nor nonentity*
> *Would be established*
> *If entity and nonentity were established. [XXV.15]*

The negative property "neither entity nor nonentity" would be established if the negated properties, entity and nonentity, were themselves established. Given their establishment, the teaching that the transcendence of suffering is neither entity nor nonentity would then be established as well. Nevertheless, since both of these objects of negation, entity and nonentity, have already been refuted, the negative property that is the negation of these two is not established either.

Refutation of the Argument
On the second issue, the treatise states:

> *If the transcendence of suffering*
> *Were neither entity nor nonentity,*
> *Who would perceive that*
> *"It is neither entity nor nonentity"? [XXV.16]*

If the transcendence of suffering were, by nature, neither entity nor non-entity, what person would perceive that "the transcendence of suffering has a nature that is neither entity nor nonentity"? Is it someone within cyclic existence, or is it rather a person who abides in the transcendence of suffering? At the stage of peace, there is no one to conduct such an examination. Moreover, the transcendence of suffering is not an object of the relative, subjective consciousness of cyclic existence. Wakefulness, on the other hand, which is the ultimate subject, does not observe any of the marks of mental construction. It would not, therefore, apprehend the transcendence of suffering to be neither entity nor nonentity.

The Buddha Is Not Established in the Way of the Four Extremes
Now it will be shown that the one who flawlessly realizes the transcendence of suffering is not established in the manner of the four extremes. Doing so will include demonstrating the lack of establishment at (1) the time of transcendence and (2) the time of abidance.

The Lack of Establishment at the Time of Transcendence
On the first issue, the treatise states:

> *When the Transcendent Conqueror has gone beyond,*
> *He is not perceived as "existent,"*
> *Nor as "nonexistent,"*
> *As "both," or as "neither." [XXV.17]*

Once the Transcendent Conqueror has passed beyond suffering, he is not perceived to be "existent" or "nonexistent," nor is he manifest as "both existent and nonexistent" or "neither existent nor nonexistent." It has already been explained that, from the very moment he appears, the Buddha is peace by nature.

The Lack of Establishment at the Time of Abidance
On the second issue, the treatise states:

> *Even as the Transcendent Conqueror remains,*
> *He is not perceived as "existent,"*
> *Nor as "nonexistent,"*
> *As "both" or as "neither." [XXV.18]*

It is not only upon his passing that the Transcendent Conqueror is beyond the four extremes. Indeed, he is not perceived to exist while he remains either because, as was explained above, the appropriated and appropriator are devoid of nature. He is not seen as nonexistent either, for there cannot be any negative property in the absence of something negated. Moreover, because existence and nonexistence are incompatible, he is not seen to be both, and since the negated properties have no establishment, he is not perceived as neither existent nor nonexistent.

Conclusion
Third, the conclusion includes (1) establishing that there is no difference between existence and peace and (2) refuting the indeterminate views.

No Difference between Existence and Peace
On the first issue, the treatise states:

> *Cyclic existence is not the slightest bit*
> *Different from the transcendence of suffering*
> *Transcendence of suffering is not the slightest bit*
> *Different from cyclic existence. [XXV.19]*

> *That which is the condition of transcendence*
> *Is the condition of cyclic existence as well.*
> *Between these two there is not*
> *The slightest bit of difference. [XXV.20]*

Neither appearance nor absence of appearance are established in the manner of the four extremes. In reality, the cyclic existence of the initial time of appearance is, therefore, not even the slightest bit different from the subsequent nonabiding transcendence of suffering. Neither is the nature of the subsequent transcendence of suffering the slightest bit different from the prior cyclic existence. How so? Because the real condition of the transcendence of suffering, that is, the freedom from the four extremes that was explained above, is also the real condition of cyclic existence. Between these two there is not even the most subtle difference. Upon examination, they are seen to be the same in not being established with any nature at all.

Indeterminate Views
The refutation of the fourteen indeterminate views begins with an identification of these views. The treatise states:

> *Views of what follows the passing, of the finite and so on,*
> *Along with those on permanence and so forth,*
> *Are based on the transcendence of suffering,*
> *The limit of the future, and the limit of the past. [XXV.21]*

Among the fourteen views, there are four that concern what follows the passing of the Thus-Gone. Respectively, they are the beliefs that he then exists, does not exist, both exists and does not exist, and neither exists nor does not exist. These four are based on and supported by [the idea of] the transcendence of suffering. Another set of four views concerns the finite and so on. Respectively, they are the beliefs that the self or the world are finite, infinite, both finite and infinite, and neither finite nor infinite. Since these views involve holding future events to occur, not occur, both occur and not occur, and neither occur nor not occur, they are based on the limit of the future. Four further views concern permanence and so forth, in the sense that these are views that the self or the world are permanent, impermanent, both permanent and impermanent, or neither permanent nor impermanent. As these are beliefs in prior existence, prior nonexistence, combined prior existence and nonexistence, and neither prior nonexistence nor prior nonexistence, they are based on the limit of the past. Finally, there are the two views that concern sameness and difference. These two views relate to the body and the life-force being identical and different, respectively. Hence, they are based on, or are made in reference to, [the concepts of] body and life-force.

Why These Indeterminate Views Are Untenable
Second, showing these indeterminate views to be untenable, the treatise states:

> *When all things are empty,*
> *What is finite and what is infinite?*
> *What is both finite and infinite?*
> *What is neither finite nor infinite? [XXV.22]*

> *What is identical and what is different?*
> *What is permanent, what is impermanent?*
> *What is both permanent and impermanent?*
> *What is neither permanent nor impermanent? [XXV.23]*

When all things are empty in essence, what then to say of views that concern distinct qualities? What to say of the view that the self or the world will, at some point, come to an end, and that these two are, thus, finite? What of the view that they will not end and, hence, are infinite? What does it mean for them to both end and not end, to be both finite and infinite? And what would it mean that they neither end nor do not end, that they are neither finite nor infinite? What does it mean for body and life-force to be the same? What does it mean for them to be different? What does it mean that the world and the self are permanent and existed throughout the past or that they did not and are impermanent? What would it mean that they both exist and do not, that they are both permanent and impermanent? Or that they neither existed nor did not exist, being neither? The refutation of the four views that are based on the transcendence of suffering have already been refuted above [in the analysis of the Thus-Gone]. Therefore, since the bases for such distinctions have no establishment in reality, these views that ascribe distinctions to them are all untenable. Know, then, that this is why they are indeterminate.

Teaching the Dharma Is Not Meaningless
On the third topic, the treatise states:

> *Complete pacification of all observations,*
> *The complete pacification of constructs, peace—*
> *Nowhere did the Buddha teach*
> *Any Dharma to anyone at all. [XXV.24]*

It may be argued. "If, upon examination, one finds that there is no transcendence of suffering, it would be meaningless to teach the Dharma that is associated with the remedies employed for the purpose of attaining the transcendence of suffering."

If there were Dharma, students, and a teacher in reality, there would also be a teaching. Ultimately, however, all observations are universally and completely pacified. The mental constructs associated with language are completely pacified, and there is peace with the pacification of all of the mind's observations. Therefore, nowhere, neither in a divine realm nor at any other place, did the Buddha ever teach any Dharma concerned with affliction and its purification to any god, human, or otherwise—not to anyone at all. Hence, this is not meaningless. As taught in the *Sūtra on the Secret of the Thus-Gone*:

> From the night of enlightenment,
> And until my passing utterly beyond,
> I do not teach any Dharma
> To anyone at all.

One might wonder: "Well, if this is the case, how did the great diversity of conventions found in the Buddha's excellent discourses manifest?"

These are not stated in terms of reality, but in terms of convention. Even conventionally they are not taught in terms of any essence of the ultimate. They are conveyed by superimposition through and through. Moreover, since for the Buddha all verbal and mental engagements are completely pacified, they are not stated by the Buddha himself. Rather, they appear as the objects of a deluded mind due to the combined power of past aspirations and the purity of the action of those to be influenced. Hence, it is taught:

> Here there is no suchness and no Thus-Gone.
> Wandering beings all see reflections.
> This is, as it were, a reflection of the Thus-Gone's
> Undefiling qualities of virtue.[209]

Thus, this chapter has ultimately shown the primordial and existential negation of mental constructs concerning the transcendence of suffering,

---

209. From the *Ornament of Wisdom Light*.

while in terms of convention it has explained freedom from adventitious stains to be similar to an illusion. Implicitly, the chapter has shown that this holds for all other phenomena as well. The *Sūtra of the King of Meditative Absorptions* teaches:

> The ultimate truth is like a dream
> And the transcendence of suffering is of the nature of a dream.
> The wise one who acts accordingly
> Is declared to possess the vow of speech.

This concludes the explanation of the twenty-fifth chapter, the analysis of nirvana, in the *Ornament of Reason*, a commentary on the *Root of the Middle Way*.

CHAPTER TWENTY-SIX

Analysis of Dependent Origination

HAVING THUS EXPLAINED that its distinctive qualities are natural emptiness, we will now turn to the dependent origination that is the basis for such distinction. Three issues pertain to this chapter as well.

THE CONTEXT OF CHAPTER 26

First, regarding the context of this chapter, the present analysis relates to certain teachings found in the sūtras, such as the following:

> Aside from the dependently originated, a bodhisattva does not see any phenomena whatsoever.

Thus, the sūtras teach relative dependent origination along with its divisions. Here, it is the meaning of such teachings that will be ascertained.

Concerning this chapter's relation to the other analyses, it was explained above that:

> That which originates in dependence
> Is taught to be emptiness.[210]

And:

> The one who sees
> Dependent origination

---

210. *Root of the Middle Way*, XXIV.18a–b.

Sees suffering, its origin,
Cessation, and the path.[211]

It may, therefore, be asked, "How is dependent origination itself to be understood ?"

The present chapter presents a reply to this question in two parts: (1) an explanation of the content and (2) a contemplation of the meaning.

THE CONTENT OF CHAPTER 26

The literal meaning of the term "dependent origination" has already been explained above. With respect to the objects that this term applies to, we have identified both their characteristics and the bearers of these characteristics. As for the way the bearers are divided, we may distinguish between the dependent origination of the external environment and the dependent origination of the beings that inhabit it. Here, the latter is our primary concern. Therefore, it is the impure dependent origination of the twelve links of existence, from ignorance to aging and death, that the treatise treats here. The explanation will cover (1) the forward arising of the links, (2) the person who is associated with their arising and reversal, and (3) the reversal of the links.

THE ARISING OF THE LINKS OF DEPENDENT ORIGINATION

On the first topic, the treatise states:

> *Due to the obscuration of ignorance, there occurs, directed at rebirth,*
> *The conditioning of the action*
> *Of the three types of formation.*
> *Thus, there is migration between the realms. [XXVI.1]*

> *Consciousness, conditioned by formation,*
> *Enters the realms.*
> *Once consciousness has entered,*
> *Name and form will manifest. [XXVI.2]*

211. Ibid., XXIV.40.

When name and form have manifested,
The six sense sources will develop.
Dependent on the six sense sources,
Contact comes into being. [XXVI.3]

It arises exclusively in dependence
On eye, form, and consciousness.
Thus, dependent on eye and form,
Consciousness will occur. [XXVI.4]

Contact is the meeting
Of eye, form, and consciousness.
Out of this meeting
Arises sensation. [XXVI.5]

Conditioned by sensation, there is craving,
Craving with respect to sensation.
When there is craving, there will be grasping,
Grasping in the fourfold way. [XXVI.6]

Grasping will initiate
The becoming of the grasper.
Absence of grasping will result
In liberation free from becoming. [XXVI.7]

Becoming is the five aggregates.
From becoming follows birth.
Aging and death, grief,
Lamentation, pain, [XXVI.8]

Mental unrest, disturbance—
All of this occurs due to birth.
Thus arises this mass
Of nothing but suffering. [XXVI.9]

The bond of ignorance, or of existence, is to be understood neither as an existential negation of awareness, nor as a mistaken cognition in the sense of a predicative negation of awareness. Rather, this is a type of cognition that conflicts with a precise understanding of the way things are. In this context, the *Śālu Sprout* speaks of "the belief in permanence and singularity in relation to the composite of the six elements." However, this is simply meant to illustrate the lack of insight into the absence of self that is entailed by such ignorance.

In terms of its divisions, ignorance includes delusion with respect to the relative cause and effect of action and the ultimate absence of self in relation to persons and phenomena. Both of these delusions are discards that are to be eliminated by seeing things exactly as they are, for these modes of apprehending conflict with that observation. As for the extremely subtle delusion that concerns the consequences of action, it is only discarded at the level of Buddhahood.

Now, such ignorance obscures the path of peace in that it hinders seeing the relative causality of actions and the ultimate absence of the two selves. This, in turn, leads to a future rebirth, insofar as the defiling actions that propel one into existence, and which are of three types of conditioning (understood as those of either body, speech, and mind, or meritorious, unmeritorious, and unshakable), are formed, thus causing migration from one realm to another.

As for the consciousness that is conditioned by formation, this is a consciousness that, due to formation, has been infused with the habitual tendencies of the aforementioned actions. As a result, this consciousness becomes capable of producing name and form. The *Sūtra on the Discernment of Dependent Origination*, in this context, identifies the link of consciousness with the six collections. The Master Vasubandhu, however, has argued that if the sūtra's statements were to be taken literally, three problems would occur. First, apart from the [resultant consciousness], there would be no separate [consciousness] to perform the infusion of habitual tendencies. Second, as the six collections become virtuous and nonvirtuous, they could not serve as the recipient of infusion. Finally, that which is infused would dissipate because it would lack a support. Vasubandhu, therefore, sees this sūtra to be using the name of the supported as a way of referring to its support, just as when there is mention of "clear faculties." He thus identifies the link of consciousness with the all-ground consciousness that is indeterminate and active together with that which performs the infusion. In accordance with its action, this consciousness then enters the various realms.

Once consciousness has entered the mother's womb, name and form will manifest. "Name" here refers to sensation, identification, formation, and consciousness, which have not yet fully developed. "Form" includes the first six of the eight stages in the development of the fetus: the oval shape, the oblong, the lumpy, the hardened , the development of legs and arms, and the development of hair on the head and body.

When name and form have manifested in this manner, the eye and the other faculties that make up the six sense sources, and which are capable of determining inner and outer objects, will develop on the seventh stage. Dependent on the six sense sources, contact will come into being.

What, then, is contact? How does it arise? To answer these questions, let us consider how the eye consciousness arises exclusively in dependence on three factors: the ruling condition of the eye, the observed condition of form, and the immediately preceding condition of attentive mental activity. Thus, the consciousness associated with the eye arises in dependence on the attention of the four factors subsumed by name and on form, its sense object.

In essence, the contact associated with eye consciousness is the determination of attractive, unattractive, and neutral objects based on the meeting of eye, form, and consciousness. Contact as such includes the contact associated with the eye up to the contact associated with the mental faculty.

Sensations that are pleasurable, painful, and neutral arise from this determination of attractive, unattractive, and neutral objects.

Sensation serves as the condition for craving. This craving expresses itself as the wish to either keep or separate from these sensations. Once craving occurs, intention and desire arise in relation to that which is sensed, and so craving develops into grasping. This grasping is fourfold in the sense that it involves grasping in relation to pleasures, views, belief in the supremacy of view and discipline, and the doctrine of self. Craving associated with the realm of desire produces grasping for pleasures, while the craving associated with the form and formless realms may engender any of the other three forms of grasping.

The presence of these four graspings allows action to gain impetus, leading to the grasper's becoming. When discerning insight prevents the craving in relation to the sensations, grasping will be absent. This, in turn, will result in liberation, and there will then not be any becoming.

Becoming is composed of physical, verbal, and mental actions. In this sense, it is of the nature of the five aggregates as subsumed under mind and matter. Because of this factor, there will also be the becoming of the future five aggregates. Hence, that this link of dependent origination is called "becoming" can also be understood as an instance of a causal factor's being named after its effect. Based on this link of becoming, there will be rebirth in a future life and aging and death as the aggregates of that life respectively age and come to an end. At the time of death, there will be grief as the mind is pained by having to separate from that which it cherishes. This grief, in turn, will be vocalized with lamentations. There will be pain and mental unrest as body and mind experience what is not desired. Such sufferings then create disturbances in the psychophysical continuum. Read differently, there will be disturbance as one is exhausted by the efforts of searching and securing. All of this is due to birth. Thus, this mass, or accumulation, of suffering is nothing but suffering in that it involves no happiness and is entirely devoid of a self and anything that belongs to a self.

The latter elements are mentioned in certain sūtras to elicit a sense of disillusionment by considering the results of the evolving of the links. Nevertheless, because they are not certain to occur, they are not counted among the links of dependent origination.

THE TYPE OF PERSON WHO ENGENDERS AND DISSOLVES THIS PROCESS

On the second topic, the treatise states:

> Formation is the root of cyclic existence,
> Therefore, the wise do not form.
> The agents of that are the unwise;
> Not the wise, for they see reality. [XXVI.10]

Karmic formations are the root of cyclic existence in the sense that they are the primary cause for consciousness and the other elements that constitute the engagement in cyclic existence. For this reason, the noble ones, who possess wisdom regarding the means for ending cyclic existence, or about karmic causality and the real nature of things, do not form any action, and so do not give rise to the roots of cyclic existence.

It might then be thought that those who have seen the truths will not take future rebirths because they do not accumulate formations. It is, however, taught that:

For the one who has seen the truth, there is no impelling.[212]

Thus, once the truth has been seen, there will be no further accumulation of action that impels one toward cyclic existence. Yet the old action that was impelled by ignorance in the past will be nourished by the craving and grasping of the noble one who is on the path of training. This will bring about further rebirth. Finally, for those beyond training, there is neither craving nor grasping so there will not be any rebirth either. Hence, it is taught:

Once free of grasping, there is no rebirth.[213]

Therefore, it is ordinary individuals—those who are unwise with respect to the means for ending cyclic existence, or with regard to karmic causality and the real condition of things—who are the agents that create the three types of formation. As is taught:

The being, or person, who is associated with ignorance forms meritorious, unmeritorious, or unshakable formations.

Why are the wise not agents of karmic formations? The wise do not engage in any karmic action, for they see reality and that sight is incompatible with the cause of karmic formation.

The Reversal of the Links

On the third topic, the treatise states:

When ignorance has ceased,
Formation does not arise either.
The cessation of ignorance is accomplished
By meditating on reality through insight. [XXVI.11]

As each of them ceases,
None of them will occur.

212. From Vasubandhu, *Commentary on the Sūtra on the Discernment of Dependent Origination.*
213. Ibid.

Thus, this mass of nothing but suffering
Will actually come to an end. [XXVI.12]

When ignorance is present, there will be formation. Therefore, when ignorance has ceased, no formation will arise either because its cause will be
missing. Thus, as each preceding cause, from formation to birth, ceases,
none of their subsequent effects, from consciousness to aging and death,
will occur either.

One may then wonder: "That may be so, but what makes ignorance
cease?"

Ignorance is the cause that establishes existence. Its cessation is accomplished by meditating, through the insight that the reality of dependent
origination is empty of both the person and phenomena. This meditation
begins on the levels of inspired conduct. Through that, one will witness
reality, just as it is. This entire mass of suffering, which does not contain
any happiness and is empty of a self and anything that belongs to a self, will
without exception ("actually" renders the Sanskrit *samyak* and "without
exception" the Sanskrit *samanta*) come to an end.

CONTEMPLATION OF THE MEANING

Second follows a few words of explanation in relation to the above. This
involves (1) ascertaining the nature of dependent origination, (2) its profound distinctions, and (3) the supremacy of the realization of dependent
origination.

THE NATURE OF DEPENDENT ORIGINATION

First, it has already been explained that "arising in dependence on various
phenomena" is the defining characteristic of dependent origination, while
the bearers of that characteristic are all outer and inner phenomena. What
we will consider here is, therefore, the teaching on (1) the outer dependent
origination of the environment and (2) the inner dependent origination
of sentient beings.

Outer Dependent Origination
First, as an illustration of outer dependent origination, we may take

the example of a crop. Its dependent origination should be understood by considering 1) its related causes, 2) its related conditions, and 3) the absence of volition. In our example, the series of developing causes is as follows: seed, sprout, shoot, stem, stalk, bud, flower, and fruit. Its conditions are earth, water, fire, wind, space, and time. Respectively, these create adhesion, moisture, maturation, unfolding, openness, and change. There is no freedom of volition in terms of causes, conditions, or effects. As it is explained:

> Without thinking, "this shall be produced,"
> Production, nevertheless, takes place.
> Likewise, there is no intention "I shall produce."[214]

Thus, the production simply takes place according to the capacity of the causes.

Inner Dependent Origination

Second, the teaching of the inner dependent origination of sentient beings covers (1) the evolution of impure dependent origination, (2) the evolution of pure dependent origination, and (3) the means for bringing about their reversal.

The Evolution of Impure Dependent Origination

The evolution of the first type of dependent origination concerns the twelve links of existence, from ignorance through aging and death. Thus, we shall consider these links in terms of (1) their individual essences, (2) the causal and conditional relationships between them, (3) how they do not involve volition, and (4) the definitive nature of their enumeration and sequence. Their individual essences and causal relationships have already been covered through the treatise's account of the way the previous links serve as the basis for the arising of subsequent links.

Concerning the related conditions, these are explained as follows:

> From a composition of six elements,
> The body is born.[215]

---

214. Śāntideva, *Entering the Activity of the Bodhisattvas,* VI.26.
215. Nāgārjuna, *Stanzas on the "Śālu Sprout Sūtra,"* 28a–b.

Thus, the elements of earth, water, fire, wind, space, and consciousness respectively provide the body with solidity, cohesion, maturation, breathing, openness in its cavities, and preservation without rotting. These are the conditions for the establishment and remaining of the aggregates.

As for the way these causes, conditions, and results do not do not involve any freedom of volition, this is easily understood from statements such as:

> It is held that these do not involve
> The arising of any thought of "I" or "mine."[216]

Fourth, in various sūtras, the Transcendent Conqueror repeatedly treats these twelve links of dependent origination as definitive in terms of their sequence and number. As for the mutual causal relationships between the links, the Listeners' collection of the words of the Buddha, as well as the treatise entitled *Entry into Wakefulness*, teach that the links are divided in three parts, encompassing three lives. Thus, two sequences of cause and effect are identified. This is as well reflected in the *Treasury of Abhidharma*:

> As for the past and the future, there are two times two,
> While in between there are eight, when all is complete.[217]

This explanation employs the example of the present life positioned between a past and a future life. The affliction of ignorance and the action of formation associated with the past life thus serve as the cause for their effect, which consists of the consciousness, name and form, six sense sources, contact, and sensation found in the present life. This, then, is one sequence of cause and effect. In addition, in the present life, the afflictions of craving and grasping and the action of becoming together bring about the effect of birth plus aging and dying in the future life. That is the second causal sequence. In this way, we arrive at two links that are exclusively causes pertaining to the past life and two links that are effects that belong to the future life alone. In between, the present life then spans eight links,

---

216. Ibid., 28c–d.
217. Vasubandhu, *Treasury of Abhidharma*, III.20b–c.

that is, five that are the effects of the past life and three that are cause of the future life.

Accepting the above explanation at face value will, however, lead to a number of problems. For one, this would conflict with the way the Transcendent Conqueror has characterized the functions of ignorance, craving, formation, and becoming. He treats the first two as those factors that, respectively, produce and nourish the accumulation of action, whereas the latter two are seen to be karmic accumulation and its gaining impetus. The explanation is also called into question by the fact that simple formations engendered by ignorance may be present even for a foe-destroyer. The notion of craving and grasping serving as causes in isolation is not reasonable either, for unless action is accumulated, craving and grasping cannot function. Nor does it make sense to see consciousness and the next four links in isolation from birth, aging, and death. These causes and effects cannot reasonably be a definitive sequence of distinct elements. The explicit meaning of the above account is, thus, subject to critique.

It is, however, also taught that the sequential causes and effects are mutually inclusive. Thus, we find the following passage:

> The past and future causes and effects, in summary,
> Can be inferred from the intermediate ones.[218]

Here, we are given two accounts of causality: summarized causes and elaborated effects versus elaborated causes and summarized effects. When both the causal and resultant factors included in the present life are elaborated, we may, with respect to their causes and effects, infer their past causes and future effects and so enumerate sixteen links. When an alternate concise causal sequence is applied with respect to this life, the number of relevant links becomes eight. The explanation is given with the following considerations in mind. The causes (craving, grasping, and becoming) and effects (consciousness, name and form, the six sense sources, contact, and sensation) included in this life may be mentioned individually because they are manifest and each performs its function. The causes found in the past life have, on the other hand, ceased, while the effects in the future life are not yet clearly established. Hence, ignorance and formation can be referred to under the general label of action and affliction, while [birth, aging,

---

218. Ibid., III.26b–c.

and death] may simply be spoken of as arising and disintegrating. What emerges is a picture where each of the three lives itself, in dependence, includes a previous, subsequent, and intermediary element. Hence, this is seen to be a way of showing each of the lives in terms of a sequence of three factors of cause and effect.

The master Asaṅga, on the other hand, operates with a system of six causal and six resultant links. He explains that the experience of emerging from one's mother's womb and living a life through to its final end is the effect of defiling action that requires a set of primary causes and effects that unfold over the course of two lives. Identifying the six causal and six resultant links with reference to these two lives, he sees this enumeration to be definitive. The six causes are, moreover, divided into distant impelling causes and close establishing causes. The first set of causes includes the basis for, the means for, and the mode of impulsion. In other words, this concerns the process of ignorance becoming the basis for formation, and formation then impelling the creation of imprints of action in the consciousness. The second type of cause is similarly to be understood in terms of the basis for, the means for, and the mode of establishment. Craving in relation to sensation is the basis for grasping in pursuit of objects, and that grasping is the means for the establishment of [becoming, that is] powerful, or unimpeded action that is able to produce the sprouts of name and form.

Also, the six effects contain distant impelled effects and close established effects. The first type includes four effects associated with the consciousness that has received the impelling energy. These are name and form, the six sources, contact, and sensation. The first two are, respectively, the initially obtained and fully developed body, and the second two constitute the character and experience of encounter. The second type consists of birth, meaning establishment, and aging and death, which are the continuum of establishment undergoing change and disintegration.

The *Compendium,* the master Nāgārjuna, and the ṭīka on *Distinguishing the Middle from Extremes,* alternatively, treat consciousness in terms of the resultant entry into the womb, elaborating five causes and seven effects. The *Collection of the Mind* and the *Secret Meaning* present ten causes and two effects by considering the four links that begin with consciousness as seminal factors that manifest their result in birth and aging and death. The *Discernment of Discrete Phenomena* explains that the twelve links are included in seven topics. Ignorance and formation are, thus, 1) that which impels; consciousness infused with karmic habitual tendencies is 2) the way the impulsion takes place; name and form plus the next three links constitute 3) that which is impelled; craving and grasping make up 4) the factors that establish the manifestation of the impelled; becoming is 5) the way the establishment takes place; birth is 6) that which is manifestly established; and aging and death are 7) the negative consequences of the established.

The master Vasubandhu summarizes this doctrine as follows:

> The impeller, how impulsion takes place, and the impelled,
> The process of establishment,
> As well as its flaws,
> Are taught by means of the twelve links.
>
> Through two links, one link,
> Four links, two links,
> One link, one link, and one link,
> The seven topics are clearly explained.
>
> Because the truth is not known as it is
> The mind is infused with action,
> And so four links are gradually impelled
> As their seeds solidify.
>
> Having arisen as impelled,
> Sensation produces craving,
> Which again gives rise to grasping.
> Its action manifests the establishment of the infused.
>
> The established is birth,
> While aging and the like are its negative consequences.
> There is, therefore, no impulsion for the one who sees the truth,
> And for the one free from craving there is no recurrence.[219]

---

219. From Vasubandhu, *Commentary on the Sūtra on the Discernment of Dependent Origination.*

These five stanzas contain a presentation, an explanation, and an argument. The presentation is found in the first stanza. The explanation is two-fold, covering both the classification and function of the links. Of these, the classification is explained in the second stanza. The way the links function as impulsion, establishment, and negative consequences is, explained in the third stanza, the fourth stanza plus the first line of the fifth, and the second line of the fifth stanza, respectively. The argument that the links function to infuse and establish in this way is delivered in the second half of the fifth stanza. The argument emerges by considering how, for those who see the truth, there is no karmic impulsion toward rebirth, while for the foe-destroyer there is an absence of the afflictions that take control of the impelled. Since becoming is treated here as a further development of the original effect of impulsion due to the influence of the establishing factors, this account sees the links as a single causal sequence.

In fact, [from Asaṅga's explanation onward,] these different presentations of causality all agree on the following. The habitual tendencies of the karmic actions that are motivated by ignorance become nourished by craving and grasping. This, in turn, leads to becoming. Thereby, name and form and other factors arise. It is with respect to the manifest establishment of these that one speaks of birth, aging, and death. Thus, they all concur in treating the links as one single instance of cause and effect. This sequence is explained in terms of the karmic effects that will be experienced in the subsequent life. Hence, this single causal sequence unfolds over the course of two lives.

One may then wonder: "Well, is that which is directly established by the consciousness or becoming of this life not birth into the intermediate state? How are the causes and effects of karmic accumulation to be classified with respect to that state?"

It is inappropriate to reply here that since [in the intermediate state one] is a corporeal being associated with the next life, [that state] should be considered included in the next life. Instead, it is taught that since [the intermediate state] is not matured, as is the case with a dream, it is not to be classified in terms of [past and future lives] at all.

One may likewise wonder: "Well, when the linking between two lives in their own distinct realm occurs, which of those two realms do these causes and effects then pertain to?"

Apart from ignorance, all the other links belong to the realm that one is being born into. Nine types of linking are possible with respect to the three realms, three of which involve birth in the realm of desire. In all the latter three cases, ignorance will pertain to the level of the resultant desire realm itself, regardless of where one is being born from. The reason is that the two higher realms are free from the desire that is characteristic of the lower realm. Therefore, no accumulation of the action that leads to rebirth in the realm of desire occurs in the higher realms. When being born from the realm of desire into one of the higher realms, the ignorance that is involved is still that of the desire realm because, since the higher realms have not yet been achieved, there is no presence of the ignorance that accumulates the action associated with those realms. Moreover, when one's rebirth involves a passage between the formless and the form realm, or when a descent occurs in relation to the concentrations and formless states, that which impels is seen to pertain to a different level than [the one one emerges from].

Turning Back Criticism
Turning back criticism involves the objections that (1) the enumeration of the links cannot be definitive, (2) their sequence is untenable, and (3) they cannot reasonably be the same or different.

The Objection That the Enumeration Is Not Definitive
As for the first, it may be argued: "Unless ignorance has a cause and aging and death have a result, cyclic existence will end up having a beginning and an end. If, on the other hand, those links themselves have causes and effects, the number of links ends up higher than stated. Moreover, why are grief and the four other negative consequences of cyclic existence not counted? And why is the abidance that is a characteristic of the conditioned not enumerated?"

Ignorance per se is the cause of delusion with respect to self and mere entities. From the beginning, it has never been absent. Hence, the cause of ignorance is precisely the previous manifestation of the continuity of this type of delusion. For this reason, the cause of ignorance is not counted separately. Thus, it is taught:

> The view of self does not need to be produced;
> It is a habit without beginning.[220]

---

220. Maitreya, *Ornament of the Sūtras of the Great Vehicle*, XIX.104a–b.

Some sūtras explain incorrect [mental activity] to be the cause of ignorance, but such accounts consider this factor to be what develops the particularities of ignorance and causes them to increase. In the context of the causality between the links, incorrect mental activity is not taught to be the cause of ignorance. As Asaṅga and his brother explain, the reason for this is that the relationship between ignorance and incorrect mental activity is similar to that between ignorance and formation. That is to say, it is not the end of incorrect mental activity that stops ignorance, but the end of ignorance that stops incorrect mental activity.

It is, moreover, not aging and death as such that produce rebirth. Rather, one takes rebirth because of the present life's action of becoming. Cyclic existence is, thus, not interrupted because until defiling cognitions have been exhausted, the effects of actions will be continuous, just like ripples on water.

Also, the statement that "from seven arise three," as well as the account of mutual causality, is simply meant to show that there will be ignorance in the subsequent life. If sensation and so on, along with aging and death, could themselves produce ignorance on their own, this would absurdly have to be the case for the noble ones too. If the statement is taken to concern the continuity of mere objects of observation, it will follow that each of the causes of the links would be the causes of the other ones as well. Therefore, in a single causal sequence, ignorance is the cause, while aging and death are the effect. This is why the scriptures explain that two of the twelve links are definitively cause and effect, while the other ten are not. Grief and the other factors are not certain to occur and abidance is not a cause of sadness. Hence, these elements are not treated as links.

The Objection That the Sequence Is Untenable

It may be objected: "If the definitive nature of the enumeration of the links is accounted for by seeing them as a single sequence of cause and effect, where six links are causes and six are results, then the sequence that appears in the sūtras cannot be definitive because there the links occur in a threefold causal sequence."

Indeed, this may be so, but if craving and so forth were taught to be subsequent to their causes, ignorance and formation, they would be lacking causes. Hence, it is explained that formation energizes consciousness, thus impelling name and form and the next three links. Therefore, while no such stages occur once the impelling power is present, the enumeration of the links explains the stages in the manifestation of the effect.

It might then be argued: "But since the power [to produce] birth, aging, and death [would also be present by the force of impulsion], why are those two links not taught [to be directly after sensation]?"

They are not taught for three reasons. First, the existence of birth, aging, and death is nominal. Secondly, craving and so on would become disconnected if those links were taught to be subsequent to birth, aging, and death. Finally, to summarize the limits of cyclic existence under negative consequences, the manifestation of birth, aging, and death is taught to be last.

The Objection That the Links Can Reasonably Be neither the Same nor Distinct

Likewise, it may be objected: "Are these twelve links that are definitive in terms of both number and sequence substantially the same or substantially different? If they are the same, they cannot be cause and effect, yet if the second is the case, it follows that there may be a stream of being that does not possess any ignorance and action."

Just as the cause of mind is mind itself, the actual causal factors are each substantially different, yet, in terms of their general classification, the links are distinct differentiations of the same essence. Hence, the implied problem is entirely irrelevant.

As for the link between two lives, this is explained by means of the example of crops growing from planted seeds. Concerning the six causal links, it is said:

> Action, craving, and ignorance
> Are field, moisture, and planting—
> Consciousness sows seeds.

As for the six effects, they are explained in terms of the arising, transformation, and protection of the sprouts of name and form and so on. In the *Sūtra on Transference of Existence*, the same issue is explained by means of eight examples. The master Nāgārjuna puts that teaching into verse:

> Like a recitation, a candlelight, a mirror, a mold,
> A magnifying glass, a seed, sourness, or a sound—

> Thus, the wise should see that the linking of the aggregates
> Takes place without any transference.[221]

This can be understood by considering the illustrative properties of the examples in general, the illustrative properties of each of them individually, and the way that the examples serve to settle dispute. As for the first issue, all of these examples serve to illustrate the way that this life is followed by a future life. A recitation comes into being because of the causes and conditions associated with the teacher and his student all being complete; a candlelight arises based on the wick and fire; a reflection occurs because of the face and a mirror; from a mold and some clay comes a cast; because of the glass, light, and some straw, there will be fire; from soil and seed comes a sprout; when one has drunk wine and the word "sour" is spoken, saliva will emerge; and because of a sound and the presence of a rock wall, an echo will occur. All of these are examples of arising due to an assembly of causes and conditions, an arising where the causes are not transferred into their effects, and yet where the effects arise without interruption. This is also characteristic of the way the aggregates of the next life arise due to the causal complex of action and affliction in this life.

Second, the examples can also be seen as illustrations of particular aspects of this arising. Thus, the teacher's teaching a recitation to his student illustrates the link between the consciousness of this life and the next. Next, just as the prior presence of candlelight makes the subsequent burning of another one possible, the causes that are included in this life are not permanent, and yet the future life is not uncaused. The mirror illustrates how the existence of this life is the reason that there is another life beyond, and yet without there being any transference between the two lives. The mold shows the way action shapes the future rebirth. The example of the magnifying glass illustrates the way cause and effect belong to the same class. The seed explains that the cessation of this life does not mean nonexistence. Sourness shows that rebirth occurs because of previously experienced karmic actions. The example of the echo shows that rebirth takes place when conducive factors have assembled and obstacles are absent, and that cause and effect are neither identical nor different.

As for the third issue mentioned above, this concerns the way that the subsequent examples serve to eliminate errors about the meaning of the

221. *Heart of Dependent Origination*, 5.

previous ones. Yet fearing an excess of words, I shall not elaborate on that here.

In the *Śālu Sprout*, moreover, there are four examples: eye consciousness, a reflection, the moon, and fire. According to the master Kamalaśīla, these illustrate how effects ensue from actions that are to be experienced in this life, upon birth, in other lives, and without certainty, respectively. Thus, he explains that these examples show the way karmic effects will be experienced in one's current life, in one's next life, in some life after that, and at some undetermined point in the future. Thus, impure dependent origination is composed of the three types of thorough affliction and the two truths. From the sixfold causal complex of action and affliction arises the sixfold effect associated with aging and death. Hence, it is taught:

> When the conditions are complete, the machinery of suffering emerges.
> This is the machinery of ignorance; it is not exhausted and it does not increase.

As a particular instance of impure dependent origination, it should be understood how ignorance with respect to the consequences of actions, the formations of nonvirtue, and the rest of the six causes produces name and form and the five other effects as associated with the lower realms.

Pure Dependent Origination

Second, as for pure dependent origination, this refers to the way that foe-destroyers who have exhausted defilements, self-realized buddhas, and bodhisattvas who have gained mastery take birth. For them, the process of dependent links does not occur as outlined above. Nevertheless, it is taught that the habitual tendencies of ignorance serve as a condition that cooperates with aspirations and causal nondefiling action. These factors lead to their taking birth by assuming a body that is of a mental nature, and this body is explained as disintegrating in inconceivable death and transference. The implications of this can be learned from the *Lion's Roar of Śrī Mālā*, the *Journey to Laṅkā*, and the *Sūtra Requested by Sāgaramati*. Thus, dependent origination evolves in three ways: as existence in the lower realms, as cyclic existence, and as pure dependent origination.

The Means for Reversing the Links

The third issue concerns the way to reverse the evolution of the links. The support for this process is a person who possesses any of the three types of potential. Following an excellent spiritual friend, such a person must begin by following an exact and complete course of study. Having gone for refuge and developed the wish to achieve his or her particular goal, the student must then persist in the process of eliminating ignorance. Ignorance in the form of delusion regarding the consequences of actions causes the first of the three processes of dependent origination mentioned above. Ignorance in the form of delusion about reality is the cause of the second process. Finally, the ignorance associated with the ground of habitual tendencies is the cause of the third process. The total elimination of all such ignorance brings about the attainment of Buddhahood and the perfection of all excellent qualities.

THE PROFUNDITY OF DEPENDENT ORIGINATION

Second, it is taught that there are five profound distinctions of dependent origination: Unless a cause has ceased, its effect will not occur. Hence, there is no permanence. The arising of an effect follows without interruption from the cessation of its cause. Thus, there is no annihilation. Different classes of existence manifest one after the other. Therefore, there is no transference. Since great effects arise from small causes, cause and effect are not equal. Virtuous actions unfailingly cause pleasure while nonvirtuous actions bring pain. Thus, the effects that occur resemble their causes. Because these issues are difficult to comprehend, they are referred to as "profound distinctions."

REALIZATION OF DEPENDENT ORIGINATION

The third issue concerns the magnificent qualities associated with the realization of dependent origination. While the sūtras and treatises explain numerous such qualities, they can be summarized into the following three. As one comes to see everything as workable, understanding how causality does not deviate or deceive, one gains confidence in the teachings and faith in the Teacher. Secondly, with the realization that, conventionally, things originate in dependence, while their nature is devoid of arising, one will abandon the extremes of permanence and annihilation, as well as one-sided views of existence and nonexistence. Thus, one will gain access to the relative and ultimate truths. Finally, knowing the means for reversing the process by which the links unfold, one will eliminate the three types of causal ignorance by practicing the relevant remedy. This will accomplish the aims of the three individuals.

This concludes the explanation of the twenty-sixth chapter, the analysis of the links of existence, in from the *Ornament of Reason,* a commentary on the *Root of the Middle Way.*

CHAPTER TWENTY-SEVEN

Analysis of Views

The analysis of views also addresses three issues.

THE CONTEXT OF CHAPTER 27

First, regarding the context, the chapter's relation to the profound sūtras can be seen by considering the following passage from the *Śālu Sprout Sūtra*:

> The one who truly sees dependent origination as it is does not
>   depend on the extremes of past and future, or on the present.

Thus, this chapter replies to the query: "What is dependence on the extremes of past and future, and how does one not depend on those?"

As for the chapter's relation to the other analyses, at this point we may hear the author inform us: In this manner, I have accurately explained that while its distinctive properties are, ultimately, emptiness beyond all mental constructs, dependent origination occurs in terms of the relative. The present chapter teaches the fruition of this realization, the attainment of the nonabiding transcendence of suffering through the relinquishment of all views.

THE CONTENT OF CHAPTER 27

The explanation of the chapter's content includes (1) identifying the objects of negation, the sixteen views that are based on the extremes of past and future, and (2) showing how the person who has realized dependent origination does not rely on such views.

The Sixteen Views

On the first issue, the treatise states:

Past existence and nonexistence,
A permanent world, and so forth—
These views depend
On the extreme of the past. [XXVII.1]

The views of existence and nonexistence
At a different time in the future,
Of the end of the world, and so forth
Depend on the extreme of the future. [XXVII.2]

One may believe that the self existed in the past, that it did not, that it both did and did not, or that neither were the case. Likewise, one may believe that the world of the self and the aggregates is permanent, impermanent, both permanent and impermanent, or that it is neither. All of the views included in these two sets of four depend on the extreme of the past because, based on the observation of the self alone and the self along with the aggregates, respectively, they take the form of beliefs in past existence, nonexistence, both, and neither.

Moreover, one may believe that, at a different time in the future, the self will exist, not exist, both exist and not exist, or that neither will be the case. Likewise, it may be held that the world of the self and the aggregates is finite, infinite, both, or neither. These two sets of four views are dependent on the extreme of the future because, based on the observation of the self alone and both the self and the aggregates, respectively, they manifest as beliefs in future existence, nonexistence, both, and neither.

How the Realization of Dependent Origination Precludes Such Views

The second issue includes showing how (1) although dependent origination is accepted in terms of the relative, one will not rely on such views and (2) there will be no such reliance because, in reality, the appropriated, the appropriator, and so forth are all entirely devoid of establishment. The first section contains (1) a refutation of the views based on the self and

(2) a refutation of the views based on the self and aggregates in general. The first of these two issues will include (1) refuting the views that pertain to the four options, such as past existence, and (2) showing how this also invalidates the four options in terms of future existence and so forth. The treatment of the first of these two issues begins with a refutation of the view that the self existed in the past. This refutation involves (1) stating the argument and (2) proving it.

Stating the Argument
On the first issue, the treatise states:

> *Saying "It existed in the past"*
> *Indeed, does not make sense.*
> *Whatever occurred in past lives*
> *Is not the same as this. [XXVII.3]*

The idea that "the self existed in the past" does not make sense because the self that was in hell in previous lives is not the same as the present human self. In scripture we do find statements such as, "At that time, I was the universal monarch by the name of Mahāsammata." Yet, such statements are simply denials of difference. They are not affirmations of sameness. Hence, there is no conflict, for what is implied is that "he was not someone else."

Proving the Argument
On the second issue, the treatise states:

> *If you think, "That itself is the self,"*
> *The appropriated would be different.*
> *Apart from appropriated,*
> *What is this self of yours? [XXVII.4]*

> *It does not make sense for there to be*
> *A self that is different from the appropriated.*
> *If different, it could reasonably be perceived*
> *In the absence of appropriation, yet it cannot. [XXVII.7]*

> *When it is held that there is no self*
> *Apart from the appropriated,*

If the appropriated is itself the self,
Your self does not exist. [XXVII.5]

The appropriated is not the self,
For it arises and disintegrates.
How could the appropriated
Ever be the appropriator? [XXVII.6]

Thus, it is not other than appropriation,
Nor are these two the same.
The self does not exist without appropriation,
Yet neither can it be ascertained as nonexistent. [XXVII.8]

It may be objected: "Your argument is not established because it is precisely the self of the past that has now become the self of this human being in the present."

If this were the case, there would not be any difference between the aggregates that in the past were appropriated in hell and those presently being appropriated as a human being. Yet those two appropriations are different in terms of what caused them, the time at which they occur, and their features. Hence, they are essentially different, so it does not make sense for there to be a single self that appropriates them both.

It might then be argued: "These appropriations occur at different times, but why should that contradict the notion that the appropriating self is one and the same?"

If there were a self that is distinct from what it appropriates, then what, apart from the appropriations, is this self of yours? If the self is different from the appropriated aggregates, it follows that it would be independent of them, and the causes for the designation of self would then be absent.

Below, it is further explained how it would not make sense for the self to be different from what it appropriates. If there were such a difference, it would be perceptible, and we could then reasonably expect to apprehend the self in the absence of the appropriated aggregates, just as we may apprehend a blanket where there is no vase. Therefore, because no such self can be apprehended, it does not exist apart from the appropriated, and so there cannot be a single self that is involved in a series of appropriations.

As a supplementary topic, it is explained that when it is said that there is no self apart from the appropriated, certain members of our own tradition may argue that the appropriated is indeed the self. Yet the characteristics that they ascribe to the self do not then have any existence. Why? Because the aggregates, which they believe to entail the self, are characterized by arising and disintegration, while the self is thought to be permanent and singular. Thus, since their characteristics are incompatible, the aggregates cannot be identical to the self.

Moreover, how could the appropriated ever be the appropriator? This would mean that object and agent were one, and nothing can take itself as an object. The cutter would, for example, then be identical with what it cuts, and this is absurd.

To conclude, the self is not different from what it appropriates because the self cannot be observed separate from the aggregates and because it would then have no cause. Yet the self is not the same as what it appropriates either because, according to such a view, the self would end up impermanent and multiple, and object and agent would become one and the same. The self does not exist independent of what it appropriates because it cannot be observed as such. Consequently, it might be thought that the self is completely nonexistent, just like the son of a barren woman. Yet since, in terms of the relative, the self is imputed based on the aggregates, it cannot be ascertained to be nonexistent either.

The View That the Self Did Not Exist in the Past
Second, the refutation of the view that the self did not exist in the past involves (1) stating the argument and (2) proving it.

Stating the Argument
On the first issue, the treatise states:

> Saying "It did not exist in the past,"
> Does not make sense either.
> Whatever was there in past lives
> Is not different from this. [XXVII.9]

Neither does it make sense to say that the self did not exist in the past because the self that was in hell in past lives is not different in essence from the self of the present human life.

Proving the Argument
On the second issue, the treatise states:

> *If it were something other,*
> *It could arise even in its absence.*
> *Likewise, that would remain*
> *And there could be birth without death there. [XXVII.10]*

> *There would be annihilation, action would be wasted,*
> *The action done by one*
> *Would be experienced by another—*
> *These and other flaws would ensue. [XXVII.11]*

> *Something previously nonexistent does not arise*
> *Because flaws would follow:*
> *The self would be a product*
> *And its arising would lack a cause. [XXVII.12]*

If the argument's establishment is questioned, it will be explained that were the present human self something other than the past self in hell, it would be pointless for these two to be dependent on one another, just like a vase and a blanket are not mutually dependent. The present self could then arise even in the absence of a past self. Likewise, just as a vase may arise without its occurrence necessitating the destruction of the blanket, the present human self could arise while the past self in hell continued to remain. Just as the blanket may arise without the vase having ceased, there could be birth in this life without the past self having died in a past life.

Moreover, if the past and present selves were different, this would mean that when the human self exists in the present, the past self of hell has been annihilated. If this is accepted, it will follow that action would go to waste because, at the time of the impelling action, the ripened effect is not present, and when the effect is experienced, the self of the agent would have been annihilated. If it is then held that pleasant and painful effects of virtuous and nonvirtuous actions performed by the former self will be experienced by the subsequent self, this means that the action created by one person will be experienced by another. If that is accepted, more flaws will ensue. Actions would be performed in vain because their effects would not be experienced by the agent that performs them. On the other hand, people would have to fear the consequences of actions that they never engaged in, including those with immediate effects.

It might then be thought: "The selves are different in substance, yet of the same continuum. Hence, these flaws are irrelevant."

Yet that is not correct either. As was explained before, there is no continuum that is essentially different from the substances of which it is composed.

If the present self were different from the past self, it would, furthermore, be a previously nonexistent self that is born into this life. Yet that cannot be argued because various flaws would ensue. How so? The self would then be a newly produced product. If the self were such a product, then the self that is born here will not have been preceded by the self of the agent and will be lacking its cause. The arising of an uncaused self is similar to the notion of there being a child of a barren woman. Since such an assertion is nonsensical, it should not be accepted that the self arises without having existed before.

Summarizing Refutation of Both and Neither

The third section presents a summarizing refutation of the remaining alternatives, both and neither. The treatise states:

> *Thus, that the self existed, did not exist,*
> *That it both existed and did not,*
> *Or neither existed nor did not exist—*
> *These views on the past are untenable. [XXVII.13]*

Thus, that the self existed, that it did not exist, that it both existed and did not, or that it neither existed nor did not exist—these views regarding the past are untenable. Combined existence and nonexistence is not feasible given that each of these options is itself impossible. Meanwhile, the negation of both is not correct either, given that the objects of negation are not established.

The Implicit Invalidation of the Views with Respect to Future Existence and so Forth

Second, showing the implicit invalidation of the four views that pertain to future existence and so on, the treatise states:

The views that "it will exist
At a different time in the future,"
Or that, "it will not exist in the future,"
Are equal to those about the past. [XXVII.14]

The views that the self will exist at some different time in the future, that it will not exist, that it both will and will not, and that neither is the case can be refuted in the same way as the views that concern the self's past existence and so forth. Thus, with the appropriate changes we get:

Saying "It will exist in the future,"
Indeed, does not make sense.
Whatever will be in future lives
Is not the same as this.

This can also be applied to the remaining arguments.

Refutation of Views Based on Self and Aggregates in General

The second issue is the refutation of the views that are based on [the self and aggregates] in general. This includes a refutation of beliefs in the four alternatives associated with (1) permanence and so forth and (2) finitude and so on. The first section includes (1) specific refutations and (2) a general refutation. Concerning the first, there are four specific refutations.

Refutation of a Permanent Self and Aggregates

First, refuting the notion of permanence, the treatise states:

If the god were the human,
It would be permanent.
The god would be unborn,
For the permanent has no birth. [XXVII.15]

If the self and aggregates associated with the future birth of a god were identical with the present self and aggregates of a human being, then the factors associated with the god would be permanent, in the sense that they also existed before. The self and aggregates associated with the god and human are, however, not identical. Hence, it does not make sense for them to be permanent. Furthermore, if the god were permanent in this way, it would also be unborn. This is entailed because the permanent has prior existence and cannot be considered previously nonexistent. Hence, it knows no birth.

Refutation of Impermanence
Second, refuting impermanence, the treatise states:

> *If the god were different from the human,*
> *It would be impermanent.*
> *If god and human were different,*
> *There could not reasonably be one stream of being. [XXVII.16]*

If the future divine self and aggregates were different from the present human self and aggregates, the factors associated with the god would be impermanent factors without any prior existence. Yet since the two sets of factors are not different, there could not reasonably be any such impermanence or absence of past existence. The self and aggregates that are associated with the god and the human are not established as different in substance because if they were, they could not reasonably make up one single stream of being, in the same way that Maitreya and Upagupta do not constitute the same continuum. Hence, since it is asserted that they do form a single stream of being, they cannot be different in substance.

Refutation of Both Permanence and Impermanence
Third, refuting the combination of permanence and impermanence, the treatise states:

> *If one part were divine*
> *And another part human,*
> *It would be permanent and impermanent.*
> *That is not reasonable either. [XXVII.17]*

Let us then assume that one part of the god's self and aggregates is divine, in the sense that with respect to this part humanity has been relinquished, while another part of its self and the aggregates remains identical with the past human. One part of the god's state would then be permanent and existent from before, whereas another part would be impermanent with no prior existence. This would contradict the god and the human's being the same in essence. Therefore, since it does not make sense for the self and aggregates to have a separate part that is human, these two cannot reasonably be both permanent and impermanent.

Refutation of the Denial of Both
Fourth, refuting the denial of both permanence and impermanence, the treatise states:

> *If permanent and impermanent*
> *Were both established,*
> *It would be possible to establish*
> *The neither permanent nor impermanent. [XXVII.18]*

If the objects of negation, the permanent and the impermanent, were both established, it would be possible to negate them, thus establishing that which is neither permanent nor impermanent. Yet, as they have already been refuted, these two neganda are not established. The denial and negation of these two is, therefore, not established either.

General Refutation
Offering a general refutation, the treatise states:

> *If something came somewhere from somewhere*
> *And then would go somewhere else,*
> *Then cyclic existence would have no beginning,*
> *Yet that is not the case. [XXVII.19]*

> *When nothing is permanent,*
> *What could be impermanent?*
> *Permanence, impermanence,*
> *And both have been dismissed [XXVII.20]*

It may be argued: "Something has been wandering in cyclic existence since time without beginning, and that something is also observed now. Therefore, the one that cycles throughout cyclic existence is permanent."

If something—a formation or a person—came somewhere from somewhere in the past and were then to go somewhere else in the future, there would be cyclic existence without beginning. Yet there is no such coming and going, neither of a person nor of formations, because the going and coming of both the permanent and the impermanent have already been refuted. That is to say, since cyclic existence is not established, there is nothing permanent that cycles. What, then, could be qualified by impermanence, by the negation of the former quality? Both permanence and impermanence, as well as the negation of these two (since the objects of negation are not established), have hereby been dismissed.

Refutation of the Finite and so Forth

The refutation of beliefs in the four alternatives associated with finitude and so forth will include (1) a refutation of finitude and infinitude, (2) a refutation of their combination, and (3) a refutation of the denial of both. The first of these sections contains arguments based on (1) the existence of other worlds and (2) continuous arising and disintegration.

Argument Based on the Existence of Other Worlds

On the first issue, the treatise states:

> *If the world had an end,*
> *How could there be another world?*
> *If the world had no end,*
> *How could there be another world? [XXVII.21]*

If the world of the present self and aggregates had an end, and so would be annihilated, how could there be another world? Indeed, that would be impossible. Therefore, since there are other worlds, the present self and aggregates cannot be finite and subject to annihilation. Moreover, if the world of the self and aggregates does not have an end and is inexhaustible, how could there be another world? Indeed, there could not. Therefore, because there are other worlds, the present one cannot be infinite and inexhaustible.

Argument from Continuous Arising and Disintegration

On the second issue, the treatise states:

This continuity of the aggregates
Is just like an oil lamp's light.
Hence, neither finitude
Nor infinitude makes sense. [XXVII.22]

If the previous were to cease,
And if, based on these aggregates,
Those aggregates would not arise,
The world would have an end. [XXVII.23]

If the previous were not to cease,
And if, based on these aggregates,
Those aggregates would not arise,
The world would be endless. [XXVII.24]

Moreover, the continuity that the aggregates partake of throughout past and future is just like the light of an oil lamp. As previous instances of light cease, subsequent instances arise. The same is the case with the aggregates, for subsequent instances arise without interruption once the previous instances cease. Therefore, it does not make sense to think in terms of finitude and annihilation or infinitude and inexhaustible permanence.

To elaborate, if the previous aggregates were to cease and then not serve as the cause for the aggregates that subsequently arise as a result, as is the case with the foe-destroyer's final moment of mind, the world would indeed have an end. Yet subsequent aggregates follow based on the previous aggregates. Hence, the world is not finite. Likewise, if the previous aggregates did not cease, and if, hence, the resultant, subsequent aggregates did not arise on the basis of the causal, previous aggregates, the world of the cause would be endless. Therefore, since the causal, previous aggregates do cease, the world is not infinite.

Refutation of Combined Finitude and Infinitude
Second, refuting their combination, the treatise states:

If one part were finite
And another part infinite,
The world would and would not have an end.
This does not make sense either. [XXVII.25]

How could one part
Of the appropriator be destroyed
And another part not be destroyed.
This does not make sense. [XXVII.26]

How could one part
Of the appropriated be destroyed
And another part not be destroyed?
That does not make sense either. [XXVII.27]

If one part of self and aggregates were to be destroyed, being finite, while another part were not, being infinite, then the world would and would not have an end. But since self and aggregates cannot reasonably be half destroyed and half not destroyed, it is not the case that the world is both finite and infinite.

How so? Well, would it be the self or the aggregates that are half destroyed and half not destroyed? If it is the self, then how could one part of the appropriator be destroyed and another part not? There is no argument that can support such an account. Moreover, this would mean that one half is the human of the past, while the other half is no longer human but a god, or that one half has disintegrated, while the other half has not. Yet that is not feasible with respect to a single essence. And again, when we search the aggregates for the self in the fivefold way, we do not find one. It is, therefore, not reasonable for one half of the self to be destroyed and the other half not.

Given the second option, how could one part of the appropriated be destroyed and the other half not? There is no proof to support such a position, and a single essence cannot be both permanent and impermanent. Finally, since the aggregates themselves have already been refuted, it is not reasonable for one half of the aggregates to be destroyed and not the other.

Refutation of the Denial of Both
On the third issue, the treatise states:

If the finite and infinite
Were both established,

It would be possible to establish
The neither finite nor infinite. [XXVII.28]

If the objects of negation, the finite and the infinite, were both established, it would be possible to negate them and establish that which is neither. Yet as these two neganda, the finite and the infinite, have already been refuted and shown to have no establishment, the negative phenomenon that is neither of them cannot be established either.

Ultimate Lack of Establishment

Thus, in terms of the relative, we may assert illusion-like dependent origination, where cause and effect are not the same, yet not different either. None of the sixteen views are appropriate in this context. Having explained how that is so, it will next be shown that since, in reality, the self, the aggregates, and so on are all not established themselves, all specific views about them are inappropriate as well. The treatise states:

Alternately, because all things are empty,
How could views of permanence and so on,
Occur in any form, anywhere,
And to anyone at all? [XXVII.29]

Alternatively, as explained above, all things originate dependently and are, therefore, empty of nature, like reflections. What, then, would be the reason for views of permanence and so on to occur in any form, at any place, and to anyone at all? Similarly, there is no reason for views about the sharpness or dullness of donkey horns to occur in any form, at any place, to anyone at all.

CONCLUDING HOMAGE

The meaning of the profound teaching of dependent origination free from all mental constructs has here been flawlessly explained, along with the fruition of realization. Knowing this to be the kindness of the Teacher, the Master now pays homage by rejoicing in the Teacher's explanation:

> *By the love of his heart, he accepts us*
> *And, so that all views may be relinquished,*
> *Reveals the sacred Dharma.*
> *To the teacher, Gautama, I prostrate. [XXVII.30]*

The words "I prostrate" present the basis for distinctions, an act of reverence in body, speech, and mind. To whom is this prostration made? To Gautama, the victorious Śākyamuni, who was born into the royal line of Gotama. The distinctive qualities of this object of veneration are found in his revealing the sacred Dharma, the peace of dependent origination that is, in reality, free from arising, ceasing, and all other such constructs. The Dharma that he teaches protects us from the abyss of all views, such as those that cherish peace and regard existence as something to reject. This Dharma is sacred insofar as it is enjoyed by those who are sacred and noble, and it is the supreme Dharma, in that it saves one from the extremes of existence and peace and is worthy of praise. The purpose of this teaching is to facilitate the relinquishment of all views, such as the sixteen described before, and thereby to eliminate the universal root of all faults. What is the motivation behind this teaching? The teaching is given out of the acceptance of nonreferential love because realizing dependent origination, which is devoid of essential nature, is the remedy against the reification that lies at the root of all suffering. As is taught:

> For those possessed by the demon of reification,
> This is the supreme healing.

This concludes the explanation of the twenty-seventh chapter, the analysis of views, in the *Ornament of Reason*, a commentary on the *Root of the Middle Way*.

THE MEANING OF THE POSTSCRIPT

This treatise on the Middle Way, the *Root of Insight*, is the vajra speech
Of the noble son of the Victorious Ones, prophesied by the Lord of the Able.
By means of the instructions transmitted in the lineage of the masters of scripture and reasoning,
And with the eye of intelligent discernment, I have here clearly explained the import of this scripture.

At the request of bright and committed individuals,
And with the wish to be of benefit, this work has been well composed.
By the merit that ensues, may all wanderers enter this path of the collection of genuine reasoning,
And, by the pacification of all ignorance and construction, thus attain the supreme stage.

This completes the *Ornament of Reason*, a commentary on the root treatise on the Middle Way composed by the noble master Nāgārjuna, the great being, who flawlessly reveals the way of transcendent insight.

The commentary was composed by Mabja Jangchub Tsöndrü, a Buddhist monk and teacher of the Middle Way, who, during the seventh five-hundred-year-cycle of the Bliss-Gone One's teaching, appeared in the land of snowy mountains. He has gone beyond the ocean of our own and other's philosophies, is wealthy in scripture and reasoning, and has no delusion with respect to the profound and the vast.

Mabja's Topical Outline

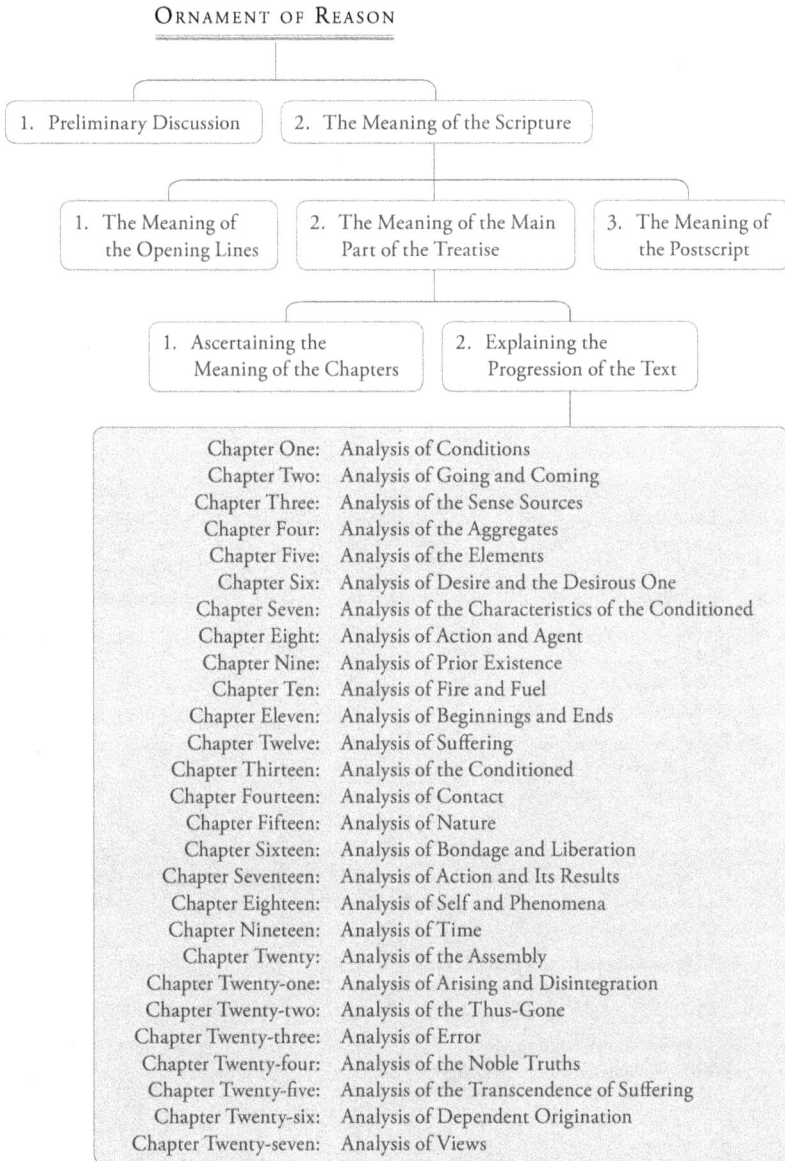

ORNAMENT OF REASON

1. Preliminary Discussion   2. The Meaning of the Scripture

1. The Meaning of the Opening Lines   2. The Meaning of the Main Part of the Treatise   3. The Meaning of the Postscript

1. Ascertaining the Meaning of the Chapters   2. Explaining the Progression of the Text

Chapter One:	Analysis of Conditions
Chapter Two:	Analysis of Going and Coming
Chapter Three:	Analysis of the Sense Sources
Chapter Four:	Analysis of the Aggregates
Chapter Five:	Analysis of the Elements
Chapter Six:	Analysis of Desire and the Desirous One
Chapter Seven:	Analysis of the Characteristics of the Conditioned
Chapter Eight:	Analysis of Action and Agent
Chapter Nine:	Analysis of Prior Existence
Chapter Ten:	Analysis of Fire and Fuel
Chapter Eleven:	Analysis of Beginnings and Ends
Chapter Twelve:	Analysis of Suffering
Chapter Thirteen:	Analysis of the Conditioned
Chapter Fourteen:	Analysis of Contact
Chapter Fifteen:	Analysis of Nature
Chapter Sixteen:	Analysis of Bondage and Liberation
Chapter Seventeen:	Analysis of Action and Its Results
Chapter Eighteen:	Analysis of Self and Phenomena
Chapter Nineteen:	Analysis of Time
Chapter Twenty:	Analysis of the Assembly
Chapter Twenty-one:	Analysis of Arising and Disintegration
Chapter Twenty-two:	Analysis of the Thus-Gone
Chapter Twenty-three:	Analysis of Error
Chapter Twenty-four:	Analysis of the Noble Truths
Chapter Twenty-five:	Analysis of the Transcendence of Suffering
Chapter Twenty-six:	Analysis of Dependent Origination
Chapter Twenty-seven:	Analysis of Views

The Relationship between the 27 Analyses as Explained in the *Ornament of Reason*

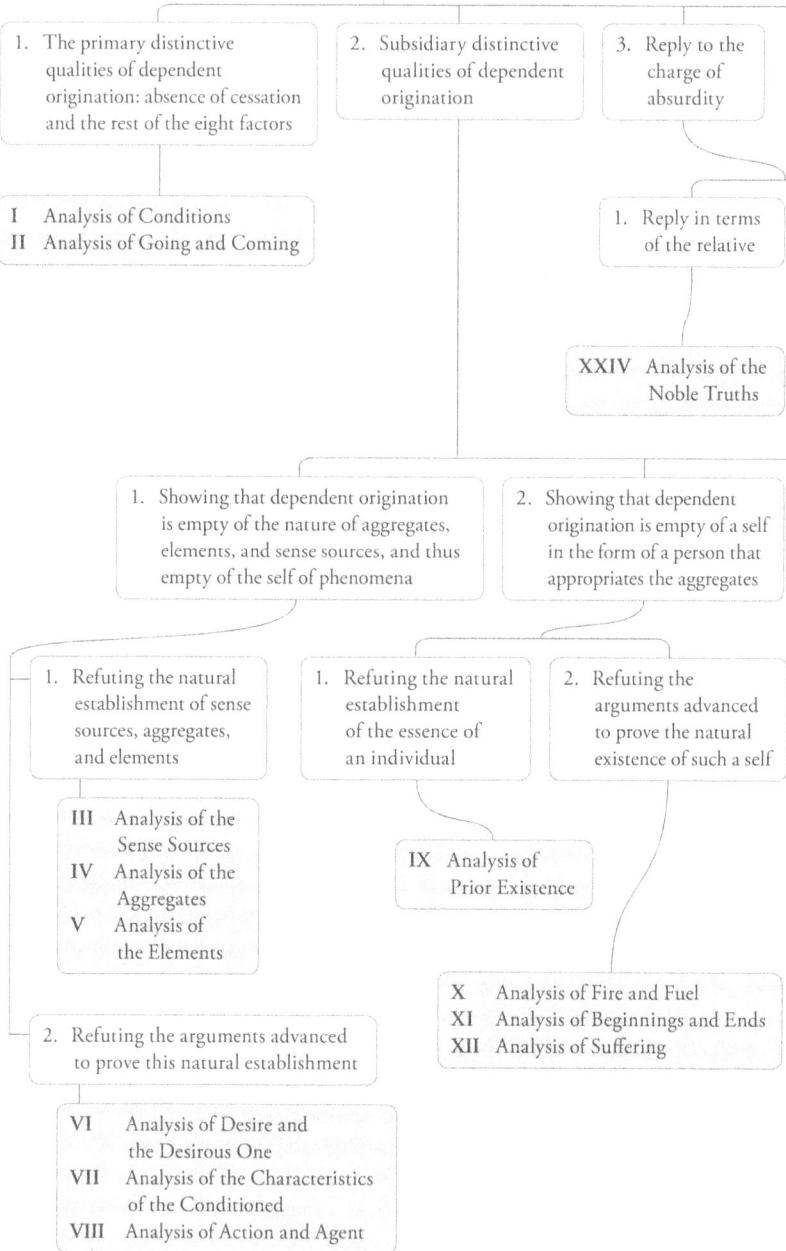

1. The primary distinctive qualities of dependent origination: absence of cessation and the rest of the eight factors

2. Subsidiary distinctive qualities of dependent origination

3. Reply to the charge of absurdity

I   Analysis of Conditions
II Analysis of Going and Coming

1. Reply in terms of the relative

XXIV   Analysis of the Noble Truths

1. Showing that dependent origination is empty of the nature of aggregates, elements, and sense sources, and thus empty of the self of phenomena

2. Showing that dependent origination is empty of a self in the form of a person that appropriates the aggregates

1. Refuting the natural establishment of sense sources, aggregates, and elements

1. Refuting the natural establishment of the essence of an individual

2. Refuting the arguments advanced to prove the natural existence of such a self

III   Analysis of the Sense Sources
IV   Analysis of the Aggregates
V   Analysis of the Elements

IX   Analysis of Prior Existence

X   Analysis of Fire and Fuel
XI   Analysis of Beginnings and Ends
XII   Analysis of Suffering

2. Refuting the arguments advanced to prove this natural establishment

VI   Analysis of Desire and the Desirous One
VII   Analysis of the Characteristics of the Conditioned
VIII   Analysis of Action and Agent

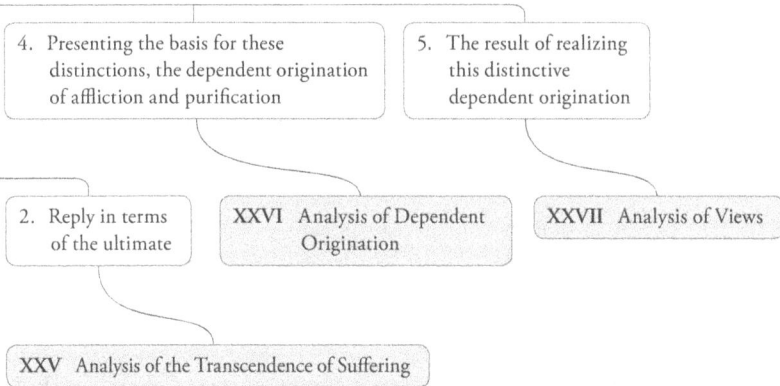

4. Presenting the basis for these distinctions, the dependent origination of affliction and purification

5. The result of realizing this distinctive dependent origination

2. Reply in terms of the ultimate

XXVI Analysis of Dependent Origination

XXVII Analysis of Views

XXV Analysis of the Transcendence of Suffering

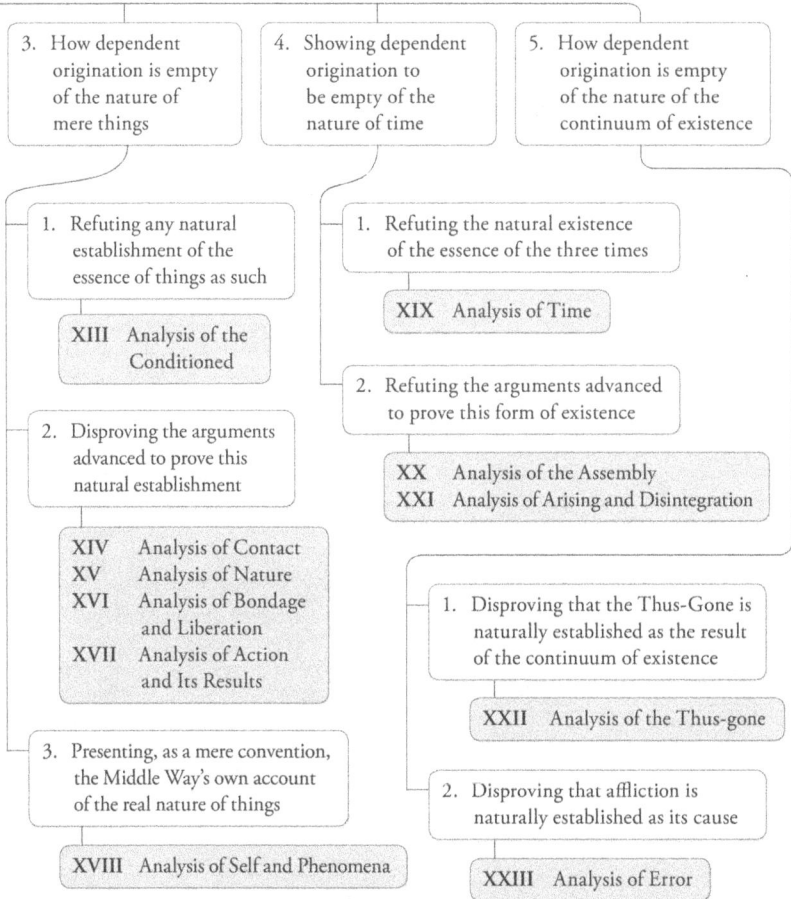

3. How dependent origination is empty of the nature of mere things

4. Showing dependent origination to be empty of the nature of time

5. How dependent origination is empty of the nature of the continuum of existence

1. Refuting any natural establishment of the essence of things as such

XIII Analysis of the Conditioned

2. Disproving the arguments advanced to prove this natural establishment

XIV Analysis of Contact
XV Analysis of Nature
XVI Analysis of Bondage and Liberation
XVII Analysis of Action and Its Results

3. Presenting, as a mere convention, the Middle Way's own account of the real nature of things

XVIII Analysis of Self and Phenomena

1. Refuting the natural existence of the essence of the three times

XIX Analysis of Time

2. Refuting the arguments advanced to prove this form of existence

XX Analysis of the Assembly
XXI Analysis of Arising and Disintegration

1. Disproving that the Thus-Gone is naturally established as the result of the continuum of existence

XXII Analysis of the Thus-gone

2. Disproving that affliction is naturally established as its cause

XXIII Analysis of Error

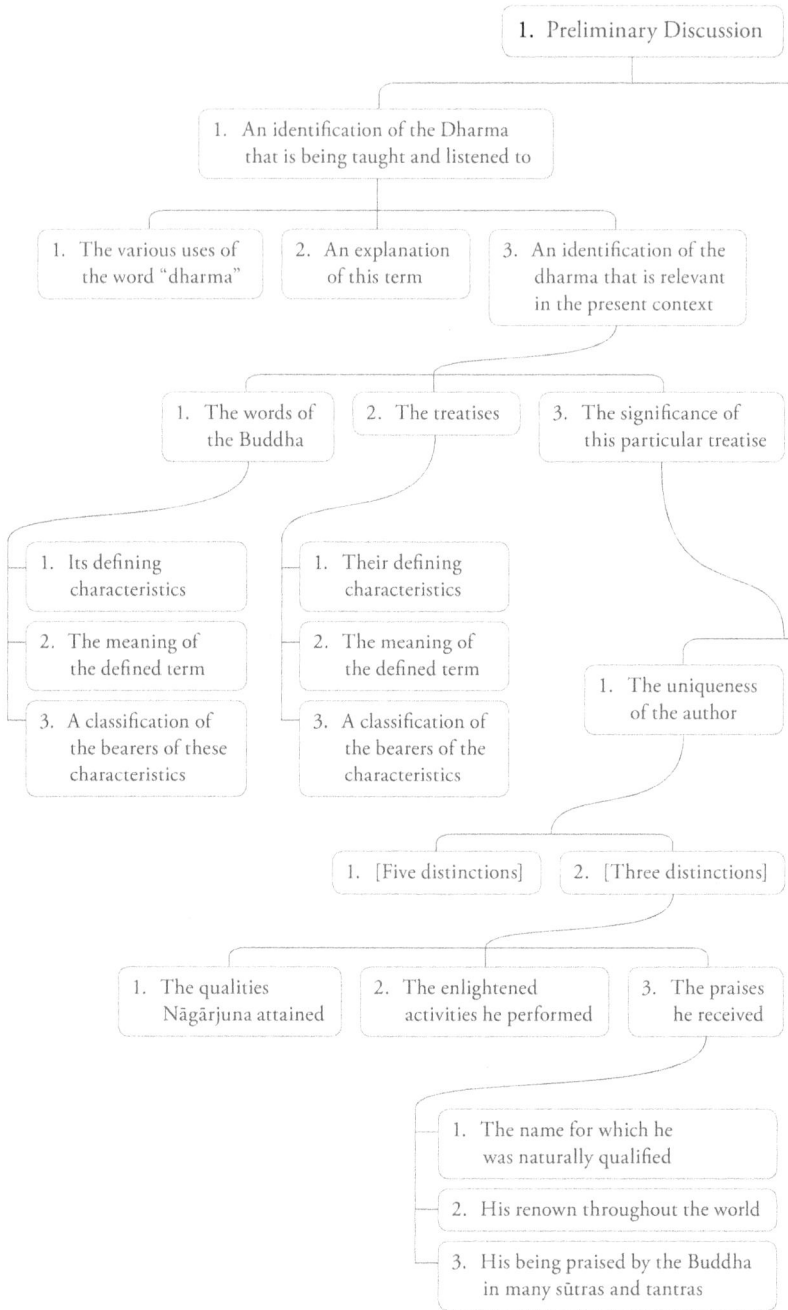

1. Preliminary Discussion

1. An identification of the Dharma that is being taught and listened to

1. The various uses of the word "dharma"

2. An explanation of this term

3. An identification of the dharma that is relevant in the present context

1. The words of the Buddha

2. The treatises

3. The significance of this particular treatise

1. Its defining characteristics

2. The meaning of the defined term

3. A classification of the bearers of these characteristics

1. Their defining characteristics

2. The meaning of the defined term

3. A classification of the bearers of the characteristics

1. The uniqueness of the author

1. [Five distinctions]

2. [Three distinctions]

1. The qualities Nāgārjuna attained

2. The enlightened activities he performed

3. The praises he received

1. The name for which he was naturally qualified

2. His renown throughout the world

3. His being praised by the Buddha in many sūtras and tantras

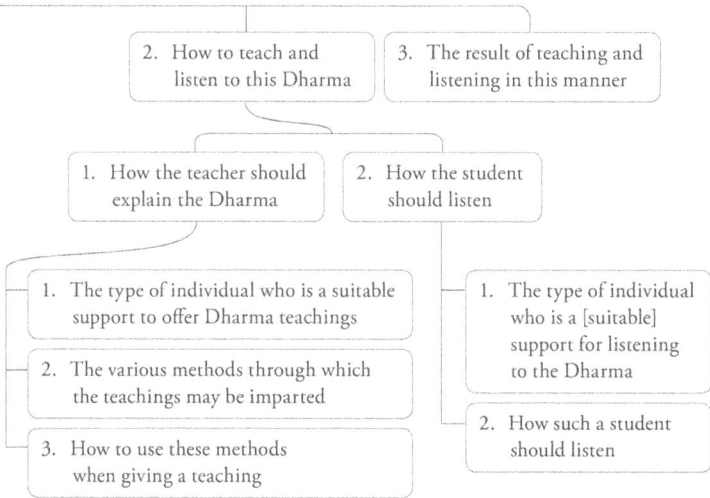

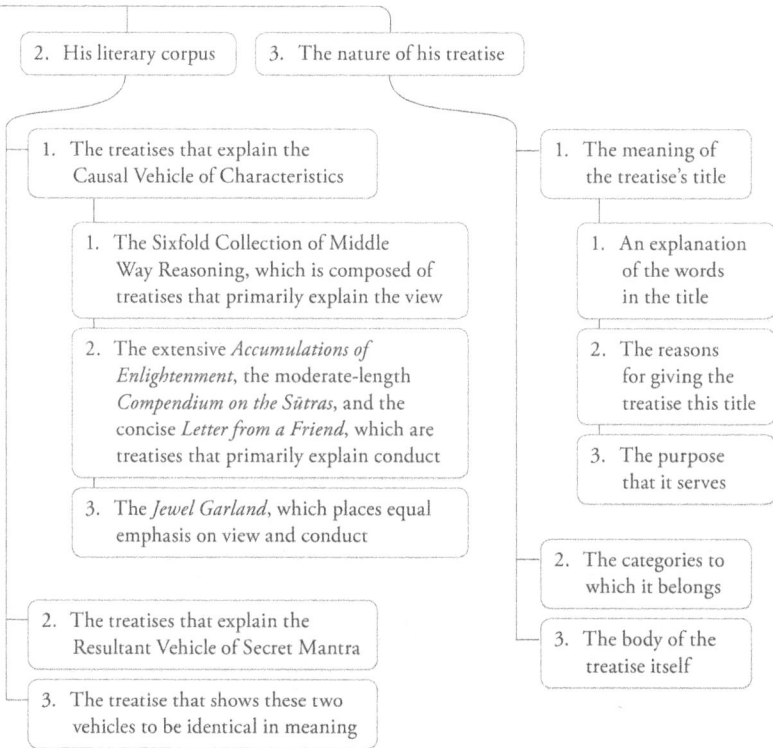

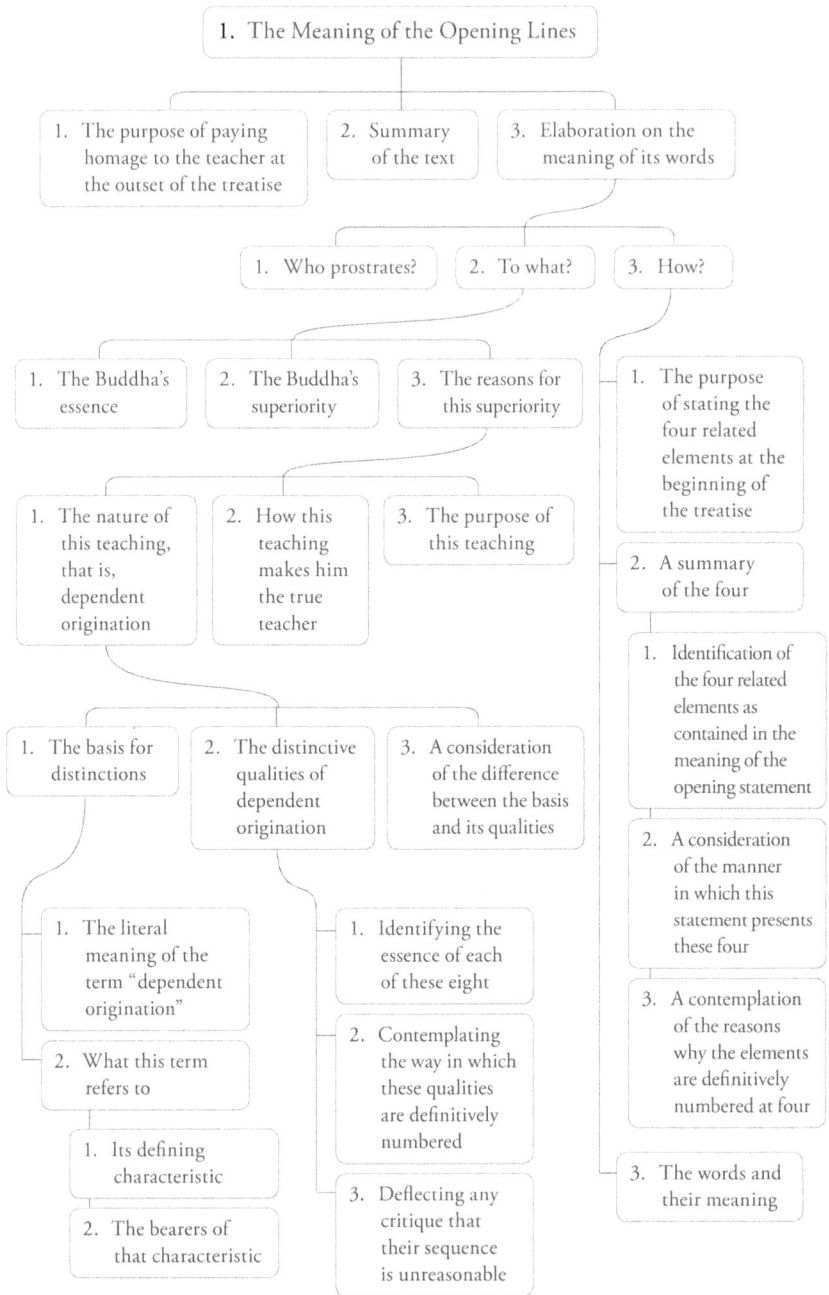

1. The Meaning of the Opening Lines

- 1. The purpose of paying homage to the teacher at the outset of the treatise
- 2. Summary of the text
- 3. Elaboration on the meaning of its words
  - 1. Who prostrates?
  - 2. To what?
  - 3. How?

1. Who prostrates?
- 1. The Buddha's essence
- 2. The Buddha's superiority
- 3. The reasons for this superiority
  - 1. The nature of this teaching, that is, dependent origination
  - 2. How this teaching makes him the true teacher
  - 3. The purpose of this teaching

1. The nature of this teaching, that is, dependent origination
- 1. The basis for distinctions
- 2. The distinctive qualities of dependent origination
- 3. A consideration of the difference between the basis and its qualities

1. The basis for distinctions
- 1. The literal meaning of the term "dependent origination"
- 2. What this term refers to
  - 1. Its defining characteristic
  - 2. The bearers of that characteristic

2. The distinctive qualities of dependent origination
- 1. Identifying the essence of each of these eight
- 2. Contemplating the way in which these qualities are definitively numbered
- 3. Deflecting any critique that their sequence is unreasonable

3. How?
- 1. The purpose of stating the four related elements at the beginning of the treatise
- 2. A summary of the four
  - 1. Identification of the four related elements as contained in the meaning of the opening statement
  - 2. A consideration of the manner in which this statement presents these four
  - 3. A contemplation of the reasons why the elements are definitively numbered at four
- 3. The words and their meaning

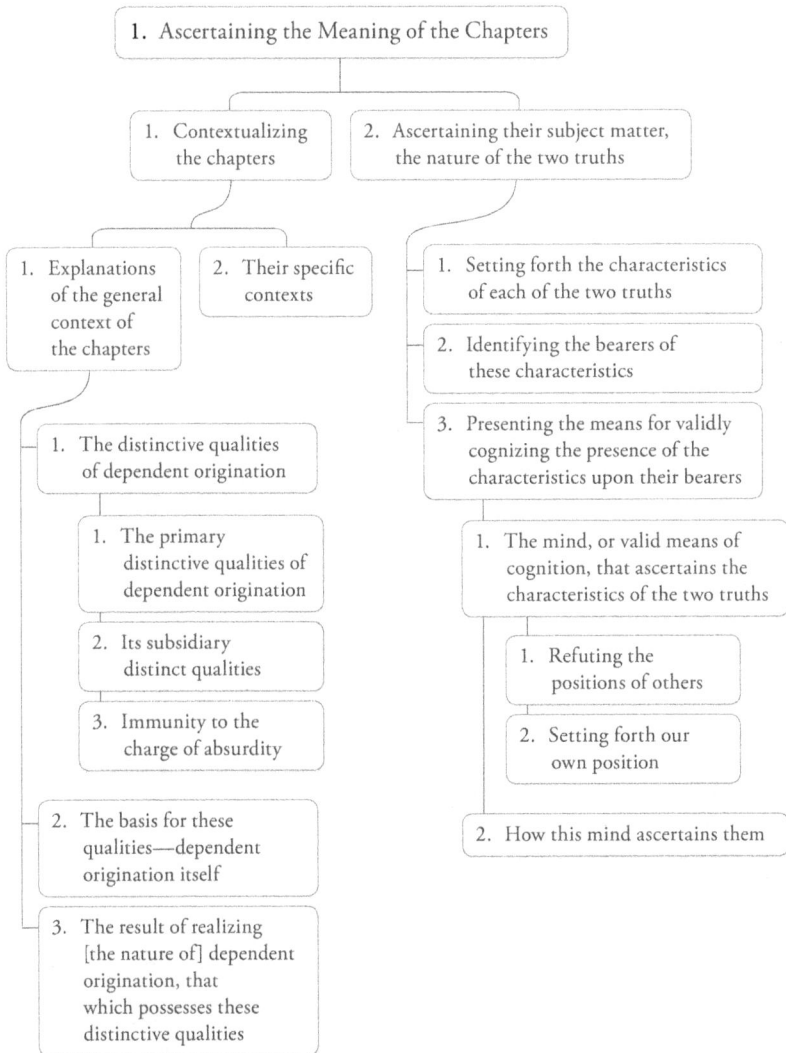

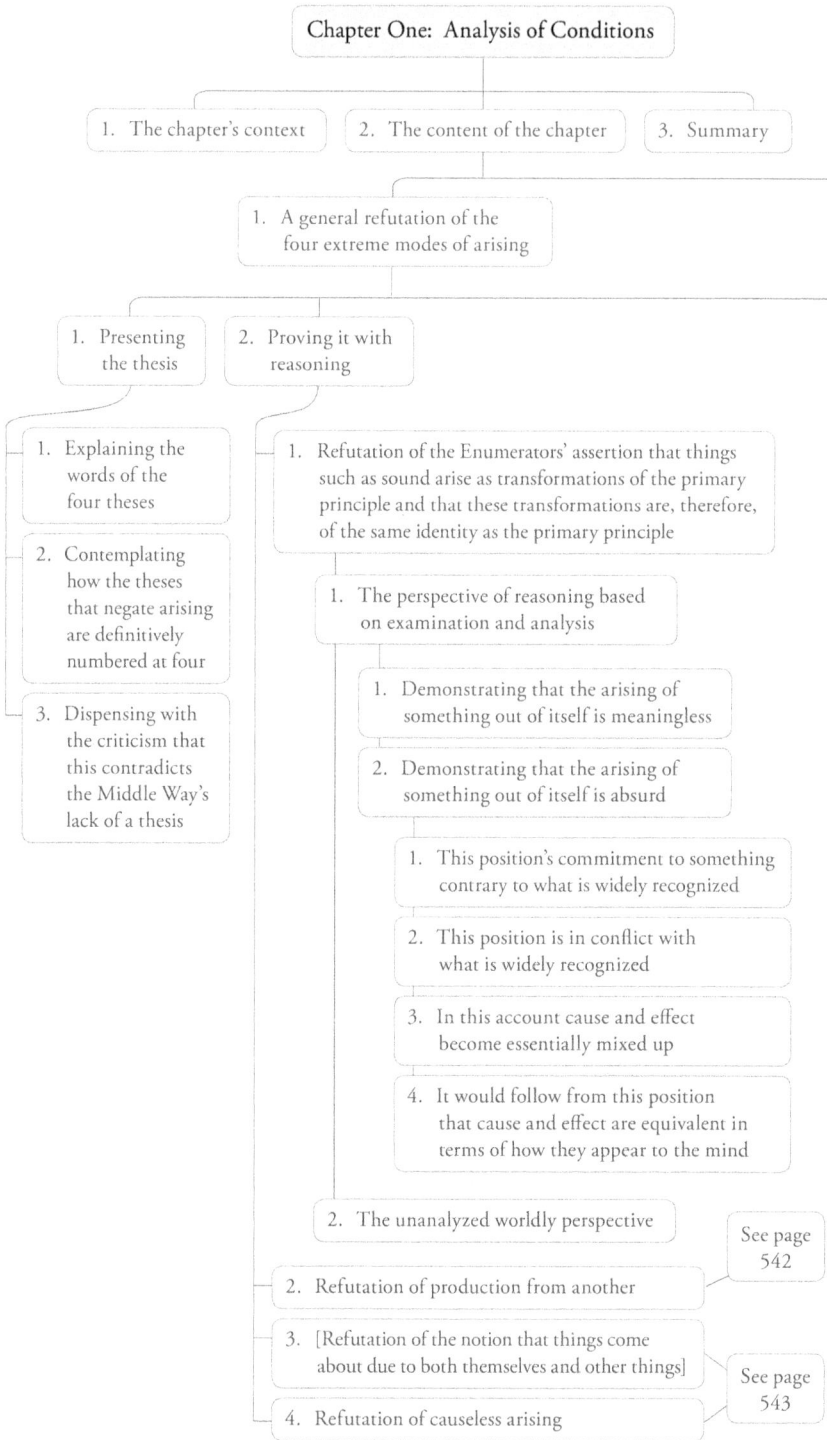

Chapter One: Analysis of Conditions

1. The chapter's context

2. The content of the chapter

3. Summary

1. A general refutation of the four extreme modes of arising

1. Presenting the thesis

2. Proving it with reasoning

1. Explaining the words of the four theses

2. Contemplating how the theses that negate arising are definitively numbered at four

3. Dispensing with the criticism that this contradicts the Middle Way's lack of a thesis

1. Refutation of the Enumerators' assertion that things such as sound arise as transformations of the primary principle and that these transformations are, therefore, of the same identity as the primary principle

1. The perspective of reasoning based on examination and analysis

1. Demonstrating that the arising of something out of itself is meaningless

2. Demonstrating that the arising of something out of itself is absurd

1. This position's commitment to something contrary to what is widely recognized

2. This position is in conflict with what is widely recognized

3. In this account cause and effect become essentially mixed up

4. It would follow from this position that cause and effect are equivalent in terms of how they appear to the mind

2. The unanalyzed worldly perspective

See page 542

2. Refutation of production from another

3. [Refutation of the notion that things come about due to both themselves and other things]

See page 543

4. Refutation of causeless arising

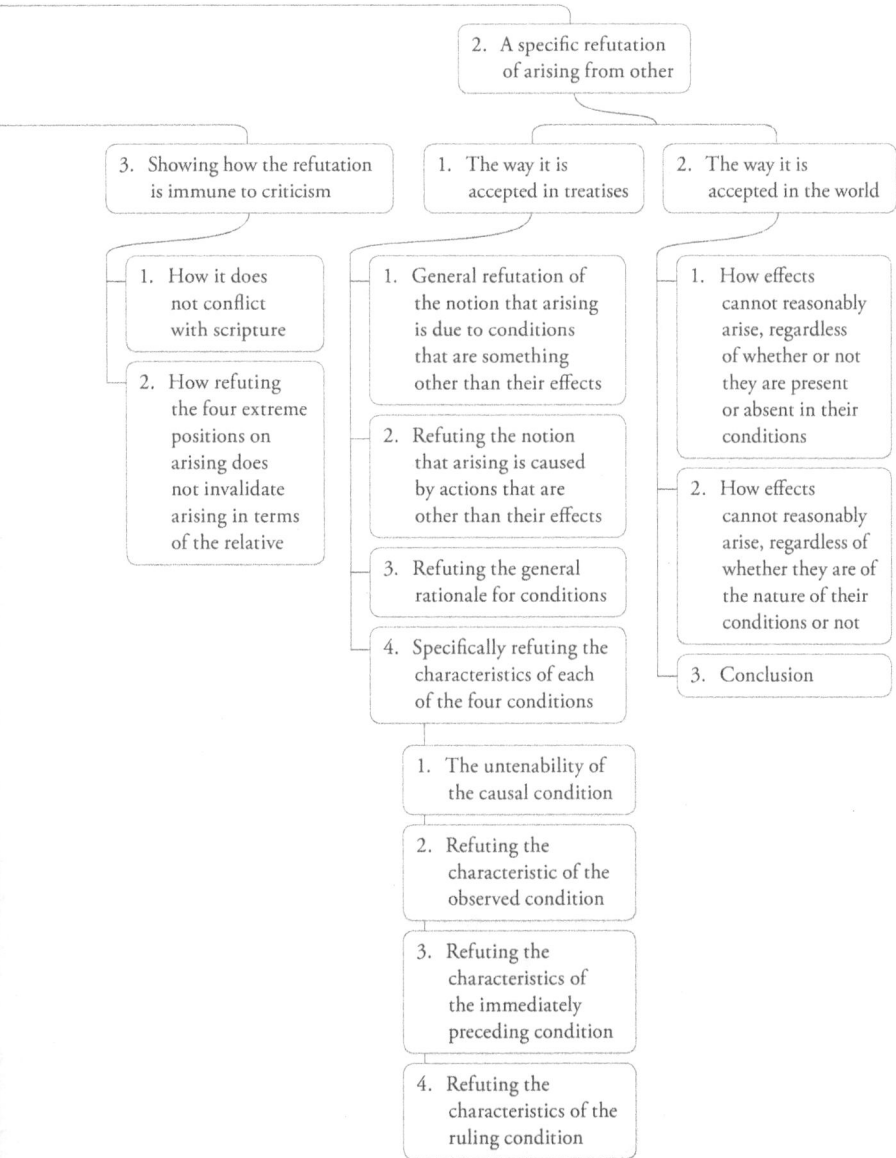

2. A specific refutation
   of arising from other

3. Showing how the refutation
   is immune to criticism

1. The way it is
   accepted in treatises

2. The way it is
   accepted in the world

1. How it does
   not conflict
   with scripture

2. How refuting
   the four extreme
   positions on
   arising does
   not invalidate
   arising in terms
   of the relative

1. General refutation of
   the notion that arising
   is due to conditions
   that are something
   other than their effects

2. Refuting the notion
   that arising is caused
   by actions that are
   other than their effects

3. Refuting the general
   rationale for conditions

4. Specifically refuting the
   characteristics of each
   of the four conditions

1. How effects
   cannot reasonably
   arise, regardless
   of whether or not
   they are present
   or absent in their
   conditions

2. How effects
   cannot reasonably
   arise, regardless of
   whether they are of
   the nature of their
   conditions or not

3. Conclusion

1. The untenability of
   the causal condition

2. Refuting the
   characteristic of the
   observed condition

3. Refuting the
   characteristics of
   the immediately
   preceding condition

4. Refuting the
   characteristics of the
   ruling condition

Continuation of Chapter 1: Analysis of Conditions ...

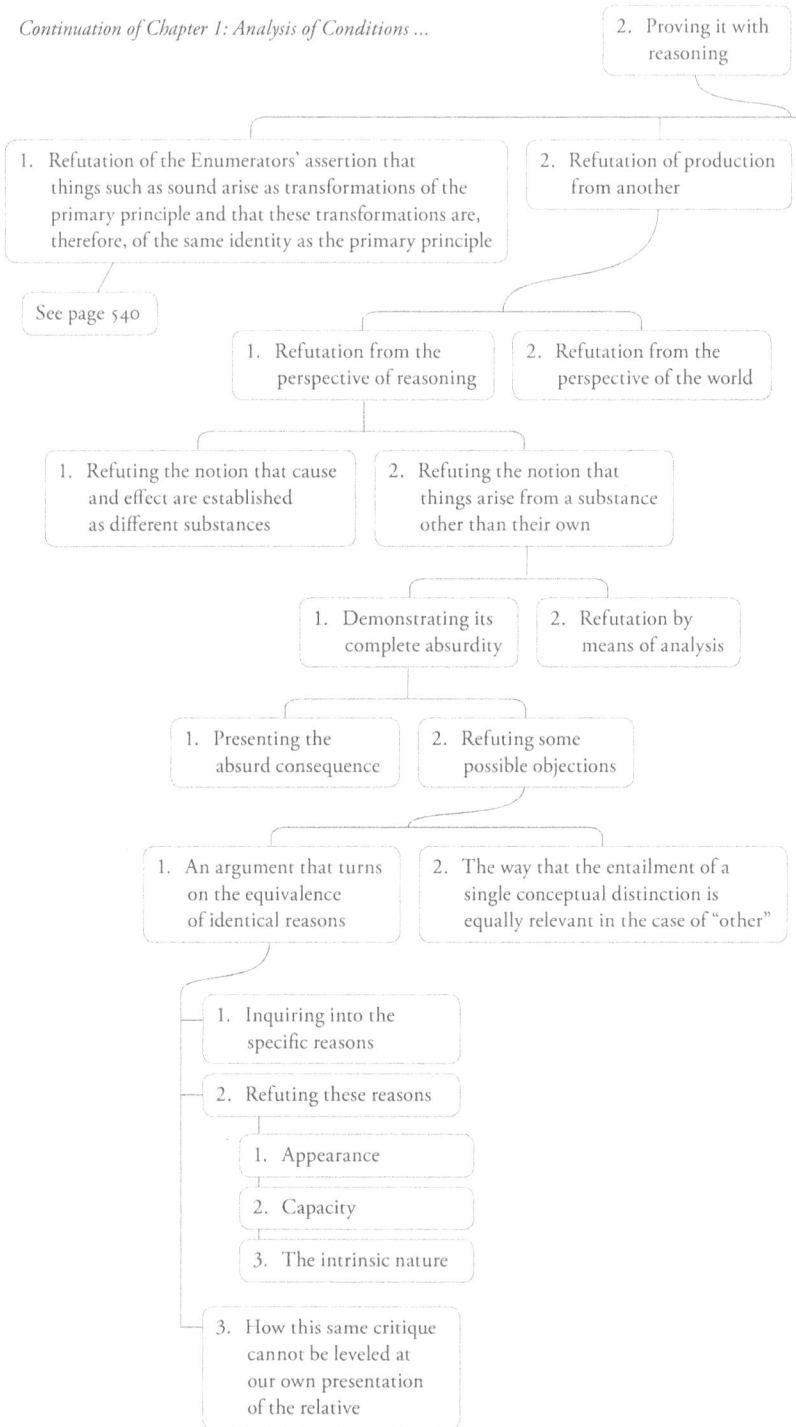

2. Proving it with reasoning

1. Refutation of the Enumerators' assertion that things such as sound arise as transformations of the primary principle and that these transformations are, therefore, of the same identity as the primary principle

2. Refutation of production from another

See page 540

1. Refutation from the perspective of reasoning

2. Refutation from the perspective of the world

1. Refuting the notion that cause and effect are established as different substances

2. Refuting the notion that things arise from a substance other than their own

1. Demonstrating its complete absurdity

2. Refutation by means of analysis

1. Presenting the absurd consequence

2. Refuting some possible objections

1. An argument that turns on the equivalence of identical reasons

2. The way that the entailment of a single conceptual distinction is equally relevant in the case of "other"

1. Inquiring into the specific reasons

2. Refuting these reasons

1. Appearance

2. Capacity

3. The intrinsic nature

3. How this same critique cannot be leveled at our own presentation of the relative

3. [Refutation of the notion that things come about due to both themselves and other things]

4. Refutation of causeless arising

1. The arguments that were explained earlier

2. Further arguments not previously supplied

1. Things would no longer occur occasionally

2. All efforts to cause an effect to occur would be futile

3. No apprehended objects could appear to the mind

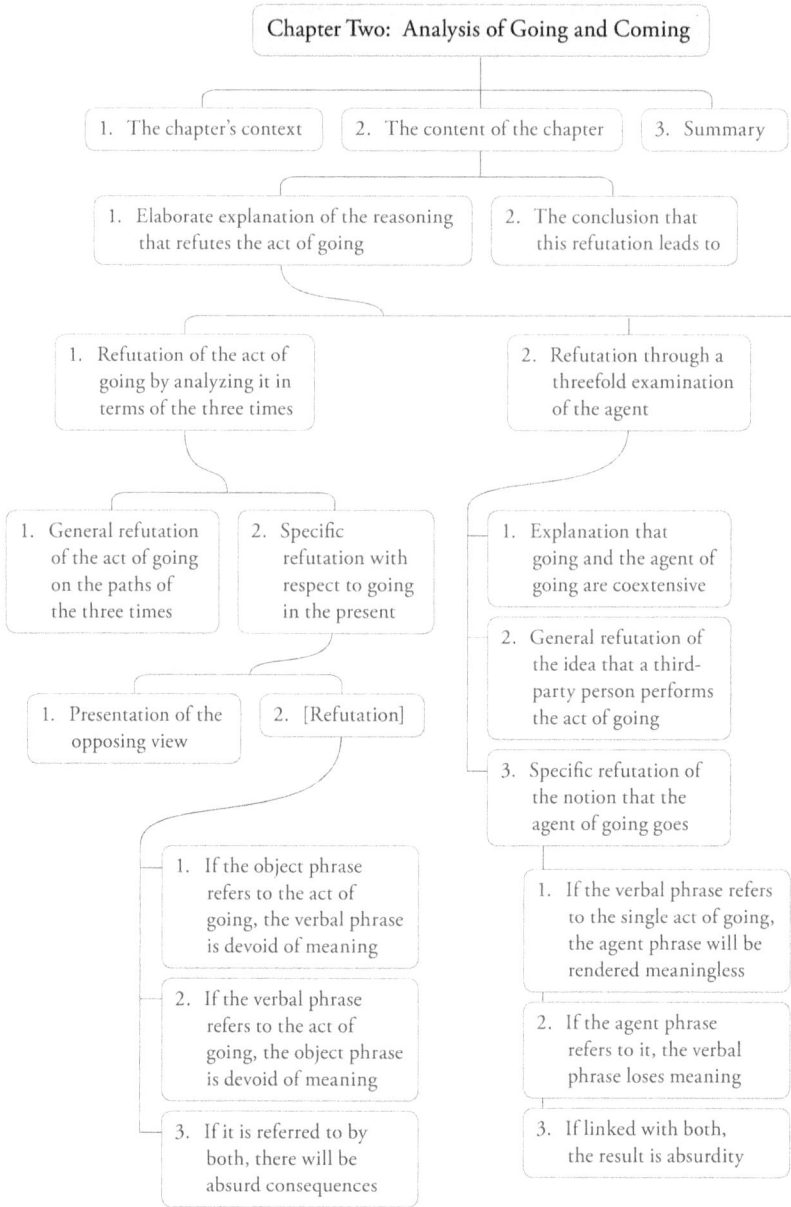

Chapter Two: Analysis of Going and Coming

1. The chapter's context

2. The content of the chapter

3. Summary

1. Elaborate explanation of the reasoning that refutes the act of going

2. The conclusion that this refutation leads to

1. Refutation of the act of going by analyzing it in terms of the three times

2. Refutation through a threefold examination of the agent

1. General refutation of the act of going on the paths of the three times

2. Specific refutation with respect to going in the present

1. Explanation that going and the agent of going are coextensive

2. General refutation of the idea that a third-party person performs the act of going

3. Specific refutation of the notion that the agent of going goes

1. Presentation of the opposing view

2. [Refutation]

1. If the object phrase refers to the act of going, the verbal phrase is devoid of meaning

2. If the verbal phrase refers to the act of going, the object phrase is devoid of meaning

3. If it is referred to by both, there will be absurd consequences

1. If the verbal phrase refers to the single act of going, the agent phrase will be rendered meaningless

2. If the agent phrase refers to it, the verbal phrase loses meaning

3. If linked with both, the result is absurdity

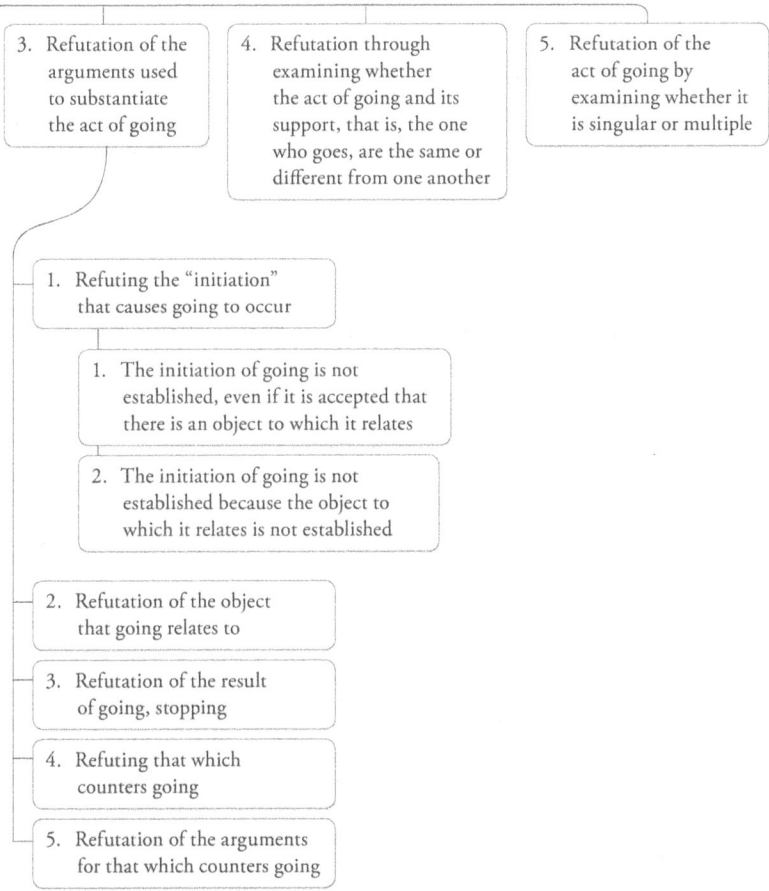

3. Refutation of the arguments used to substantiate the act of going

4. Refutation through examining whether the act of going and its support, that is, the one who goes, are the same or different from one another

5. Refutation of the act of going by examining whether it is singular or multiple

1. Refuting the "initiation" that causes going to occur

   1. The initiation of going is not established, even if it is accepted that there is an object to which it relates

   2. The initiation of going is not established because the object to which it relates is not established

2. Refutation of the object that going relates to

3. Refutation of the result of going, stopping

4. Refuting that which counters going

5. Refutation of the arguments for that which counters going

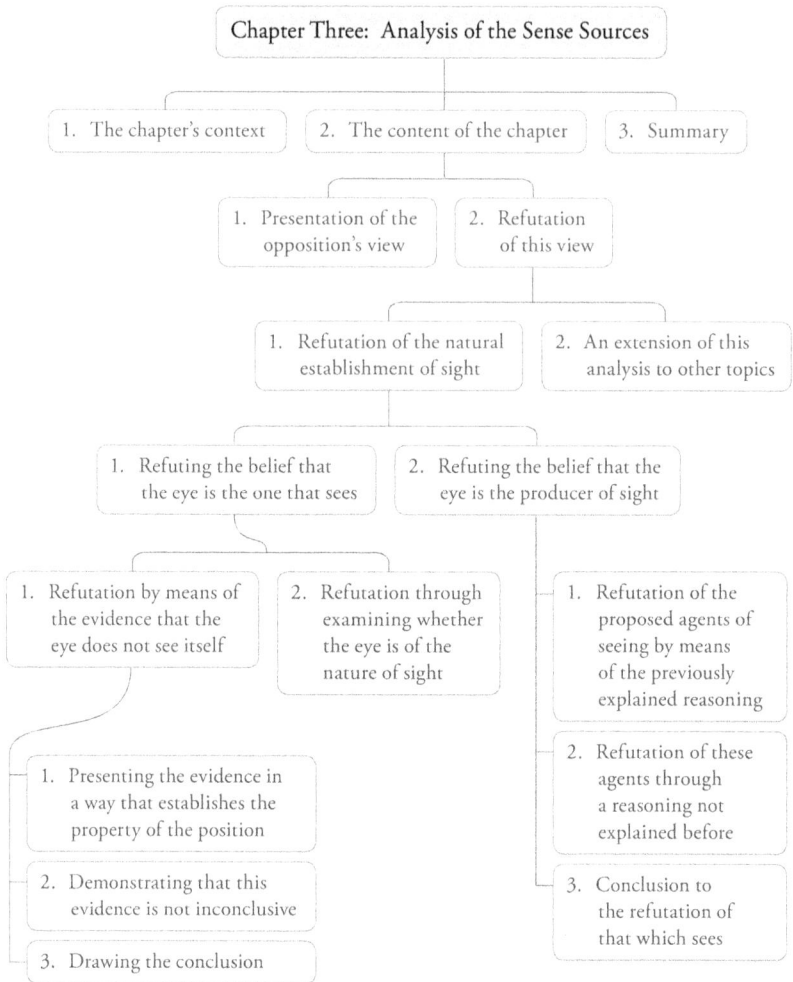

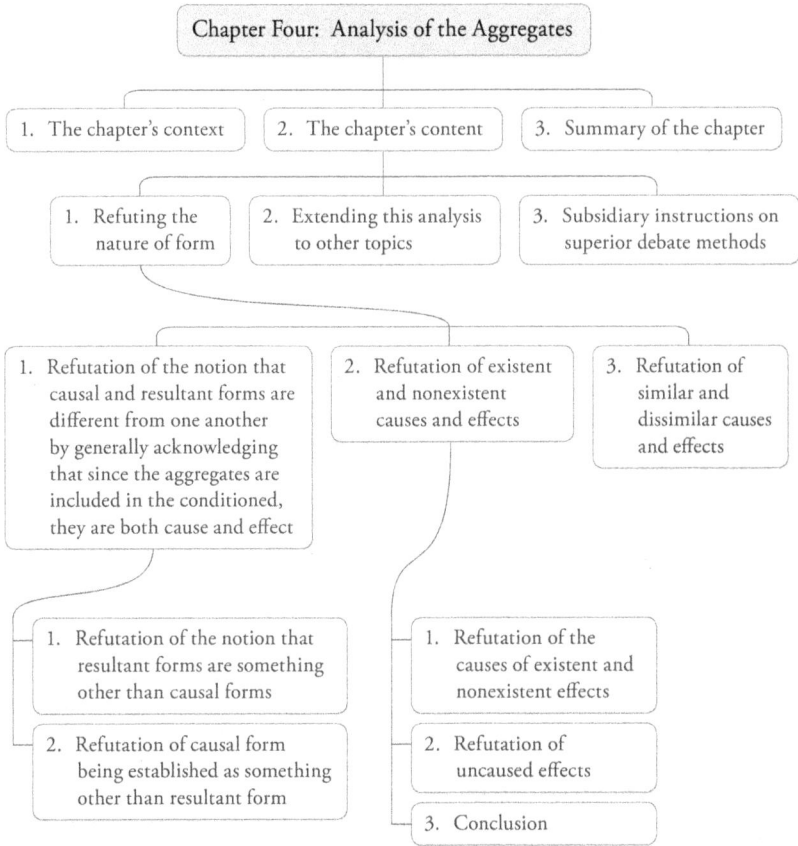

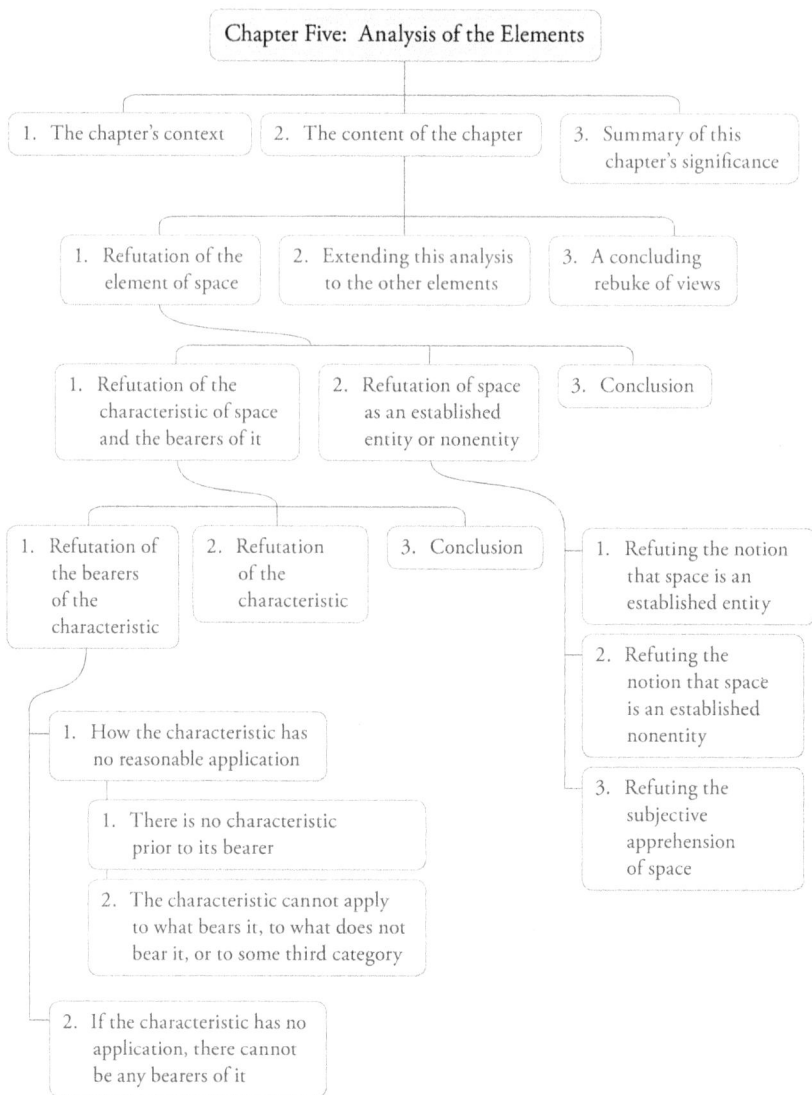

Chapter Six: Analysis of Desire and the Desirous One

1. The chapter's context

2. The content of the chapter

3. Summary[1]

1. Refutation of desire and the desirous one

2. Extension of this analysis to other topics

1. Refutation of the notion that desire and the desirous one occur in sequence

2. Refutation of the notion that they coexist

1. The consequence that these two will then lack mutual dependence

2. The untenability of identical and different things occurring in coexistence

1. General refutation of the coexistence of identical and different things

2. Specific refutation of the coexistence of different things

1. Desire and the desirous one are not established as different and are, therefore, not coexistent

2. If they were different, it would be meaningless to prove their natural existence by referring to coexistence

3. If their difference depends on their coexistence, difference and coexistence become mutually dependent

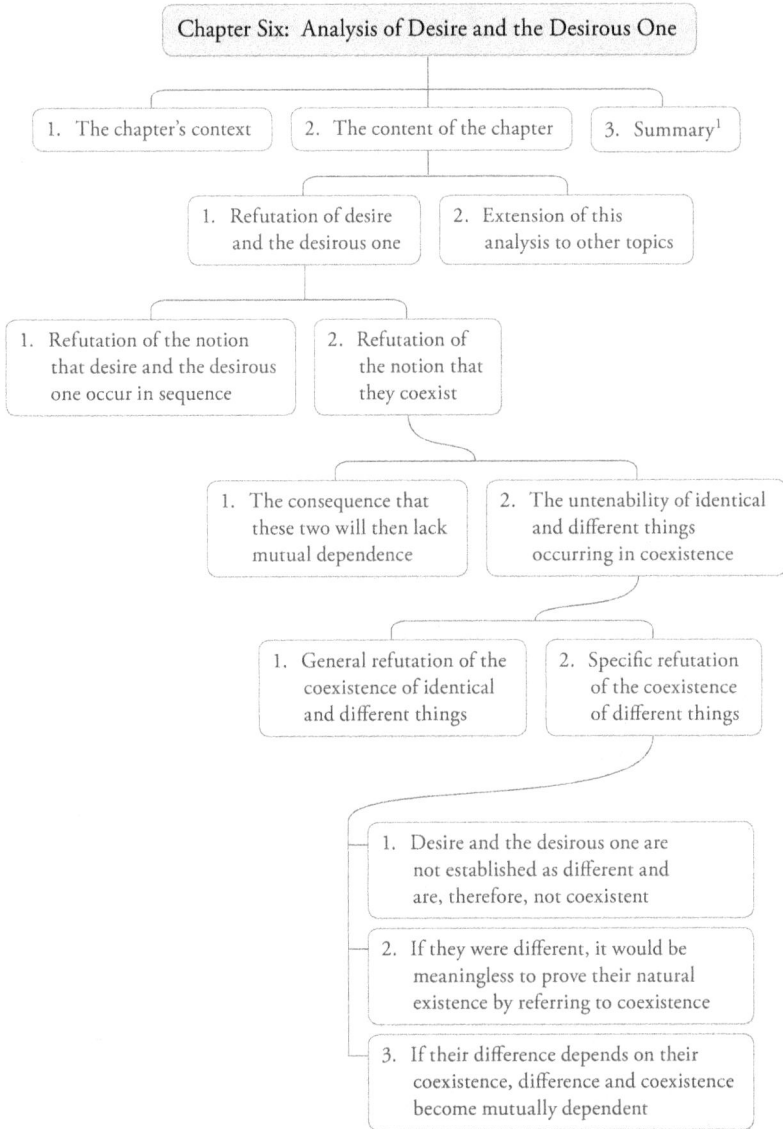

1. The precise location of this section is not obvious from the text (see p. 228 n. 117).

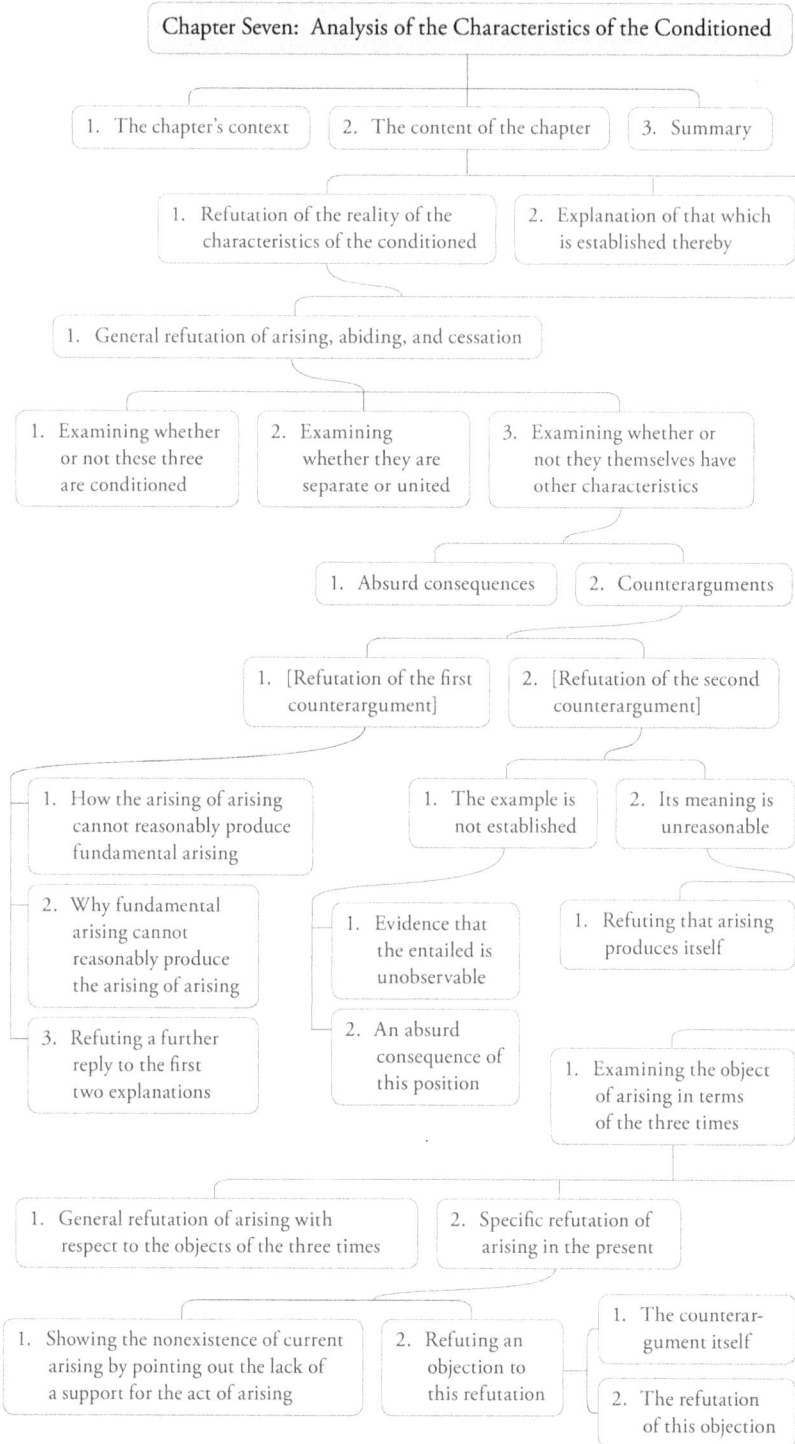

Chapter Seven: Analysis of the Characteristics of the Conditioned

1. The chapter's context

2. The content of the chapter

3. Summary

1. Refutation of the reality of the characteristics of the conditioned

2. Explanation of that which is established thereby

1. General refutation of arising, abiding, and cessation

1. Examining whether or not these three are conditioned

2. Examining whether they are separate or united

3. Examining whether or not they themselves have other characteristics

1. Absurd consequences

2. Counterarguments

1. [Refutation of the first counterargument]

2. [Refutation of the second counterargument]

1. How the arising of arising cannot reasonably produce fundamental arising

1. The example is not established

2. Its meaning is unreasonable

2. Why fundamental arising cannot reasonably produce the arising of arising

1. Evidence that the entailed is unobservable

1. Refuting that arising produces itself

3. Refuting a further reply to the first two explanations

2. An absurd consequence of this position

1. Examining the object of arising in terms of the three times

1. General refutation of arising with respect to the objects of the three times

2. Specific refutation of arising in the present

1. The counterargument itself

1. Showing the nonexistence of current arising by pointing out the lack of a support for the act of arising

2. Refuting an objection to this refutation

2. The refutation of this objection

3. Rejection of the criticism that this refutation contradicts scripture

2. Individual refutation of each

1. Refutation of arising

2. Refutation of abiding

3. Refutation of impermanence

1. Recalling what was previously explained

2. Reasoning that has not been explained before

2. Refuting that it produces something else

2. Examining whether arising itself has a further arising

3. Dispensing with the criticism that this is irreconcilable with dependent origination

1. Refutation of abiding with reference to the refutation of arising

2. Abiding in terms of the three times

3. Refutation by examining whether what abides is currently ceasing or not

4. Whether abiding itself has a further abiding

1. Refutation with reference to causal arising, which has already been refuted

2. Refutation by examining cessation in terms of the three times

3. Refutation by examining whether or not what ceases is currently abiding

4. Refutation that considers whether cessation is brought about by the initial state itself, or by some other state

5. Whether or not that which ceases is a thing

6. Whether or not cessation itself has a further cessation

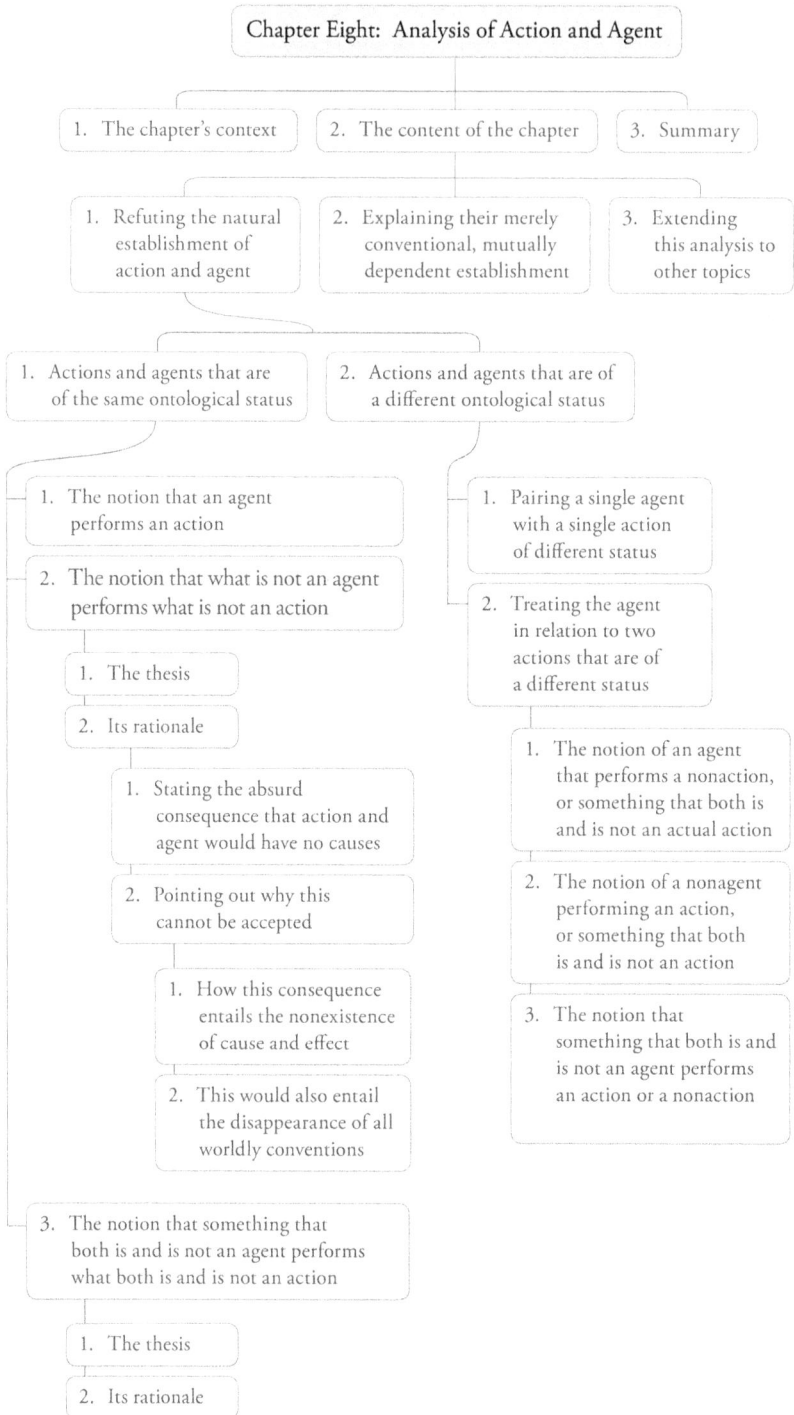

Chapter Eight: Analysis of Action and Agent

1. The chapter's context

2. The content of the chapter

3. Summary

1. Refuting the natural establishment of action and agent

2. Explaining their merely conventional, mutually dependent establishment

3. Extending this analysis to other topics

1. Actions and agents that are of the same ontological status

2. Actions and agents that are of a different ontological status

1. The notion that an agent performs an action

2. The notion that what is not an agent performs what is not an action

1. Pairing a single agent with a single action of different status

2. Treating the agent in relation to two actions that are of a different status

1. The thesis

2. Its rationale

1. Stating the absurd consequence that action and agent would have no causes

2. Pointing out why this cannot be accepted

1. The notion of an agent that performs a nonaction, or something that both is and is not an actual action

2. The notion of a nonagent performing an action, or something that both is and is not an action

1. How this consequence entails the nonexistence of cause and effect

2. This would also entail the disappearance of all worldly conventions

3. The notion that something that both is and is not an agent performs an action or a nonaction

3. The notion that something that both is and is not an agent performs what both is and is not an action

1. The thesis

2. Its rationale

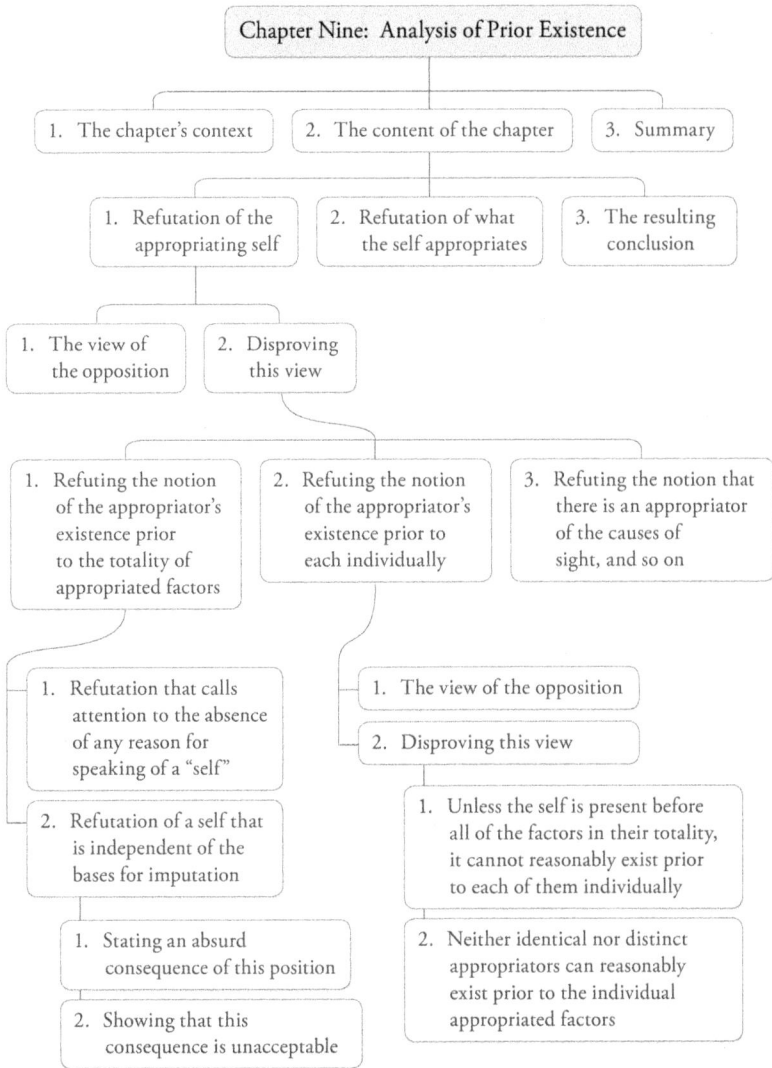

Chapter Ten: Analysis of Fire and Fuel

1. The chapter's context

2. The content of the chapter

3. Summary[2]

1. Refuting the notion that fire and fuel are established by nature

2. Extending this reasoning to other topics

3. A concluding rebuke of views

1. Refuting the essences of fire and fuel by examining whether they are the same or different

2. Refuting the arguments that are advanced to support these views

3. Summary of the meaning of these refutations

1. Refuting that fire and fuel are the same

2. Refuting that fire and fuel are different

1. Refutation of dependence

1. Why neither sequential nor simultaneous fire and fuel can be dependent

1. Fire would be independent of fuel

2. Why neither established nor unestablished fire and fuel can be dependent

1. Fire would be observable independent of fuel

3. Drawing the conclusion

2. Fire would be causeless, and so on

2. Refuting the use of perception as proof

3. Neither of these two consequences can be questioned

2. There would be no contact between the two

1. The consequences

2. How these consequences are unquestionable

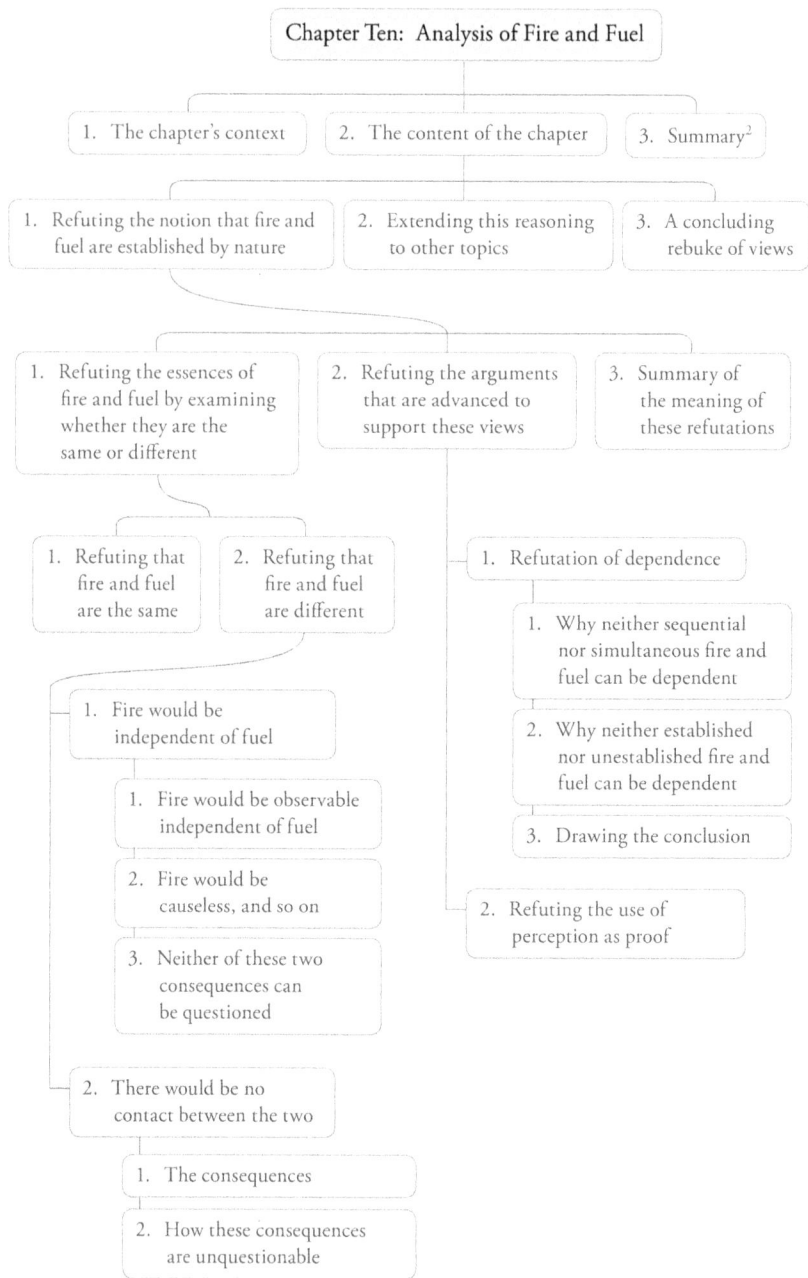

2. In this chapter the summary appears to be contained in the section on "Extending the Reasoning to Other Topics."

Chapter Eleven: Analysis of Beginnings and Ends

1. The chapter's context

2. The content of the chapter

3. Summary[3]

1. Refuting the natural existence of cyclic existence

2. Applying this refutation to other topics

1. Cyclic existence has no beginning, end, and middle

2. Birth, on the one hand, and aging and death, on the other, can be neither sequential nor simultaneous

1. Presentation

2. Explanation

3. Conclusion

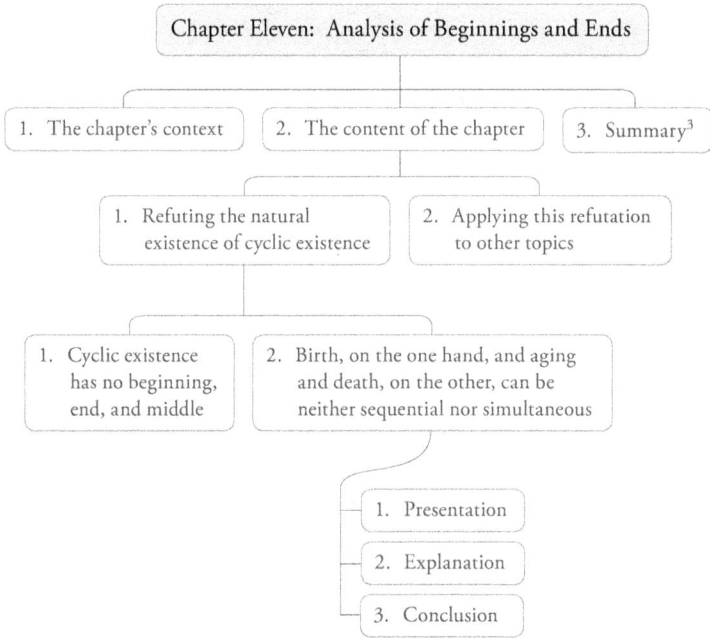

3. In this chapter there is no separate, final summary. Instead, the summary appears to be included in the explanation of stanza XI.6.

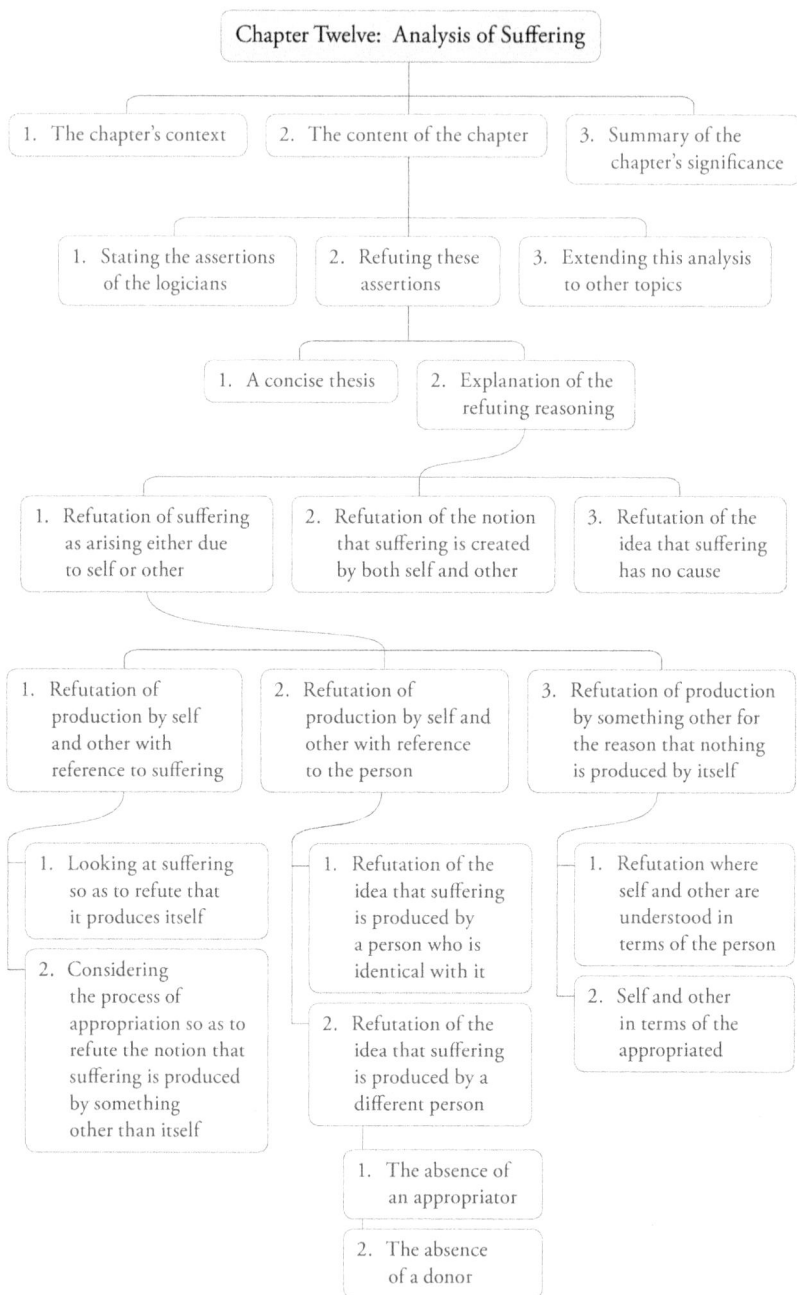

Chapter Twelve: Analysis of Suffering

1. The chapter's context

2. The content of the chapter

3. Summary of the chapter's significance

1. Stating the assertions of the logicians

2. Refuting these assertions

3. Extending this analysis to other topics

1. A concise thesis

2. Explanation of the refuting reasoning

1. Refutation of suffering as arising either due to self or other

2. Refutation of the notion that suffering is created by both self and other

3. Refutation of the idea that suffering has no cause

1. Refutation of production by self and other with reference to suffering

2. Refutation of production by self and other with reference to the person

3. Refutation of production by something other for the reason that nothing is produced by itself

1. Looking at suffering so as to refute that it produces itself

2. Considering the process of appropriation so as to refute the notion that suffering is produced by something other than itself

1. Refutation of the idea that suffering is produced by a person who is identical with it

2. Refutation of the idea that suffering is produced by a different person

1. Refutation where self and other are understood in terms of the person

2. Self and other in terms of the appropriated

1. The absence of an appropriator

2. The absence of a donor

Chapter Thirteen: Analysis of the Conditioned

1. The chapter's context

2. The content of the chapter

3. Summary[4]

1. Using scripture to establish that there is no nature

2. Refuting a different exegesis

1. Presenting the view of the opposition

2. Disproving the view of the opposition

1. Change cannot be used as an argument for the natural existence of mere phenomena

2. Emptiness is not established

1. Nature and change are contradictory

2. In reality, change as such has no establishment

1. Refuting the belief that emptiness can withstand analysis

2. Showing how this refutation does not contradict scripture

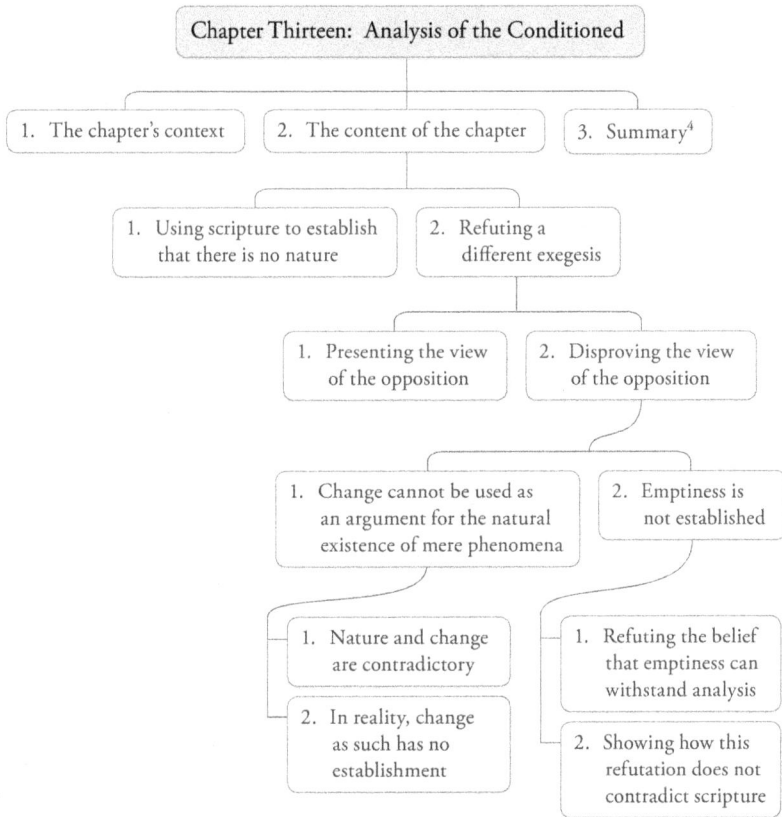

4. Note that in this chapter the concluding summary is not explicit as a separate section.

Chapter Fourteen: Analysis of Contact

1. The chapter's context

2. The content of the chapter

3. Summary[5]

1. Presentation of the thesis that there is no contact between conditioned phenomena

2. Explanation of the rationale for this thesis

3. Conclusion

1. The absence of contact due to lack of difference

2. The infeasibility of contact whether things are the same or distinct

1. Presentation of the evidence by demonstrating a reverse entailment

2. Application of the evidence to all phenomena

3. Establishment of the evidence

1. Things that are mutually dependent cannot reasonably be different

2. The universal "difference" has no establishment

3. Drawing the conclusion

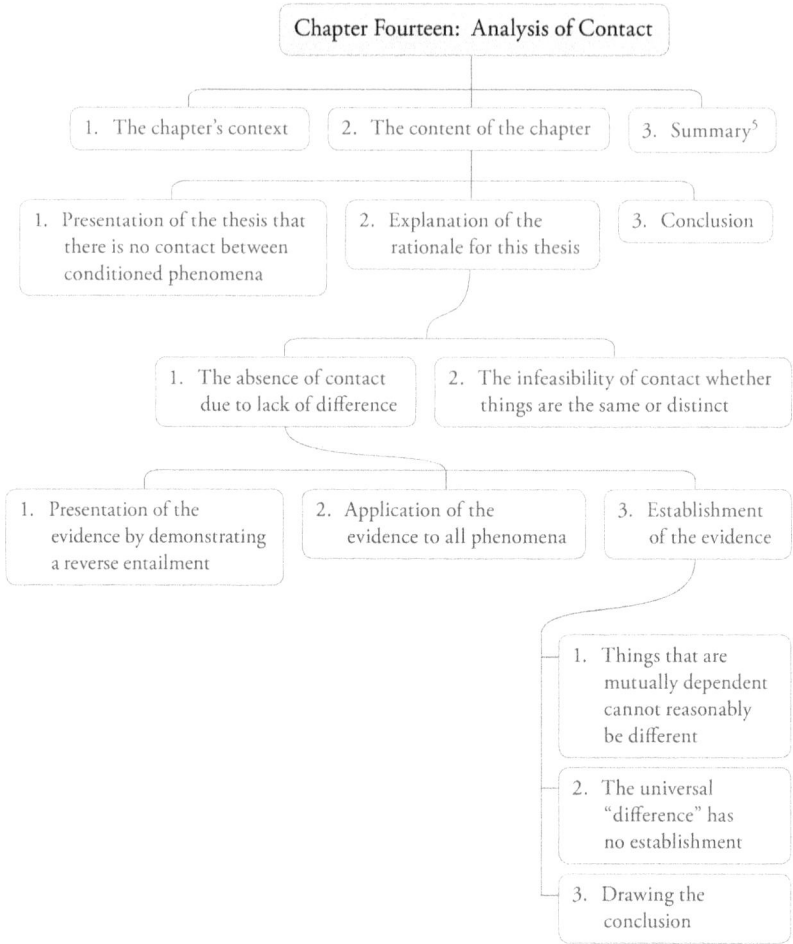

5. Note that in this chapter the concluding summary is not explicit as a separate section.

Chapter Fifteen: Analysis of Nature

1. The chapter's context | 2. The content of the chapter | 3. Summary[6]

1. Refutation of the mental constructs of the four extremes | 2. A concluding rebuke of views | 3. Instructions on applying one's mind to the Middle Way

1. Refutation of nature and other-nature | 2. Refutation of entity and nonentity

1. Refutation of nature | 2. Refutation of other-nature | 1. A refutation using reasoning | 2. Refutation by means of scripture of definitive meaning

1. Negating the notion that nature originates dependently | 2. Negating the notion that nature undergoes change | 1. Refutation of entity | 2. Refutation of nonentity

1. It is pointless for nature to arise due to causes and conditions | 2. Nature and arising due to causes and conditions are incompatible | 1. Presenting an absurd consequence | 2. Demonstrating its entailment | 3. Showing that the refutation of nature is indisputable

1. An absurd consequence | 2. Why the consequence cannot be accepted | 3. Our own approach in terms of the conventional

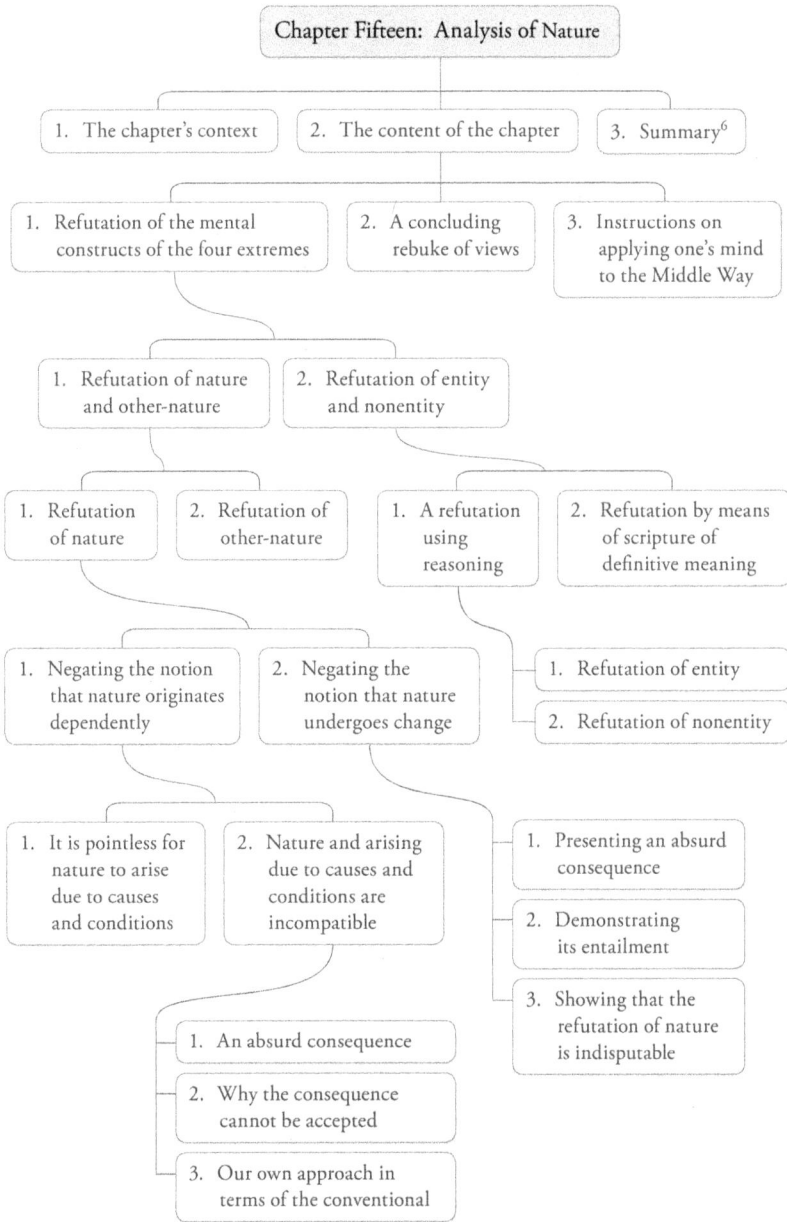

6. Note that in this chapter the concluding summary is not explicit as a separate section.

Chapter Sixteen: Analysis of Bondage and Liberation

1. The chapter's context

2. The content of the chapter

3. Summary[7]

1. Refutation of the nature of cyclic existence and transcendence

2. Refutation of bondage and liberation

3. Rebuttal of the criticism that such refutations render aspiring to the fruition and applying oneself to the causal path meaningless

1. Refutation of cyclic existence

2. Refutation of the transcendence of suffering

1. General refutation

2. Individual refutations

1. Refutation of the cycling of appropriated aggregates

2. Refutation of the cycling of an appropriating person

1. Refutation of bondage

2. Refutation of liberation

1. Refuting the cycling of a person that is independent of the aggregates and substantially existent

2. Refuting the cycling of a person who is dependent on the aggregates and whose existence is an imputation

1. Bondage cannot occur whether appropriation is present or absent

2. There is no bondage prior to that which is bound

3. The activity of binding is refuted through an examination of the three times

1. The one that cycles is itself not established

2. There is no appropriation

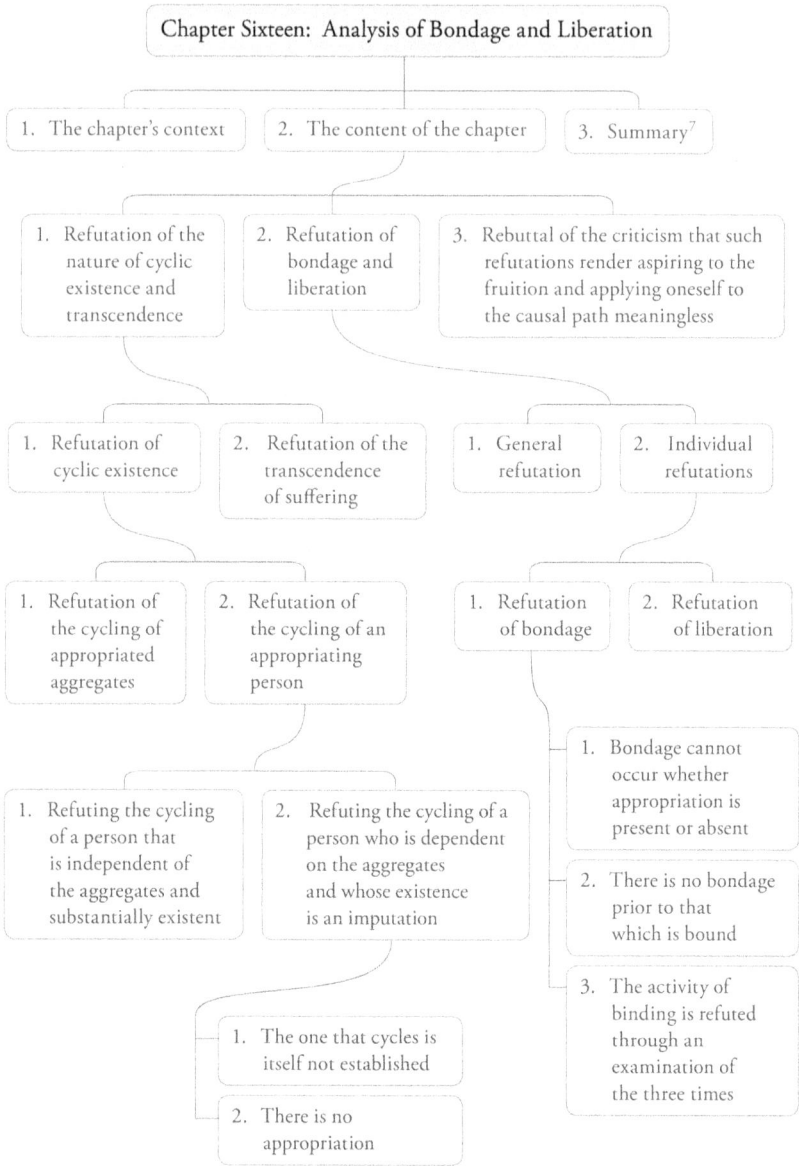

7. Note that in this chapter the concluding summary is not explicit as a separate section.

Chapter Seventeen: Analysis of Action and Its Results

1. The chapter's context

2. The content of the chapter

3. Summary[8]

1. Objections to this presentation

2. Replies to these objections

See next page 562

1. Setting forth the nature of action and its result

2. Showing that the presentations are not flawed by permanence and annihilation

1. The divisions of action

2. The effects of action

1. Stating the criticism

2. Presenting replies to this criticism

1. A concise classification

2. Elaborating on this classification

3. Further expanding this classification

1. Reply by appealing to a concordance between cause and effect

2. A refutation of that reply

3. Reply by asserting the substance of nondissipation

1. Presentation

2. Explanation

3. Conclusion

1. Presentation of the essence of nondissipation using an example

1. How causes produce their effects

2. How this does not imply either permanence or annihilation

2. The divisions of nondissipation

3. The nature of nondissipation

4. The classification of nondissipation as a discard

5. The rationale for the above classification

6. The qualities of nondissipation

7. The arising of nondissipation

1. Its arising in this life

2. The arising of nondissipation at the time of the linking between two lives

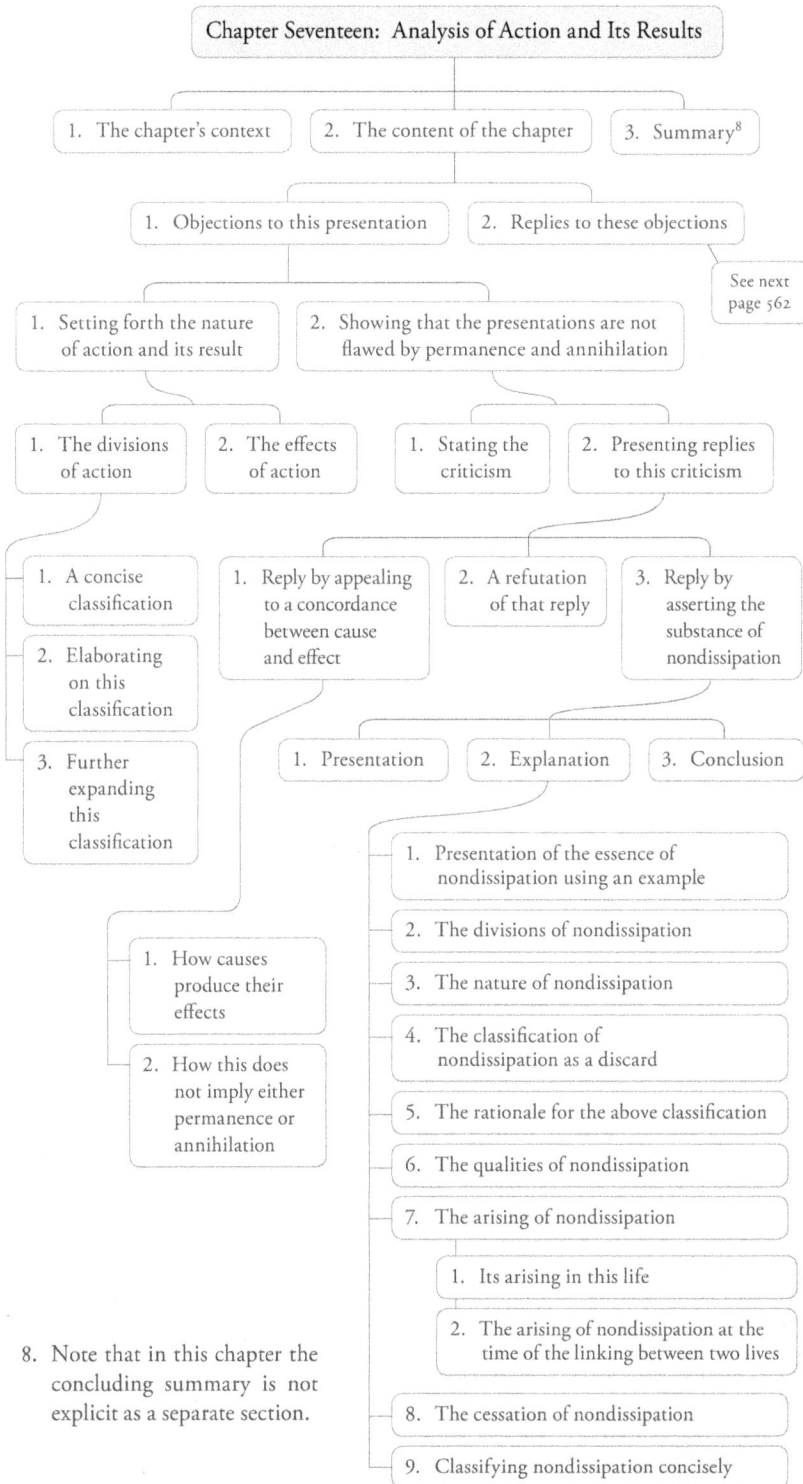

8. Note that in this chapter the concluding summary is not explicit as a separate section.

8. The cessation of nondissipation

9. Classifying nondissipation concisely

Continuation of Chapter Seventeen: Analysis of Action and Its Results ...

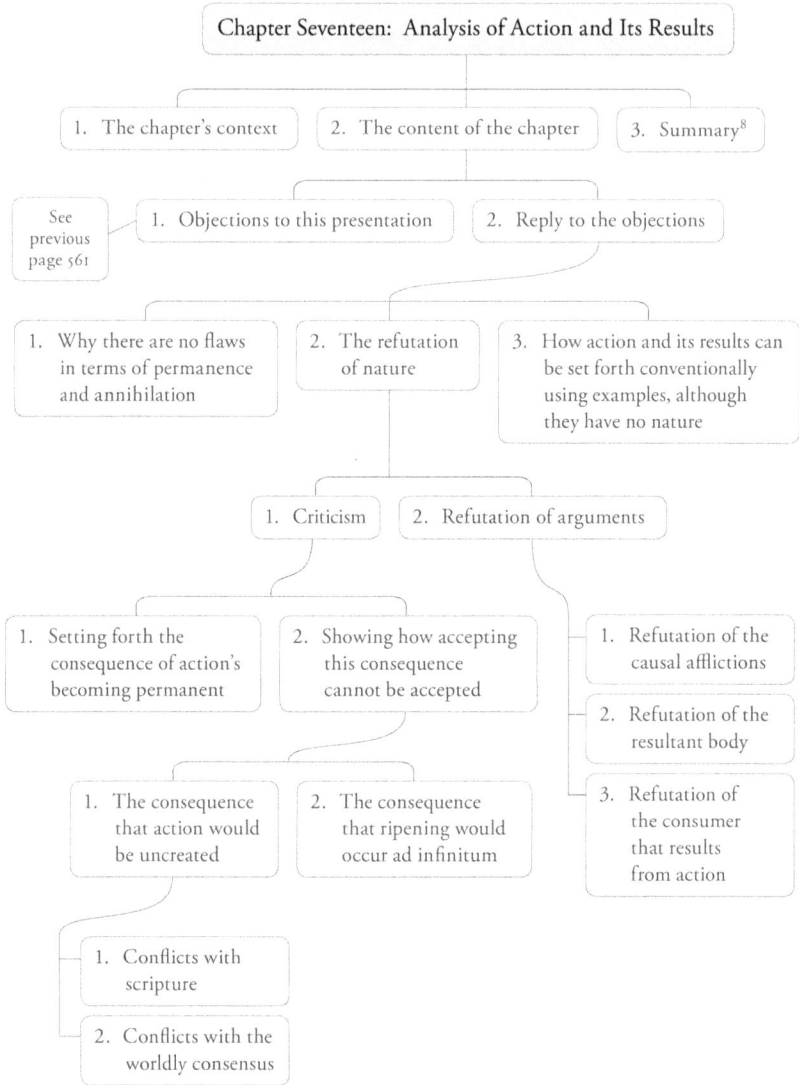

Chapter Seventeen: Analysis of Action and Its Results

1. The chapter's context

2. The content of the chapter

3. Summary[8]

See previous page 561

1. Objections to this presentation

2. Reply to the objections

1. Why there are no flaws in terms of permanence and annihilation

2. The refutation of nature

3. How action and its results can be set forth conventionally using examples, although they have no nature

1. Criticism

2. Refutation of arguments

1. Setting forth the consequence of action's becoming permanent

2. Showing how accepting this consequence cannot be accepted

1. Refutation of the causal afflictions

2. Refutation of the resultant body

3. Refutation of the consumer that results from action

1. The consequence that action would be uncreated

2. The consequence that ripening would occur ad infinitum

1. Conflicts with scripture

2. Conflicts with the worldly consensus

8. Note that in this chapter the concluding summary is not explicit as a separate section.

Chapter Eighteen: Analysis of Self and Phenomena

1. The chapter's context

2. The content of the chapter

3. Summary[9]

1. How to access reality

2. The nature of reality

3. The results of realization

1. Refuting the notions of "I" and "mine"

2. The effect of this refutation

2. Showing that this refutation does not contradict scripture

1. The ultimate

1. How the ultimate cannot be taught in terms of an essence of its own

2. How the ultimate is taught by means of superimposition

3. The characteristics of that teaching

2. The relative

1. Refutation of the appropriating self by showing that it is neither identical to, nor different from, the appropriated aggregates

2. Explaining how the appropriated aggregates that belong to the self are refuted thereby

1. How subjective grasping is renounced

2. Dispensing with objections to this refutation

3. How the cessation of grasping brings about liberation

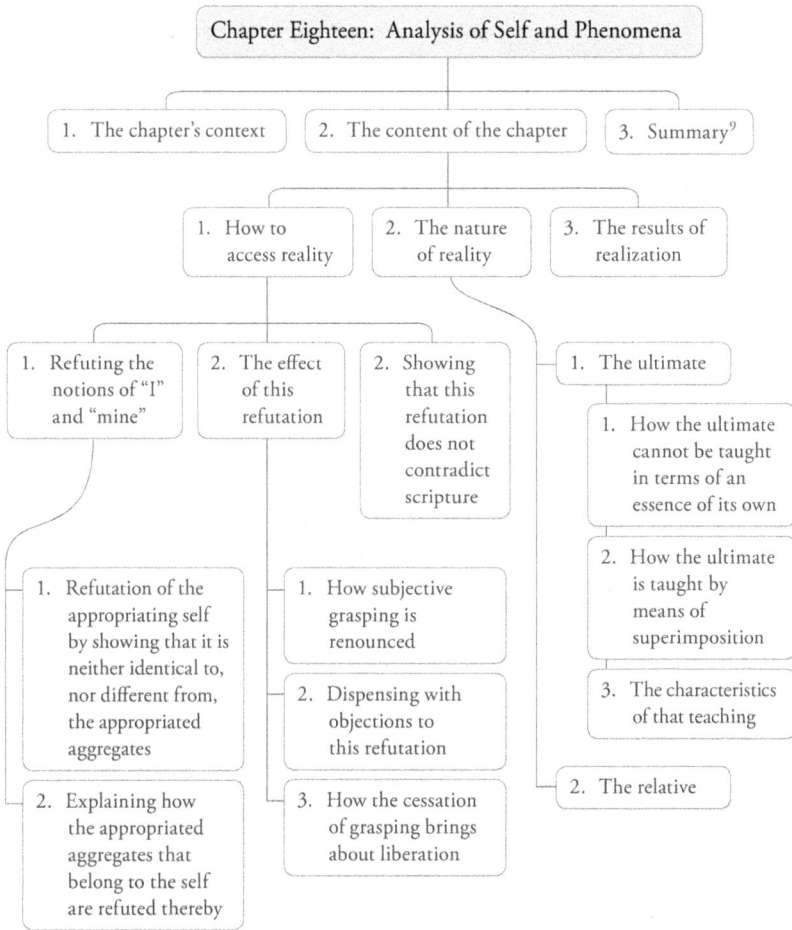

9. Note that in this chapter the concluding summary is not explicit as a separate section.

```
                  ┌─────────────────────────────────────┐
                  │  Chapter Nineteen:  Analysis of Time  │
                  └─────────────────────────────────────┘
        ┌──────────────────────┬──────────────────────────┐
┌─────────────────────┐ ┌──────────────────────────┐ ┌─────────────────┐
│ 1. The chapter's     │ │ 2. The content of the     │ │ 3. Summary[10]  │
│    context           │ │    chapter                │ │                 │
└─────────────────────┘ └──────────────────────────┘ └─────────────────┘
                              ┌──────────────┴──────────────┐
              ┌───────────────────────────────┐ ┌───────────────────────────────┐
              │ 1. Showing the natural existence│ │ 2. Refuting the arguments for  │
              │    of time to be flawed         │ │    time's natural existence    │
              └───────────────────────────────┘ └───────────────────────────────┘
          ┌───────────────────────────────┐     ┌───────────────────────────────┐
          │ 1. Refutation of present       │     │ 1. Refuting time with          │
          │    and future time             │     │    reference to extent         │
          └───────────────────────────────┘     └───────────────────────────────┘
              ┌───────────────────────────┐      ┌───────────────────────────────┐
              │ 1. Refuting dependence     │      │ 2. Refuting time with          │
              │    on the past             │      │    reference to entities       │
              └───────────────────────────┘      └───────────────────────────────┘
              ┌───────────────────────────┐
              │ 2. Refuting the absence    │
              │    of such dependence      │
              └───────────────────────────┘
              ┌───────────────────────────┐
              │ 3. Drawing a conclusion    │
              └───────────────────────────┘
          ┌───────────────────────────────┐
          │ 2. Extending the refutation    │
          │    to other topics             │
          └───────────────────────────────┘
```

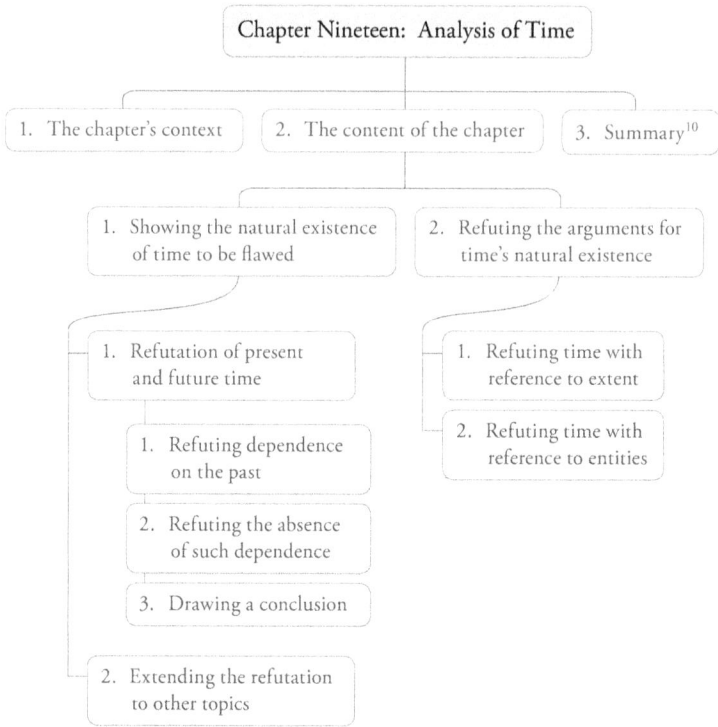

10. In this chapter, the concluding summary appears to be included in the explanation
    of stanza 4.

```
┌─────────────────────────────────────────────┐
│  Chapter Twenty: Analysis of the Assembly     │
└─────────────────────────────────────────────┘
```

| 1. The chapter's context | 2. The content of the chapter | 3. Summary[11] |

| 1. Refutation of the notion that production occurs due to an assembly of causes and conditions | 2. Refutation of the belief that production occurs due to a cause | 2. Conclusion to the refutations |

1. Refutation of arising effects by considering the effect

 1. Effects that arise based on assemblies that precede their effects

 2. Effects that arise based on assemblies that are simultaneous with them

 3. Effects that arise based on assemblies that are subsequent to them

2. Refutation of arising effects by considering the cause

1. Whether or not it is supplied to the effect, a cause cannot produce anything

2. Refuting the notion that effects are produced by causes that are not different from them

3. Causes can produce neither effects that have arisen, nor those that have not

4. Causes cannot produce effects that are seen or unseen

5. Regardless of whether or not the two come into contact, causes cannot produce effects

6. Causes cannot produce anything, whether they are empty or not empty of their effects

7. Whether or not they themselves are empty, effects cannot arise

8. Effects are produced neither by causes that are identical to them, nor by those that are different

9. Neither existent nor nonexistent results are produced

10. Conclusion regarding causality's proven lack of nature

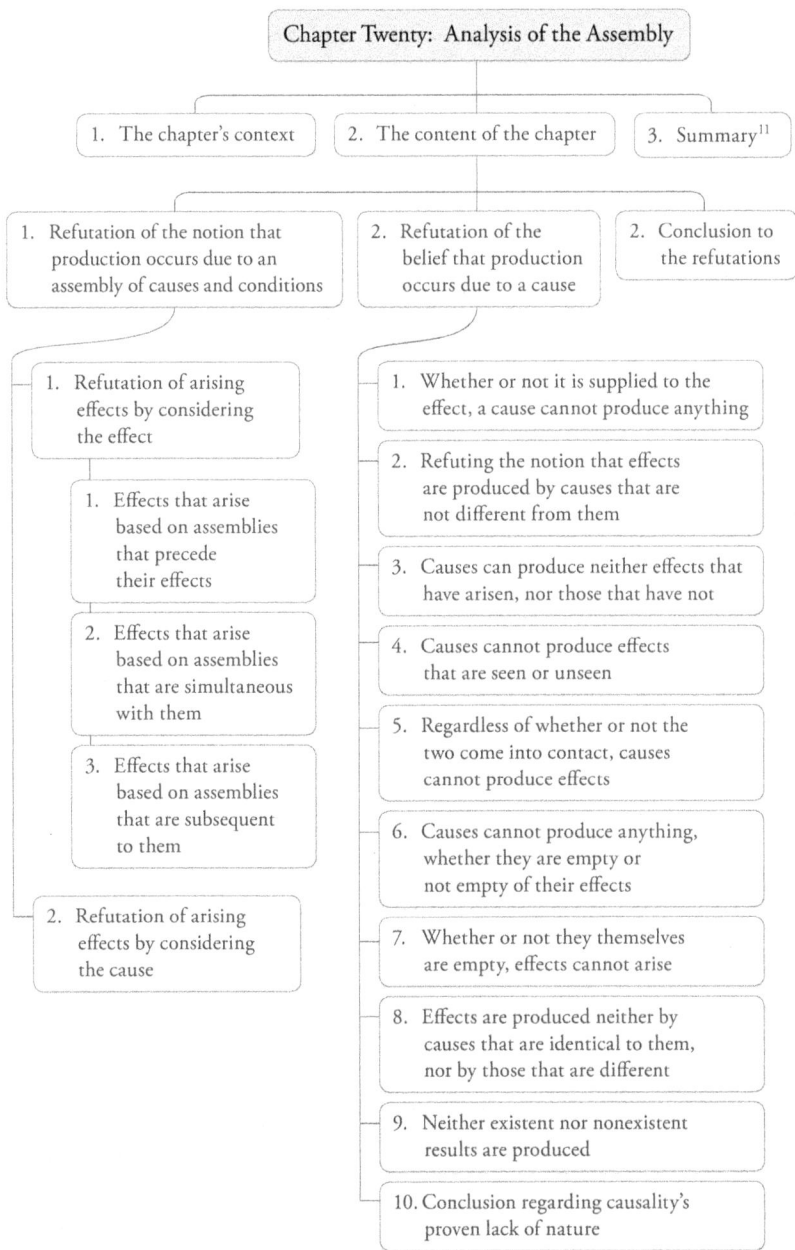

11. Note that in this chapter the concluding summary appears to be identical with the "Conclusion to the refutations" above.

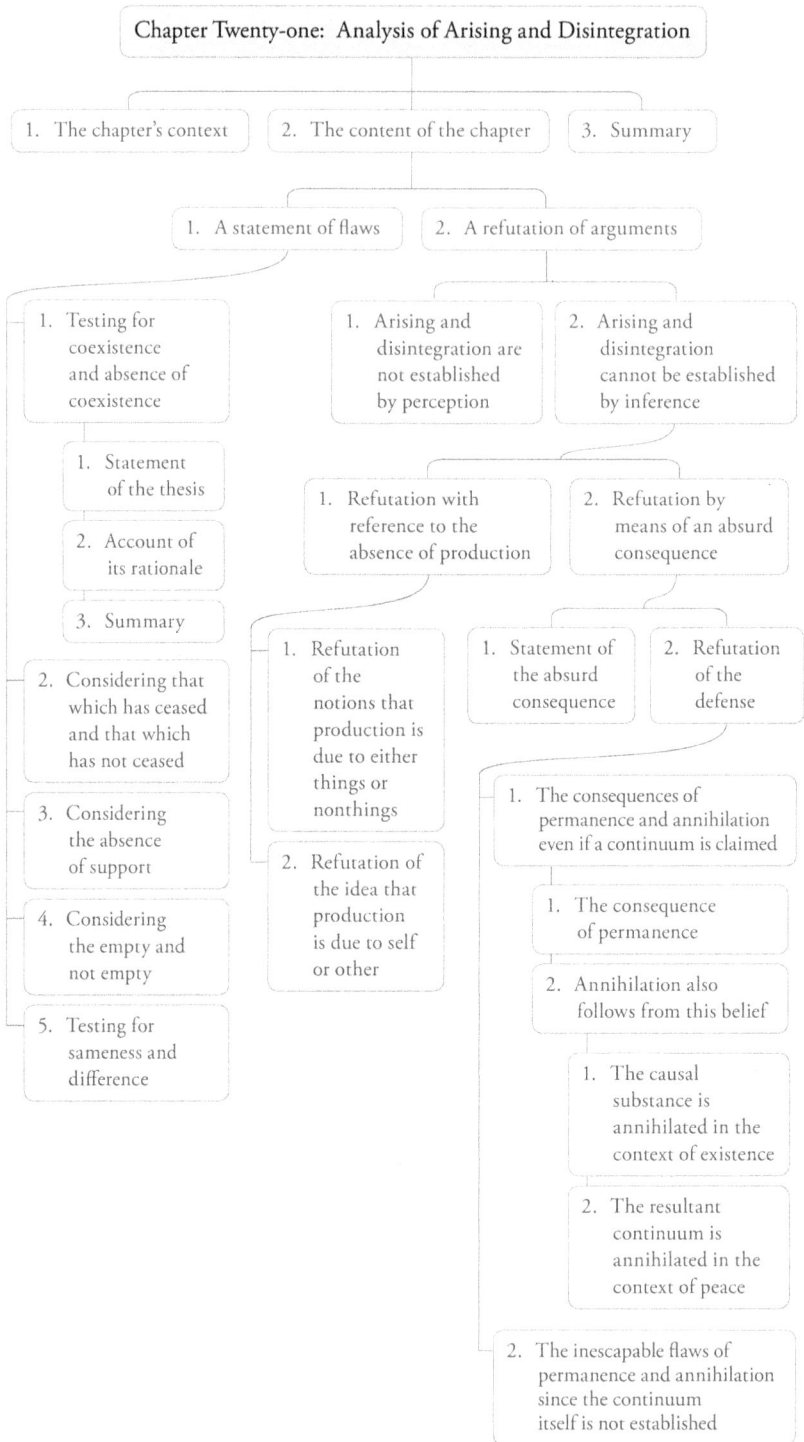

Chapter Twenty-one: Analysis of Arising and Disintegration

1. The chapter's context

2. The content of the chapter

3. Summary

1. A statement of flaws

2. A refutation of arguments

1. Testing for coexistence and absence of coexistence

1. Arising and disintegration are not established by perception

2. Arising and disintegration cannot be established by inference

1. Statement of the thesis

2. Account of its rationale

3. Summary

1. Refutation with reference to the absence of production

2. Refutation by means of an absurd consequence

2. Considering that which has ceased and that which has not ceased

1. Refutation of the notions that production is due to either things or nonthings

1. Statement of the absurd consequence

2. Refutation of the defense

3. Considering the absence of support

4. Considering the empty and not empty

2. Refutation of the idea that production is due to self or other

1. The consequences of permanence and annihilation even if a continuum is claimed

1. The consequence of permanence

2. Annihilation also follows from this belief

5. Testing for sameness and difference

1. The causal substance is annihilated in the context of existence

2. The resultant continuum is annihilated in the context of peace

2. The inescapable flaws of permanence and annihilation since the continuum itself is not established

Chapter Twenty-two: Analysis of the Thus-Gone

1. The chapter's context

2. The content of the chapter

3. Summary[12]

1. Refuting the notion that the Thus-Gone is established by nature

2. Establishing that he is, therefore, beyond all beliefs

3. Extending this analysis to other topics

1. Showing that the appropriating person who is the Thus-gone lacks establishment

2. Showing that the aggregates that are appropriated by him lack establishment

3. Drawing a conclusion

1. The reality of the Thus-Gone is beyond all mental and verbal constructs

2. It is a flaw to apprehend it as confined to such constructs

1. Refuting the substantial existence of the person by pointing out that the person does not exist in relation to the appropriated in any of the five ways

2. Refuting the nominal existence of the person by pointing out that the person does not exist in relation to the appropriated in any of the five ways

1. There is no basis for this designation

2. He cannot be established as either a self-entity or as an entity that is of another nature

3. There is no appropriation

1. Presentation

2. Explanation

1. Refuting the notion of self-entity

2. Refuting the belief in an entity that is established as the nature of other

2. Conclusion

1. Prior to the appropriated, the appropriator does not exist

2. There could be no appropriation by an appropriator who has no prior existence

3. Without an appropriation, there cannot be something appropriated

4. There is no appropriator without appropriation

12. Note that in this chapter the concluding summary is not explicit as a separate section.

Chapter Twenty-three: Analysis of Error

1. The chapter's context

2. The content of the chapter

3. Summary[13]

1. Refutation of affliction itself

2. Refutation of its proof, the pursuit of the method that eliminates affliction

1. General refutation of the three poisonous afflictions

2. Individual refutations of these three

1. Dependent origination

2. Absence of support

3. Lack of cause

4. Nonobservation

1. General presentation

2. Proof through reasoning

1. Refutation of the self being the support

2. Refutation of the notion that the mind is the support

1. How a support in the form of the afflicted mind cannot be established since it does not relate to the afflictions in any of the five ways

2. How, as an aside, the afflictions are not established either since they do not relate to the afflicted in any of the five ways

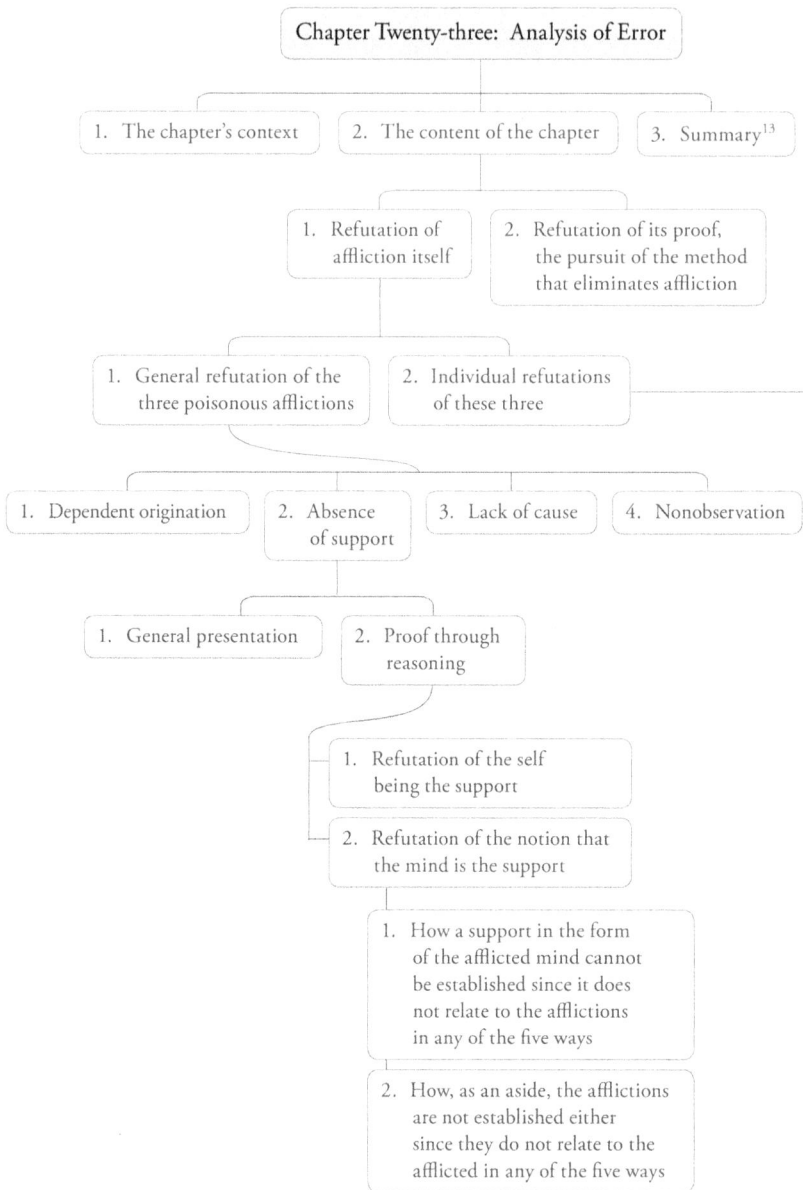

13. Note that in this chapter the concluding summary is not explicit as a separate section.

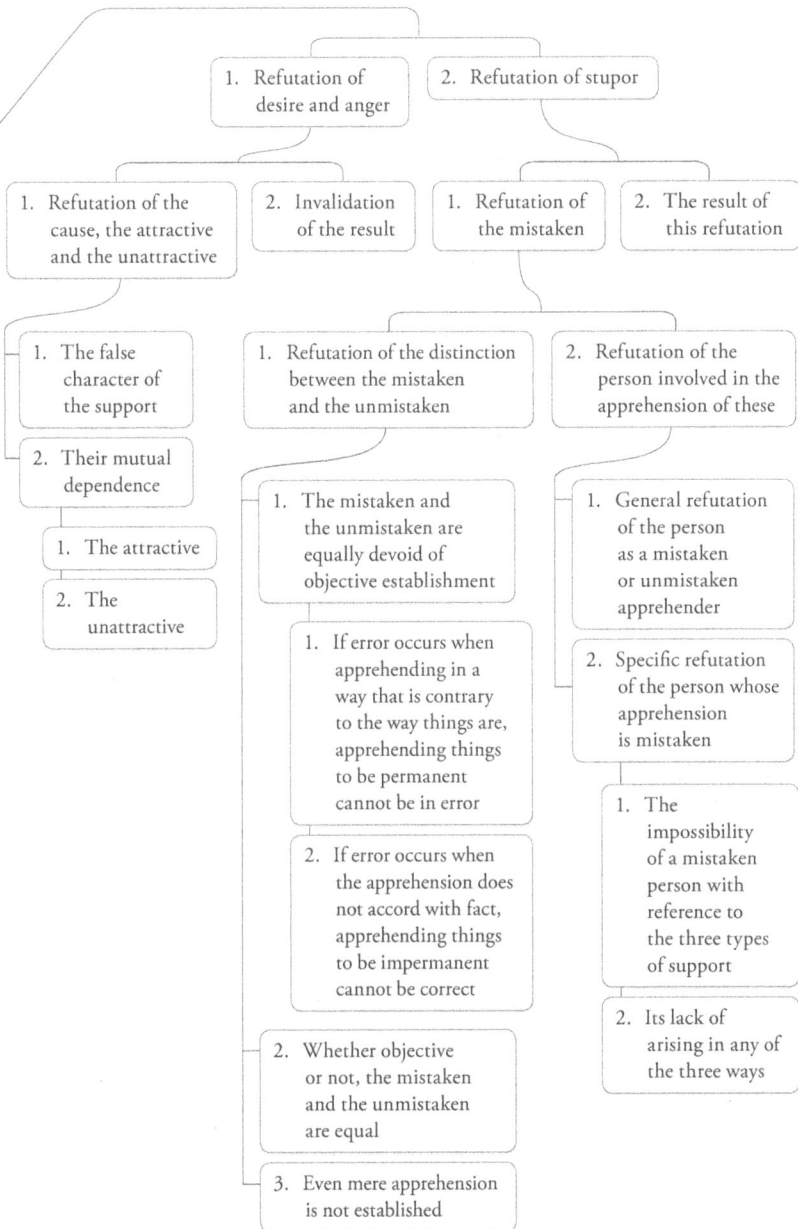

1. Refutation of desire and anger

2. Refutation of stupor

1. Refutation of the cause, the attractive and the unattractive

2. Invalidation of the result

1. Refutation of the mistaken

2. The result of this refutation

1. The false character of the support

2. Their mutual dependence

1. The attractive

2. The unattractive

1. Refutation of the distinction between the mistaken and the unmistaken

2. Refutation of the person involved in the apprehension of these

1. The mistaken and the unmistaken are equally devoid of objective establishment

1. General refutation of the person as a mistaken or unmistaken apprehender

2. Specific refutation of the person whose apprehension is mistaken

1. If error occurs when apprehending in a way that is contrary to the way things are, apprehending things to be permanent cannot be in error

2. If error occurs when the apprehension does not accord with fact, apprehending things to be impermanent cannot be correct

1. The impossibility of a mistaken person with reference to the three types of support

2. Its lack of arising in any of the three ways

2. Whether objective or not, the mistaken and the unmistaken are equal

3. Even mere apprehension is not established

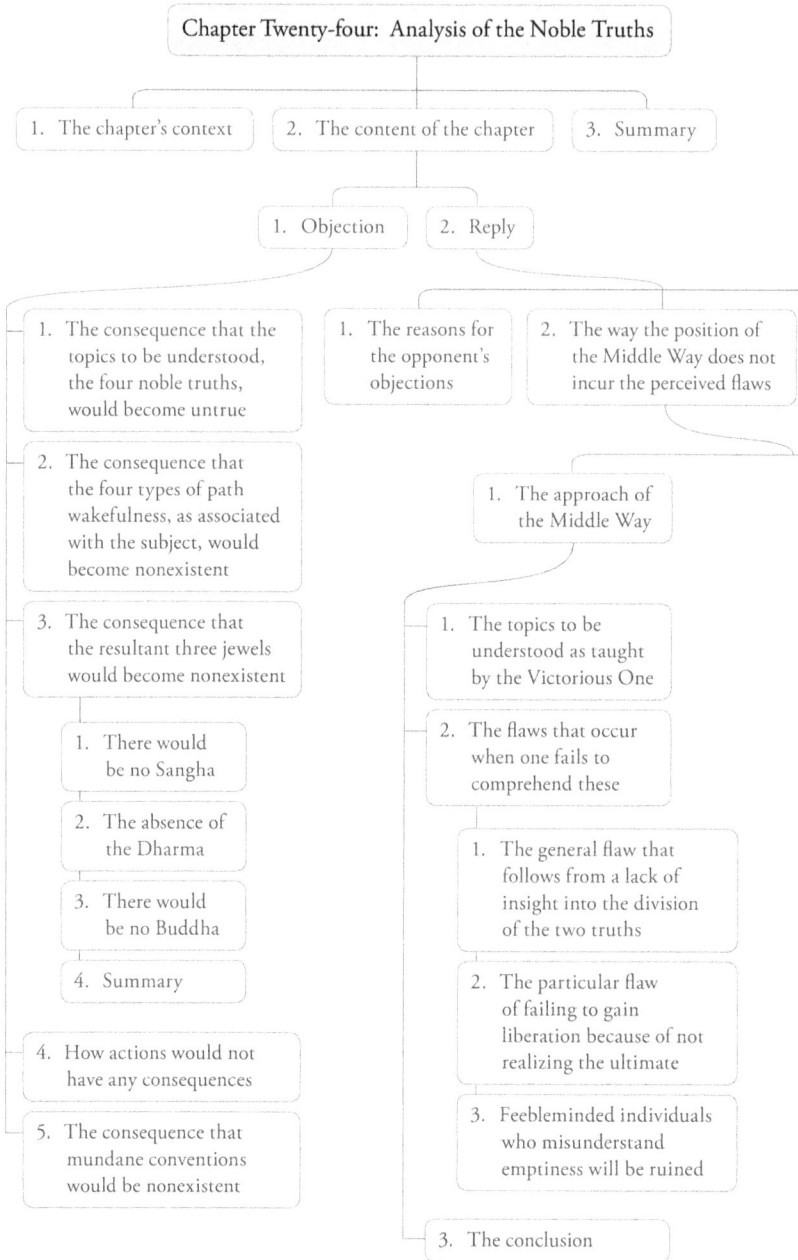

Chapter Twenty-four: Analysis of the Noble Truths

1. The chapter's context

2. The content of the chapter

3. Summary

1. Objection

2. Reply

1. The consequence that the topics to be understood, the four noble truths, would become untrue

2. The consequence that the four types of path wakefulness, as associated with the subject, would become nonexistent

3. The consequence that the resultant three jewels would become nonexistent

1. There would be no Sangha

2. The absence of the Dharma

3. There would be no Buddha

4. Summary

4. How actions would not have any consequences

5. The consequence that mundane conventions would be nonexistent

1. The reasons for the opponent's objections

2. The way the position of the Middle Way does not incur the perceived flaws

1. The approach of the Middle Way

1. The topics to be understood as taught by the Victorious One

2. The flaws that occur when one fails to comprehend these

1. The general flaw that follows from a lack of insight into the division of the two truths

2. The particular flaw of failing to gain liberation because of not realizing the ultimate

3. Feebleminded individuals who misunderstand emptiness will be ruined

3. The conclusion

3. The supremacy of
   Middle Way realization

2. How it is free
   from flaws

3. Why denying the Middle
   Way would be a mistake

1. The basis for the
   flaws is not accepted

2. The bases for flaws
   and benefits

3. How the criticism
   is, therefore,
   unreasonable

1. The consequence that causality
   becomes nonexistent

2. The topics to be understood
   would become untrue

3. There would be no
   subject of the path

4. How the resultant three
   jewels would be nonexistent

5. How it would not make sense
   for actions to have consequences

6. How neither mundane nor
   transcendent conventions
   would make any sense

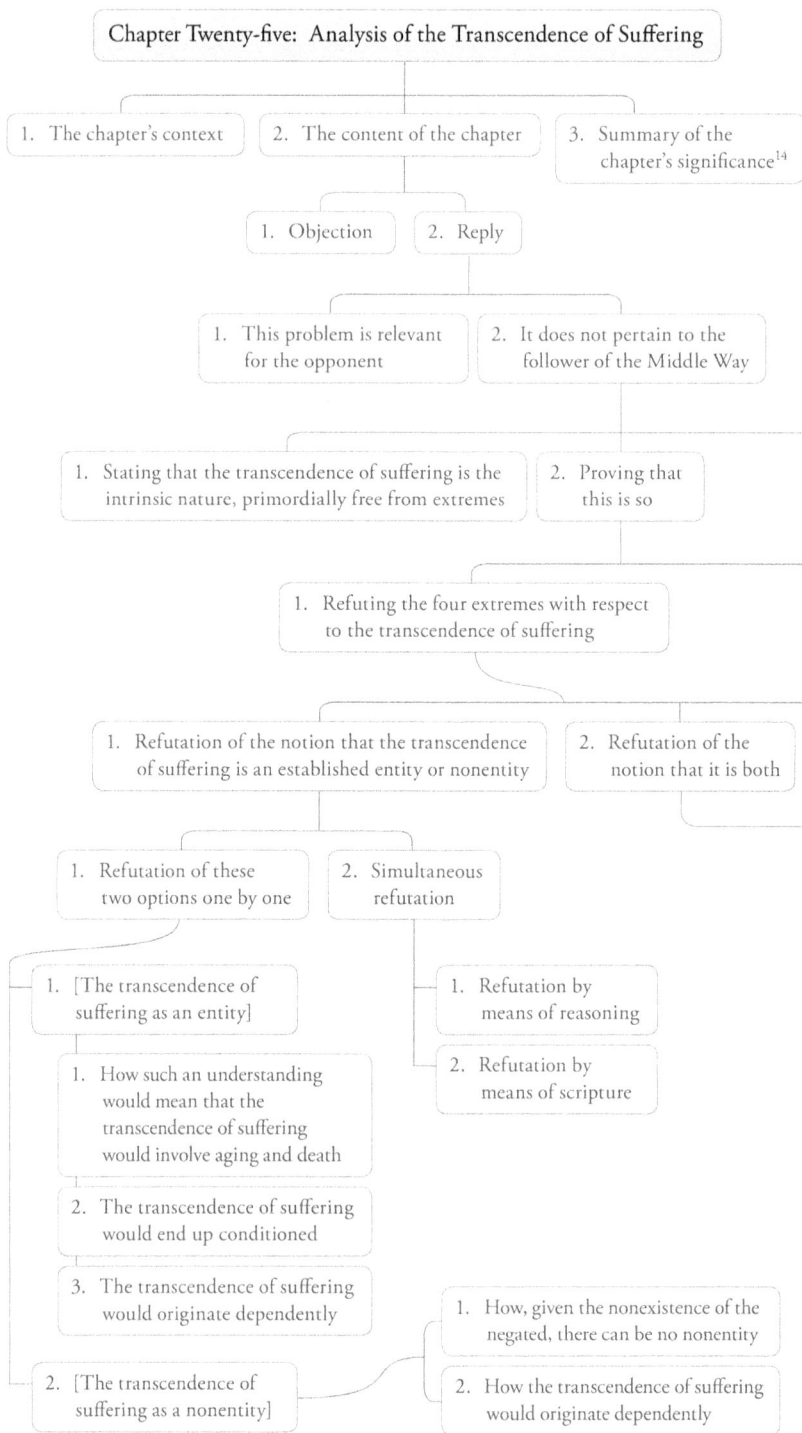

Chapter Twenty-five: Analysis of the Transcendence of Suffering

1. The chapter's context

2. The content of the chapter

3. Summary of the chapter's significance[14]

1. Objection

2. Reply

1. This problem is relevant for the opponent

2. It does not pertain to the follower of the Middle Way

1. Stating that the transcendence of suffering is the intrinsic nature, primordially free from extremes

2. Proving that this is so

1. Refuting the four extremes with respect to the transcendence of suffering

1. Refutation of the notion that the transcendence of suffering is an established entity or nonentity

2. Refutation of the notion that it is both

1. Refutation of these two options one by one

2. Simultaneous refutation

1. [The transcendence of suffering as an entity]

1. Refutation by means of reasoning

2. Refutation by means of scripture

1. How such an understanding would mean that the transcendence of suffering would involve aging and death

2. The transcendence of suffering would end up conditioned

3. The transcendence of suffering would originate dependently

1. How, given the nonexistence of the negated, there can be no nonentity

2. How the transcendence of suffering would originate dependently

2. [The transcendence of suffering as a nonentity]

3. Deflecting the objection that it would then be meaningless to teach the Dharma

2. Showing that a Buddha who has realized this is not established in the manner of the four extremes

3. The ensuing conclusion

3. Refutation of the notion it is neither of these two

1. The lack of establishment at the time of transcendence

1. Establishing that there is no difference between existence and peace

2. The lack of establishment at the time of abidance

2. Refuting the indeterminate views

1. A demonstration of the absurdity of this position

1. An identification of these views

2. How the transcendence of suffering would turn out to be dependently originated

1. Presenting the criticism

2. Showing these indeterminate views to be untenable

2. Refuting the arguments

3. Refuting that the transcendence of suffering is both entity and nonentity by referring to its being unconditioned

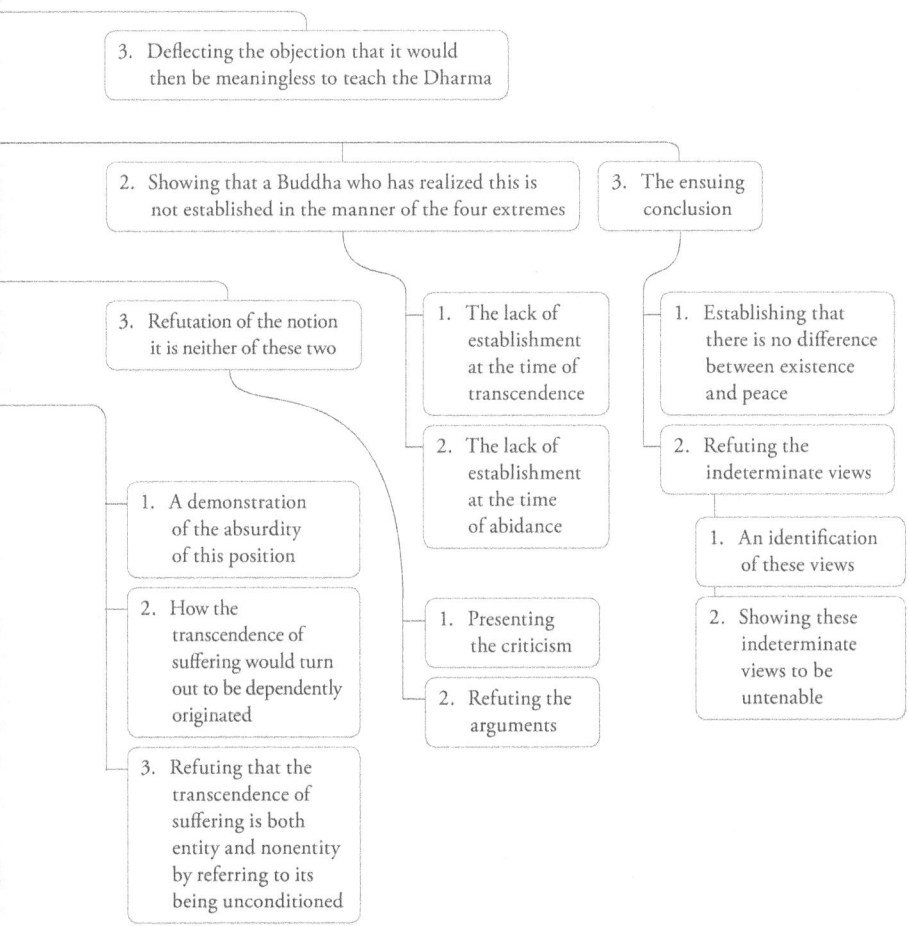

14. In this chapter, the concluding summary is included in the explanation of stanza 24.

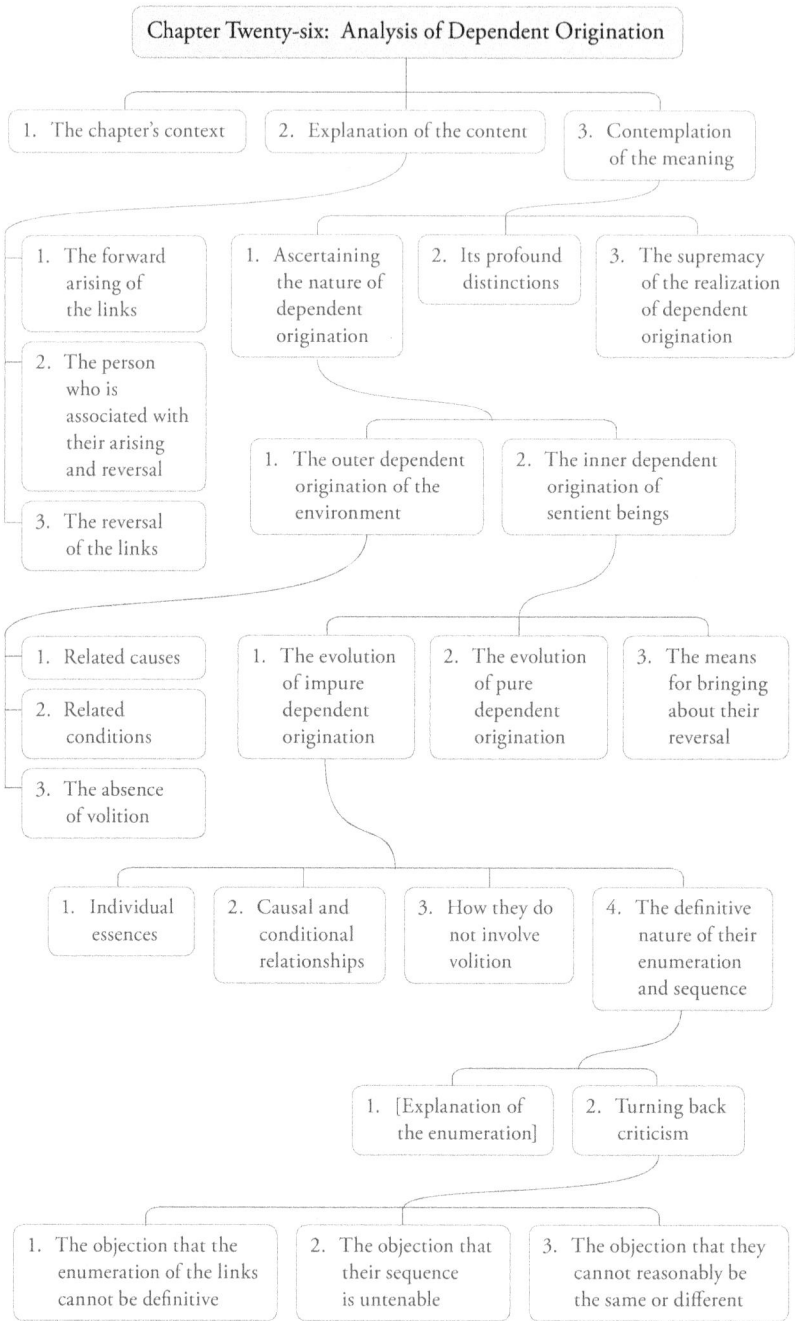

Chapter Twenty-six: Analysis of Dependent Origination

1. The chapter's context

2. Explanation of the content

3. Contemplation of the meaning

1. The forward arising of the links

2. The person who is associated with their arising and reversal

3. The reversal of the links

1. Ascertaining the nature of dependent origination

2. Its profound distinctions

3. The supremacy of the realization of dependent origination

1. The outer dependent origination of the environment

2. The inner dependent origination of sentient beings

1. Related causes

2. Related conditions

3. The absence of volition

1. The evolution of impure dependent origination

2. The evolution of pure dependent origination

3. The means for bringing about their reversal

1. Individual essences

2. Causal and conditional relationships

3. How they do not involve volition

4. The definitive nature of their enumeration and sequence

1. [Explanation of the enumeration]

2. Turning back criticism

1. The objection that the enumeration of the links cannot be definitive

2. The objection that their sequence is untenable

3. The objection that they cannot reasonably be the same or different

Chapter Twenty-seven: Analysis of Views

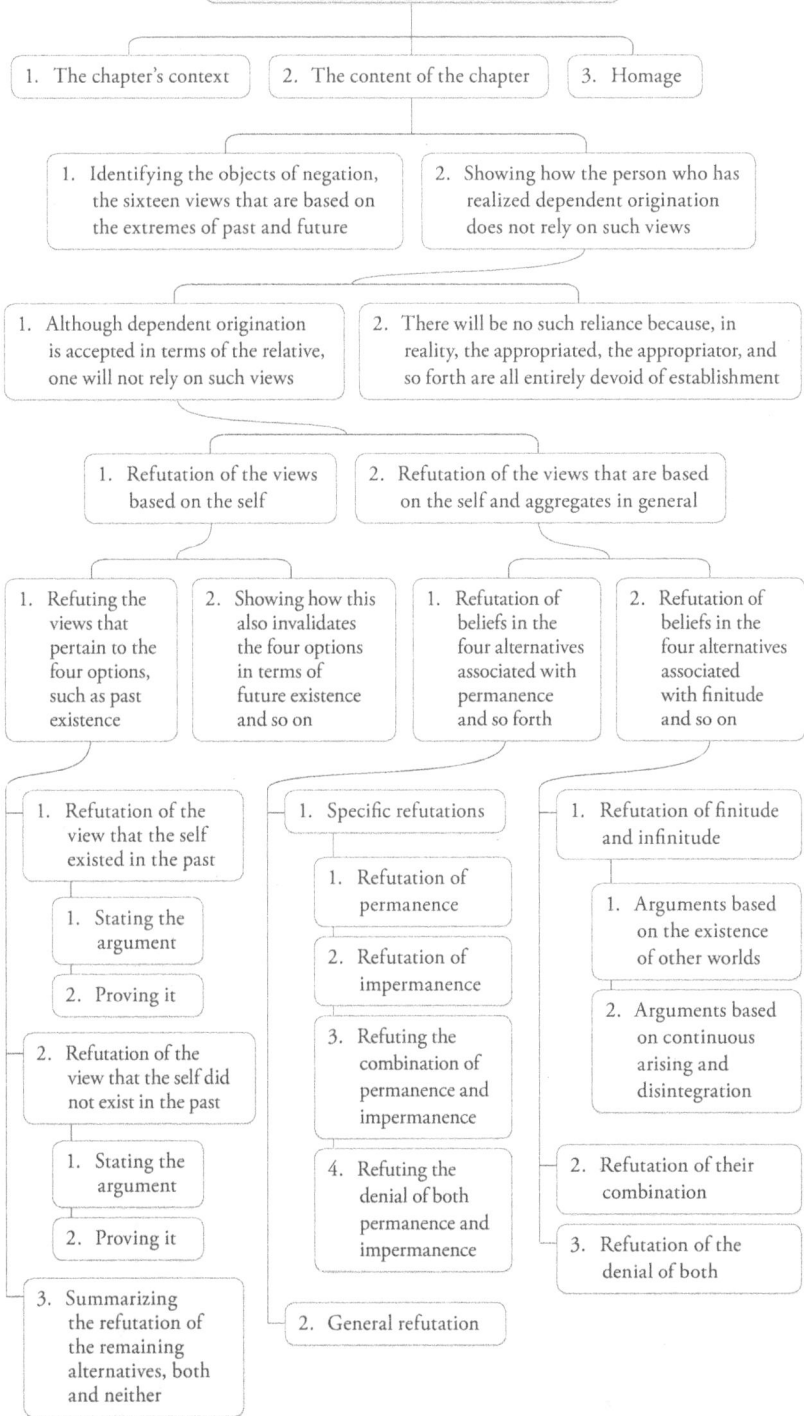

1. The chapter's context

2. The content of the chapter

3. Homage

1. Identifying the objects of negation, the sixteen views that are based on the extremes of past and future

2. Showing how the person who has realized dependent origination does not rely on such views

1. Although dependent origination is accepted in terms of the relative, one will not rely on such views

2. There will be no such reliance because, in reality, the appropriated, the appropriator, and so forth are all entirely devoid of establishment

1. Refutation of the views based on the self

2. Refutation of the views that are based on the self and aggregates in general

1. Refuting the views that pertain to the four options, such as past existence

2. Showing how this also invalidates the four options in terms of future existence and so on

1. Refutation of beliefs in the four alternatives associated with permanence and so forth

2. Refutation of beliefs in the four alternatives associated with finitude and so on

1. Refutation of the view that the self existed in the past
  1. Stating the argument
  2. Proving it

2. Refutation of the view that the self did not exist in the past
  1. Stating the argument
  2. Proving it

3. Summarizing the refutation of the remaining alternatives, both and neither

1. Specific refutations
  1. Refutation of permanence
  2. Refutation of impermanence
  3. Refuting the combination of permanence and impermanence
  4. Refuting the denial of both permanence and impermanence

2. General refutation

1. Refutation of finitude and infinitude
  1. Arguments based on the existence of other worlds
  2. Arguments based on continuous arising and disintegration

2. Refutation of their combination

3. Refutation of the denial of both

Works Cited

Canonical Scripture

Guhyasamāja Root Tantra (Sarvatathāgatakāyavākacittarahasya-guhya-samāja-nāma-mahākalparāja). D 442.[222]

Instructions to Kātāyana (Kātāyanasūtra), contained in the *Minor Precepts of the Vinaya.*

Jewel Cloud (Ratnamegha). D 231.

Jewel Mound (Ratnakūṭa). D 45–93.

Journey to Laṅkā (Laṅkāvatāra). D 107.

Lion's Roar of Śrī Mālā (Śrīmālādevīsiṃhanāda-sūtra). D 92.

Minor Precepts of the Vinaya (Vinayakṣudrakavastu). D 6.

Mother of the Victorious Ones (The extensive, the intermediate, and the concise Prajñāpāramitā sūtras). D. 8, 9, and 12.

Ornament of Wisdom Light (Sarvabuddhaviṣayāvatārajñānālokālaṃkāra) D 100.

Root Tantra of Mañjusrī (Mañjuśrī-mūlatantra). D 543.

Śālu Sprout, The (Śālistambha-sūtra). D 210.

Sūtra of Instruction to the Listeners (Mañjuśrīvikrīḍita-sūtra; Mañjuśrī-vikurvaṇaparivarta-sūtra). D 97.

Sūtra of the Elephant's Strength (Hastikakṣya-sūtra). D 207.

Sūtra of the Great Cloud in Twelve Thousand Stanzas (Mahāmegha-sūtra). D 232.

Sūtra of the Great Display (Lalitavistara-sūtra). D 95.

Sūtra of the Great Drum (Mahābherīhārakaparivarta-sūtra). D 222.

Sūtra of the King of Meditative Absorptions (Sarvadharmasvabhāvasamatā vipañcita-samādhirāja-sūtra). D 127.

Sūtra of the Meeting of Father and Son (Pitāputrasamāgama-sūtra). D 60.

Sūtra of the Source of Jewels (Ratnākara-sūtra). D 124.

---

222. Enumeration according to *sDe dge* edition of the Tibetan *Tripiṭaka.*

Sūtra on the Discernment of Dependent Origination (Pratītyasamutpādādi vibhaṅganirdeśa-sūtra). D 211.

Sūtra on the Secret of the Thus-Gone (Tathāgatācintyaguhyanirdeśa-sūtra). D 47.

Sūtra on the Taming of the Demons (Māradamana-sūtra). D 97.

Sūtra on the Ten Grounds (Daśabhūmika-sūtra). D 44.

Sūtra on Transference of Existence (Bhavasaṃkrānti-sūtra). D 226.

Sūtra Requested by Anavatapta, King of the Nāgas (Anavataptanāgarāja-paripṛcchā-sūtra). D 156.

Sūtra Requested by Sāgaramati (Sāgaramatiparipṛcchā-sūtra). D 152.

Sūtra Requested by the Son of the Gods, Susthitamati. (Susthitamatideva-putraparipṛcchā-sūtra). D 80.

Sūtra Requested by Upāli (Upāliparipṛcchā-sūtra). D 68.

Sūtra Taught by Akṣayamati (Akṣayamatinirdeśa-sūtra). D 175.

Sūtra That Shows the Nonarising of All Phenomena (Sarvadharmāpravṛtti-nirdeśa-sūtra). D 180.

Vajra Cutter, The (Vajracchedikā-sūtra). D 16.

Verses of the Dharma (Dhammapada). In Radhakrishnan 1996.

Indian Treatises

Āryadeva. *Four Hundred Stanzas (Catuḥśatakaśāstra)*. D 3846.

Asaṅga. *Grounds of the Bodhisattvas (Bodhisattvabhūmi)*. D 4037.

_____. *Grounds of Yogic Practice (Yogācārabhūmi)*. D 4035–42

Candrakīrti. *Clear Words (Mūlamadhyamakavṛtti-prasannapadā)*. D 3860.

_____. *Entering the Middle Way (Madhyamakāvatāra)*. D 3861.

_____. *Exposition of Entering the Middle Way (Madhyamakāvatāra-bhāṣya)*. D 3862.

_____. *Commentary on the Sixty Stanzas of Reasoning, The (Yuktiṣaṣṭikā-vṛtti)*. D 3864.

Dharmakīrti. *Commentary on Reliable Means of Cognition (Pramāṇa-vārttika)*. D 4210.

Dīpaṅkaraśrījñāna. *Accessing the Two Truths (Satyadvayāvatāra)*. D 3902.

Jayānanda. *Logic Hammer (Tarkamudgara)*. D 3870.

Jñānagarbha. *Commentary on Discerning the Two Truths (Satyadvaya-vibhaṅgakārikā-vṛtti)*. D 3882.

_____. *Discerning the Two Truths (Satyadvayavibhaṅga-kārikā)*. D 3881.

Kātyāyanīpūtra. *Entry into Wakefulness (Jñānaprasthāna)*. Taishō Shinshū Daizōkyō 1543 and 1545.

Maitreya. *Distinguishing the Middle from Extremes (Madhyāntavibhāga)*. D 4021.

_____. *Distinguishing Phenomena from Their Intrinsic Nature (Dharma-dharmatāvibhāga)*. D 4022.

_____. *Ornament of Manifest Realization (Abhisamayālaṁkāra)*. D 3786.

_____. *Ornament of the Sūtras of the Great Vehicle (Mahāyānasūtrālaṁkāra)*. D 4020.

_____. *Supreme Continuity (Mahāyānottaratantra-śāstra, Ratnagotra-vibhāga)*. D 4024.

Nāgārjuna. *Accumulations of Enlightenment (*Bodhisambhāra)*. Extant in Chinese translation: Taisho 1660.

_____. *Commentary on the Enlightened Mind (Bodhicittavivaraṇa)*. D 1801.

_____. *Compendium on the Sūtras (Sūtrasamuccaya)*. D 3934.

_____. *Detailed Examination (Vaidalyasūtra)*. D 3826.

_____. *Establishing Conventions (*Vyavahārasiddhi)*. Not extant.

_____. *Five Stages (Pañcakrama)*. D 1802.

_____. *Heart of Dependent Origination (Pratītyasamutpādahṛdaya)*. D 3836.

_____. *Jewel Garland (Rājaparikathā-ratnamāla)*. D 4158.

_____. *Letter from a Friend (Suhṛllekha)*. D 4182.

_____. *Praise to the Incomparable (Nirupamastava)*. D 1119.

_____. *Praise to the Supramundane (Lokātītastava)*. D 1120.

_____. *Rebuttal of Objections (Vigrahavyāvartanī)*. D 3828.

_____. *Root of the Middle Way (Prajñā-nāma-mūlamadhyamaka)*. D 8324.

_____. *Seventy Stanzas on Emptiness (Śūnyatāsaptati)*. D 3827.

_____. *Sixty Stanzas of Reasoning (Yuktiṣaṣṭikā)*. D 3825.

_____. *Stanzas on the Śālu Sprout Sūtra (Śālistambaka-kārikā)*. D 3985.

Śāntideva. *Entering the Activity of the Bodhisattvas (Bodhicaryāvatāra)*. D 3871.

Secret Meaning (Vivṛtaguhyārthapiṇḍa-vyākhyā). D 4052.

Sthiramati. *Explanatory Commentary on Distinguishing the Middle from Extremes (Madhyāntavibhāgaṭīkā)*. D 4032.

Vasubandhu. *Commentary on the Sūtra on the Discernment of Dependent Origination (Pratītyasamutpādāvibhaṅga-bhāṣya)*. D 3994.

_____. *Explanation of the Treasury of Abhidharma (Abhidharmakośa-bhāṣa)*. D 4090.

_____. *Reasoned Exposition (Vyākhyāyukti)*. D 4061.

_____. *Treasury of Abhidharma (Abhidharmakośa)*. D 4089.

Tibetan Treatises

rMa bya byang chub brtson 'grus. 1975. *dBu ma rtsa ba shes rab kyi 'grel pa 'thad pa'i rgyan*. Rumtek: rGyal ba Karma pa.

_____. 2006a. *Root Verses of the Appearance of Reality, an Ornament of the Six Collections of Middle Way Reasoning (dBu ma rigs pa'i tshogs kyi rgyan de kho na nyid snang ba'i rtsa ba)*. In dPal brtsegs bod yig dpe rnying zhib 'jug khang, 2006, vol. 13: 745–48.

_____. 2006b. *dBu ma rigs pa'i tshogs kyi rgyan de kho na nyid snang ba*. In dPal brtsegs bod yig dpe rnying zhib 'jug khang 2006, vol. 13: 754–820.

dPal brtsegs bod yig dpe rnying zhib 'jug khang. 2006. *bKa gdams gsung 'bum phyogs bsgrigs*. Khreng tu'u: Si khron dpe skrun tshogs pa, Si khron mi rigs dpe skrun khang.

Modern Works and Translations

Doctor, Thomas. 2009. "In Pursuit of Transparent Means of Knowledge—the Madhyamaka Project of rMa bya byang chub brtson 'grus." *Journal of the International Association of Buddhist Studies* 32, nos. 1–2: 419–41.

_____. n.d. "Refuting the Undeniable, Affirming the Intolerable—rMa bya byang chub brtson 'grus on Experience, Rationality, and the Freedom from Extremes." PhD diss., Université de Lausanne.

Dunne, John D. 2004. *Foundations of Dharmakīrti's Philosophy*. Boston: Wisdom Publications, 2004.

Katusura, Shoryu, and Mark Siderits. Forthcoming. Translation of, and commentary to, the *Mūlamadhyamakakārikās*.

Khunu Rinpoche 1999. *Vast as the Heavens, Deep as the Sea: Verses in Praise of Bodhicitta*. Boston: Wisdom Publications.

Radhakrishnan, Sarvepalli. 1996. *The Dhammapada: With Introductory Essays, Pali Text, English Translation and Notes*. New York: Oxford University Press.

Ruegg, David Seyfort. 2000. *Three Studies in the History of Indian and Tibetan Madhyamaka Philosophy*. Vienna: Arbeitskreis für tibetische und buddhistische Studien, Universität Wien.

Tsong khapa, rJe. 2006. *Ocean of Reasoning*. Trans. Geshe Ngawang Samten and Jay Garfield. New York: Oxford University Press.

Vose, Kevin. 2009. *Resurrecting Candrakīrti—Disputes in the Tibetan Creation of Prāsaṅgika*. Boston: Wisdom Publications.

Williams, Paul. 1985. "Rma bya pa Byang chub brtson 'grus on Madhyamaka Method." *Journal of Indian Philosophy* 13: 205–25.

Index

moving. *See* going
mundane relative truth
two kinds of, 126–28
See also relative truth

N
Nāgārjuna
activities of, 95–96
distinguishing features of, 94
followers of, 91
literary corpus of, 93, 99–103
Madhyamaka philosophy and, xii
Madhyamika School and, ix
praises of, 96–99
qualities of, 95
Root of the Middle Way and, xi
works by on Secret Mantra, 103
works by that show the Causal and
Resultant Vehicles to be identical in
meaning, 103
See also *Accumulations of
Enlightenment; Commentary on the
Enlightened Mind; Compendium on
the Sūtras; Detailed Examination;
Establishing Conventions; Five Stages;
Heart of Dependent Origination;
Investigation of the World; Jewel
Garland; Letter from a Friend;
Praise to the Incomparable; Praise
to the Supramundane; Rebuttal
of Objections; Seventy Stanzas
on Emptiness; Six Collections of
Reasoning;* Sixfold Collection
of Middle Way Reasoning; *Sixty
Stanzas on Reasoning*
natural emptiness
of all constructed phenomena related
to mind and cognized objects, 374
of all phenomena that are observed by
insight, 93, 99, 137, 374
conditioned phenomena and, 307–8
of dependent origination, 463
dependent origination and, 124–25,
468
of existence and peace, 334
as free from permanence and annihilation, 381
of phenomena, 326–27

as taught by proponents of the Middle
Way, 467
of the ultimate, 381
See also emptiness
natural existence, 309–11
nature (of a thing)
analysis of, 322–33
arising of
Mind Only Proponents on, 324
Proponents of Differences on, 324
refutation of, 323–27
change and, 309–10, 327–29
dependent origination and, 323–27
emptiness and, 326–27
true, 326–27
See also essence
negation
identification of that which is negated
and, 114–16
negative properties and, 311
object of negation and, 311
See also eliminative negation; existential negation; indicative negation;
predicative negation
nihilism
accusation of, 243, 263, 307, 366
natural existence and, 333
things' being devoid of nature and, 307
nirvana. *See* liberation
noble truths. *See* four noble truths
nonconceptual wakefulness of the noble
one's equipoise, 126, 129, 326. *See also*
wakefulness
nondissipation, 354–59
nonentities, refutation of, 329–31
nothingness. *See* nihilism

O
observed condition
definition of, 162
refutation of, 167–68
One Hundred Thousand Verse Sūtra, 96
Ornament of Manifest Realization
(Maitreya), 93
Ornament of Reason, Tibetan version of,
xii–xiii
*Ornament of the Sūtras of the Great
Vehicle* (Maitreya), 93, 106, 509